D1457531

ISLAM AND TRAVEL IN THE MIDDLE AGES

ISLAM & TRAVEL
IN THE MIDDLE AGES

HOUARI TOUATI

Translated by Lydia G. Cochrane

The University of Chicago Press
Chicago and London

HOUARI TOUATI is a director of studies at the École des hautes études en sciences sociales, Paris. His most recent book is *L'armoire à sagesse: Bibliothèques et collections en Islam* (2003), which has been translated into both Italian and Turkish.

LYDIA G. COCHRANE has translated more than three dozen books from French and Italian, most recently Rémi Brague's *The Legend of the Middle Ages: Philosophical Explorations of Medieval Christianity, Judaism, and Islam* (2009), published by the University of Chicago Press.

The University of Chicago Press, Chicago 60637
The University of Chicago Press, Ltd., London
© 2010 by The University of Chicago
All rights reserved. Published 2010
Printed in the United States of America

19 18 17 16 15 14 13 12 11 10   1 2 3 4 5

ISBN-13: 978-0-226-80877-2 (cloth)
ISBN-10: 0-226-80877-7 (cloth)

The University of Chicago Press gratefully acknowledges a subvention from the government of France, through the French Ministry of Culture, National Center of the Book, in support of the costs of translating this volume.

Originally published as *Islam et voyage au Moyen Âge: Histoire et anthropologie d'une pratique lettrée* © Éditions du Seuil, Octobre 2000.

Library of Congress Cataloging-in-Publication Data
Touati, Houari.
  [Islam et voyage au Moyen Âge. English]
  Islam and travel in the Middle Ages / Houari Touati ; translated by Lydia G. Cochrane.
    p. cm.
  In English; translated from French.
  Includes bibliographical references and index.
  ISBN-13: 978-0-226-80877-2 (cloth : alk. paper)
  ISBN-10: 0-226-80877-7 (cloth : alk. paper)   1. Travel—Religious aspects—Islam.
2. Muslim travelers—History—To 1500. 3. Muslim pilgrims and pilgrimages.
4. Emigration and immigration—Religious aspects—Islam. 5. Travelers' writings, Arabic—Islamic Empire—History and criticism. 6. Travel, Medieval.
I. Cochrane, Lydia G.   II. Title.
  BP190.5.T73T6813 2010
  910.4—dc22

                                                           2009042971

♾ The paper used in this publication meets the minimum requirements of the American National Standard for Information Sciences—Permanence of Paper for Printed Library Materials, ANSI Z39.48-1992.

CONTENTS

According to postmodern intellectuals of the diaspora, exile is intellectually fertile in that it permits them a certain distance from the theater of the world that enables them to participate in all of the places of culture without enclosing them within any one in particular. Rarely voluntary, exile is also a source of instability, fragility, and confusion, as illustrated by the tragic end of Walter Benjamin before a frontier that remained inaccessible to him, or the resigned return of Theodor W. Adorno to "the rotten house."

Although they traveled in a Muslim world that they described as one coherent "house" (*dār*), the men of letters whom the reader of the present volume is invited to meet say that they, too, have known exile. Just like foreign visitors to their land, those men of letters felt unrooted and far from home, which means that they suffered from a sense of dissociation. But because they traveled in order to know, some among them gave a cognitive foundation to their experience of expatriation, while others gave it an ethical content. All shared a neo-Stoic perspective and followed the paths of knowledge as an asceticism that was both physical and intellectual. By their incessant coming and going through the "empire of Islam" (*mamlakat al-islām*), a spatiotemporal entity that the geographers promoted to the rank of a frame of intelligibility and meaning, they wove a vast web that became part of classical Islamic culture. Thus, thanks to their efforts, the voyage, more than a means for acquiring knowledge, became the prime modality for creating it.

According to whether they gave cognitive primacy to the ear or to the eye, those same men of letters made the journey a methodological necessity. Their use of the world was based on two models of knowledge that were both concurrent and congruent: "audition," or hearing (*samā'*) for religious, philological, and historical knowledge, on the one hand; and, on the other, sight (*autopsia, 'iyān*), or the visual constatation that is typical of most of the rational disciplines, but also of mysticism. In concrete terms, those two paradigms combined and were divided in different ways, the genesis and forms of development of which this book attempts to describe. Because such men shared legal training, they made juridical science the discipline that brought together all other disciplines, both religious and secular. In Islam, all epistemology is legal. With the translation of the Greek corpus, that strictly Islamic gnoseology was combined with Aristotelian epistemology, both in order to compare the two and to appropriate the basic assumptions of the latter.

The inquiry pursued in *Islam and Travel in the Middle Ages* draws from history and from the sociology of the sciences, and there were some critics of the French edition who found it incomplete and would have liked it to be an archaeology of Islamic knowledge. That was not its aim, even though Michel Foucault has not been neglected. By remaining tightly bound to the study of travel for scientific and literary ends, its objective was a more modest one, but one with considerable influence: removing a literary practice from the sociological contingency in which it is almost always enclosed in order to study that practice as a mechanism of a characteristic mode of the production of knowledge.

Those who sought a treatment of the peregrination of the *hajj* in this book were disappointed as well. Despite its importance, that ritual journey brought no specific sort of objective knowledge, unless it was fortuitous, as, for example, when a man of letters met another of his kind along the way and, according to the formula, "took knowledge" from him. The absence of the *hajj* in these pages can be justified when we think that the voyage in search of knowledge was constructed as a break with that peregrination and declared that sort of travel to be equally, if not more, important. Other ritual journeys are mentioned in the book, but they merit inclusion only to the extent that they had intellectual consequences. This is true of the experimental wanderings of the mystics and of the sojourn in the frontier marches. The mystics debated at length which of the two sources of sense information—the visual or the auditory—was more pertinent to a survey of the supernatural. As for the sojourn on the frontier, this book shows that it was by no means motivated as a response to the need to defend the territories of Islam from external aggression. If it was not in order to fight, why should the religious men of letters of the time generally, and the transmitters of religious traditions among them in particular, have flocked to the frontiers? I suggest that, first and foremost, they were attempting to use their ritualized presence to breathe symbolic efficacy into a representation of the territories of Islam as a coherent dogmatic space.

That means that the majority of the traveling men of letters of the period crossed and recrossed the central and peripheral lands of Islam without judging it necessary to go beyond Islam's borders. Does that mean that classical Islamic culture refused to look elsewhere than at itself? Certainly not. Compared to that of its neighbors, its curiosity regarding the known external world seems astonishingly rich. But what did Islam know of Western Europe? The question has preoccupied scholars of the modern age. The answer is: almost nothing, simply because there was not much to learn. As the heir to Hellenistic conceptions of the inhabited world, that tropism long contaminated the perception of the external world of classical Islam, which continued to pay very little attention to that part of the *oikoumene*. Moreover, it remained more preoccupied with Byzantium, India, and China of that era, which it judged to be more civilized and more cultivated. A study of the discursive and narrative products that travelers of the classical Muslim world brought back from those lands, which were so near but culturally so distant, would be a welcome adjunct to this book.

Houari Touati
Algiers, September 2009

ACKNOWLEDGMENTS (2000)

The present work benefited, in its first year of preparation, from the financial support of the Alexander von Humbold Stiftung, and I wish to express my gratitude to that foundation. My thanks go also to George R. Khoury, Avram Udovitch, and Frank E. Vogel, the first for having welcomed me at the Seminar für Sprachen und Kulturen des Vorderen Orients of the University of Heidelberg, the second for having welcomed me to Princeton University and allowed me the opportunity to work in Firestone Library, and the third for having invited me to Harvard University, where I completed my bibliography at Widener Library. Much of the material utilized in this book formed a part of my seminar at the École des hautes études en sciences sociales, and I hope that the students and the colleagues who gave me an opportunity to think through those materials will also find thanks in these lines. For reading the manuscript, in part or in whole, and giving me their suggestions, my gratitude goes to Lucette Valensi, Jean-Claude Schmitt, François Hartog, Françoise Micheau, and Richard Figuier. Finally, my gratitude to Anne Varet-Vitu, the cartographer at the Center of Historical Demography of the EHESS, who helped me to establish the travel itineraries in this book.

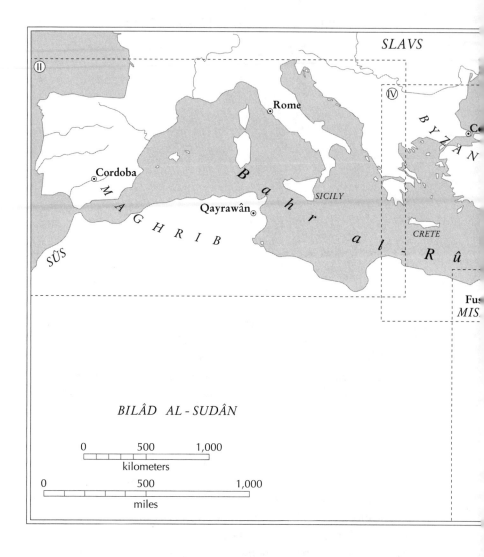

SLAVS

(II)

Rome

(IV)

B Y Z A N

C

Cordoba

M
A
G
H
R
I
B

B
a
h
r

SICILY

CRETE

SÛS

Qayrawân

a
l

R

û

Fus
MIS

BILÂD   AL - SUDÂN

0   500   1,000
      kilometers

0   500   1,000
      miles

Regions and cities of Islam according to the geographer Muqaddasī (tenth century). The Muslim world is divided into four regions: region I is discussed in chapter 2; regions II and III in chapter 3; and region IV in chapter 5. Map courtesy of Dick Gilbreath, University of Kentucky Cartography Lab.

KHAZAR   TURKISTÂN

                                        Aral
                                        Sea   (III)

ople

                                                                    Samarkand
                    Ardabîl
        Mawsil   Marw
M   Shârastân   AL - MASHRIQ   FARGHÂNA
            AQÛR   RIHÂB   Nîsâbûr
                                    DAYLAM
RUS   Damascus   Hamadân

        Baghdâd   (I)
    SHÂM   IRÂQ   Ahwâz
                            Shîrâz   Sirjân
                    Bahr   FÂRS   KIRMÂN
            ARABIAN   Fâris
                                                                    Mansûra

        Mecca
                PENINSULA

    Bahr al-Qulzum   Bahr
                                                            al-Sîn
ÛBA
                Zabîd
    AL - HABASHA

·◟ INTRODUCTION ◞·

Muslim men of letters of the Middle Ages were mad for travel. This is why they cultivated the art of travel with such a passion. For most of them, the voyage was the prime test of their lives. Because travel brought them, through suffering, into learning as a way of life, Muslims saw it as a figure for metamorphosis, coupled with an experience of the painful. They probably would not have appreciated the fact that some people thought travel a kind of "servitude," a "burden" on meaningful work causing an "incidental loss of weeks or months" that subjected them to "periods of hunger, exhaustion, sickness perhaps; and always the thousand and one dreary tasks which eat away the days to no purpose."[1] The relationship of men of letters with travel went beyond that. After all, initiation defines an experience, not a body of knowledge.[2] They went even farther: they

---

1. Claude Lévi-Strauss, *Tristes tropiques* (Paris: Plon, 1955), 13; quoted from *Tristes Tropiques*, trans. John and Doreen Weightman (New York: Atheneum, 1974), 17.

2. Recently, however, the anthropologists have taught us that hermeneutic and pragmatic situations that confront them in the field presuppose that experience: see Jean Bazin, "Interpréter ou décrire: Notes critiques sur la connaissance anthropologique," in *Une école pour les sciences sociales: De la VIe section à L'école des hautes études en sciences sociales*, ed. Jacques Revel and Nathan Wachtel (Paris: Cerf and Éditions de l'école des hautes études en sciences sociales, 1996), 401–20. See also Remo Guidieri's interesting introduction to the French translation of Bronislaw Malinowski, *A Diary in the Strict Sense of the Term* (New York: Harcourt, Brace & World, 1967): *Journal d'ethnographe*, trans. Tina Jolas (Paris: Seuil, 1985). Reversing Lévi-Strauss's perspectives, James Clifford understands what he calls "the institutionalization of fieldwork" in the late nineteenth and early twentieth centuries "within a larger history of 'travel'": *Routes: Travel and Translation in the Late Twentieth Century* (Cambridge, MA: Harvard University Press, 1997), 64. For an analysis of the tension between ethnology and travel, see also Marc Augé, "Voyage et ethnographie: La vie comme récit," *L'homme* 151 (1999): 11–19.

thought travel a necessary mechanism of their scientific institution. The idea that "the truths which we seek so far afield only become valid when they have been separated from this dross"—the "servitudes" of travel—was completely foreign to them.[3] It might even have seemed to them dangerous, because it bore within it disturbing effects that clouded their epistemological horizon. Subscribing to it (by means of the book, for example) meant to some extent endangering the voyage or precipitating its end.

In other words, the attachment of Muslim men of letters to travel had little to do with superstition, nostalgia, or tradition but was rather a matter of method.[4] Firmly tied to a world in which intellectuality and adventure were closely linked, they worked collectively to defend the principle that one cannot truly inhabit knowledge without shipping off on a trip. It is my intention to paint the portrait of that close coupling, using materials from the eighth to the twelfth centuries—one of the most fertile periods of Islam. The terminus a quo is the birth and development of the *rihla* as a voyage in search of knowledge; the terminus ad quem is the appearance of the *rihla* as a travel narrative. There are two peak moments, but the timing of the *rihla*-voyage and the *rihla*-narrative presents problems. The two are so different that the first question that springs to mind is why Muslim men of letters arrived at the idea of composing *rihla*-narratives only quite a long time after they had been traveling far and wide. The reasons for that hiatus are not uniquely time related, as one might guess, and they need to be inventoried and explicated. But first we need to examine the reasons for the *rihla*-voyage and explain why Muslim men of letters felt the need to use it as a symbol of high intellectuality.

What is there in the Islamic way of traveling and obtaining cognitive, discursive, and narrative results that is so particular and original that it merits having a book written about it? Although the Muslim experience functioned with the same means as the Western experience of travel and writing about travel, it was nonetheless profoundly different. One cannot say of Muslim travel that "the voyage is *always* a movement toward the other, a face-to-face with the other."[5] This is something that the West can say, whether it worked out its identity within a relationship to the past or

3. Lévi-Strauss, *Tristes tropiques*, 14; Weightman translation, 17.
4. To say, for example, "More than all other peoples, because they were nomads out of atavism, Arabs were great travelers," as Paule Charles-Dominique does in *Voyageurs arabes: Ibn Fadlān, Ibn Jubayr, Ibn Battūta et un auteur anonyme* (Paris: Gallimard, 1995), xi, has to be attributed to ineptitude.
5. Jean Céard, "Voyages et voyageurs à la Renaissance," in *Voyager à la Renaissance*, actes du colloque de Tours, 1983, ed. Jean Céard and Jean-Claude Margolin (Paris: Maisonneuve et Larose,

to the future, to what is foreign to it or to nature, and whether or not it conceived of travel writing and its heir, ethnology, as a "hermeneutics of the other."[6] For the West, the voyage to Greece or to Italy constituted a trip back through time in which, thanks to stones and the dead, it entered into dialogue with those whom it took to be its ancestors: the Greeks and the Romans.[7] The exotic voyage—in particular to the New World—allowed the West to establish another alterity that raised questions about its own age and singularity. In Islam, travel and the discourse that travel produced did not draw their meaning from a historical and anthropological relationship with the other. Rather than from a hermeneutics of the other, meaning derived from an exegetic construction of sameness. Although the voyagers whose peregrinations we will follow in this book were well aware of Ptolemy's geography,[8] their aim was not to push back the known frontiers of the *oikoumene*, but rather to define a geographically delimited space that some called the "abode" (the "house" or the "territory") of Islam (*dār al-islām*) and others the "empire" (*mamlaka*) of Islam. What was at stake in this construction was to make sure that this georeligious and geopolitical unity become a space that dogmatically guaranteed the truth of a "living together" willed by God. To attain that aim, our voyagers traveled incessantly back and forth in that space for nearly four centuries. In the long run, they ended up saturating it with Islamism.

Because they identified with this task, the founders of Islamic learning showed a distinct dislike of transgressing the geographical frontiers that they themselves had set up to serve as religious and cultural barriers

---

1987), 593–611, esp. 605. For a recent illustration of this explanation, see Jean Chesneaux, *L'art du voyage: Un regard (plutôt . . .) politique sur l'autre et l'ailleurs* (Paris: Bayard, 1999).

6. Michel de Certeau, *L'écriture de l'histoire* (Paris: Gallimard, 1975), 231; trans. Tom Conley as *The Writing of History* (New York: Columbia University Press, 1988), 218ff.

7. It is interesting to see how Hermann Harder analyzes the voyage to Italy as "a collective work of a great homogeneity": *Le président de Brosses et le voyage en Italie au dix-huitième siècle* (Geneva: Slatkine, 1981), 435.

8. I might recall that this effort to create "sameness" is, at least in part, accomplished with the epistemological and hermeneutical instruments that Muslims felt no compunction about seeking outside the Muslim community, notably among the "people of the Book" and the Greeks. This means that there is no obsession about "closure," "suture," or "autism" in their efforts, but, rather, a simple desire to construct an identity—that is, to draw a line between what makes me "me" in my full singularity and others. It is a way of constructing an "egocentrism." There is also the Greek way of doing so. The Greeks chose another modality for self-definition: instead of the principle of sameness, they privileged that of difference. This, however, did not stop their ethnocentrism from being total. At the same time, they showed no hesitation about borrowing gods, technical innovations, and know-how from "Barbarians": see Arnaldo Momigliano, *Alien Wisdom: The Limits of Hellenization* (Cambridge: Cambridge University Press, 1975); trans. Marie-Claude Roussel as *Sagesses barbares* (Paris: La Découverte, 1979).

around the space of law, peace, and salvation that bore the name of *dār al-islām*.[9] As the canonical seat of the *umma*, "a well-defined entity that can at times be hard to grasp,"[10] that space stood opposed, as water to fire, to the rest of the inhabited world, which was in turn qualified, religiously, as the "territory of Infidelity" (*dār al-kufr*), or, in a more bellicose spirit, as the "territory of war" (*dār al-harb*).

It did of course happen that the artisans of this association between a text (that of Islam as a religion) and a space (that of the Islamic "empire") traveled elsewhere. It must be said, however, that although they occasionally ventured outside their own area, they never did so for reasons of intellectual or cultural curiosity (let alone for religious reasons), as André Miquel has so well demonstrated in his engaging human geography of the medieval Muslim world.[11] Most of those who did travel outside the domain of Islam did so as ambassadors or as part of a governmental mission.[12] In 842, "the caliph Wāthiq, having seen in a dream that the wall erected by Alexander the Great between our lands and Gog and Magog had been breached, sought out a person capable of going to that place and examining the state in which it was." That man was the famous Sallām the Interpreter.[13] When Ibn Butlān "traveled among the Bulgars of the Volga"

9. This is shown by Bernard Lewis in *The Muslim Discovery of Europe* (New York: Norton, 1982, 2001); trans. Annick Pélissier as *Comment l'Islam a découvert l'Europe* (Paris: Gallimard, 1990). See also André Miquel, "L'Europe vue par les Arabes jusqu'en l'an mil," in *Lumières arabes sur l'Occident médiéval*, actes du colloque "Civilisations arabe et Européenne: Deux cultures complimentaires," ed. Henri Loucel and André Miquel (Paris: Anthropos, 1978), where Miquel speaks of a "poorly known Europe" and a "Europe conceived as a series of *membra dijecta*." It is interesting to see a Moroccan man of letters on an official voyage to France appeal, as late as the mid-nineteenth century, to the medieval juridical principle of "the interest of Muslims": see Susan Gilson Miller, ed. and trans., *Disorienting Encounters: Travels of a Moroccan Scholar in France in 1845–1846: The Voyage of Muhammad as-Saffār* (Berkeley: University of California Press, 1992).

10. Gustave E. Von Grunebaum, *Studien zum Kulturbild und Selbstverständnis des Islam* (Zurich: Artemis, 1969); trans. Roger Stuvéras as *L'identité culturelle de l'Islam* (Paris: Gallimard, 1973), 78; in English translation as *Islam: Essays in the Nature and Growth of a Cultural Tradition* (New York: Barnes & Noble, 1961).

11. André Miquel, *La géographie humaine du monde musulman jusqu'au milieu du 11e siècle*, 4 vols. (Paris: Mouton, 1967–).

12. Speaking of a later age and of the ulemas of Egypt and Syria in the Mamluk era, Henri Laoust writes: "The sovereign charged them with a number of political missions, often of a most delicate sort. . . . It is rare that an embassy sent to Baraka Khān, to the Franks, or to the Mongols did not include within its ranks one or more jurisconsults": see Henri Laoust, *Essai sur les doctrines sociales et politiques de Takī-d-Dīn Ahman b. Taimīya, canoniste hanbalite, né à Harrān en 661/1262, mort à Damas en 725/1328* (Cairo: Institut Français d'Archéologie Orientale, 1939), 41–42.

13. We know the travel account of Sallām the Interpreter thanks to the ninth-century geographer Ibn Khurdādhbeh: see *Kitāb al-masālik wa'l-Mamālik (Liber viarum et regnorum)*, ed. M. J. de Goeje (Leiden, 1889). On the same narrative, see Ernest Zichy, "Le voyage de Sallām, l'interprète,

between 921 and 923, he did so as an "envoy of the caliph Muqtadir to the king of the Saqāliba."[14] "Officially, he was supposed to be perfecting, shaping, and refining the Islamic faith of that people. In reality, the idea was to circumvent an obstacle. The commerce of the Bulgars . . . passed through there, descending the Volga, through [the lands of] another people. These were the Khazars, partially Judaized vassals of the major enemy, Constantinople." A century later Abū Dulaf claimed to have gone to China in similar circumstances.[15] Four centuries later a traveler from the Maghreb, Ibn Battūta, also went to China, and before that to Constantinople, as a member of an embassy. When these travelers were not diplomats or members of a mission, they were prisoners, as was Hārūn ibn Yahya, who provided Islam with its first description of Constantinople at the end of the ninth century,[16] or merchants, as was the author of *Relation of China and India*, written in 851, which offers particular interest, since "no text known today can contradict it."[17]

The one text that contrasts with this concordant picture is the *India* of Bīrūnī (d. 442/1050). The problem is that he describes India, which he knew intimately, not as he had seen it, but as he had heard and read about it. He quite obviously gives hearing—and even more the book—methodological primacy over sight. This means that the reader is invited on a voyage to an India of books and culture, a "fundamental India"[18] rather than a real one. That eminent medieval savant thus perpetuated a tradition that reaches back to another great literary voyage, the translation movement of the 'Abbāsid golden age. Nor was Bīrūnī the only writer who showed an interest in India. Muslim men of letters from Andalusia to Iraq dreamed of conquering the wisdom of that distant yet congenial part of the world. Why such enthusiasm? From the mid-eighth century,

à la muraille de Gog et Magog," *Körösi Csoma Archivum* 1 (1921–25): 190–204. Against all expectations, this traveler went not to China, but to the Caucasus, returning by way of the Urals.

14. Ahmad ibn Fadlān, *Voyage chez les Bulgares de la Volga*, trans. Marius Canard (Paris: S.P.A.G. [Papyrus], 1988); trans. Richard N. Frye as *Ibn Fadlan's Journey to Russia: A Tenth-Century Traveler from Baghdad to the Volga River* (Princeton: Markus Weiner, 2005).

15. For a French translation of this travel narrative, see "Voyage de Abū Dulaf Mis'ar bin Muhalhil," in *Relations de voyages et textes géographiques arabes, persans et turks relatifs à l'extrême Orient du VIIIe au XVIIIe siècles*, ed. and trans. Gabriel Ferrand, 2 vols. (Paris: Leroux, 1913–14), 1:208–29.

16. Afanasii Vasiliev, "Hārūn ibn Yahiā and His Description of Constantinople," *Seminarium Kondakovianum* 5 (1932): 149–63; Mehmed Izeddin and Paul Therriat, "Un prisonnier arabe à Byzance au IXe siècle: Haroun ibn Yahiā," *Revue d'études islamiques* 15 (1941–47): 41–62.

17. *Ahbār as-Sīn wa' l-Hind, Relation de la Chine et de l'Inde rédigée en 851*, trans. Jean Sauvaget (Paris: Belles Lettres, 1948).

18. Louis Renou, *L'Inde fondamentale: Études d'indianisme réunies et présentées par Charles Malamoud* (Paris: Hermann, 1978).

Indian wisdom possessed an aura rivaled only by the Greek scientific and philosophical corpus and the Persian political and literary traditions. When the great 'Abbāsid century divided the "categories of the nations" into two sorts—the "nations having cultivated the sciences" and the "nations not having cultivated the sciences"[19]—it in effect decided that, of all the peoples outside its borders, only the Greeks, the Persians, and the Hindus had wisdom to transmit to Islam. In contrast, no contemporary peoples—neither the Rūm (Romans; more accurately, Byzantines)[20] nor the Chinese, Turks, Kurds, or Blacks (held to be, at most, gifted representatives of *Homo faber*) could satisfy its intellectual curiosity. With the blacks at the bottom of the scale and the Rūm and the Chinese at the top, such peoples took their places among the "manual nations."

Out of sheer necessity, the present book is not dedicated to rare frontier figures like Bīrūnī. It concerns another class of travelers, who were just as indefatigable, but who bear more weight on a numerical, sociological, and intellectual scale of importance, and whose actions were more decisive in the construction of Islamic identity. Those travelers moved only within the limits of the "abode of Islam." That there were so many of them and that they never went elsewhere is precisely what seems to me to make them interesting as a subject for study.

In order to verify that allegation, I have divided my investigations, concentrating on the points of view of Tradition, language, and space. The activities of the traditionists will show how a field of knowledge—here, that of traditions related to the Prophet—produced a genuine epistemology of the voyage that ended up, after an entire series of inflections, investing the entire field of Islamic knowledge, religious as well as secular. In the process, I will show how the traditionists gave to the *umma*—the emotional community of Muslims—a dogmatic foundation that synchronized its ideal of life with the one represented by the Qur'an *and* the *Sunna*—that

---

19. On this basic division, see Ibn Sā'id (d. 462/1070), *Kitāb tabakāt al-uman (Livre des catégories des nations)*, trans. Régis Blachère (Paris: Larose, 1935).

20. One of the most enlightened minds of the ninth century, Jāhiz (d. 255/868) contested the Romans' and the Byzantines' filiation from the Greeks and claimed that Islam was more worthy to be the latter's intellectual heir. In the eleventh century, Ibn Sā'id, who was Andalusian, stated, however, that they were among the "civilized nations." Thus, it is not by chance that we see the first translation from Latin into Arabic in Andalusia: see Ibn Juljul (d. after 994), *Les générations des médecins et des sages: Tabqat al'atibba' wal-hukama': Écrit composé en 377-H. par Abu Dawud Sulaiman ibn Hassan ibn Gulgul Al-Andalusi*, ed. Fu'ad Sayyid (Cairo: Institut Français d'Archéologie Orientale, 1955). For a more recent summary of this question, see Charles Burnett, "The Translating Activity in Medieval Spain," in *The Legacy of Muslim Spain*, ed. Salma Khadra Jayyusi, 2 vols. (Leiden: Brill, 1992), 2:1036–58.

is, Islamic Tradition. Philology offers proof of the difficulty of the conceptual tools of the study of traditions (*hadīth*) within Islamic knowledge: by going into the desert to gather the language in its pure form from the mouth of the Bedouins, then returning to store their gleanings in dictionaries and lexicons, linguists certainly behaved in exactly the same way as their traditionist colleagues. And the traditionists, by tying the Arabic language (for religious reasons) to the purest Bedouin idiolects, made that version of Arabic the language of Islam and of its basic knowledge. When later geographers followed the same path, they made use of a notional apparatus borrowed from the law to establish sight as a principle of knowledge of the domain of Islam, deployed for politico-dogmatic reasons as a unified, centralized space.

Tradition, the language, and the space of Islam would have been enough to satisfy our purposes if a class of men of letters—the mystics—had played only a minor part in the definition of Islam. Mystics, who were by vocation great travelers, instead played an essential role in a culture that is, in the final analysis, the product of a miracle. To the extent that they conceived of their learning as a systematic pacing out of space, they cannot be ignored. Sharing with the geographers the dogmatic and legal principle that an ascertained fact trumps all other evidence, they made the voyage the principal instrument of their hermeneutics of space. This enabled them to travel throughout "the abode of Islam," turning it into a spiritual space wherever their wanderings took them.

Other forms of travel with more ritualistic aims were added to these peregrinations that provided a basis for knowledge. One of these—a journey to the frontiers of Islam—deserves special consideration, because it offered the traveler a chance to defend the territories of Islam, at times by force of arms and, at other times, in a totally symbolic and ritual manner. Because such visits produced their share of accounts, both oral and written, they contributed to the voyage in its dogmatic function as a machine for producing writings. As did earlier or contemporary cultures, medieval Islam combined rituality and intellectuality. Studying a journey to the border areas can project new light on the knowledge travel brings.

Thus far all that I have done is to sketch out the framework for a response to *why* the voyage became an act that helped to found Islam. *How* that occurred remains to be investigated. To do so requires interrogation of the voyage in light of the anthropological and epistemic codes of medieval Islamic intellectuality.

From an anthropological point of view, there was a strong tension between the two orders of literacy and orality within learned culture in

Islam. Beginning in the eighth century, debate focused on whether the book could replace the master and function as the depository of his authority. The global response was negative: the master continued to reign supreme, following the theory that books do not speak for themselves, but always require an authority to enable them to speak. By opting for the master against the book, Islamic culture instituted the rule that no one accedes to the scholar's condition by his own authorization. Filiation was the only way. Hence the Muslim men of letters of the Middle Ages decided that authorized knowledge was the only legitimate knowledge, and that the only authorized knowledge was genealogical. That structure explains the importance of the voyage: candidates for learning who hoped to become inscribed within a prestigious genealogy of scholarship were advised to connect themselves to the most renowned masters of their time, those for whom, as the medieval biographical dictionaries put it, "one packs his bags and loads up the beasts."

That response is doxological. Despite its prescriptive tone, however, it did not stifle the development, in its shadow, of a "marginal solution" that permitted the book to make a place for itself in the general apparatus of medieval higher education. Thanks to an entire set of expedients, juridical ones in particular, the book as a didactic and scientific support emerged from its marginality as early as the ninth century. Borne along by a prodigious scientific and literary tide, it eventually became established as a basic tool for knowledge. The success of the book made its diehard opponents worry that its broad socialization might threaten the principle of the voyage, and in the long term that may well be what happened. In the middle term, however, just the opposite took place. A state-supported bibliophilia, backed by the formation of an international market for books, considerably enlarged the circle of travel between the ninth and tenth centuries.[21] The anthropological explanation—which, after all, could just as well be applied to China in the sixth century or Europe of the seventeenth century[22]—would be insufficient if we failed to pursue an interrogation

21. Thanks to financial support from the state and from private sources, expeditions were even organized to go as far as Byzantium and India in order to seek out the treasures of "the wisdom of the ancients." But if such enterprises did indeed have Muslims as backers, their agents were generally non-Muslims, Christians for the most part.

22. China, which had great voyagers, behaved in much the same fashion as Islam. Its travelers abroad were at first diplomats, emissaries, or prisoners of war. Chinese men of letters went abroad only when, beginning in the fourth century, Buddhism became established in their homeland and they had to go to India in search of the sacred books they needed. At that point a great movement of pilgrimage began, which, continuing for over six centuries, "can be regarded as one of the most considerable events of the history of the civilization of the world." Holy travelers

of the voyage that it implies and solve the riddle of how the epistemic foundation of medieval Islamic culture functioned. It is true that the symbolic order of that culture gave Islamic learning—'ilm—its structure and its codes of genealogically constituted knowledge. "Hearing" functions as a primordial institution within that structure. Under the name of *samāʿ*, a term that can also be rendered as "audition," it became one of the principal internal institutions of medieval learned culture. That the organ (the ear) connected with it was made a source of understanding leads to a paradigm known, for commodity's sake, as "the listening paradigm." We can measure the importance of the voyage within this paradigm by recalling that it functioned by genealogical transmission from master to disciple.

The fact that Tradition was organized by this sort of paradigm did not prevent the secular disciplines from claiming "audition" as a founding and organizing principle. Nor did it prevent the emergence of another paradigm, *'iyān*, at once concurrent and congruent to it, which, like *autopsia* among the ancient Greeks,[23] designates the act of seeing with one's own eyes. Thus, the primacy of hearing and sight as principal sources of sense knowledge became established in medieval Islam; *'iyān* was incorporated into the voyage as well, giving rise to a novel principle of knowledge and description. But, just like hearing, it first had to combat the book, challenging it not in the name of the master, but in the name of the personal and direct experience of the observer.[24] To the extent that this encounter between the ear and the voyage and the eye and the voyage need to be set in historical context, this book also attempts to tell that story.

who were not satisfied with going to India also traveled "throughout the Buddhist world." But they hardly ever ventured outside that religious space. In the middle of the eleventh century, the voyages to India ended, thanks to the local triumph of Islam and the rapid decline of Indian Buddhism. See Edouard Chavannes, ed. *Les voyageurs chinois* (Paris: Comité de l'Asie Française, 1904).

23. Defining "autopsy," Marcel Detienne writes that it is "not, to be sure, the autopsy of gloved, white-cloaked acolytes whom a police inquest obliges to inspect the corpus delicti, but that of a witness who is all eyes." Marcel Detienne, *Dionysos mis à mort* (Paris: Gallimard, 1977), 51; quoted from *Dionysos Slain*, trans. Mireille Muellner and Leonard Muellner (Baltimore: Johns Hopkins University Press, 1979), 20.

24. It is interesting to note the extent to which the renewal of the voyage and the travel narrative in Europe of the Renaissance occurred on a similar basis. It was in obedience to the credo of Latin peoples of *experientia magistra rerum* and *unus testis oculatus, valet auritos decem* (which can be found in identical terms and cited proverbially in Islam) that the renewal took place. See François-Marc Gagnon, *Experientia est rerum magistra: Savoir empirique et culture savante chez les premiers voyageurs au Canada*, Questions de culture, Institut Québécois de Recherche sur la Culture (1981); and Norman Doiron, *L'art de voyager: Le déplacement à l'époque classique* (Sainte-Foy, Quebec: Presses de l'Université de Laval, 1995), 49–60.

·⟨ 1 ⟩·

INVITATION TO THE VOYAGE

W hy did Islamic men of letters invent the voyage? And just who were these men of letters? To what use did they put their travels? In order to answer these questions, the great Orientalist Ignaz Goldziher, working in the late nineteenth century, accepted the thesis that it was specialists in Tradition who initiated the *rihla*-voyage in the early eighth century. He states that the traditionists made use of the voyage as a war machine to combat the opposing party of "reasoners" (the *as'hāb al-ra'y*, or "people of opinion") in the task of collecting, authenticating, and harmonizing the sayings of the Prophet.[1]

That conception of travel, far from dying out, has continued to gather support from many scholars.[2] Some went so far as to state that the origin of the voyage, as a literary practice, is much older than that, and that travel was inextricably intertwined with the history of Islam from the start.[3] The

1. Ignaz Goldziher, *Muhammedanische Studien*, 2 vols. (Halle: Niemeyer, 1889–90), 2:33–34, 176–80; trans. Lèon Bercher as *Études sur la tradition islamique: Extraites du tome II des Muhammadanische Studien* (Paris: Adrien-Maisonneuve, 1952), 40–41, 218–22; trans. C. R. Barber and S. M. Stern as *Muslim Studies: Muhammedanische Studien*, 2 vols. (London: George Allen & Unwin, 1967).

2. See, in particular, Nabia Abbot, *Qur'anic Commentary and Tradition*, vol. 2 of *Studies in Arabic Literary Papyri*, 3 vols. (Chicago: University of Chicago Press, 1967), 40–43; and G. H. A. Juynboll, *Muslim Tradition: Studies in Chronology, Provenance and Authorship of Early Hadīth* (Cambridge: Cambridge University Press, 1983), 66–70.

3. "Migration, pilgrimage and travel in Islam are as old as the religion itself. The Prophet Muhammad made his famous archetypal *Hijra* (Migration) from Mekka to Medina in AD 622 . . . ; the *Hajj* (Pilgrimage) of Farewell enacted by the Prophet in AD 632 provided the paradigm for all future pilgrimages to the sacred *Ka'ba* in Mekka; while a much quoted *hadīth* portrays the Founder of Islam counselling his followers that they should seek knowledge even as far as China. The concept of *Rihla* (Travel) in search of knowledge thus became . . . ," etc., Ian Richard Netton

great treasury of modern Orientalism, *The Encyclopaedia of Islam*, bears the mark of this double misunderstanding.[4] The question is how the traditionists could have possibly created an institution like the *rihla*-voyage at a time when they themselves did not yet exist as a group.

We have no serious proof that attests to the collective existence of these specialists in Tradition before the late eighth century. As for the "prophetic science" that they promoted, all evidence seems to attest that it attained its maturity only in the first half of the ninth century. If they made use of certain genealogical and doctrinal arrangements to give themselves older origins, and if they took care to give their enterprise an aura of the prestige of the past, that is simply another episode in the "invention of tradition."[5] As shown by one of the oldest sources, the *Tabaqāt* of Ibn Sā'id (d. 230/845), a biographical dictionary that, it is worth recalling, participated in the enterprise of shaping learning through a genealogy of sources, those whom the traditionists took to be their ancestors displayed a pronounced aversion to what became the procedures and the customs of their self-proclaimed heirs. First among these was 'Abd-Allāh ibn Mas'ūd (d. 32/652), the founding figure of religious intellectuality at Kufa. One person who came to join his study circle and listened to him for an entire year asserts that only once did he hear him say, "The Prophet said . . ." At that point, "seized by overwhelming regret," he apologized for his statement, saying that he could not remember whether the Prophet had truly said "something more than that, that approximated that, or that fell short of that."[6] Another disciple reports having seen him, on another occasion, apologize for having said, "I heard the Prophet say . . ." When the master realized his mistake it was too late: the damage had been done.

---

writes in the introduction to a collective work, *Golden Roads: Migration, Pilgrimages and Travel in Medieval and Modern Islam*, ed. Ian Richard Netton (Richmond UK: Curzon, 1993), x.

A similar idea is well established among Muslim scholars. One of them, criticizing Ignaz Goldziher, writes that "the *rihla* began in the era of the Companions of the Prophet. When the latter died and the wars of conquest scattered the troops of the warriors for God among the Companions in the newly Islamized regions, the *rihla* arose": Ziyād M. Mansūr, in the introduction to his edition of the *Kitāb al-Mu'jam* of Abū Bakr al-Ismā'īlī (d. 425/1033) (Medina: Maktaba al-'Ulum wa-al-Hikam, 1990), 1:102.

4. See I. R. Netton, "Rihla," in *Encyclopédie de l'Islam*, new ed. (Leiden: E. J. Brill; Paris: Maisonneuve et Larose, 1966), 8:545–46; and in *The Encyclopaedia of Islam*, new ed., ed. E. J. Van Donzel (Leiden: Brill, 1966), .8:528ff.

5. As Eric Hobsbawm reminds us, "'Invented tradition' is taken to mean a set of practices, normally governed by overtly or tacitly accepted rules . . . which seek to inculcate certain values and norms of behaviour by repetition, which automatically implies continuity with the past"—real or invented: Eric Hobsbawm, "Inventing Tradition," in *The Invention of Tradition*, ed. Eric Hobsbawm and Terence Ranger (Cambridge: Cambridge University Press, 1983, 1992), 1.

6. Ibn Sā'id, *Tabaqāt*, ed. Karl Vilhelm Zettersteen (Leiden, 1909), 3:156.

"He trembled all over, as did his clothing." He nonetheless took the time to rectify: "I think that he said approximately that, or something close to it."[7] The disciple in question, 'Aqlama ibn Qays (d. 62/681), was a Qur'an scholar and a jurisconsult, and at the death of his master his name was suggested to replace him, which involved being subject to close questioning. The Arabic text uses the term nas'al,[8] a verbal form derived from the root s.'a.l. The use of that verb implies use of the casuistic method of masā'il, the equivalent of the Latin quaestiones, a technique that had taken over entire fields of learning from theology to medicine. It was not really the preferred method of the traditionists, who inclined instead toward procedures that they derived from the verb haddatha (to transmit, relate, inform, narrate) and its nominal form hadīth (transmission, tradition, information, oral relation). The term hadīth was still used to speak of secular narratives and did not yet have the specialized meaning within their conceptual apparatus that later traditionists gave it.[9]

This means that the sage in question was not teaching the hadīth in the sense that the traditionists understood the term. Otherwise it would be difficult to understand why his disciple Ibrāhīm al-Nakha'ī (d. 96/714) should have asked him, one day, whether he knew the "hadīth that had come to him from the Prophet." The master is reported to have answered, "Yes, but I prefer to say: 'X said, Y said, and Z said'; I find that easier (than to say 'The Prophet said')."[10] Nor can we say that Nakha'ī was a specialist in Tradition in the strict sense, or that his own students were. When, at his death, his disciples asked two of their company to carry on the master's teachings, it was not in order to teach them the traditions. One of them states: "When Ibrāhīm died, we thought only A'mash (d. 148/765) capable of succeeding him. We went to see him and we interrogated him on 'the licit and the illicit' [an expression meaning 'law'], but he knew little about it. Then we interrogated him on the farā'id [the part of jurisprudence that treats successions and teaches what is due to each heir], and we saw that he possessed them. Next we went to see Hammād (d. 120/730) and we interrogated him on the farā'id, about which he knew little, and on 'the licit and the illicit,' of which he had full command. We therefore studied the farā'id from A'mash and law from Hammād."[11]

7. Ibid., 3:157.
8. Ibid., 6:59.
9. We find the term used by a transmitter of ancient Arab tales of that epoch cited in Isbahānī, Kitāb al-Aghānī, ed. Ibrahīm Ibyarī (Cairo:Dār al-Sha'b, 1969–), 9:249.
10. Ibn Sa'd, Tabaqāt, 6:190.
11. Ibid., 6:232.

One eyewitness reports that he entered the Great Mosque of Kufa in the company of the judge of that city and saw Ḥammād "surrounded by his companions," all seated in a circle animated by "their boisterousness and their loud voices." The scene, which displeased the magistrate, is a good indication that the two men were not watching a session of the transmission of traditions but a disputation circle,[12] and that such circles did not much like those who made a profession of collecting traditions. A'mash is reported to have said that if he had had dogs, he would not have hesitated to set them on *aṣ'ḥāb al-ḥadīth*, or tradition seekers.[13] A generation earlier, another great jurist in Medina, no less a personage than the grandson of the first caliph of Islam, demonstrated his hostility toward the enthusiasm for collecting *ḥadīth*. He reportedly attempted to turn one of his disciples away from the practice by telling him that when the second caliph of Islam saw that traditions attributed to the Prophet were proliferating in Medina, he gave orders to destroy by fire all the "supports" on which they had been written down. This means that to speak of a "world of traditionists" that existed "throughout the eighth century" seems more than a bit anachronistic.[14]

On the other hand, the disaffection that the doctors of the late seventh and early eighth centuries showed regarding prophetic traditions was not accompanied by an absolute refusal to use them. In order to elaborate their doctrines, the jurists of the age felt it necessary to base them on Tradition. Thus, it is not impossible that one of their number, a doctor from Basra installed in Syria named Abū Qilāba (d. 105?/723?), made the trip to Medina, where he reportedly waited for several days until a specialist in traditions returned to that city in order to collect a *ḥadīth* that he had heard of directly from him. The source tells us that the Iraqi jurisconsult made the trip in the hope of obtaining just "one *ḥadīth*." This fits with other evidence that the same doctor from Basra displayed circumspection about improper transmission of this type of material. One of his disciples tells us that when his master had transmitted more than three traditions at one time, he thought he had said too much.[15]

12. Ibid., 6:175.

13. Khaṭīb al-Baghdādī, *Sharaf Aṣḥāb al-Ḥadīth*, ed. Muḥammad Saʿīd Khāṭib Ogiu (Ankara: Dār iḥyā al-Sunnah al-abawīyah, 1972), 131.

14. Régis Blachère, *Le Coran*, 3 vols. (Paris: Maisonneuve, 1947–50), 1:82. A similar anachronism can be found in Hichem Djaït, who describes Ibn Masʿūd surrounded by "a group of companions, all 'reciters,' exegetes, *traditionists*, ancestors of Islamic knowledge at Kufa": Hichem Djaït, *La grande discorde: Religion et politique dans l'Islam des origines* (Paris: Gallimard, 1989). 134.

15. Ibn Saʿd, *Tabaqāt*, 7:185; Abū Nuʿaym, *Hilyat al-Awliyāʾ*, 10 vols. (Cairo: Maktabat al-Khānjī, 1932–38); new ed., 10 vols. (Beirut: Dār al-Kitāb al-ʿArabī, 1967–68), 2:287; Dhahabī, *Siyar*

When the great Medina jurist Zuhrī (d. 124/741) first arrived in Damascus in 701, he encountered the same determination to respect Tradition.
In the Umayyad capital, one of the first study circles that he frequented
was that of an eminent doctor who had connections at court. He learned
there that the caliph was eager to know what laws had been passed in the
time of 'Umar I (r. 634–44), one of the "Rightly Guided" caliphs, regarding
the status of a slave concubine who had borne her master's child. Zuhrī
won his sovereign's favor by providing the information requested, but he
lost that of his master, who was hostile to the reigning dynasty.[16]

Although we are now at the threshold of the second century of the existence of Islam, the voyage was only beginning to develop around the first
study circles constituted in the larger urban centers of the Hejaz (Mecca,
Medina), Iraq (Basra, Kufa), and Syria (Damascus). Still, there were a few
men of letters who were already genuine "*tour*ists." This was true of 'Ikrima
(d. 105/723). He was an indefatigable traveler whose peregrinations took
him to the Hejaz, Iraq, Persia, and Yemen, and even as far as Khurasan
and Transoxiana.[17] The judge of Kufa at the time said of him, admiringly,
that he had never known anyone who had visited a greater number of
"horizons" in his quest for knowledge.[18] Ayyūb al-Sikhtiyānī (d. 131/748),
a doctor in Basra, reports how he met him: "I wanted to go see 'Ikrima,
wherever he might be—he traveled much—when one day, when I was in
the marketplace of Basra, I saw a man on a donkey (and heard) people crying, 'It's 'Ikrima! It's 'Ikrima!' A crowd of people then surrounded him. I
came closer in order to ask him the questions lodged in my heart, but I
could not do so. They had flown from my mind. So I placed myself next
to his donkey, and as people questioned him, I memorized his responses
to them."[19]

Mak'hūl (d. 112/730), whom the Syrian school of law considers its founding master, was also one of the great travelers of the time. Leaving Egypt,
he passed through the entire Middle East from Syria to Iraq, including the
Hejaz. When he got to Iraq, he spent several months at the court of the

---

A'lām al-Nubalā', ed. Shu'ayb al-Arna'ūt et al., 25 vols. (Beirut: Mu'assasat al-Risālah, 1982–83),
4:470.

16. His master, Sa'īd ibn al-Musayyab (d. 94/712), one of the "seven jurists" of Medina, held it
against him to have dealt with the "iniquitous" Umayyads: see Shukr-Allāh al-Qawjānī, *Al-Zuhrī*,
extracted from Ibn 'Asākir, *Tārīkh madinat Dimashq*, ed. 'Alī Shīrī, 40 vols. (Beirut: Dār al-Fikr,
1995–96), 14:15.

17. Ibn Khuthayma Zuhayr ibn Harb, *Kitāb al-'Ilm*, MS no. 3830, Zāhiriyya, Damascus,
fol. 193a.

18. Ibid., fol. 188a.

19. Ibn Sa'd, *Tabaqāt*, 5:213.

grand judge of that city, observing his decisions.[20] At Medina he joined the circle of a master who had earned from his contemporaries the title of "jurisconsult of the jurisconsults."[21] There he met other men of letters, in particular, from Iraq.[22] He is the first man of letters whose travel narrative, albeit in fragments, appears in ninth-century sources:

> Fragment 1: I was in Egypt the slave of a woman of the tribe of Hudayl, and that woman gave me my freedom. But I did not leave Egypt before having gathered all the knowledge that could be found there. Then I went to the Hejaz, and from there to Iraq, with the same purpose and with the same success. Next I traveled toward Syria and thoroughly examined that land. . . . I have never left a land without thinking that there was a knowledge hidden within it that I had not heard. . . . I traveled throughout the earth in search of knowledge. . . . Then I met [the judge] Sha'bī; he was without peer.
>
> Fragment 2: I frequented [the judge] Shurayh [d. 78/697] with assiduity for several months without interrogating him; I was satisfied with hearing him pass judgment.[23]

That was the start, after which the men of letters of Islam made incessant journeys within the empire. For a long time the Middle Ages resonated to the sound of their mounts' hooves.

The *'ilm*, an Onomastic Emblem

Mak'hūl said of the Kufa judge whom he had frequented that he had never known any man more knowledgeable than he "in matters of past *Sunna*."[24] It would seem normal for a great judge to be an authority on what should, in practical terms, furnish the traditional rules of law. It seems in fact in-

---

20. Ibn Khuthayma, *Kitāb al-'Ilm*, fol. 188b. The *Tabaqāt* of Ibn Sa'd often shows the presence of "searchers for knowledge" in the courts of the judges: see *Tabaqāt*, 6:175–76, for example.

21. This was Sa'īd ibn al-Muysayyab (d. 94/712). On the juridical doctrine of this doctor, see Hāshim Jamil 'Abd-Allah, *Fiqh al-Imām Sa'īd ibn al-Musayyab*, 4 vols. (Baghdad: Jumhurīyah al-'Irāqīyah, 1974–75).

22. Ibn Sa'd, *Tabaqāt*, 5:90.

23. Ibn Khuthayma, *Kitāb al-'Ilm*, fol. 188b. Ibn Khuthayma (d. 243/857) and Ibn Sa'd, *Tabaqāt*, 6:92, both include the second fragment. The first was used, in the second half of the ninth century, by Abū Dāwud al-Sijistānī (d. 275/888): Abū Dāwud Sijistānī, *Jāmi' al-Sahīh*, 9 vols. in 19 pts. (Baduz: Jam'iyat al-Maknaz al-Islāmī, 2000–2001), 1:274. See also Dhahabī, *Kitāb Tadhkirat al-huffādh*, 3rd ed., 2 vols. (Hyderabad: Dairatu L-Ma'arif-il-Osmana, 1955), 1:108; and Dhahabī, *Tahdhīb Kitāb al Kabā'ir* ('Ammān: al-Urdun; al-Maktabah al-Islāmīyah, 1996), 572. Goldziher, *Études sur la tradition islamique*, 40, quotes this fragment from Abū Dāwud.

24. Ibn Sa'd, *Tabaqāt*, 6:177.

conceivable that the application of the law not demand a reactivation of the *Sunna*, the *usus* of the "community of Muslims" as that community had been organized by Muhammad and his immediate successors. One might then conclude that the professionals of law and of religion, like this magistrate, would have sought to glean from it their doctrinal elaborations. The development of a social life that was becoming more and more complexly tangled as the empire grew, now stretching from Asia to Europe and to Africa, demanded the regulation of relations between individuals and groups within the framework of consistent legal norms and more or less unified rituals. The judges were officials named by the sovereigns. Without going so far as to take it for granted that, from that time on, they followed a line determined by the state, it is likely that their political masters' preoccupations helped to shape the development of jurisprudence in the direction of the *Sunna*.[25] The considerable role that jurists allied to the Umayyad dynasty played in that alliance between law and Tradition is a familiar tale. They made that contribution thanks to their authority as judges, their competence as jurisconsults, and their talents as professors.

With the coming to power of the 'Abbāsids, the movement for drawing juridical materials out of the *Sunna* led to the first major attempts to put them in written form. That enterprise of dogmatic elaboration produced such collections as the *Summa of Traditions* of Ma'mar ibn Rāshid (d. 153/770),[26] and the *Book of Traditions* of the judge Ibn Abī Dhi'b (d. 159/775). Those two works are unfortunately lost, and we can judge them only by what the Middle Ages happened to retain of them. It is known, for example, that, contrary to what their titles suggest, these two compendiums were not collections of traditions, but rather works of law, divided into chapters, as was the jurists' practice.[27] Another lost work, the *Major Summa* of Sufyān al-Thawrī (d. 161/777), also seems to have belonged to the same category of juridico-traditionist works. Although a bibliographer who consulted this work in the mid-tenth century reports that it was composed "in the manner of the (books of) *hadīths*," it is possible that it contained a choice of traditions capable of serving as a doctrinal source. Before he was a traditionist, the author of this work was an eminent jurist who founded a school of law that lasted until the early eleventh century.

25. On ways of using the notion of *Sunna* in the Umayyad age, see Patricia Crone and Martin Hinds, *God's Caliph* (Cambridge: Cambridge University Press, 1986), 59–79.

26. 'Amr ibn 'Alī al-Ja'dī, *Tabaqāt Fuqahā' al-Yaman*, ed. Fu'ād Sayyid (Beirut: Dār al-Kitāb al-'Ilmīyah, 1981) 67.

27. As noted by Ibn al-Nadīm in *Fihrist*, ed. Ridā al-Māzindarānī (Beirut: Dār al-Masīrah, 1988), 225.

Sufyān al-Thawrī's desire to compare his juridical doctrine with the Tradition came from the influence of the juridical tendencies of the Hejaz.[28]

Although these academic and professional milieus supportive of the Tradition did not conceive of their activities in collecting *hadīth* as independent from their juridical constructions, we would have to admit that the "science of traditions" (*'ilm al-hadīth*) was born out of their concerns. Such circles brought together several generations of men of letters, whose sole preoccupation was to search out, collect, and compare traditions by traveling from one region to another in the Muslim world.[29] For that reason, they took on the title of *muhaddith*, which distinguished them from the jurists (*fuqahā'*) and from the other doctors of law (*'ulamā*). Despite the state persecutions that they suffered during the years 827–56, the ninth century was their golden age.[30]

To diffuse their materials, these specialists in the Tradition followed the model of the *Musnad*, a type that drew its name from the fact that the *hadīth* such works contained were linked by a chain of guarantors going back to a Companion, who himself relied on the authority of the Prophet. But the practical—and notably the juridical—use of these *Musnad* was so awkward that the most daring and the most competent specialists composed their own *Musannaf*,[31] works that were thematically divided into chapters.[32] This did not stop renowned jurists from continuing to compose collections of the *Musnad* type up to the late tenth century.

28. Thawrī left Kufa to live in Mecca, where he was exposed to that city's school of law. Shāfi'ī (d. 204/819), in whose opinion "Malik ibn Anas [his master] and Sufyān al-Thawrī were equal in matter of the transmission of the knowledge [*'ilm*] of the Hejaz," said that if the one had not been in Medina and the other in Mecca, "the *'ilm* of the Hejaz would have disappeared": Ibn Abī Hatīm, *Ādāb al-Shāfi'ī wa-manāqibuh* (Beirut: Dār al-Kutub al-'Ilimīyah, 1963), 205, 210.

29. G. H. A. Juynboll has shown the extent to which the compilations of these early traditionists bear the mark of the jurists' milieus from which they sprang: see G. H. A. Juynboll, "Some Notes on Islam's First *Fuqahā*, Distilled from Early *Hadīth* Literature," *Arabica* 39 (1992): 287–314.

30. On the persecution of this group, see Walter Melville Patton, *Ahmed ibn Hanbal and the Mihna: A Biography of the Imām including an Account of the Mohammedan Inquisition Called the Mihna, 218–234 A.H.* (Leiden, 1897); Wilfred Madelung, "The Origins of the Controversy Concerning the Creation of the Koran, in *Orientalia Hispanica: Sive Studia F. M. Pareja Octogenario Dicata*, ed. J. M. Barral (Leiden: Brill: 1974); John Abdallah Nawas, *Al-Ma'mūn: Mihna and Caliphate* (Nijmegen, 1992); and Nimrod Hurvitz, "Ahmad b. Hanbal and the Formation of Islamic Orthodoxy" (Ph.D. dissertation, Princeton University, 1994), esp. 203–57.

31. The oldest of the *Musannaf* that have come down to us is that of the Yemenite 'Abd al-Razzāq, *al-Musannaf*, ed. Habīb al-Rahmān al-A'zamī (Karachi, 1972).

32. On this model, see Ignaz Goldziher, *Muhammedanische Studien*, 2:228–29; *Études sur la tradition islamique*, 286–88. Muhammad ibn Yahyā al-'Adanī was one of the first to use the *Musnad* model, according to Bahā' al-Dīn Jandī, *Al-Sulūk fī Tabaqāt 'Ulamā' al-Yaman*, ed. Muhammad ibn 'Alī ibn al-Husayn al-Akwa' al-Hiwalī (San'a: Maktabat al-Irshād, 1993, 1995), 154.

To the extent that they promoted a new field of knowledge, the traditionists developed a gnoseological theory in which the only "science" (*'ilm*)
was that of religion, and the only science of religion was that of the traditions. Conceived of as a knowledge based in learning, that *'ilm* was defined
as constructed on the base of the *hadīth*—that is, of sayings attributed
to the Prophet. It soon made the *Sunna*, which forms Islamic Tradition,
properly speaking,[33] a principle of authority, conferring on it a dogmatic
status that at times placed it on the same level as the word of God, if not a
right of abrogation. But far from taking credit for its invention, the traditionists took refuge behind the prestigious doctors of the past and spoke
in their name. This sacralization of Tradition was accomplished by the
prestigious elders of the late seventh century. The great jurist and traveler Mak'hūl (d. 112/730), whom we have already met, was credited with
the rule according to which "the Qur'an needs the *Sunna* more than the
Sunna does the Qur'an."[34] One of his contemporaries is considered the
source of the principle that "the *Sunna* is judge of the Qur'an, but the contrary is not true."[35] In order to give such principles a firm foundation, the
traditionists were led, as early as the end of the eight century, to invent
out of whole cloth the idea that Tradition, as they understood it, was in

33. "The *hadīth* is an oral communication that is traced back to the Prophet. The *Sunna* is
the *usus* in force in the ancient Muslim Community touching on a point of law or of religion":
Goldziher, *Études sur la tradition islamique*, 13. On the older meanings of the term, see G. H. A.
Juynboll, "Some New Ideas on the Development of *Sunna* as a Technical Term in Early Islam,"
Jerusalem Studies in Arabic and Islam 10 (1987): 97–118; reprinted in G. H. A. Juynboll, *Studies on
the Origins and Uses of Islamic Hadīth* (Brookfield, VT: Variorum, 1996). See also Fazlur Rahman,
"Concepts of Sunna, *Ijtihād* and *Ijma'* in the Early Period," *Islamic Studies* 1, no. 1 (1962): 5–21.
Modern studies are dominated by the "veritative" approach given them by Joseph Schacht in *The
Origins of Muhammadan Jurisprudence* (Oxford: Clarendon Press, 1950); and in Schacht, "A Revalu-
ation of Islamic Tradition," *Journal of the Royal Asiatic Society* (1949): 143–54. Michael Cook states
that "Schacht's discovery of the spread of *isnād* is in fact a highly ambivalent contribution to
knowledge," and that, in his opinion, "the choice is between Schacht and Shāfi'ī": Michael Cook,
Early Muslim Dogma: A Source-Critical Study (Cambridge: Cambridge University Press, 1981), 116.
See also N. J. Coulson, "European Criticism of *Hadīth* Liberature," in *Arabic Literature to the End
of the Umayyad Period*, vol. 1 of *The Cambridge History of Arabic Literature*, ed. A. F. L. Beeston et al.
(Cambridge: Cambridge University Press, 1983), 317–31; Juynboll, *Muslim Tradition*; and J. Robson,
"Hadīth," in *Encyclopédie de l'Islam*, new ed. (1966), 3:24–30; and in *The Encyclopaedia of Islam*, new
ed. (1966), 3:23ff. In a more apologetic spirit, see Muhammad Mustafa A'zami, *Studies in Early
Hadīth Literature with a Critical Edition of Some Early Texts* (Beirut: al-Maktab al-Islāmī, 1968).
34. Dārimī, *Sunan*, 2 vols. (Beirut: Dār Ihyā' al-Sunna al-Nabawāyah, 1975), vol. 1, hadīth
no. 586.
35. Khatīb al-Baghdādī, *Sharaf Ashāb al-Hadīth*, 82. On this sacralization of tradition, see Ibn
Qutayba, *Mukhtalaf al-Hadīth* (Cairo: Maktabat al-Kullīyāt al-Azharīyah, 1966); trans. Gérard
Lecompte as *Le traité de divergence du Hadīth d'Ibn Kutayba (m. 276/889)* (Damascus: Institut Français, 1962); and Khatīb al-Baghdādī, *Al-Kifāya fī 'ilm al-Riwāya* (Beirut: Dār al-Kitāb al-'Arabī,
1985), 8–16.

circulation from the first century of Islam. An exemplum credited to a disciple of a doctor by the name of Abū Mijlaz (d. 101/719) presents a man of letters who calls for less attention to traditions and more focus on the Qur'an in the master's study circle. The master, offended, is reported to have responded, "What brings us together here does not seem to me of less importance than the study of the Qur'an."[36] In the hands of the traditionists what might, at the limit, be merely a rhetorical argument became a principle. A Basra jurist with similar ideas is quoted on what his master, Abū Qilāba (d. 105?/723?), said: "If you are teaching the *Sunna* to someone and he says, 'Drop this and tell me what there is in the Book of God,' know that such a man has lost his way."[37] Still, we are told by the traditionist sources themselves that when that same doctor had delivered "more than three traditions," he considered that he had transmitted enough.[38] The truth of the matter is that fewer traditions were in circulation in the early eighth century than at the end of that century.[39]

Even supposing that the primacy of Tradition over the Qur'an was already established by the age of Abū Qilāba, we have enough examples to show that not everyone accepted that primacy as a rule throughout the eighth century.[40] At the end of the eighth century, a good many doctors opposed the forced move to sacralize the *Sunna*.[41] In the traditionist camp,

---

36. Khatīb al-Baghdādī, *Sharaf Ashāb al-Hadīth*, 83.

37. Ibn Saʿd, *Tabaqāt* 7:184; Dhahabī, *Siyar*, 4:472.

38. Ibn Saʿd, *Tabaqāt*, 7:185; Abū Nuʿaym, *Hilyat al-Awliyā'*, 2:287; Dhahabī, *Siyar*, 4:470.

39. On the occasion of his first voyage in 796–97, for example, Ahmad ibn Hanbal met ʿAbd al-Rahmān ibn Mahdī (d. 198/813), and under the authority of the latter, he wrote down six or seven hundred traditions. On his second voyage, he took about a thousand traditions from the same source; see Hurvitz, "Ahmad b. Hanbal," 287.

40. A late but possibly creditable narrative—it is reported without comment by a jurist of a rival school of law—relates that the doctors of Kufa went to see Abū Hanīfa (d. 150/767) to dissuade him from presenting reasoning by analogy (*qiyās*) as a source of the law, arguing that it was the work of the devil. The great Iraqi jurist is reported to have responded: "What I say has nothing in common with analogy. It is entirely in the Qur'an, since God has said, 'Nothing have we omitted from the Book'" (Qur'an 6:38). "What I say is analogy only for those to whom God has not granted comprehension of the Qur'an": Shaʿranī, *Kitāb al-Mizān*, ed. ʿAbd al-Rahmān ʿUmayrah (Beirut: ʿĀlam al-Kutub, 1989), 1:18.

41. To contest the new dogmatic principle, traditionists in Syria based their arguments on the tradition in which the Prophet is supposed to have said, "When you receive a *hadīth*, compare it with the Book of God; if it turns out to be in conformity [with it], take it on, and if it departs from it, reject it." Subjecting the chain of transmission of one tradition to criticism, the Iraqi traditionist Yahyā ibn Muʿīn (d. 233/847) notes that his Syrian editors relate it according to Yazīd ibn Rabīʿa, who was in fact unknown (*majhūl*). The traditionist asserted that, according to Abū al-Ashʿat, no one of that name was known. The latter is himself given in the chain of guarantors as having received the tradition in question from the Companion of the Prophet Thawbān. As Ibn Muʿīn notes, all of the *hadīth* that have Thawbān as the terminus of their chain of authority are reported according to Abū Asmā' al-Barqī, who, as it happens, was absent from the chain of

not all adhered to this movement with a good conscience.[42] It seems that what was needed was the authority of someone like Shāfiʿī (d. 204/819) if the idea that the *ḥadīth*, which is not the eternal word of God, nonetheless remains of divine inspiration, was to triumph. "It is God," Shāfiʿī pronounces, "who has imposed on believers the obligation to conform to his Revelation and to the traditions of his Messenger."[43] Allah had conferred the privilege of associating God's word with human speech on Muhammad alone. This is the basis of the dogmatic rule that makes obedience to the prescriptions of the Messenger of God an act of faith. Can Tradition claim powers of abrogation over the Qur'an? Yes, certain scholars responded. Without removing the word of God from the grip of Tradition, Shāfiʿī supports the contrary opinion, saying that only the Qur'an abrogates the Qur'an. But since Tradition alone can elucidate the Book of God, it is the obligatory gateway to comprehension of God's word.[44] This was the thesis that ended up winning,[45] but not to the exclusion of the counterthesis of the abrogation of the Qur'an by Tradition, which continued to have active partisans throughout the Middle Ages.[46] The divisions between the two camps remained within the profession, however. The traditionists and their allies presented a united face to the outside world, insisting that in no event could one accede to God without passing

transmission of this particular tradition. The critic concludes that therefore the *ḥadīth* was apocryphal. See Tirmidhī, *Jāmiʿ al-Saḥīḥ*, ed. Muhammad ibn ʿAbd Allāh ibn al-ʿArabī, 13 vols. in 5 pts. (Al-Azhar: al-Matbāʿah al-Misrīyah, 1931–34), 10:132–33.

42. When he was stricken with blindness, Hārūn ibn Maʿrūf (d. 231/845), a specialist on the *ḥadīth* from Khurasan, interpreted his misfortune as the sign of divine punishment. In a dream he heard someone say to him, "He who manifests more interest in Tradition than in the Qur'an is punished": Dhahabī, *Siyar*, 11:130.

43. Shāfiʿī, *Risāla*; trans. Lakhdar Souami as *La Risāla: Les fondements du droit musulman* (Paris: Actes Sud, 1997), 92.

44. Shāfiʿī argues this point of view in his famous *Risāla*. Suyūtī, on the other hand, attributes to Shāfiʿī a solution that makes the abrogation of the Qur'an by Tradition possible: see Suyūtī, *Al-Itqān fī ʿUlūm al-Qurʾān*, 2 vols. (Cairo: Matbaʿat al-Maʿahid, 1935), 2:21. Goldziher alludes to him without referring to the thesis expounded in the *Risāla*.

45. The thesis is defended in the *Book of Revenues* of the judge Ibn Sallām (d. 224/838), for example, where that author clearly indicates that "the *Sunna* is explicative of Revelation": Ibn Sallām, *Kitāb al-Amwāl*, ed. Muhammad Khalīl Harrās (Beirut: Dār al-Kutub al-ʿIlmīyah, 1986), 541. Commenting on the rule, Ibn Qutayba later explained that "the *Sunna* makes the Qur'an explicit and exposes what God wanted to say in His Book": trans. Lecompte, *Le traité de divergence*, 320.

46. "Most Moderns," writes Abū Bakr al-Hāzimī (d. 584/1188), "lean toward the validity of the abrogation of the Qur'an by the *Sunna*": *Al-iʿtibār fī al-Nāsikh wa-al-Mansūkh min al-akhbār*, ed. Muhammad ʿAbd al-ʿAzīz (Cairo, n.d.), 52. With more pondered judgment Ibn al-Jawzī (d. 597/1200) speaks of it as a marginal solution: *Nāsikh al-Qurʾān* (Damascus: Dār al-Thaqāfah al-Arabīyah, 1990), 119.

through his Prophet and, consequently, without passing through them. They used that extraordinarily powerful dogmatic chain to bind up Sunnite Islam to our own day.

If the *'ilm* of the traditionists was a form of religious knowledge in its earlier stages,[47] it was not just any form of religious knowledge, but a knowledge of traditions. Hence, it was focused on collecting, transmitting, meditating, and studying all sorts of prophetic exempla. When the traditionists, as we have seen, declined responsibility for the invention of the *'ilm,* they credited its creation to "Pious Ancients." In the beginning of the ninth century, one account was transmitted, credited to a doctor of the first half of the eighth century, stating that when 'Atā ibn Abī Rabāh (d. 115/733), the great master of the juridical school of the Hejaz, wanted to teach, he always asked his listeners if they preferred to hear about the *'ilm* (that is, traditions) or about *ra'y* (his own juridical "opinions" and those of his masters.).[48]

In the Umayyad age, to say of the law that it is *ra'y* was a commonplace: the equivalence *ra'y* = law is well attested in the mid-eighth century. In 748 a doctor from Medina on his way to Egypt was stopped by a local judge who wanted to know who held authority in Medina in questions of *ra'y* after the death of Rabi'a ibn 'Abd al-Rahmān (d. 130/747), called "the Reasoner."[49] The doctor answered that authority had passed on to Mālik ibn Anas (d. 179/795). Despite his attachment to Tradition, Mālik does not hesitate to speak, in his *Epitome of the Law*—the oldest example of the genre that has come down to us—of his own personal *ra'y.*[50] This means that at the time, the notion had not yet been polluted by all of the prejudices that distorted it in the ninth century.

At the beginning of the eighth century, the pair *'ilm-ra'y* was operational, even before the traditionists had come into existence.[51] But whereas in the

47. Ibn Sa'd, *Tabaqāt*, 6:345.

48. Ibid., 5:345.

49. Ibn 'Abd al-Barr, *al-Intiqā fi fadā'il a'imma al-thalāthah* (Cairo: Maktabat al-Qudsī, 1931), 262.

50. Abdel-Magid Turki, "Le *Muwatta'* de Mālik, ouvrage de *fiqg*, entre le *hadīth* et le *ra'y*: Ou comment aborder l'étude du mālikisme Kairouanais au IV/Xe siècle," *Studia Islamica* 86 (1997): 5–36. See also *Al-Muwatta of Imam Malik ibn Anas: The First Formulation of Islamic Law*, trans. Aisha Abdurrahman Brewley (London: Kegan Paul, 1989).

51. When did *ra'y* first appear as a technical term, standing in contrast to the *'ilm* in Islamic culture? Contrary to Ignaz Goldziher and Joseph Schacht, who see a late origin for the famous tradition in which the Prophet, giving instruction to Mu'ād ibn Jabal, recommends that he use his "personal reasoning" (*ijtihād al-ra'y*), M. M. Bravmann opts for an earlier origin and offers philological arguments in support of his stand. He shows that the term, in its technical acception of a hermeneutic process by which new "procedures" and new "norms" were created, existed as

early eighth century the two terms were more or less equivalent, at the beginning of the ninth century they stood opposed to one another like antinomic entities.[52] This semantic tour de force arose out of the growing rivalry between the traditionists and the jurists, notably those of the Iraqi school. The tension that shook the two rival camps was not just dogmatic, but also social and statutory. Jāhiz (d. 255/868), always a sharp observer of the society of his time, depicted the social effects of this rivalry in a famous passage of his *Book of the Animals*: "One occasionally encounters one of those men in search of religious traditions and Qur'anic interpretation; he frequented the jurists for fifty years, yet he enjoys no consideration and was not named to the functions of *qadi*. All he would need to do, however, would be to study the books of Abū Hanīfa and his competitors and spend one or two years learning the books of stipulations to have people take him for a governor when they pass before his door."[53]

Both the *ra'y* and the *'ilm*, along with other terms, gave rise to new discursive and ritual formations, standing in opposition to *jahl* (ignorance) and in connection with *'amal* (works of piety). If the relation *'ilm-jahl* drew meaning from the antagonism between knowledge and ignorance (in particular, scriptural knowledge and ignorance), the relation *'ilm-'amal*, to the contrary, was based on the actualization of theoretical knowledge in social practices. Just how did all these discursive and ritual formations involve travel? In differentiated ways. The voyage played an important role in the first but was somewhat less important in the second. And if, in the first, travel derived from a theory of knowledge, in the second it was related to a theory of action.[54] In one case its status was epistemological; in the other it was axiological.

---

early as the epoch of the caliph 'Umar I (r. 634–44): see M. M. Bravmann, *The Spiritual Background of Early Islam: Studies in Ancient Arab Concepts* (Leiden: Brill, 1972), 185.

52. When the traditionists appeared on the scene, the term *ra'y*, which had had positive connotations, came to be associated with *hawā*, or errant speech. It is not by chance that the traditionist Dārimī (d. 255/868) speaks of the *ra'y* in the chapter of his *Sunan* on "avoiding *hawā*."

53. Jāhiz, *Tahdhīb Kitāb al-Hayawān*, ed. 'Abd al-Salām Muhammad Hārūn, 7 vols. (Cairo: Maktabat al-Khanjī, 1938–45); selections trans. Lakhdar Souami as *Le Cadi et la mouche: Anthologie du Livre des animaux* (Paris: Sindbad, 1988), 184.

54. The ideology that saw the voyage in search of prophetic traditions as a religious obligation was the subject of a work by the Iraqi traditionist Abū Bakr al-Ajūrī (d. 360/970). The work's title is an entire program in itself: "The Book of the Obligation of the Search for *'ilm*": Abū Bakr Ajūrī, *Kitāb Fard Talab al-'Ilm*, ed. Leonard T. Librande, *Bulletin d'études orientales* 45 (1993): 89–159. It should be noted that the prophetic tradition according to which "the voyage in search of *'ilm* is a legal obligation" was judged to be apocryphal by the more scrupulous of the traditionists. Its first editors were Ibn Māja (d. 273/870), *Sunan*, ed. Mohammad Fu'ād 'Abd al-Bāqī, 2 vols. (Cairo: 'Isā al-Bābī al-Halabī, 1972), 1:81; and Abū Bakr Bazzār (d. 296/908), *Musnad*, ed. M. Zīn-Allāh, 5 vols. (Beirut: Muassasat 'Ulm al-Quran, 1988), 1:172.

In saving the *'ilm* by "works," the traditionists gave it a practical aim that was both its foundation and its norm. This is why they were in advance of society, not only as guardians of the *'ilm*, but also as its "vivificators." Tirmidhī (d. 279/892), one of the authors of the canonical "Six Books" of Tradition, relates that a famous doctor of the latter half of the eighth century was fond of saying to his disciples that "a scholar who practices and teaches his science is particularly praised in the heavens."[55] It is not certain that the two men were thinking of the same *'ilm*—we have already seen that doctor's dislike of the collection of traditions—but Tirmidhī cites the statement of that master as an echo of a *hadīth* he himself had edited, according to which scholars are praised by all the beings of the heavens and the earth, "including the fishes in the water." Drawing on that capacity to bring the heavens closer to the earth, the traditionists claimed dogmatic functions of *representation*.[56] When cast in the modality of time, that function made the traditionists the sole true heirs of the Prophet. It raised them up in the presence of an absence: the prophet Muhammad, physically dead, was nonetheless living thanks to them. The *Corpus traditionum* gave him a substitute corporeal envelope. This led one of the masters among the critics of traditions, Hākim al-Nīsābūrī (d. 405/1014) to say about Tirhidhī's *Summa*: "Having this book at home is like having as a guest a prophet with whom one can converse."[57] Even earlier, one doctor, who had been asked why he remained continually closed in at home, responded that he found pleasure in "the company of the Prophet," thus letting it be understood that if he never went out it was because he was absorbed by the reading of books of prophetic traditions.[58] In the modality

55. Tirmidhī, *Jāmi'*, 10:159.

56. In the dual sense in which Louis Marin understands the term "representation" as having an "effect and power of presence" and as an "effect of subject," which he explains as a "power of institution, authorization, and legitimation as resulting from the functioning of the framework reflected onto itself." The representation has "a double power—that of rendering anew and imaginarily present, not to say living, the absent and the dead and that of constituting its own legitimate and authorized subject by exhibiting qualifications, justifications, and titles of the present and living to being": Louis Marin, *Le portrait du roi* (Paris: Minuit, 1981), 16; quoted from the English translation by Martha Houle as *Portrait of the King* (Minneapolis: University of Minnesota Press, 1988), 6.

57. Dhahabī, *Kitāb Tadhkirat*, 1:634.

58. Khatīb al-Baghdādī, *Al-Jāmi' li-Akhlāq al-Rāwī wa Adab al-Sāmi'*,MS no. 505, Mustalah al-Hadīth, Dār al-Kutub, Cairo, fol. 176b. We shall see elsewhere that the traditionists often communicated with the Prophet in dreams. In 934, when the traditionist Tabarānī (d. 360/970) found himself in the "desert of Isfahan," he consulted the Prophet in a dream about the authenticity of a certain number of *hadīth*s: Ibn Manda, *Juz' fihi Dhikr Abā al-Qāsim . . . al-Tabarānī*, ed. Kamāl Yūsūf Hūt (Beirut: Muassasat al-Rayyan, 2001), 112–13. On this sort of contact with the Prophet,

of space, the function of representation predisposed the traditionists to mediation between heaven and earth. When one of them was asked who were the *abdāl*, the "substitute saints" who were the pillars of the world's order and spiritual equilibrium, he is reported to have responded, "If these were not the transmitters of prophetic traditions, I cannot see who they could be." As anonymous champions of intercession and of the struggle between good and evil, the *abdāl* had chosen as their dwelling place the border areas of Islam, from which they watched over Muslims. Combined with that myth, the pair *'ilm-'amal* gave rise to the ideology of the sojourn at the frontier that will be discussed later. As formulated by the traditionists in the late eighth century, the meritorious sojourn at the frontier functioned with a dual valence. It exalted the salutary contents of the *'ilm*, but at the same time it permitted the traditionists to make use of the social resonance that they needed in their role as a specialized body located at the meeting point between the past and the present and the heavens and the earth.

A Catastrophic Theory of Knowledge

One way that the traditionists justified the institution of the voyage consisted in stressing the idea of the imminent disappearance of the *'ilm*. The pessimism that resulted from that belief shaped the idea of a need (and a pressing one) to find a Noah's Ark to safeguard Tradition and shelter it from the ravages of oblivion. Because the entire Muslim Middle Ages succumbed to the phantasm of a Great Forgetfulness, it cultivated—in a fine display of unanimity—a veritable cult of memory. In this general mobilization, the voyage appeared to be essential to ward off forgetfulness. But, the traditionists asserted, it was the "Pious Ancients" who initiated that conception of time worthy of Hesiod, destroying everything that came to lodge in its folds. Time's erosion, dramatized within a narrative, had supposedly been announced by the Prophet, who is reported to have declared his own century "the best of all" but said that the centuries to come in following ages were less certain, passing through in an inexorable decline until the day when men would be faced with a fatal "adversity."[59] Like

see M. J. Kister, "The Interpretation of Dreams: An Unknown Manuscript of Ibn Qutayba's *'Ibārat al-Ru'ya*," *Israel Oriental Studies* 4 (1974): 67–103; reprinted in Kister, *Society and Religion from Jāhiliyya to Islam* (Brookfield, VT: Variorum, 1990), chap. 24, esp 78–79.

59. Ibn 'Abd al-Barr, *Jāmi' Bayān al-'Ilm wa-fadlih*, ed. 'Abd al-Rahmān Muhammad 'Uthmān, 2 vols. (Medina: al-Maktabah al-Sulfiyah, 1968), 1:188.

everything else caught on the cutting edge of time's irreversibility, the *'ilm* was projected to undergo the same decline.[60]

Belief in the disappearance of the *'ilm* long haunted the minds of Muslims. The prose writers and the traditionists claimed that the first caliph of Islam soon felt the fears that such a belief inspired. At the death of Muhammad, the Bedouin tribes of the Arabian Peninsula in large part broke the ties of allegiance that linked them to the young, prematurely orphaned *umma*. In order to force them back into the fold, the caliph Abū Bakr carried on an all-out war, in the course of which many of those who had known the Prophet and learned the revelation from him perished. Fearing that the Qur'an might disappear along with its "bearers," the caliph decided that the Revelation should be written down as soon as possible.[61] Instead of dissipating, however, the unbearable belief in the effacement of Islamic knowledge continued to exist among even the most literate of the Companions of the Prophet. One ninth-century source tells us that when 'Umar, the second caliph of Islam, died, some thought that "nine-tenths of the *'ilm*" had disappeared with him.[62] The more cultivated Companions probably passed on their fear to their disciples of the next generation, known as the "Successors" (*Tābi'ūn*). A text in dialogue form shows one of these reacting with horror as he learns that his master is about to die:

> "Why are you weeping?"
>
> "I am weeping for the *'ilm* that I have been hearing from you and that will disappear with you."
>
> "Do not weep: the *'ilm* will not disappear [a variant adds: "until the final judgment; and he who seeks it will know that it is the Qur'an and the *Sunna*"]. He who will seek it will find it. Solicit it as Abraham solicited it when he inter-

60. In this sense, 'Abd-Allāh ibn 'Abbās (d. 68/687), the young cousin of the Prophet and one of the most learned among his entourage, is crediting with having told his disciples that a time would come in which every passing year would be more "miserable" (or more "iniquitous") than the one before it. He is quoted as adding, "And I am not speaking of a year more fertile than another or of a sovereign better than another, but of your scholars, of your pious men, and of your doctors, who will depart, one after the other, and whom you will not be able to replace": Dārimī, *Sunan*, 1:65. For the Syrian jurist Awza'ī (d. 157/773), who transmits this story, the prophecy had already come true in his epoch and the *'ilm* had already begun to come apart, fragment by fragment, like "a rope whose strands unravel one knot at a time."

61. It was a scribe who had been in the service of Muhammad, Zayd ibn Thābit, who was charged with reviewing the various partial collections that were already extant, to which he was to add many fragments of the Revelation conserved only in memory. On the formation of the vulgate Qur'an, see Régis Blachère, *Introduction au Coran* (Paris: Maisonneuve, 1947), 4–135.

62. Ibn Khuthayma, *Kitāb al-'Ilm*, fol. 189b.

rogated God because he did not know and said, 'I give myself into the hands of God. He shall guide me.'"[63]

The dialogue is an invitation to travel. In fact, it later states that, before he died, the master recommended to his pupil that he move on elsewhere to continue his search for knowledge. In contrast to that soothing approach, another account written down toward the mid-ninth century, in which a no less imposing figure appears—the cousin of the Prophet—proposes that efforts to save the *'ilm* should be redoubled "before it disappears." Its disappearance, this account prophesies, will be the consequence "of the departure (to the other world) of its own."[64]

This anxiety gripped the eighth century like a truth of life and death importance.[65] Fear of "the disappearance of the *'ilm*" was soon held to be a widely shared, collective sentiment, even at the highest level of the state. One report describes Abd al-Malik (685–705) as having been persuaded of the "rapid death" of the *'ilm*. In order to prevent that death, the Umayyad caliph is reported to have recommended to those who possessed it to share it widely.[66] A credible source—a letter from Medina of the first half of the eighth century—states that 'Umar II (r. 717–20), the most pious of the Umayyad sovereigns and the most cherished by the Sunnite doctors, ordered his governor in Medina, in a correspondence that has become famous, to "search out what exists in the way of traditions or of *Sunna* of the Prophet . . . and to transcribe all of it." The caliph is reported to have told his emir: "I fear the ruin of the *'ilm* and the disappearance of the scholars [*durūs al-'ilm wa dhahāb al-'ulamā*]."[67]

These anxiety-laden representations were aimed at making the *'ilm* a *teleological knowledge*. In the sense in which it had an origin and a goal, the *'ilm* diminished or shrank as its distance from its source of emission increased. Mālik ibn Anas (d. 179/795) was one of those who defended the

63. Ibn 'Asākir, *Tārikh madinat Dimashq*, 5:120; 6:359–60.

64. Ibn Khuthayma, *Kitāb al-'Ilm*, fol. 189b; Ibn 'Abd al-Barr, *Jāmi' Bayān al-'Ilm*, 1:184.

65. Mircia Eliade devoted many a page to this theme of a universal sense of the aging of the world, but it should be recalled that Eliade studied the Islamic mind up to the early twentieth century.

66. Ibn 'Abd al-Barr, *Jāmi' Bayān al-'Ilm*, 1:149.

67. Mālik (d. 179/795), *Muwatta'*, in the recension by Shaybānī (d. 189/804), ed. 'Abd al-Wahhāb 'Abd al-Latīf (Beirut, n.d.), 330; in English translation as *The Muwatta of Imam Malik Ibn Anas in the Narration of Imam Muhammad Ibn al-Hasan ash-Shaybani* (London: Turath: 2004). Malik, himself a native of Medina, obtained his information from one of his masters in that city. A ninth-century source states that this caliph charged the judge Zuhrī to seek out and put into writing the prophetic traditions that circulated in Syria: Tirmidhī, *Mukhtasar al-shamā'il al-Muhammadiyah* (Cairo: Maktabat al-Ādāb, 1987), 125.

idea that "the *'ilm* diminishes without ever growing." According to him, "It has not stopped diminishing after the prophets and the (revealed) Books."[68] In his youth Mālik is reported to have heard one of his Medina masters acknowledge that belief. The master, after having transmitted a hundred or so traditions to a circle of listening young men of letters, turned to his disciple and asked him how many of them he had committed to memory. Hearing that his disciple, a man who later would be called "the imam of Medina," had retained only forty or so, the master, upset, covered his face with his hands and lamented: "My God! How much has memorization diminished."[69] The old Medina master expressed a similar regret to another disciple from Egypt, who heard him predict "the disappearance of the *'ilm* and of those who put it into operation."[70] Outside the Hejaz and Syria, the belief seems to have been widely shared among Iraqi men of letters of the early eighth century. One doctor in Kufa is reported to have said that the *'ilm* had already disappeared. Less categorical, one of his colleagues in Basra thought that remains of it still subsisted, even if "in defective provisions sacks."[71] The shrinking of knowledge necessarily diminished the ranks of those who possessed it.

The Genealogical Structure of Knowledge

How to avoid the danger of loss that hovered over the *'ilm*, or at least what remained of the *'ilm*? What could be done to preserve this knowledge from corruption and transmit it in its original purity? In order to resolve those grave problems, the traditionists developed the idea of instituting Islamic knowledge as *a genealogical knowledge*. They decided that the constitution and the transmission of knowledge must take place within a framework of direct affiliation. Rules were gradually put into place during the eighth century and cast in final form only in the following century. As in other

68. Dhahabī, *Kitāb Tadhkirat*, 1:211
69. Dhahabī, *Siyar*, 5:97.
70. Ibn ʿAsākir, *Tārīkh madinat Dimashq*, 11:77.
71. Ibn ʿAbd al-Barr, *Jāmiʿ Bayān al-ʿIlm*, 1:175. The same author relates that Muhammad ibn Sirīn (d. 110/728) had a premonitory awareness of the approaching end of the *'ilm* when, one day, a man came to tell him that he had seen in a dream a bird descend from the heavens and attack a fat sheep, which he partly devoured before flying back to where he had come from. "This," the jurist is reported as sighing, "is the end of the scholars!" Ibid., 1:189. It should be recalled that the Middle Ages credited this Basra scholar with a key to dreams: see Muhammad ibn Sirīn *Taʾbīr al-Ruʾya*; trans. Yusuf Siddiq as *Le grand livre de l'interprétation des rêves* (Beirut: Dār al-Bouraq, 1993, 1999). According to a mid-ninth-century source (already cited), Mujāhid (d. ca. 721) was also of the opinion that genuine scholars had disappeared, leaving only "learners" (*mutaʿallimūn*): Ibn Khuthayma, *Kitāb al-ʿIlm*, fol. 192a.

areas, the traditionists abused recourse to the past to tie their "discovery" to an original source. They argued the principle of the trauma caused by the battle of Siffin.[72] At the time of that inaugural break, the various politico-religious parties in competition made such an abusive use of traditions that the more scrupulous among the doctors became aware of the danger that Tradition would be perverted. Muslim (d. 261/874), one of the most famous traditionists of all times, was among those who adhered to that theory. He explains that the first transmitters of traditions "did not interrogate their informers on their chains of transmission [sanad]. But when the *Great Discord* took place, they began to say to them: 'Name your men to us!' When they saw that the latter were Sunnites, they took their traditions; but when they saw that they were 'innovators,' they rejected their traditions."[73]

Without giving additional support to this narrative explication, which multiplies anachronisms,[74] It should be stressed, following Goldziher, that the politico-religious factions, struggling among themselves, indulged in an abundant forgery of traditions.[75] Far from dissipating, that tendentious activity continued to the second century of Islam. One indication of this is the many traditions favorable to the rise of the 'Abbāsids as members of the House of the Prophet that a traditionist from Khurasan, Nu'aym ibn Hammād (d. 229/844) collected in a work entitled *The Book of Political Disorders*.[76] One might theorize that in order to remedy the mystifications of one party and the forgeries of the other, the most conscientious among

72. To recall the facts: the battle of Siffin, which took place on 26 July 657, constituted a rupture that continues to trouble Islam, still segmented into a majority Sunnism, a minority Shiism, and a residual Kharijism. For a recent summary of the situation, see Djaït, *La grande discorde*.

73. Muslim, *Al-Jāmi' al-Saḥīḥ*, ed. Fu'ād 'Abd al-Bāqī, 4 vols. (Beirut, 1985), 1:11; Ibrāhīm ibn Ya'qūb Jūzjānī, *Aḥwāl al-Rijāl*, ed. Ṣubḥī al-Badrī Samarrā'ī (Beirut: Muassasat al-Risālah, 1985), 36.

74. Some Orientalists have cast doubt on this origin and substituted two other ones. For Joseph Schacht, the practice of the *isnād* developed following the "third civil war," prompted by the assassination of the Umayyad caliph Walīd II in 743: Schacht, *The Origins of Muhammadan Jurisprudence*, 36. According to G. H. A. Juynboll, the point of departure was the "second civil war," set off by 'Abd-Allāh ibn al-Zubayr in 683. Juynboll develops this point of view in several articles, notably "The Date of Great Fitna," *Arabica* 20 (1973): 142–59; and "Some Notes on Islam's First Fuqahā."

75. Goldziher, *Études sur la tradition islamique*, 88–132.

76. Nu'aym ibn Hammād, *Kitāb al-Fitan*, ed. Suhayl Zakkār (Mecca: al-Maktabah al-Tijārīyah, 1991). Nor did the Umayyad party lack scholars who collected traditions favorable to its cause: "I have seen," Mas'ūdi writes in the year 324/935, "in Tiberias, a city of the Jordan Valley in Syria, in the dwelling of a freedman of the house of Umayya, a scholar and man of letters belonging to the sect of the 'Uthmāniyya, a book of about three hundred leaves entitled the 'Book of Proofs of the Imamate of the Umayyads and of the unfolding of the volume of their merits'": Mas'ūdī, *Kitāb al-Tanbīh wa-al-ishāf*, ed. M. J. de Goeje (Leiden: Brill, 1967), 433.

the redactors of traditions began to establish rules for their collation.[77]
They demanded that the transmitters of traditions give their sources;
later, however, they opined that, in order for a tradition to be acceptable,
it must be linked to the Prophet by a continuous chain of transmitters.
These clarifications, however, did not stop people from inventing, falsifying, or extrapolating traditions for religious or political ends. That the re-
forms took a good deal of time to become accepted, even among the most
highly reputed collators, changes nothing.

Since we always seek a name to accompany the first occurrence of an
experience, 'Abd-Allah ibn 'Abbās (d. 68/687) is credited with having been
one of the first to demand that traditions be transmitted along with the
names of those who had passed them on.[78] A generation later in Kufa the
rule began to be established in the circles formed by the disciples of 'Abd-
Allah ibn Mas'ūd (d. 32/652). In this extract A'mash (d. 148/765) asks his
master to transmit his traditions to him with their chains of guarantors:
"I said to Nakha'ī [d. 96/714]: 'When you tell me a narration according to
your masters, give me its chain of guarantors.' He answered me: 'When I
say: 'Abd-Allah ibn Mas'ūd said (a thing), that means that I heard it from
more than one of his companions. But when I say So-and-So told me, that
means that it was that person alone who transmitted it to me.'"

To transmit tradition in this manner seems to have been a novelty in
Kufa at the end of the seventh century. Another account shows that same
Nakha'ī interrogating a man of letters to know how he preferred to have
oral traditions gathered from him, with or without chains of transmission.
As the traditionists themselves bear witness, the rule was fairly well as-
similated by the doctors of that epoch. In the years from 710 to 729, in
Basra itself, the city where the rule is reported to have been born, a doctor
complains of the little attention paid to the need to associate traditions
with their guarantors. When, half a century later, a representative of the
juridical school of Medina claimed that his master and compatriot, Zuhrī
(d. 124/741), was the first doctor who collected and transmitted traditions
with their chains of guarantors (*sanad*), he thought that the interiorization
of the rule was a recent phenomenon.[79] It is true that the great Medina

77. In his *The State of Men*, Ibrāhīm ibn Ya'qūb Jūzjānī (d. 259/872) declares that he is beginning his inventory with the Kharijites "because they are the first blameworthy innovation to have
appeared in Islam": Jūzjānī, *Aḥwāl al-Rijāl*, 33.

78. Muslim, *Al-Jāmi' al-Saḥīḥ*, with the commentary of Nawawī, 1:81.

79. Hārith Sulaymān Dārī, *Al-Imām al-Zuhrī wa-āthāruhu fi al-sunnah* (Mawsil: Maktabat
Barsān, 1985), 316–17. For a critique of that thesis, see Michael Cook, *Muḥammad* (Oxford: Oxford
University Press, 1983, 1996, 2001), 66.

scholar worked hard to impose the new rule in Syria, where he had moved. Several narratives show him scandalized by abusive use of the phrase "The Prophet has said." The doctor reproached the traditions of the "people of Syria" for having the inconvenient fault of having "no halter and no muzzle."[80] In this manner, he appeals to the pastoral metaphor of the halter tied to the ring through the nose of the camel, to the end of which the bridle was attached, a symbol for the *sanad* that linked, through a series of names, the tradition in question with its prophetic source. That image returns later in the great transmitters, Shu'ba ibn al-Hajjāj (d. 160/776), for example. That Basra jurist and traditionist was fond of saying that "any tradition that is not preceded by the expressions 'So-and-So has told us' or 'So-and-So has informed us' is like a man who finds himself surrounded by 'beasts without muzzles.' "[81] An earlier specialist in traditions had made use of the image of the ladder to explain the extent to which a tradition without guarantors was useless: "To solicit traditions without *isnād*," he explains, "is like trying to climb up to a terrace or get down from it without a ladder."[82] Their successors drew other metaphorical resources from this symbolism of ascension in order to throw light on Tradition.

But what could be a simple means of checking accuracy among the ancients acquired a dogmatic status among their successors. During the second half of the eighth century, the *sanad* became a religious obligation. 'Abd-Allāh ibn al-Mubārak (d. 181/797), a jurist and traditionist from Khurasan, is credited with having set forth the rule that "the *isnād* is an integral part of religion." Otherwise, he claimed, "anyone could say anything."[83] One of his own masters had already stipulated that "the *isnād* is the weapon of the believer."[84] The sacralization of Tradition was thus reinforced by the sanctification of its mode of transmission.[85] Those who initiated this dogmatic coup quite naturally came to consider the technique

80. Ibn 'Asākir, *Tārīkh madinat Dimashq*, 11:72.

81. Ibn Hibbān, *Kitāb al-Majrūhīn*, 3 vols. (Hyderabad: Matba'ah al-Azīzīyah), 1:27.

82. Ibn Rajab, *Sharh 'ilal al-Tirmidhī* (Baghdad: Matba'at al-Anī, 1396/1976, 88; Suyūtī, *Tadrīb al-rāwī* (Cairo, 1307 AH/1889), 359. Sufyān ibn 'Uyayna (d. 198/813) may have been alluding to this response one day when his brother suggested that he get rid of the crowd of knowledge seekers who flocked to his house by giving them *hadīth* without *isnād*. Taking offense, the great Kufa traditionist appealed to his many listeners, crying out, "Listen to that man! He wants me to climb up on the roof of the house without a ladder": Khatīb al-Baghdādī, *Al-Kifāya*, 557.

83. Muslim, *Al-Jāmi' al-Sahīh*, 1:11.

84. Khatīb al-Baghdādī, *Sharaf Ashāb al-Hadīth*, 42.

85. Ibn Rahawayh (d. 238/852), one of the great traditionists of Khurasan, often cited the words of the 'Abbāsid governor of that area, 'Abd-Allah ibn Tāhir (d. 230/844), who claimed that "the *isnād* is a miracle of God in favor of the Muhammedan community": Zurqānī, *Sharh al-Mawāhib*, 8 vols. (Cairo: al-Matba'at al-Azharīya al-Misrīya, 1908–10), 5:435

of the genealogical transmission of traditions to be exclusive to Muslims. The critic of tradition Ibn Hibbān (d. 354/965) translated that singularity in terms that were those of the "catastrophic" theory of knowledge discussed above: "Without the *isnād*," he claimed, "falsifications of all sorts would have altered the religion [of Muhammad] as was the case in the other nations [of the Book]."[86] Taking up the idea, one of his colleagues and contemporaries stated, more emphatically: "If it had not been for the *isnād*, the torch of Islam would have been extinguished long ago."[87]

In point of fact, the Jews had used this same procedure well before the Muslims, and they expected the same efficacy from it. Under the title of the "chain of Tradition" (*shalshelet ha-qabbalah*), they invented a literature that related chronologically the transmission of the Law and rabbinic doctrine. Its object was to note "the succession of exceptional minds that passed on the torch of the oral law to one another through the ages" and to establish "the existence of an uninterrupted chain of teaching and authority from the Bible, through the Talmud, and often up to the epoch of the authors themselves."[88] Compared to the Islamic *silsila*, however, the Jewish *shelshelet* remained feebly structured. In order to consolidate its apparatus, the doctors of Medieval Judaism were led, in Islamic lands, to examine the Muslim model of genealogical transmission and to use it as an example. The Muslim model had, in fact, attained a degree of technical focus and sophistication that was incomparably higher than in all older genealogical systems, to the point of seeming a characteristic singularity of Islam.

Far from embracing the technique as an inherited institution, Muslims saw it as a privilege that God had granted to Muslims, to the exclusion of Jews and Christians, fallen from their scriptural prestige, as a way to keep his message and that of his Prophet free from all impurity. In scrutinizing the Qur'anic text, the sanctifiers found the scriptural foundations for their assertions. Interpreting verse 44 of surah 44, "It is a Reminder for

86. Ibn Hibbān, *Kitāb al-Majrūhīn*, 1:25.

87. Hākim al-Nīsābūrī, *Ma'rifat 'ulūm al-Hadīth* (Beirut: al-Maktabah al Tijārīyah lil-Tibāhna al Nashr, 1966), 6.

88. Yosef Hayim Yerushalmi, *Zakhor: Histoire juive et mémoire juive* (Paris: La Découverte, 1984, 1991), 47–48. For a parallel between the two traditions, Jewish and Muslim, see Gerson D. Cohen's introduction to his critical edition and English translation of Abraham ibn Daud, *Sefer Ha-Qabbalah: The Book of Tradition* (Philadelphia: Jewish Publication Society of America, 1967), 50–57. It seems that the Jews themselves were influenced, in this connection, by the Greeks, if one can believe E. J. Bickerman, "La chaîne de la tradition pharisienne," *Revue biblique* 59 (1952): 44–54. For an attempted comparison in the domain of Islamic studies, see Josef Horovitz, "Alter und Ursprung des *isnād*," *Der Islam* 8 (1918): 39–47; and Horovitz, "Noch Einmal die Herkunft des *isnād*," *Der Islam* 11 (1921): 264–65.

you and your folk," one of their number found in it an allusion to the genealogical mode of transmission that was being put into place, saying, "I hold this from my father, who holds it from his father, who holds it from his." The ending of the phrase "or any remnant of knowledge" in verse 4 of surah 46 was also interpreted as an allusion to the *isnād*.[89]

Had the rule that stated that a *hadīth* must have a fixed "body" called *matn* and a "chain of guarantors" (*silsislat al-sanad* or *isnād*), defined as an "uninterrupted chain" (*ittisāl*), been put into place by the mid-eighth century? No. Many doctors of the time still practiced the *irsāl*, a procedure consisting of the transmission of traditions with incomplete chains of guarantors—which was just what their followers of the ninth century reproached them for, though without completely disqualifying them.[90] In fact, the rule was not established before the mid-ninth century. Hence, despite the prestige attached to the rigor of their procedures, many doctors transmitted *hadīth* with "interrupted" chains (*mursal, mawqūf*) that the specialists of tradition of the ninth, tenth, and eleventh centuries subjected to stringent criticism.[91] The critical criteria that had been applied to them owed the better part of their elaboration to Bukhārī (d. 256/869) and Muslim (d. 261/874), the two great collators of this type of material. These two traditionists were the first to define the rigorous conditions for receiving a *hadīth*, stipulating, among other rules, the need for an "uninterrupted chain" of guarantors defined as "worthy of trust" who were contemporaries and had received the information that was transmitted directly and successively.[92]

The system of constraints that was put into place forced the *'ilm*, which was already an authorized form of knowledge, to become an *authoritarian*

89. Khatīb al-Baghdādī, *Sharaf Ashāb al-Hadīth*, 39.

90. The doctors of later ages reproached their earlier colleagues for the more serious fault of having used the technique of *tadlīs* to do a cosmetic cover-up of their chains of transmission: see Goldziher, *Études sur la tradition islamique*, 43–44; Dārī, *Al-Imām al-Zuhrī*, 417–22.

91. Such critics included Abū Dāwud al-Sijistānī, *Kitāb al-Marāsi* (Riyad: Dār al-Sumay'ī, 2001); and Ibn Abī Hātim, *Al-Marāsil fī al-Hadīth*, ed. Subhī al-Sammarrā'ī (Bagdhad: Maktabat al-Muthaan, 1967). In the ninth century, one traditionist, Abū Zur'a al-Rāzū, stated that "Mālik almost always practiced the *irsāl* by relying on sure people": Dhahabī, *Siyar*, 13:79. See also Ibn 'Abd al-Barr, *Al-Tamhīd li-mā fī al-Muwatta' min al-Ma'ānī wa'l-Asānid*, ed. Mustafā ibn Ahmad 'Alawī and MuhammadAbdal-Kabīr Bakrī, 17 vols. (Rabat, 1967). The traditionists completed the chains of transmission of many *hadīth*s of the *mursal* variety, such as those of Mālik, following the rule dictated by Ibn Hibbān (d. 354/965) that stated, "we are not obliged to take the 'interrupted' information as either proof or information 'cut off'": *Kitāb al-Thiqāt*, ed. 'Abd'l-Mu'īn Khān, 3 vols. (Hyderabad: Dār al-Fikr, 1973–83), 1:12.

92. It is true that the ground work for this task had been done by Shāfi'ī, who had declared the principal rules of receivability of traditions in the late eighth century in his famous *Epistle*: see the French translation by Lakhdar Louami, *La Risāla: Les fondements du droit musulman*.

knowledge. After the mid-ninth century, no one could complain that the Iraqi great doctors were taking liberties with the transmission of traditions: "A doctor of Kufa who died in the mid-eighth century complained that X, Y, and Z transmitted *hadīth*, at one time in one way and another time in another way. I spoke of the problem before my master, and he answered me: 'If they had transmitted them as they had heard them, it would have been preferable!'"

The collector of traditions who relates this scene in the early ninth century offers other examples of first transmitters operating in a similar way, at times adding (and their honesty was not in question) at the end of the tradition, "Or as he is reported to have said." Some of them went so far as to recognize that they were not transmitting the very words of the Prophet, but only the content and sense of his statements.[93] By the end of the eighth century, such "liberties" were no longer permitted. They belonged to a bygone age of the living Tradition. With the aid of the weight of the written word, the reformulated Tradition operated in a new way. In order to bring uniformity to their material and exert their control over it, the traditionists fixed it into acts of language that could no longer be changed or modified, as had been the case with transmission by memory. Nothing illustrates the role of writing in fixing the *Corpus traditionum* better than the words credited to Dhū al-Rumma (d. 117/735), asking the grammarian 'Īsā ibn 'Umar (d. 149/766) to write down his poems. He states: "I prefer to entrust my poems to books rather than to memory. The Bedouin who has forgotten one word or another will spend all night struggling to find it again. If his attempt fails, he will inevitably put another word of the same size in the place of the forgotten word; then he will declaim the poem—thus altered—before his listeners. Now, the book does not forget, and it does not substitute one word or an expression for another."[94]

Echoes of praise for the virtues of the written word can be found in recent scholarship. Thanks to the works of Jack Goody, we know that writing, as distinct from oral transmission, operates by formalization and de-

---

93. Dārimī, *Sunan*, 1:96–97.

94. Jāhiz, *Tahdhīb Kitāb al-Hayawān*; Souami translation, 148. This does not mean, however, that this restriction had become constraining for everyone. The traditionists, who continued to trust their memory, were often criticized by their colleagues. The Iraqi critic of traditions Darāqutnī, for example, said of his compatriot Abū Qulāba, the Ascetic (d. 276/889), that he was "trustworthy," but that he made many mistakes in his *hadīth* because he transmitted them from memory: Dhahabī, *Kitāb Tadhkirat*, 1:579. See also Goldziher, *Études sur la tradition islamique*, 241–50.

contextualization.[95] Formalization is both linguistic and intellectual, and because it fixes and standardizes verbal statements in durable forms, it was the object of bitter struggles between the representatives of the two traditions of oral memory and written memory. The outcome of the conflict was fatal to the living Tradition.

Who was authorized to transmit Islamic knowledge? According to the traditionists, following the jurists in this, they were persons of *thiqa*.[96] That word originally designated "a tie, a tether, a cord with which one attaches or ties up something"—and we should remember that genealogy is also a form of linkage. Having become a synonym for confidence, the term eventually took on a juridical meaning and came to apply to any person worthy of trust or confidence; someone who was called *ma'mūn* because he could be relied upon,[97] or called *'ādil* because he was of unquestioned probity.[98] Muslim (d. 261/874) later said the *thiqa* were people known for their *sidq*, a term that refers both to "verity" and "sincerity," and for their *amāna*, which meant "sureness."[99] Making use of medical metaphors, the critics of traditions qualified their own transmissions as "healthy" (which meant "authentic") calling those they denounced "suspect," "sick," and "weak." Muslim, who treats "transmission" as evidence, puts it into a juridical content: "In the same way that the evidence of a person who is not honest is not receivable, corrupt information is not accepted. It remains without value. For although the words 'information' and 'testimony' are different,

95. Jack Goody, *The Domestication of the Savage Mind* (Cambridge: Cambridge University Press, 1977); in French translation as *La raison graphique: La domestication de la pensée sauvage* (Paris: Minuit, 1979); and Goody, *The Interface between the Written and the Oral* (Cambridge: Cambridge University Press, 1987); trans. Denise Paulme as *Entre l'oralité et l'écriture* (Paris: Presses Universitaires de France, 1994).

96. Ibn Ja'd al-Jawharī (d. 230/844) was the first traditionist to have noted down the rule that states, "Only the *thiqa* have the right to pass on the words of the Prophet." He attributes the paternity of this rule to another doctor of the late seventh century: Dārimī, *Sunan*, 2:662.

97. This is the definition of the term given by Yahiā ibn Sa'īd (d. 198/813): Jūzjānī, *Ahwāl al-Rijāl*, 37. Before him Ibn 'Awn al-Basrī (d. 151/768) had it from one of his masters that "this science (of traditions) is a debt." This means that the person contracting the debt had to know "with whom he is dealing": 'Abd al-Razzāq, *al-Musannāf*, 5:334.

98. Bayhaqī (d. 458/1065) transmits a tradition is which he has the Prophet say that "the *'ilm* is transmitted from one *ādil* to another": Bayhaqī, *al-Sunan al-Kubrā*, ed. Muhammad 'Abd al-Qādir 'Atā, 11 vols. (Beirut: Dār al-Kutub al-'Ilmīyah, 1994), 10:354.

99. His contemporary Muhammad ibn Hātim gives exactly the same definition of the *thiqa*: Khatīb al-Baghdādī, *Sharaf Ashāb al-Hadīth*, 40. A century later, Ibn Hibbān (d. 354/965) stipulated the "five conditions" by means of which one could recognize a *thiqa* in a "Book of Reliable Men": *Kitāb al-Thiqāt*. On the ways that other traditionists diverged from the method of classification of Ibn Hibbān's *thiqa*, see 'Abd al-Hayy Kattānī, *Al-Risāla al-Mustatrafa* (Damascus, 1964), 147.

they are associated semantically in the majority of cases. This is why the information of the person who is without morality is unreceivable for the generality of men of science, just as is his testimony."[100]

From this attempt to discriminate between good and the bad transmitters there arose an entire scientific discipline designated by the periphrasis "knowledge of men." The medieval sources depict Shu'ba ibn al-Hajjāj (d. 160/776) as one of the first critics in Iraq who attempted an "inquiry about men."[101] They show him traveling about, both to gather traditions and to assure himself of the reliability of their guarantors.[102] These sources have left us a narrative in which the traveler relates the troubles that he has endured in order to verify the paths of transmission of the *hadīth* that states that "anyone who does his ablutions correctly, performs two prostrations, and gives himself into the hands of God will have pardon (for his sins)" on the day of the Last Judgment. He continues:

> X has transmitted this *hadīth* to me, telling me that he had it from Y, who himself had it from Z. I asked him: "Who is Y?" My question angered him. But in the presence of A, I remarked to him, "Either you will tell me who he is, or I will burn everything that I have from you!" At that point A intervened to tell me that the man in question was in Mecca. I then set off for Mecca, *not at all in order to make the pilgrimage*, but to verify the *hadīth* in question. There I interrogated Y, who indicated to me that he had it from another, whom he named. By the intermediary of [one of his compatriots encountered in Mecca] I learned that the latter had not made the pilgrimage that year. I then left for Medina, and there I met that man, who told me: "The *hadīth* is from your home town; it was So-and-So who transmitted it to me." At the mention of the latter's name, I exclaimed: "What is this *hadīth* that jumps from Kufa to Medina, then to Basra?" Once again I set off to Basra in order to interrogate that man . . . who told me: "It was [a Syrian] who communicated it to me." At the mention of [the Syrian's] name, I said: "How precious is this *hadīth*! If I had received something similar from the Prophet, I would hold it dearer than my family, my goods, and the whole world."[103]

100. Muslim, *Al-Jāmi' al-Sahīh*, 1:7.
    101. He is credited with drawing up the first known "inventory of masters" (*mashyakha*): Heinrich Schützinger, *Das Kitāb al-Mu'gam des Abū Bakr al-Ismā'īlī* (Wiesbaden: Steiner; Mainz: Deutsche Morgenländische Ges, 1978), 19.
    102. Hākim al-Nīsābūrī, *Su'ālāt Mas'ud 'Alī al-ijai* (Beirut: Dār al-Gharb, 1988), 87.
    103. Ibn 'Asākir, *Tārīkh madinat Dimashq*, 6:513.

This account is perhaps authentic, given that as early as the late eighth century Shu'ba was widely recognized as a hunter after knowledge. In one contemporary source we can see the same specialist of Tradition tell a man of letters to whom he had just transmitted a tradition: "I have given it to you without counterexchange, while in my time we would ride our mounts to Medina or elsewhere for less than that."[104]

The route that Shu'ba traveled in this narrative is interesting in that it establishes an inventory and a geography. Five cities stand out: two are in the Hejaz (Mecca and Medina), two in Iraq (Basra and Kufa), and one in Syria (Damascus). The first two are religious centers, the last one is the political seat of the empire. The two Iraqi cities were emerging cultural centers.

When Damascus became the center of political decision, the role of Medina shrank. Because Syria had dealt a severe blow to the Hejaz by taking over command of the Islamic empire, it was felt necessary to conciliate Iraq by giving it a role that never stopped growing. From the early eighth century, the eminent spiritual and cultural function of Basra—the native city of our traveler—and Kufa, its sister city and rival, is an attested fact. Medina, which had lost its political hegemony, became instead a center for studies. Islamic intellectuality, more solidly linked than it had been to the Revelation that was the focus of its meditation, stood opposed to poetry as an eminently urban phenomenon. The need to provide exegesis of the Qur'an, to define a juridical system capable of regulating social and public life, to create a grammar of the Arabic language, and to promote an art of oratory necessary both to the state and to the competing politico-religious parties (Kufa was the cradle of Shiism) seemed the necessary outcome of an expectation deeply rooted in urban life. As symbols of the "birth of the Islamic city,"[105] Basra and Kufa were the first to take the initiative in responding to that expectation and satisfying its needs. Without a historical past or a homogeneous population (their inhabitants were a mixture of Arabs from the Hejaz and from Yemen, with Iranian and Khurasanian minorities), those two cities succeeded in eclipsing other

---

104. 'Abd al-Razzāq, al-Musannāf, 5:285.

105. I am quoting the title of Hichem Djaït, Al-Kūfa: Naissance de la ville islamique (Paris: Maisonneuve et Larose, 1986), in which see, in particular, the bibliographic references to Kufa. On Basra, see Charles Pellat, Le milieu basrien et la formation de Gāḥiz (Paris: Maisonneuve, 1953). For each of the cities discussed, see the entries and the exhaustive bibliographies about them in The Encyclopaedia of Islam. For general reflection on the intellectual role of the cities up to the mideighth century, see Régis Blachère, Histoire de la littérature arabe des origines à la fin du XVe siècle, 3 vols. (Paris: Maisonneuve, 1964, 1966, 1984), 3:805–10.

urban centers with a prestigious urban past, such as Ctesiphon, in replac-
ing Mecca and Medina, the two original centers of Islam, and in rivaling
Damascus in political importance.

Although Mecca, Medina, and Damascus were active centers for the
study of law and traditions in our voyager's day, it was above all in Kufa
and in Basra that Islamic culture emerged from an earlier formlessness and
achieved classicism. As Hichem Djaït declares, "Kufa excelled in the recuperation of the Arabic poetic patrimony, in exegesis of the Qur'an, in law,
and in genealogy, while Basra, more rationalist and more critical, invented
Arabic grammar and was a major center of Mu'tazilite speculation." The
supremacy of those two Iraqi cities over other centers of Islam did not
weaken until Baghdad was created. Moreover, it was by taking over their
legacy that the 'Abbāsid capital became the intellectual center of the medieval world.

To return to our voyager, his movements define a political, religious,
and cultural space. It is a space that was both in the process of becoming structured and expanding. At the time, Islam was not completely
Islamized, at least not under the form that later became its own during
a large part of the Middle Ages. Islam was in the process of becoming,
pulling itself away from its Arab condition and giving itself a cultural identity that was centered no longer on being Arabic but on the Qur'an. The
growth of the criticism of traditions was thus a product, on its dogmatic
side, of the enterprise of the fabrication and unification of the Islamic
space. Subjected to regulation, that criticism was both an advance within
the text and a geographical itinerary. It took place according to a precise
order, dictated by the order of succession of the guarantors in the chain
of transmission by means of which the tradition to be verified had been
handed down.

Even supposing that Shu'ba is reliable when he writes of his travels, we
need to wait until around the beginning of the ninth century to see the
"knowledge of men" blossom into an autonomous discipline and be cast
in a stable literary form. Like the search for traditions, the new discipline
needed to have its specialists travel in order to inquire about the guarantors of their own age. The oldest treatise of "knowledge of men" that has
come down to us dates from the early ninth century.[106] The times were
already ripe for the development of the literary genre of the biographi-

---

106. Yaḥyā ibn Mu'in (d. 243/847), *Tārīkh*, ed. Ahmad Muhammad Nūr Sayf (Damascus: Dār
al-Ma'mūn lil-Turāth, 1986?). That dictionary has come down to us in the recension of another
great traditionist of the latter half of the ninth century, Dārimī (d. 280/893).

cal dictionary.[107] The product of the genealogical structure of knowledge, these works seem specifically connected to the constitution of Islamic knowledge. No prior culture, and no contemporary culture, produced bio-bibliographic compendiums with as much diligence or regularity. A sort of *Who's Who*, they were to the intellectual world of medieval Islam what civil identity is to citizens of the modern world, defining not only identity but also filiation.

Once the traditionists had institutionalized the genealogical principle as the mode of transmission of the *'ilm*, they made the search for "elevated *isnād*s" one of the principal motivations for the "voyage in search of knowledge." They believed that, in order to get as close as possible to the Prophet in the genealogical sense, they needed to produce the "highest" possible chains of transmission. Searching for "proximity with the Prophet,"[108] observes 'Iyād (d. 544/1149), the judge of Ceuta, "was the method of people of the profession and their doctrine; it was also the goal of their efforts and their sufferings. Someone who held even just one high *hadīth* saw voyages multiply in his direction." This statement, coming from the Muslim West, seems to echo that of a traditionist of the East, Hākim al-Nīsābūrī (d. 405/1014). That Khurasanian doctor was of the opinion that those who sought traditions only "ride their mounts" to go in search of high *isnād*s. "If they were willing to be content with low *isnād*s," he adds, "they would have found people to transmit them to them in their own lands."[109] It seems that this was why Bukhārī (d. 256/869) started off his *Summa* with the *hadīth* that declares that "acts have worth only by intention." He had received that statement from a traditionist in Mecca who had received it in Medina from the mouth of Mālik ibn Anas (d. 179/795), the great authority on traditions of his age. According to Dhahabī (d.748/1347), "Bukhārī made this *hadīth* the opening of his *Summa* because of the unique nature of its chain of transmission: each of its transmitters declaring explicitly that he had heard it from the mouth of the person who had transmitted it to him, with never an interval in the chain or the formula 'according to.'"[110]

107. Biographical dictionaries were composed by Wāqidī (d. 207/822), his pupil Ibn Sa'd (d. 230/845), Khalīfa ibn Khayyāt (d. 240/854), Bukhārī (d. 256/869), Ibrāhīm ibn Ya'qūb Jūzjānī (d. 259/872), and Muslim (d. 261/874).

108. Ibn Salāh, *Muqaddima*, ed. 'Ā'isha 'Abd al-Rahmān (Cairo: Wizārat al-Thaqāfah, 1974), 378. Ibn Aslam al-Tūsī (d. 242/856) is thought to have published a variant of this principle in which "proximity in the *isnād* is proximity in relation to God": Abū Bakr al-Ismā'īlī, *Kitāb al-Mu'jam*, 1:104.

109. Hākim al-Nīsābūrī, *Ma'rifat 'ulūm al-Hadīth*, 8.

110. Dhahabī, *Siyar*, 10:261.

In the mid-eighth century, the doctors who held "high chains of guarantors" were sought after everywhere. At that time, a jurist and traditionist of Basra, Maʿmar ibn Rāshid (d. 153/770), was particularly solicited
"because no one among his companions of Basra, Kufa, or the Hejaz possessed *isnād*s as high as his were."[111] In the following generation, a doctor
in Fustāt was reputed to possess "the highest prophetic traditions of his
epoch."[112] Searchers for traditions everywhere were on the alert for these
holders of "high chains." In the same way that there were doctors interested in sacralizing the *isnād*, there were others, in the mid-ninth century,
who claimed that "the search for high chains of guarantors proceeded out
of Tradition."[113]

The race to chase down the "high chains" was not solely guided by a
desire to see one's name figure in the most highly reputed genealogies of
transmission of Tradition of a certain time or a certain region. In other
words, that race simply illustrates the connection between the paradigm
of hearing and the voyage. It also settles another problem of a great dogmatic and epistemological importance: that of having seen the Prophet or
not. Historically speaking, the Companions of the Prophet were the only
Muslims to have seen and/or heard the founder of Islam. Having drawn
revealed knowledge from its source, they are canonically credited with an
excellence that they are alone in holding within the Muslim community.
Having seen and/or heard the Prophet procures a dogmatic prestige that
gives its holder a position of human exemplarity and makes him a source
of knowledge. However, only the very first generations of Muslims prof-
ited, or could profit, from that status. Death, Karl Marx tells us, is the
hard-won victory of the species over the individual. In order to fool death's
natural law, Islamic culture called on the ancient Arab personage of the
muʿammir, the person endowed with macrobiosis, or prodigiously long life.
Fearing the dangers of this sort of invention, Islamic culture eventually
resolved to establish its principle of continuity on a less hazardous base.
At that point, the only way that later generations of Muslims could at-
tach themselves to the Prophet and his Companions was to turn Tradition

111. Ibid., 7:9. The traditionist went to live in Yemen.
112. Ibid., 8:159–60.
113. Ibid., 11:311. There is a variant in Suyūṭī, *Tadrīb al-rāwī*, 183: "The search for high *isnād* is
a tradition [*sunna*] of the ancients; the disciples of ʿAbd-Allāh ibn ʿAbbās [d. 68/687] went from
Kufa to Medina in order to learn from ʿAmrū [?] and hear from his mouth." At the same time,
another traditionist, Muhammad ibn Aslam of Tūs (d. 242/856), used the symbolism of the ascension to declare that "elevation in the *isnād* is a mark of proximity to God": Abū Bakr al-Ismāʿīlī,
Kitāb al-Muʿjam, 1:104. See also Khaṭīb al-Baghdādī, *Al-Jāmiʿ*, fols. 11a–13b, which contains several
examples reflecting the same position.

into a written corpus and provide it with procedures of authentification. The "high chains," which are one of these procedures, draw credit from hearing as much as from *autopsia*, or direct observation—that is, from the two canonically recognized sources of sense-based knowledge. We have already seen the connection between these highly prized genealogies and hearing. What remains to be done is to untangle their relationship with the principle of *autopsia*. In the establishment of that relationship, Tradition took recourse, as was its custom, in an explication that mixed narrative arguments and the rhetoric of the example. Tradition gave certain narratives a normative meaning by exemplifying them. In one of these narrations, it is said of a "golden chain" (*silsilat al-dhahab*) of Tradition that it is so perfect that its holder can almost hear the Prophet in person speaking to him. The accent is on hearing here, but other narratives stress visual experience. Another chain, a second narrative tells us, permits its possessor to "raise the curtain on the Prophet to see him [conversing] with his Companions placed around him."[114] A third narrative with a *mu'ammir* as its hero combines the virtues of hearing and vision.[115] These exempla reported by voyagers with a certain reputation give full force to the central idea of this chapter, which is that Islamic Tradition is a product of the voyage. The jurisconsults of the time gave a legal foundation to the dual movement in space and in time that resulted in truth in the context of the attestation of one person's testimony by another's. In order to lend validity to that form of testimony, they placed it in the category of specific cases in which "the application takes the place of foundation." They then compared the person giving indirect testimony to a messenger (*rasūl*) who comes to bring information—in this case his testimony—to the court. The judge must accept his deposition, acting *"as if* [the witness] *had been present* [at the place in which the events on which he is testifying took place] and had personally seen [them]." Sarakhsī (d. 490/1096), one of the major authorities on Hanafite law, comments: "Consider this in connection with the rules of transmission of traditions that make it possible to receive the report [*khabar*] of a unique transmitter to a unique transmitter, as is the case of the doctrine of our juridical school, which has come down from

---

114. Khāṭīb al-Baghdādī, *al-Jāmi' li-Akhlāq al-Rāwī wa Adab al-Sāmi'*, ed. Muhammad 'Ajaj al-Khaṭīb, 3 vols. (Beirut: Mu'assasat al-Rislah, 1996), 2:173. Another example: "To have [such a chain] is like seeing the Prophet."

115. A traditionist from Khurasan who died in the mid-ninth century relates that during a voyage in Syria he met the son of a macrobiot who revealed to him how his father had met the Prophet: "I saw him," he told his son, "as I see you." The traditionist counted the channels by which this narrative came to him as "the highest of his chains of transmission": ibid., 2:169.

'Alī," the cousin and son-in-law of the Prophet.[116] Hearing substitutes for
autopsia here. It can do so and give the best account of itself only if it is
connected with the voyage.

Thus, when the founders of Islamic knowledge gave their scientific
enterprise a genealogico-juridical framework, the voyage became one
of its principal attributes. It entered into that framework as part of its
foundation. This is not only because it procured power and prestige, but
also because it had the ability to bring together those who held parcels of
knowledge into a chain of solidarity that guaranteed authenticity to the
whole, to the point that it appeared to be an expression of the principle
of genealogy on which the *'ilm* was constituted as a symbolic and discursive formation. Did not the voyage, like genealogy, also act as a connection? Did it not set into action the dialogic continuity between "bearers of
knowledge," bringing them together in time and in space? When Khatīb
al-Baghdādī (d. 463/1070) challenged the idea that one can put on the same
plane a *hadīth muttasil* that presents a continuous chain of links attaching
it to the Prophet and a *hadīth mursal* with a "relaxed" or "shortened" genealogy of transmission, he says exactly that: "If the legal decision concerning the two types of *hadīth* were the same," and he observes, "the collectors
of traditions would have no need to endure the burdens of the voyage to
go to far-off lands to meet scholars to 'audition.' "[117]

By the eighth and ninth centuries, hearing was an important paradigm
of knowledge. Although the traditionists, its most enthusiastic support-
ers, played an essential role in shaping it, they were not its exclusive initiators. I suspect the *rāwī* and the *nassāb* of also having had something to do
with its invention.[118] Both of these groups belonged to the ancient class
of men of letters of pre-Islamic Arabia. The *rāwī*s, as rhapsodists,[119] and

116. Sarakhsī, *Kitāb al-mabsūt* (Beirut: Dār al-Ma'rifah, [1970s]), 16:138. 'Alī was believed to
have received this doctrine from the Prophet. It should be kept in mind that if all the Sunnite
juridical schools admitted indirect testimony, they nonetheless diverged about the number: one
witness seemed sufficient to the Mālikites, but at least two were necessary for the Hanafites and
the Shāfi'ites.

117. Khatīb al-Baghdādī, *Al-Kifāya*, 402. Ibn Hibbān (d. 354/965) goes so far as to sustain that
"one cannot base oneself on the *mursal* as a proof; similarly, the *munqati'* cannot be considered
as proof": *Kitāb al-Thiqāt*, 1:12. For a recent discussion of the techniques of the *muttasil* and the
mursal, see Juynboll, "Some Notes on Islam's First *Fuqahā.*"

118. This does not seem to me to contradict the possible connections between the Muslim
silsila and the Jewish *shalshelet* that have been suggested above.

119. According to the prose writer Ibn Kalbī (d. 206/821), unlike the Persians, who celebrated
their gorious acts by means of architectural monuments, "to immortalize their great deeds the
ancient Arabs had recourse to the technique of rhythmic poetry and language with rhyme and
assonance. These constituted their archives; their monuments": Jāhiz, *Tahdhīb Kitāb al-Hayawān*;
Souami translation, 185.

the *nassāb*, as genealogists and transmitters of historical narrations, in fact constituted two essential mechanisms of tribal memory. Far from disappearing along with their ancient social regime, they continued, with the coming of Islam, to work as they always had done.[120] In the new culture their intellectual role was in fact considerably increased.[121] Moreover, the prose writers of the eighth century operated in continuity with their ancient function. Thus, it does not seem inopportune to take a look at how their heirs also came to lodge their investigations within the framework of the paradigm of hearing.

120. On this question, see the recent study by Rina Drory, "The Abbassid Construction of the Jāhiliyya: Cultural Authority in the Making," *Studia Islamica* 83 (1996): 33–50.

121. The connections between these "tribal savants" and the first ulemas are historically attested. The first commentators of the Qur'an, for example, could not have done without the philological erudition of the *rāwī*. Famous men of letters shifted from the ancient model of the tribal sage to that of the ulema. At Medina, for example, there was Zuhrī (d. 124/741), who, before he studied law with Sa'id ibn Musayyab (d. 94/712) and 'Ubayd-Allah ibn 'Abd-Allah (d. 99?/717?), had been the disciple of a locally known genealogist. His master, 'Ubayd-Allah ibn 'Abd-Allah, had himself been a *rāwī* of poetry. The same is true of another great local jurist, Abū Zinād (d. 131/748). At Kufa, the judge Sha'bī (d. 103/721) was first a transmitter of poetry. He was the brother-in-law of the Shiite poet A'sha of the Hamdān. At Basra there were men of letters who, like the Qur'an exegete Qatāda (d. 108/726), had been genealogists or transmitters of poetry and of ancient Arab narratives. Still at Basra, Shu'ba (d. 160/776), who is described as one of the founders of the "science of the knowledge of men," was first a transmitter of poetry. In his youth he had known Tirimmāh (d. 125/742), the great Syrian poet established in Kufa.

2

THE SCHOOL OF THE DESERT

Linguists and Bedouins

Addressing the 'Abbāsid caliph al-Ma'mūn (r. 813–33) in the preface to his *History of the Kings of the Arabs of Antiquity*, Pseudo-Asma'ī writes:

> You have commanded me to gather up all the narratives and the traditions concerning the kings of the ancient Arabs; all that can be known about their politics, their wisdom, their poetry, their prayers, and their manner of administrating what God has delivered over to them as well as their remarkable deeds. Despite all my efforts, I have found that there was little information concerning them. To find what relates to them is difficult because of the disappearance of their narratives and the effacing of their traces. I have nonetheless made my mount sweat traveling among the Bedouin tribes in order to interrogate the transmitters of ancient narratives and the memorizers of the "Happy Days" about such topics. Among those whom I have been able to approach, I have interrogated the genealogists at the same time that I gathered what the long-lived old men had from their ancestors, with the result that, when all was said and done, despite all my efforts, I collected only a small quantity of narratives. By which I have obeyed the august imperial decree.[1]

---

1. Pseudo-Asma'ī, *Tārīkh Mulūk al-'Arab*, ed. Muhammad Hasan Al Yasin (Baghdad, 1959), 3.

Although modern philologists and paleographers deny that this chronicle was the work of the great Basra philologist,[2] it is clear that its anonymous author offers an accurate pastiche of the method typical of prose
writers and philologists of the eighth century. The new class of secular
men of letters, of which Asma'ī was a founder, often pushed its own members, body and soul, onto the dusty roads to knowledge. Emerging in part
at least from the religious world, that class certainly did not exclude all
religious consideration from its linguistic inquiry. But at the same time,
the specificity of its activities permitted it to demote pious motives as
the sole source of creation and justification of a domain of knowledge. Its
emergence, albeit partial, from religion thus enabled it to give sufficiently
forceful backing to secular curiosity and interests to justify the linguistic
investigations that its members undertook among the Bedouins. Thus,
like the collectors of traditions who went to Mecca and Medina with the
sole aim of meeting transmitters of *hadīth*, philologists and prose writers
went to those same holy places of Islam, not to carry out their ritual obligations, but uniquely in the hope of meeting Bedouins and being able to
interrogate them on their speech, their poetry, and their traditions. We
have narratives that portray Abū 'Amr ibn al-'Alā' (d. 154?/770?), held to
be the founder of the philological school of Basra, in Mecca, gathering
verse from a member of the Banū 'Udhrā tribe, poetry to which Arab tradition attaches the invention of courtly love. Similarly, his contemporary
and compatriot Hasan ibn Ja'far al-Diba'ī, who, it seems, "never took to
the road, never went anywhere for any reason without having on him his
wooden tablets," is shown filling one of those tablets with verse declaimed
by a Bedouin in front of the Kaaba.[3]

Not only the great masters from the big cities of Iraq, but scholars in
other Muslim provinces in search of information about the Arab language
also sought out Bedouins. One anecdote is significative of the increased
number of such excursions. We are in Kufa in the study circle of the lexicographer Ibn al-A'rabī (d. 231/845).[4] The master is explaining some dif-

2. Franz Rosenthal, "From Arabic Books and Manuscripts," pt. 1, "Pseudo-Asma'ī on the
Islamic Arab Kings," *Journal of Asian and Oriental Studies* 69 (1949): 90–91; François Déroche,
"À propos du manuscrit 'Arabe 6726' BN, Paris (Al-Asma'ī, *Tārīkh Mulūk al-'Arab al-Awwalīn*),"
Revue d'études islamiques 58 (1990): 209–12.
3. Abū Muhammad Sarrāj, *Masāri' al-'Ushshāq*, 2 vols. (Beirut: Dār Bayrūt lil Tibā'ah wa-al-
Nashr, 1958), 2:75, 204.
4. A great book lover, this philologist and specialist in Qur'anic readings founded one of the
largest libraries of his age in Kufa: Ibn Khallikān, *Wafayāt al-A'yān*, 8 vols. (Cairo, 1948); ed. Insān
'Abbās, 8 vols. (Beirut: Dār Thāqāfa, 1968–72), 1:204; trans. William MacGuckin, baron Slane, as
Ibn Khallikān's Biographical Dictionary, 4 vols. (Paris, 1842–71).

ficult verses to about a hundred people of various nations. Two listeners who are whispering to one another finally annoy him: he interrupts them and asks one of them: "Where are you from?" "From Andalusia," answers one intimidated candidate for wisdom. "And you?" "From Isbījāb" (in the Sind). Astonished to see that his school attracts pupils from the outer limits of the Muslim world (and perhaps proud of having listeners from such distant lands), the learned linguist declaims some impromptu verse, which all his students dutifully noted down.[5] Some of these young people who came from distant lands acquired a reputation as a philologist or a grammarian in Iraq. In particular, they came from the eastern regions of the Muslim world, as did the famous Akhfash of Balkh (d. 215/830) and Abū Ḥātim al-Sijistānī (d. 255/868),[6] both of whom settled in Basra, attaching themselves to Ibn al-Aʿrabī's school of grammar and language.

From its founding,[7] the Basra school developed a purist conception of language that made Bedouin speech both its literary ideal and its linguistic standard.[8] Enthusiasm for Bedouin speech reached its height under the reign of caliph Hārūn al-Rashīd (r. 786–809). In Basra, two pupils of the master played a fundamental role in the promotion of this linguistic purism: Abū ʿUbayda (d. 210?/825?) and Asmaʿī (d. 213/828). But the school of Kufa was not excluded from this movement to promote Bedouin speech, in the person of two of its most eminent representatives, Kisāʾī (d. 183?/799?) and Farrāʾ (d. 207/822). It is known that the first of these, besides having studied under masters in Kufa, frequented the study circle of Khalīl

5. Ibn Khallikān, *Wafayāt al-Aʿyān*, 4:308.

6. Sayrafī, *Akhbār al-Naḥwiyīn al-Basriyīn*, ed. Muhammad Ibrahim Bannā (Cairo: Dār al-iʿtisām, 1985), 103; Ibn al-Nadīm, *Fihrist*, ed. Riḍā al-Māzindarānī (Beirut: Dār al-Masīrah, 1988), 64.

7. One ninth-century source describes the study seminar of Abū ʿAmr ibn ʿAlā (d. 154?/770?) in Basra as frequented by "searchers for knowledge, men of letters, Bedouin connoisseurs of clear and correct languages, and delegations come from the desert": Ibn al-Nadīm, *Fihrist*, 42. That same source shows another member of the school of Basra "who was not a Bedouin" traveling in the desert in the mid-eighth century and "learning from the Bedouins, connoisseurs of the Arab language": ibid., 48. Abū Bakr al-Sūlī (d. 335/946) wrote a *Kitāb Akhbār Abū ʿAmrū ibn al-ʿAlā* that unfortunately has not come down to us: Ibn Khallikān, *Wafayāt al-Aʿyān*, 4:359.

8. Qiftī, *Inbāh al-Ruwwāt*, ed. Muhammad Abū al-Faḍi Ibrāhīm, 3 vols. (Cairo: al-Hayah al-Misrīya al-ʿĀmmah lil Kutub, 1981), 2:106, 377. That linguistic ideal did not become established without hesitation and polemics, however. In Basra itself there were learned linguists who rejected the claimed purity of language of the Bedouins. We are told that the Qurʾan specialists and grammarians ʿAbd-Allāh ibn Ishāq (d. 117/735) and ʿĪsā ibn ʿUmar (d. 149/766) "spoke against the Bedouin Arabs" and attacked their reputation as connoisseurs of pure language. The second of these is even reported to have denounced the great poet Nābigha al-Dhubyānī for solecisms that displayed defects of language. Unlike Abū ʿAmr ibn ʿAlā, the two nonconformists preached, in imitation of Iraqi jurists of their age, a more speculative approach founded on analogical reasoning.

ibn Ahmad (d. 175/791) in Basra and spent time with the Bedouins of the Hejaz.[9] It seems that the rivalry between the two school did not exclude convergences, or frequentation of the masters of the adversary school: just as Kisā'ī went from Kufa to Basra to study, Abū Zayd al-Ansārī (d. 214/829), another great figure of the Basra school who studied with its founder, went to Kufa to frequent its masters.

Still, the Basra school deserves credit for having developed a method, which consisted in going to seek out grammatical, lexical, and rhetorical materials among the Bedouins. The lexicographer Ibn Durayd (d. 321/933) relates an anecdote that speaks to that point. Among a group of men of letters and book buyers gathered in the booksellers' quarter of Basra in a shop that, as was true of all bookshops, also functioned as a reading room and a literary club was a man from Kufa, the seat of a rival school of philology, as we have seen. As the man leafed through the *Reform of the Language* of the Kufa grammarian Ibn al-Sikkīt (d. 245/854), he praised the work's author and, taking advantage of the opportunity, lectured the others on the superiority of the Kufa linguists over those of Basra.[10] The Basrans listening to him were scandalized to hear such statements being made in their town, and they loudly accused the man of provocation. The affair seemed to them so serious that they brought it to Riyyāshī (d. 257/870), a representative of the Basra school of philology who lived in the neighborhood. Riyyāshī, who had been the pupil of Asma'ī and of Abū Zayd al-Ansārī, dismissed the outsider's offensive remarks scornfully: "We have learned the language of gazelle hunters and jerboa eaters; they have learned their [language] from the inhabitants of cultivated lands [*Sawād*] and makers of white flour."[11] In other words, the linguists of Basra had acquired knowledge from the Bedouins, and those of Kufa from sedentary peasants. The language of the Bedouins was reputed to be more pure, clearer, and more beautiful. According to Riyyāshī, it was thanks to his

9. Dhahabī, *Siyar A'lām al-Nubalā'*, ed. Shu'ayb al-Arna'ūtī et al., 25 vols. (Beirut: Mu'assasat al-Risālah, 1982–83), 11:132.

10. On the Kufa school, see Mahdī Makhzūmī, *Madrasat al-Kūfa wa Manhajuhā fī Dirāsāt al-Lughah wa-'l-Nahw* (Baghdad: Matba'at Dār al-Ma'rifah, 1374 AH/1955).

11. Ibn al-Nadīm, *Fihrist*, 64; Ibn al-Anbārī, *Nuzhat al-Albāb fī Tabaqāt al-Udabā'*, ed. Muhammad Abū al-Fadi Ibrāhīm (Cairo: Dār nahdaf Misr, 1967), 200. Two or three generations earlier, Abū Muhammad al-Yāzidī (d. 202/817), a disciple of the founder of the Basra school, had treated colleagues in Kufa with the same opprobrium: "We (in Basra) have always done our best to draw consequences from analogy with the original language of the Arabs (the Bedouins), until the day when people started to form analogies based on the language of the old men of Qatrubbul," a region of Iraq known for its fine wines: Anbārī, *Nuzhat*, 83.

masters that the most unchanged variants of the Bedouin language had become "the depository and the guardian of the Arab linguistic ideal in its inimitable perfection."[12]

Bolstered by this nostalgic conception of language, the scholars of Basra began to study the Bedouins' speech. Basra, situated at the edge of the desert, was all the more appropriate for that enterprise because it was a crossroads for Bedouin caravans from Bahrain, Yamāma, and the Nejd. Even before the learned linguists of Basra went to the Bedouins in order to collect speech data, their poetry, their genealogies, and their "propitious days," the Bedouins came to them, thanks to the requirements of economic exchange.

The Bedouins who frequented Basra camped in an area three miles outside the city known as the Mirbad, which functioned as a trading center for the entire region.[13] That was where the linguists chose to settle because, as with Arab fairs before Islam (and like the suqs of Morocco studied by the anthropologist Clifford Geertz), far from being a simple place for commercial exchanges, the Mirbad was a space for communication and in itself a veritable cultural institution, where poets and itinerant singers came to recite their works. Ru'ba (d. 145/762)[14] recited his poems there before audiences made up of members of the Bedouin tribe of the Tamīm. Farazdaq and Jarīr[15] engaged in ferocious poetic jousts there under the arbitrage of such experts as the poet and tribal lord Rā'ī (d. 90?/709).[16] It was thus here that Asma'ī (d. 213/828) came to seek the *gharīb al-lugha*, "the rare and obscure words" used by the Bedouins. One narrative shows him telling his master about one of his excursions into the suq: "One day I went to see Abū 'Amr ibn al-'Alā'. When he saw me, he asked me, 'Where are you coming from, Asma'ī?' 'From Mirbad,' I responded. 'Show me what you have brought back,' he said. Then I read to him what I had noted on my tablets. After having meditated on six rare words, the meanings of which

12. Jamel-Eddine Bencheikh, *Poétique arabe: Essai sur les voies d'une création* (Paris: Anthropos, 1975), 55.

13. On this "caravan halt" and its cultural role, see Charles Pellat, *Le milieu basrien et la formation de Gāhiz* (Paris: Maisonneuve, 1953); and Régis Blachère, *Histoire de la littérature arabe des origines à la fin du XVe siècle*, 3 vols. (Paris: Maisonneuve, 1964, 1966, 1984), 3:527.

14. Blachère, *Histoire de la littérature arabe*, 3:527.

15. On these two poets of tribal particularism, see ibid., 3:484–94, 497–505. More than Farazdaq, however, "Jarīr remained attached to his native desert for his entire life"; "all his life, he was the spokesman and the champion of the Qaysites against the Yemenites."

16. Shalaqānī, *Riwāyat al-lughah* (Misr: Dār al-Ma'ārif, 1971), 69. Both expressed their preference for Farazdaq. See also Blachère, *Histoire de la littérature arabe*, 3:479–82.

were unclear to him, he exclaimed, 'You have become an expert in *gharīb*, Asmaʿī!' "[17]

Abū 'Ubayd ibn Sallām (d. 224/838), a linguist and jurist from Herāt, in what is now Afghanistan, provides another illustration of this effort to collect hapax in usage among the Bedouins. In 795 a trip to Iraq also took him to Basra, Kufa, and Baghdad. Asmaʾī, his principal reference, was also one of his masters.[18]

But it was not just linguists who frequented the Mirbad. Prose writers and poets came there to perfect their mastery of the Arabic language. The famous Jāhiz (d. 255/868), born in Basra and a student of Asmaʿī and his co-disciples, learned "the purity of the language" there from the mouths of its presumed speakers.[19] The poet Abū Nuwās (d. 200/815), who studied under the direction of one of Asmaʿī's codisciples, did the same. Jāhiz walked in the steps of one of the principal founders of Arabic prose; Abū Nuwās in those of Bashshār ibn Burd, the man who revolutionized Arabic poetry.[20]

Some of the Bedouin informants who frequented the Mirbad became well known. Ibn al-Nadīm's *Catalogue* gives an entire list of them. Such men did not hesitate to attend the linguists' study circles. We know, for example, that the circle of Yūnus ibn Habīb (d. 183/799) attracted "students in language and purists from among the Bedouins and from the desert."[21] The circle of the founder of the Basra school was never without Bedouin informers. One of these seems to have known the speech habits of the Hejaz so well that all the linguists in Basra referred to his judgments and explanations when it was a question of words or expressions from that area.[22] There were even women among these privileged informers. One narrative shows Abū Hātim al-Sijistānī interrogating a woman who was well known to collectors of linguistic information about a variety of grain for which he knew only the Persian term.[23] Ibn al-Nadīm's *Catalogue* gives an entire list of woman informers.[24] We learn that the more cultivated

17. Yāqūt, *Muʿjam al-Buldān*, ed. Ferdinand Wüstenfeld, 7 vols. (Leipzig, 1855–73; reprint, 6 vols. in 11 pts., Frankfurt: Institute for the History of Arabic-Islamic Science, 1994), 2:202.
18. Ibn Sallām, *Al-Gharīb al-Musannaf*, ed. Muhammad al-Mukht 'Ubaydi (Carthage: al-Muʾassasah al-Watanīyah, 1989–).
19. Pellat, *Le milieu basrien*.
20. The prose writer in question is the political writer Ibn al-Muqaffaʿ (d. ca. 762); he and his contemporary Bashshār ibn Burd were both trained in Basra.
21. Anbārī, *Nuzhat*, 49.
22. Jāhiz, *Al-Bayān waʾl-Tabyīn*, ed. 'Abd al-Salām Muhammad Hārūn, 4 vols. (Cairo: Maktabat al-Khānjī, 1968), 3:225.
23. *Al-Amālī*, 3:540; Ibn Manzūr, *Lisān al-ʿArab*, 15 vols. (Beirut: Dār Sadir, 1955–56), 1:8.
24. Ibn al-Nadīm, *Fihrist*, 70.

Bedouins, after having frequented the circles of the city masters, might themselves begin to teach and compose linguistic monographs. The *Catalogue* cites several prototypes of such works.

In Basra, Kufa, and Baghdad, Bedouins of that sort were considered to be the repositories of the speech habits of their tribes and became familiar figures in the study circles and literary salons. Their powers of judgment were acknowledged everywhere. When the 'Abbāsid vizier Yaḥyā the Barmecide, an enlightened man who played a major role in the development of knowledge by his patronage, held a debate between Sībawayh (d. 180?/796?), representing the Basra school, and Kisā'ī (d. 183?/799?), the leading figure in the rival school of Kufa, the best Bedouin connoisseurs of desert speech habits were called in. They voted for the Kufa representative. Sībawayh emerged from this contest totally dejected. If his biographers can be believed, the "great affliction" of having undergone this humiliation was the cause of his death soon after. To defend his memory, his followers claimed that the judges were partisan, "Arabs of the Hutma, among whom Kisā'ī had stayed to take their language."[25] In another polemical exchange that had been organized in Basra between Asma'ī, the local master of philology, and Dabī, representing Kufa philology, it was a young man of the Banū Sa'd tribe, known for his vast store of memorized Bedouin poetry, who was asked to judge between the two.[26]

The Stay in the Desert

The Basra scholars were not content to collect samples of speech from Bedouins from the desert, or Bādīya, the steppes of Suria and Iraq, who came to their cities: they also took themselves into the desert to gather them from the mouths of other Bedouins, the authenticity of whose speech they judged to be intact because they had lived far from the centers of urban life. They looked down on mixed populations of Arabs and non-Arabs, to the point of thinking them a threat to the purity of the Bedouins' language. This means that in the corrupting cities, the privileged informers became themselves suspect and unworthy of trust. Their

25. Khatīb al-Baghdādī, *Tārīkh Baghdād*, 14 vols. (Cairo, 1931), 12:195; Qiftī, *Inbāh*, 2:273.

26. Qiftī, *Inbāh*, 3:303. The anonymous *Kitāb al-Majālis*, written in the tenth century, offers a number of examples of the arbitration of Bedouin experts: see *Kitāb al-Majālis al-Madkhra li'l-Ulama bi'l-Lugha*, microfilm no. 232, Ma'had a-Makhtūtāt al-'Arabiyya (Institut Arabe des Manuscrits), Cairo. On these Bedouin informers, see Régis Blachère, "Les savants irakiens et leurs informateurs bédouins aux IIIe–IVe siècles de l'Hégire," in *Mélanges offerts à William Marçais* (Paris: Maisonneuve, 1950), 37–53, esp. 37–48; reprinted in Blachère, *Analecta* (Damascus: Institut Français de Damas, 1975), 31–42.

long stays among the sedentary population and the city dwellers were held against them. There are many anecdotes that show Basra scholars scolding their Bedouin informers either for having mispronounced a word, made a grammatical mistake, or given an inaccurate meaning for a word, or for being unable to understand and explicate a poem of their contributors.

Abū 'Amr ibn al-'Alā', the founder of the school, seems to have been one of the first to travel in the desert. He had lived in the Hejaz, studying in Mecca and in Medina; in Yemen, where his father had taken refuge for political reasons; and in Syria.[27] In a narration transmitted by the mystic Tustarī (d. 283/896) he connects his experience of the desert with the persecutions of the pitiless governor of Iraq, Hajjāj (694–714). In this fragment he tells us: "We fled Hajjāj by taking refuge in the Desert of the Arabs [Bādiya]. We stayed there for a while, moving from one place to another. One day as I was coming out of one of these places, I heard an old Bedouin declaiming verse [on patience, announcing the death of the tyrant]."[28] A fanatical admirer of the pure language of the pre-Islam Bedouin poets, he mistrusted the quality of the language of the modern poets, whose compositions he disliked. Before his disciples he often compared the poetry of the earlier men to "pieces of brocade," whereas that of the later ones was like "pieces of raw wool." He seems to have remained faithful to that opinion, making it a rule to support his philological commentaries only with citations from the poets of the jāhiliyya, the epoch of Arabic paganism.[29] He is reported to have gathered together and written down such a massive amount of ancient Bedouin poetry that a room in his house was barely large enough to hold it all.[30] A narrative that shows him in Mecca in the process of interrogating a nomad who was passing through allows us a glimpse of his investigations.[31] Another narrative shows him, again in Mecca, pursuing other aspects of his investigations and subjecting a Bedouin from Oman to a genuine interrogation:

27. Shams al-Dīn Jazarī, Ghāyat al-Nihāya fī Tabaqāt al-Qurrā', ed. Gotthelf Bergstrasser, 2 vols. (Cairo: Maktabat al-Khānjī, 1932–35), 1:289.

28. Tustarī, Tafsīr al-Qur'ān al-adhīm (Misr: Matba'at al-Sa'ādah, 1329 AH/1908), 123. There is a variant reading in 'Abd al-Ghānī ibn Sa'id, Kitāb al-Mutawārīn, MS no. 3807, Zāhiriyya, Damascus, fol. 22a, that states that 'Abū 'Amr's father was an Umayyad functionary.

29. Ibn Rashīq, Al-'Umda fī Mahāsin al-Shi'r wa-adabihi wa-Naqdihi, ed. Muhammad Muhyī al-Dīn 'Abd al-Hamīd, 2 vols. (Cairo: al-Maktabah al-Tijārīyah al-Kubrā, 1963–64), 90–91. He made an exception for his contemporary Jarīr, whose poetry he liked.

30. Abū 'Amr ibn al-'Ala's biographers relate that he burned this poetic and lexicographical material in a crisis of repentance for past errors. The tension between the sacred and the profane with which linguistic studies was imbued proved psychologically unbearable to this master of philological and Qur'anic studies.

31. Sarrāj, Musāri' al-'Ushshāq, 1:204.

"What tribe do you come from?"

"From the Asads."

"Which, in particular?"

"The Nahd."

"What region are you from?'

"From Oman."

"And where does the purity of your speech come from?"

"We live in an isolated land."[32]

After this exchange, Abū ʿAmr asks the man to describe his homeland and tell him how its inhabitants lived. Rather than just questioning his informer about his tribe's speech habits, he asks ethnographic questions about the social and material life of his interlocutor's people (their modes of production, their foods and diet, their habitat, and more) and about the ecological milieu in which they lived. Everything about the Bedouins' natural setting interested him. His questions focused on the morphology of the soil, the climate, plants, domestic and wild animals, and even insects. He remained a scholar, however, operating as a linguist, not as an ethnographer, a geologist, or a zoologist. After an interview he would sift through these various themes and write them down in separate monographs, just as Asmaʿī, for example, wrote a *Book of Trees*, a *Book of Palm Trees*, and a *Book of Plants*.[33] Such inventories might in turn be included in larger works, such as the *Book of Descriptions* of Nadr ibn Shumayl (d. 204/819), another member of the Basra school. This work is divided into five volumes: 1, "The Creation of Man, Nobility, Generosity, and Women"; 2, "Dens, Habitats, Mountains, and Hills"; 3, "Camels"; 4, "Cattle, Birds, the Sun, the Moon, the Night, the Day, Milks, Wells, Basins, Beverages . . ."; and 5, "Cultivated Plants, the Vine, Trees, the Wind, Clouds, Rain." It is evident that little preconceived or rigorous order presides over the organization of these lists. That absence of rigor is true of both the monographs and the compendiums of the period.

Abū ʿAmr's students continued to make a stay in the desert a constituent part of their work of collecting sociohistorical and linguistic materials. ʿAbd Allāh ibn Saʿīd al-Umawī, "who was not a Bedouin," is described as a voyager of the desert and a collector of tribal speech patterns from

---

32. Suyūtī, *Al-Muzhir fī ʿUlūm al-lugha*, 2 vols. (Cairo, 1325 AH), 1:92; Abū ʿAlī Qālī, *Dhayl al-Amālī wa-al-Nawādir*, vol. 3 of *Kitāb al-Amālī*, 3 vols. (Cairo: Dār al-Kutub al-Misrīyah, 1324 AH/1926), 86.

33. These three texts are available in Auguste Haffner and Louis Cheiko, eds., *Dix anciens traités de philologie arabe*, (Beirut: Imprimerie Catholique, 1914).

the mouth of *fusahā* of pure and correct speech.[34] Abū Zayd al-Ansārī
(d. 214/829) claims that he had only three authorities: the master of the
Basra school, a prose writer from Kufa, and the Bedouins of the desert.[35]
In the introduction to his *Book of Precious Things*, for example, he indicates
that all of the "transmissions" consigned to his pages came to him from
his Kufa master and some "Bedouin Arabs." Among the latter, the groups
most cited are the Banū Kulayb, the Banū ʿUqayl ("men and women"), the
Banū Tamīm, and the Banū Asad.[36] Defining his approach elsewhere, he
notes that when he states "the Arabs said," he is referring to what he gathered among the Banū Bakr (the tribe of origin of the Prophet), the Banū
Kilāb, the Banū Hilāl, and more generally the inhabitants of Nejd (which
included Tamīms and Rabīʿas, segments of the Banū Asad, and others),
and in Medina and its environs.[37]

Of the many students of the master of the Basra school, it was incontestably Asmaʿī (d. 213/828) who knew the desert, its inhabitants, and its
poetry best. Thanks to his prodigious memory, he was reputed to know
by heart several thousand poetic works, which explains the nickname "the
devil of poetry,"[38] given to him by Hārūn al-Rashīd in homage to his virtuosity. Like his own master, however, he valued only the archaic poets.

The anecdotes concerning Asmaʿī's stays in the desert are scattered
through his successors' treatises on language. In one of these, we see him
traveling with a copyist who might also have been an assistant.[39] In another,
he is depicted paying court to a beautiful Bedouin woman near a well, reciting verse to her.[40] In a third account, he is interrogating an adolescent of
the Banū Asad tribe, and in a fourth, he encourages a member of the Banū
ʿAmir tribe to recite local poems. A fifth report shows him among the
Banū ʿAnba conversing with a Bedouin woman. Some of these anecdotes
describe him in highly unusual situations. In one of them he uses a variety
of ingenious arguments to persuade a group of young Bedouin women who

34. Ibn al-Nadīm, *Fihrist*, 48; Azharī, *Tahdhīb al-Lugha*, ed. Mohammad Hasan Al Yasin
(Baghdad, 1959), 1:11–12. Among the tribes whose narratives and rare terms he collected his biographers cite the Banū al-Hārith, a segment of the Kaʿb: Qiftī, *Inbāh*, 2:120.

35. Azharī, *Tahdhīb al-Lugha*, 1:21.

36. Abū Zayd al-Ansārī, *Kitāb al-nawādir fi al-lughah*, ed. Muhammad ʿAbd al-Qadir Ahmad
(Cairo: Dār al-Shuruq, 1981), 142.

37. Ibn Hazm, *Jamharat ansāb al-ʿArab*, ed. ʿAbd al-Salām Muhammad Hārūn (Misr: Dār al-
Maʿārif, 1962), 264.

38. Anbārī, *Nuzhat*, 113. In his study circle, his biographers remark, he never had written notes
before his eyes, but taught from memory in the ancient manner.

39. Khatīb al-Baghdādī, *Tārīkh Baghdād*, 9:363.

40. Ibid., 1:327; Sarrāj, *Musāriʿ al-ʿUshshāq*, 2:221.

are playfully exchanging snatches of poetry to permit him to take notes on what they are saying. They refuse to let him come too near, so he seeks out a discreet place from which he can listen to them and jot down their songs. An old man who sees him watching the young women and who cannot conceive that anyone could be interested in their childish games chides him: "How dare you write down the statements of those miserable dwarfs [*adnā*]?" And of course as the old man is scolding the linguist, he adds to his list a word that he did not know and that he notes immediately on his tablet: *dānī*, plural *adnā*, a term signifying "stupid, imbecile," but also "vile, low, worthy of scorn."[41]

Accounts of Asmaʿī among the Bedouins are so numerous that a certain number of men of letters specialized in their transmission. The Basra scholar was an insatiable collector of language, as noted by one Bedouin who was astonished to see Asmaʿī writing down all of his explanations.[42] The most famous work treating his collections is *The Narrations of Asmaʿī* of Raba 'ī (d. 329/940).[43] One might legitimately suspect that the many more or less romantic anecdotes featuring this great philologist at work in the desert are the work of late medieval authors, but there is an Egyptian papyrus that, according to Nabia Abbott, dates to the early ninth century, which attests that tales of the sort circulated during his lifetime or at least among his immediate pupils.[44] One of Asmaʿī's codisciples, Abū Zayd al-Ansārī (d. 214/829), a great traveler, made several trips into the desert. Explaining his method for collecting linguistic data to one of his students, he states: "I do not say, 'The Arabs said' unless I have heard it from the Bedouin tribes of the Bakr, the Banū Kalb, the Banū Kilāb, or those who live in the upper or lower Sāfila; otherwise I do not say, 'The Arabs said.'"[45] Following in their masters' footsteps, Asmaʿī's pupils, like those of Abū Zayd, continued to travel in the desert.[46]

When these linguistic pioneers arrived in the desert, the Bedouins received them in the same way that exotic societies welcome anthropologists—that is, with a mixture of amused surprise and curiosity. Asmaʿī,

41. Qālī, *Kitāb al-Amālī*, 1:40.

42. Rabaʿī Abūʾl-Hasan, *Al-Muntaqā min Akhbār al-Asmaʿī*, ed. Izzeddine al-Tanoukhi (Damascus: Ibn Zeydoun, 1936), j.

43. The *Akhbār al-Asmaʿī* have come down to us in the abridged version of Dayāʾ al-Dīn al-Maqdisī (d. 643/1245), *al-Muntaqā min Akhbār al-Asmaʿī*, ed. ʿIzz al-Dīn Tānūkhī (Damascus: Matbaʿat Ibn Zaydn, 1936).

44. Nabia Abbott, *Language and Literature*, vol. 3 of *Studies in Arabic Literary Papyri* (Chicago: University of Chicago Press, 1967), 79 (document 4).

45. Suyūtī, *Al-Muzhir*, 1:91

46. Ibn al-Nadīm, *Fihrist*, 54.

who had plenty of experience in the matter, tells how the language collectors operated in the desert:

> I was on a donkey, which I energetically spurred on, in search of hapax
> [*gharīb*] related to traditions, poetry, and language when in the territory of
> Dariyya [not far from Medina], I saw a sort of roof resembling a large parasol
> of woven hair that sheltered a horse. The shaded space also served as a place
> for camels to rest and as an enclosure for sheep. I got off near a well that was
> nearby. I filled the drinking trough with water for my donkey, when a young
> man came out of the house nearby. He approached me and greeted me. When
> I responded to his greeting, he said to me: "I see here someone whose clothes
> are those of a city dweller but whose language is that of a Bedouin!" I an-
> swered: "As far as the clothes are concerned, you have seen correctly. As for
> the language, where is the purity of your expressions? The ease with which
> you express yourselves? The natural capacity that you have to make [fine]
> speeches? The spontaneity with which you enrich meanings? We [city dwell-
> ers] with our impoverished expression torture the language without ever
> attaining the aim we seek and expressing what is in our hearts." [After offering
> him hospitality, the young man with the noble air asked,] "What makes you
> come into this rough and harsh land?" "The desire for the fine manners [*adab*]
> that adorn those who hold them for their beauty," Asmaʿī answered. "And that
> is the only reason for your coming here? added the young man, astonished." "I
> have no greater care, no deeper desire, and no more pressing wish!"[47]

This text is interesting for more than one reason, as it dramatizes
the city dwellers' idealized representation of the Bedouin world. Men of
letters from the big cities did not take off for the school of the desert
uniquely in order to collect instances of the "clear and pure language" of its
inhabitants. Thanks to their contact with the Bedouins, they also learned
about an ethico-cultural manner of living in this world centered on the
muruwwa, a notion that covers an entire set of social and individual rules
having to do with courage, magnanimity, constancy, generosity, and good
will. In doing so, linguists and writers portrayed the Bedouin world as the
site of an admirable masculine humanity. It is understandable that urban
elites felt the urge to become *zarīf*[48]—that is, models of refinement and

---

47. Rabaʿī AbūʾlʿAlāʾ, *Kitāb al-Fusūs*, ed. ʿAbdʾ al-Wahhāb al-Tāzī Suʿūd, 3 vols. (Mouhammadia, Morocco, 1993), 2:314.
48. On this ideal, see Susanne Enderwitz, "Du *Fatā* au *Zarīf*, ou comment on se distingue?"
Arabica 36, no. 2 (1989): 125–42.

spiritual elegance—by seeking out civility in the wild Bādiya and among its "spare and rough" inhabitants.

Despite the criticisms of the Basra linguists, who claimed to be closer to the Bedouins than their Kufa colleagues, the Kufa scholars also hastened to the desert to listen to its inhabitants. As with Basra, Bedouin caravans regularly came to Kufa for provisions.[49] The Bedouins who regularly frequented the city in the late eighth and early ninth centuries were the Banū Saʿd, the Banū ʿUqayl, and the Banū Asad. Ibn al-Aʿrabī (d. 231/845), for example, made inquiries among the two first groups, and Ibn Kunnāsa among the third.[50] A certain number of eminent members of the school made the voyage into the desert. Abū ʿAmrū al-Shaybānī, who died at the age of one hundred in 821, was one of the very first to do so. A linguist who died at the end of the ninth century reports that Abū ʿAmrū al-Shaybānī traveled extensively in the desert with a companion, carrying with him two containers of ink, and that they returned only after having exhausted this supply by taking notes on his "auditions" among the Bedouins. He is in fact credited with having collected the poetry of some eighty tribes.[51] Before him, the famous Hammād (d. 160?/776?), called "The Transmitter" (Rāwiya), who in his time was considered one of the greatest connoisseurs of archaic poetry, made the trip into the desert. His biographers portray him investigating among the Banū Asad and the Banū ʿUqayl.[52] We are told that his methods were closest to those of his colleagues from Basra, from whom he attracted some of his students.[53] One of these, Khalaf al-Ahmar (d. 179?/795?), was also known as a collector of archaic poetry and stayed among the Bedouins.[54]

The greatest desert traveler from Kufa clearly remains Kisāʾī (d. 183?/799?). After studying with the masters of his home town, he went first to Baghdad, then to Basra, where he followed the teaching of the famous Khalīl ibn Ahmad (d. 175/791), the author (or partial author) of the first

49. Like the Mirbad section of Basra, the Kunāsa of Kufa was the place for unloading and reloading camel caravans (Massignon) that linked that city to the Bādiyat. A place of exchange between city dwellers and nomads, "it became an important center of Bedouin poetry, much like the Mirbad of Basra, but on a smaller scale": Hichem Djaït, *Al-Kūfa: Naissance de la ville islamique* (Paris: Maisonneuve et Larose, 1986), 278.

50. Qiftī, *Inbāh*, 3:132, 161.

51. Ibn al-Nadīm, *Fihrist*, 68; Anbārī, *Nuzhat*, 1:96. He was also a recognized and much-appreciated transmitter of prophetic traditions.

52. Azharī, *Tahdhīb al-Lugha*, 1:21.

53. He is reported to have said one day regarding a word: "I have heard a thousand Bedouins say the contrary of what Asmaʿi has collected": Anbārī, *Nuzhat*, 151.

54. Qiftī, *Inbāh*, 2:260; Suyūtī, *Bughyat al-Wuʿāh fī Tabaqāt al-Lughawīyīn*, ed. Muhammad Abū Ibrāhīm, 2 vols. (Cairo: Matbaʿat ʿĪsā al-Bābī al-Halabī, 1964–65), 1:554.

dictionary of the Arabic language. One day, his biographers tell us, Kisā'ī
made the acquaintance of a Bedouin who frequented the master's circle,
and the man reminded him that he was neglecting the purity of language
(fasāḥa) that he had come to Basra to seek. That purity, the Bedouin reminded him, was among the Asad and the Tamīm Bedouins of the Kufa
region. The scholar was persuaded to go into the desert, when he learned
that the great lexicographer with whom he had come to study had gained
his knowledge of the language "from the tribes of the deserts of the Hejaz,
the Nejd, and the Tihama." Carrying with him a large amount of ink and
paper, "he entered into the Bādīya," returning with a considerable quantity of linguistic and poetic data.[55] The travel narrative contained in manuscript no. 232, Cairo, tells about Kisā'ī's sojourn in the Kufa desert to put
himself to the school of the Bedouins. It shows him experiencing both an
intellectual initiation and a rupture with the family milieu. At the end of
his stay among the Bedouins, he was both a changed man and a jubilant
one: "Hunger and fatigue have so strongly changed the shade of my face
and the color of my skin that I look like one of them," he reported. After
having learned his hosts' language and their poetry, he returned to Kufa,
but delayed his return home so that his master and his fellow students
could appreciate the transformation that he had undergone in his contact
with his Bedouin educators. Although his family had nearly given up hope
of ever seeing him again, he went first to the mosque where his master
had his study circle. Before all the members of the circle, he displayed the
learning that he had brought back from the desert, and it was only when
his master had confirmed his achievement that he returned home. This as-
tonishing account of a trip in the desert—the most complete known—has
the merit of showing the extent to which any quest for knowledge is an
overwhelming intellectual experience and initiation. Kisā'ī went into the
desert a student and came back out of it a young scholar.[56] He offers proof
of this complete change in two ways: he bears signs of it on his person as
proof of his virtuosity, and he carries proof of it in his transcriptions and
his notebooks. If he feels it imperative to display such proofs to his master
and his fellow students, it is because they are validated only by being seen
and recognized by competent persons.

55. Anbārī, Nuzhat, 69; Yāqūt, Mu'jam al-Buldān, 13:169. Qiftī cites several anecdotes concerning his stay among the Bedouins and shows him transcribing their sayings: Qiftī, Inbāh, 2:273.
When he returned from the desert he settled in Baghdad, and the caliph Hārūn al-Rashīd designated him the preceptor of his son Amīn, who was later caliph, between 809 and 813.
56. Anonymous, Kitāb al-Majālis, fols. 98b–101b.

Kisāʾī encouraged the idea of a stay among the Bedouins as an essential step in any pursuit of philology. His principal student, Farrāʾ (d. 207/822), was obliged to follow the same road that had led his master into the desert. When, toward the end of his life, Farrāʾ had become a fixture at the court of al-Maʾmūn (r. 813–33), the caliph charged him with composing a book that would summarize the basic treatises on grammar and everything "that he had heard from the Bedouins."[57]

During the second half of the ninth century, even though a stay in the desert remained a much-appreciated move, it was less frequently said that linguists, collectors of poetry, or genealogists had made such a trip. By then scholars were more preoccupied with putting into order the considerable material that their elders had gathered together and had often left in near-total disorder. These later scholars were responsible for what might be called the "Alexandrian moment" in the study of the Arabic language and its products. For many of them, the library replaced the school of the desert. After the figure of the "great transmitter" (*rāwiya*) of the eighth century and of the author (*muʾallif*) that emerged around the beginning of the ninth century, came the time of the editor (*musannif*). The new figure was a library man. He worked on a library and he worked in the library: after the extraordinary rise of the book at the end of the eighth century, sovereigns, princes, and the powerful of this world called on his skills in order to constitute or administer their libraries, which were often modeled on that of Alexandria. His role was to gather books, publish editions, and comment on texts so as to set down the lessons to be drawn from them. This means that his activities were both technical and intellectual. They were those of a bibliographer, an editor/publisher, and a mediator between the works, their authors, and their readers. From a technical point of view, he collated the "recensions" in circulation, establishing the text by comparing copies and variants and making choices. Intellectually, he was taking on an immense role, because he was the one who decided what should or should not be published, commented on, or protected by his authority. By the same token, he oriented the intellectual culture of his time and manipulated the reader into accepting the meaning that he preferred. Feared because of his powers, he rendered all written production

---

57. Anbārī, *Nuzhat*, 99. This work later became the *Kitāb al-Hudūd*, which students were willing to pay a high price for even during the life of its author: Yāqūt, *Irshad al-Arīb ilā Maʿrifat al-Adīb (Muʿjam al-Udabāʾ)*, ed. David Samuel Margoliouth (1913–29); ed. Ihsān ʿAbbās, 7 vols. (Beirut: Dār al-Gharb al-Islāmī, 1993), 6:2814; in English translation as *The Irshad al-arib ilá maʿrifat al-ardib; Or, Dictionary of Learned Men of Yáqút*, 2nd ed., ed. D. S. Margoliouth, 5 vols. (London: Luzac, 1923–31).

problematic because he could decide that a particular work was authentic and another one was a pastiche, or that one version of a work was worthy of being transmitted and another version unworthy. His preferred operations were sorting, classification, and putting into circulation statements that he often took pains to decontextualize completely. All of this generated specific sorts of works, the most recurrent of which are the collection, the anthology, and the dictionary. This job of putting things into writing gave Islamic culture a new sort of man of letters, unknown before the ninth century: the polygraph. The many offerings that the bookseller Ibn al-Nadīm noted in his *Catalogue* in 997 included one of a tenth-century prose writer whose collection of anecdotes regarding Arabic poets from pre-Islamic antiquity to his own day ran to "60 volumes." He also lists a collection of "5,000 sheets" containing nothing but the sample verse lines in use among the philologists, a collection of spicy anecdotes about the poets of Islam of "more than 5,000 sheets," a dictionary of poets of "more than 1,000 sheets," a dictionary of the grammarians of Basra of "more than 3,000 sheets," a dictionary of Arabic singers of "more than 1,600 sheets," and a collection of love poetry of "more than 3,000 sheets." All in all, this particular polygraph had produced a work of "over 20,000 sheets."[58] An effort such as this would be unthinkable without the existence of good libraries and a flourishing paper industry. The one fed the other in a dizzying chain of transformations.

There were also political reasons that inspired the great philologists and prose writers of the ninth and tenth centuries to devote themselves to the intense activity of compilation, to the point of neglecting inquiry in the desert. A great insecurity followed the advance of the Qarmatians from Bahrain toward the Hejaz, Iraq, and Syria. Launched in 890, this extremist movement shook the heart of the empire, paralyzing commerce, leading to the depopulation of entire regions, and creating raids on the caravans of pilgrims on their way to Mecca. The terror of believers reached its peak in 930, when the insurgents violated the shrine of the Kaaba and stole the Black Stone. City people came to view the Bedouins who followed the Qarmations in their politico-religious action in a different light from their eighth-century romantic representation as "great transmitters." Their image was no longer that of men with a fierce sense of honor and an unshakable loyalty, or that of a generous and hospitable people, but as faithless, lawless robbers as greedy as they were ferocious. An agitated age suddenly recalled that the Qur'an had called them frank "hypocrites."

58. Ibn al-Nadīm, *Fihrist*, 147–49.

Another change—a literary one this time—made the Bedouins "of pure and correct speech" less appealing to the aesthetic tastes of the men of letters of the big cities of Iraq. Whereas, in the early ninth century, listening to Bedouin eloquence was still considered a great pleasure, by the end of the century some agreed with Ibn Bassām (d. 302/914) that their "words are not beautiful,"[59] without encountering any objection. The time had past when, asked what people was the best, someone like Ibn al-Muqaffaʿ (d. ca. 762), an intellectual of both Persian and Arabic culture, could respond: the Bedouins. The Bedouin Arabs, he states, are "the wisest among the people because of the authenticity of their state of nature [fitra], the equilibrium of the structure [of their humors?], the exactitude of their thought, and the subtlety of their intelligence."[60] This ideal portrait of the nomadic Arab was widely shared among urban men of letters of the time. When the caliph al-Mahdī (r. 775–85) asked why the Bedouins were described in contradictory terms—"avidity and avarice"; "generosity and prodigality"—the prose writer from Kufa Haytham ibn ʿAdī (d. 207/ 822), the author of several monographs on linguistics, ethnography, history, and genealogy of the Bedouin Arabs, responded by relating an unusual adventure that he had had in the desert. He asked a Bedouin woman for hospitality and was welcomed. When her absent husband returned, he was worried because he had nothing to offer his guest to eat. But in order not to break the sacrosanct rule of hospitality, he killed his guest's mount and prepared the meat for him to eat. The host then left, returning only the following day. The story does not report whether the writer slept well after having eaten his own camel, but he was relieved to see the Bedouin return in the morning with several camels. They were for him, and were intended to make up for what he had lost the night before.[61] Bedouin mythology was saved! We are at a time when identification with the Bedouin ideal was so strong that one Basra scholar who had stayed in the desert for several years returned to the city so enamored of his hosts that he oiled his son's skin and made him stay in the sun so that the boy would take on their skin color. The story ends badly, however, as the child died of sunstroke.[62]

59. Johann Fück, *Arabiya: Untersuchungen zur arabischen Sprach- und Stilgeschichte* (Berlin: Akademie-Verlag, 1950); trans. Claude Denizeau as *ʾArabīya: Recherches sur l'histoire de la langue et du style arabe* (Paris: Didier, 1955), 139.

60. Tawhīdī, *Kitāb al-Imtāʿ wa-al-Muʾānasa*, ed. Ahmad Amīn and Ahmad Zayn, 2 vols. (Cairo: Matbaʿat Lajnat al-taʾlīf, 1958), 1:72–73. This presentation of the men of the desert continues with a long dissertation in praise of the fine qualities of the Bedouins in which the romanticism of the great urban men of letters of the eighth century is quite evident.

61. Ibn Khallikān, *Wafayāt al-Aʿyān*, 6:107–8.

62. Yāqūt, *Irshād (Muʾjam al-Udabāʾ)*, 6:297.

The same linguist had another student who liked to be called "the Bedouin" or "the Black Man." He oiled himself to tan in the sun and increase his "resemblance to the Bedouins, so as to justify his nickname."[63]

Faithful to this enthusiasm for the Bedouins, the fine minds of the first half of the ninth century continued to admire everything that came from the desert. Jāhiz (d. 255/868), who was to Arabic prose of the ninth century what Ibn al-Muqaffaʿ had been for the eighth century, was one of this admiring throng. In his *Book of Animals* he goes so far as to state that, where knowledge of the animal world was concerned, Muslims had learned nothing from the Greeks that the Bedouins did not already know. On a less serious note, there is an anecdote that shows him offering a Persian friend (who knew Arabic well and spoke it eloquently) to forge a genealogy for him attaching him to some Bedouin tribe, so as to enhance his oratorical and rhetorical talents.[64]

A Geography of Pure Language

Of course not all the tribes that inhabited the desert could boast of the same purity of language. According to whether they lived in self-sufficient isolation or in areas of mixed open land and settlement, their speech was reputed to be unchanged or corrupted by solecisms. On the basis of that "archaeological" concept of language, the grammarian Ishāq ibn Ibrāhīm al-Fārābī (d. 350?/961?)—not to be confused with his compatriot, the philosopher—drew up a linguistic geography of the pure and the impure. This is how it went:

> Among all the Bedouin tribes, the ones whose speech has been collected, to which one refers when the Arabic language is in question, and whose idioms have been collected, there are the Qays, the Tamīm, and the Asad. Almost everything authoritative concerning the Arabic language comes from them. People rely on them for the *gharīb* [rare words] and the *iʿrāb* and the *tasrif* [diacritics]. Next come the Hudhayl, some [segments] of the Kināna and the Tāʾiyyīn. . . . The speech of other tribes has not been much gathered. All in all, no language has been taken from either the sedentary [populations] or the nomads who live in the parts of the desert situated near the foreign nations. It is thus that the language of the Lakhmids and the Judhām has not been gathered

---

63. Ibid., 7:662; Anbārī, *Nuzhat*, 349; Suyūtī, *Bughyat*, 498.
64. Yāqūt, *Irshād (Muʿjam al-Udabā)*, 6:57. There was also word of a man so eloquent that he was nicknamed "the Bedouin": Qiftī, *Inbāh*, 1:27.

because of their proximity to the inhabitants of Egypt and the Copts [*sic!*]. Neither has the language of the Qudāʿa been taken, or the Ghassān and the ʿIyād, for the same reasons of proximity to the inhabitants of Syria, and for all the more reason, because most of them are Christians and read Hebrew. Similarly, neither had language been taken from the Taghlib and the Yaman, who were neighbors of the Byzantines in Mesopotamia, or from the Bakr, who live near the Copts and the Persians, or from the ʿAbd al-Qays and the Azd of Oman, who were mixed, in the Bahrain area, with Hindus and Persians, or from the inhabitants of Yemen because of their mixture with the Hindus and the Ethiopians, or from the Banū Ḥanīfa and the inhabitants of Yamāma, or the peoples of Thaqīf and of Ṭāʾif because of their mixing with the merchants of Yemen who lived among them, or from the cities of the Hejaz, for those who gathered language found that their inhabitants had already been mixed with other nations and their speech was already corrupt.[65]

Isḥāq ibn Ibrāhīm al-Fārābī sets up a hierarchy here among the dialects of the tribes who live in the central regions of the Arabian Peninsula, whom he considers to be paragons of the Arabic language, and the other Bedouin tribes. In reality, as time went by, one tribe or another, one region or another, was taken as the prime example of "purity of language" (*fasāha*) in the context of eloquence, hapax, or poetry. In poetry, for example, Abū ʿAmr ibn al-ʿAlāʾ had other preferences. In his opinion, the poets who displayed the greatest clarity and limpidity were from a region in the mountain chain that lies at the western edge of the Arabian Plateau along the Red Sea between Mecca and the border of Yemen, the land of the Hudhayl, the Thaqīf, and the Azd. Fārābī, on the other hand, put those tribes at the bottom of his hierarchy of linguistic excellence, reproaching them for their contacts with the populations of Yemen. It is true, however, that he was writing in the tenth century. Although their land was near the merchant center of Ṭāʾif, three days from Mecca by foot, the Hudhayl, whom he scorns, had been considered in the two first centuries of Islam to have a dialect of great linguistic purity.[66]

65. Suyūṭī, *Al-Muzhir*, 1:211.

66. Ḥassān ibn Thābit (d. 660 or 673), the poet of the Prophet of Islam, held the Hudhayl to be possessed of the greatest purity of language of his day: Ibn Rashīq, *Al-ʿUmda*, 88. Before 790, Shāfiʿī (d. 204/819)—who had not yet decided to become a jurist—is reported to have lived among them for years. He gathered from their transmitters of poetry "narratives of the happy days of the Arabs" and genealogies. Despite his young age, he was considered a refined connoisseur of Hudhayan poetry. His talents as an expert are reported to have been recognized by the great Asmaʿī. He was said to know more than ten thousand lines of verse, "with their declinations [*iʿrāb*], their rare words [*gharīb*], and their themes [*maʿānī*]": Suyūṭī, *Al-Muzhir*, 1:160 (citing Khaṭīb

The inhabitants of the merchant city of Thaqīf, neighbors to the Hud-hayl, were also considered to possess a language of high quality, as were their neighbors in Mecca, but Fārābī places them on the side of linguistic impurity. That idea goes against the dogmatically founded truth that if the Qur'an,[67] which represents an impeccable incarnation of the linguistic norm of the Arabs, was revealed to a member of the tribe of the Quraysh of Mecca, it was because it was, at least in part, revealed in the language of that tribe. Consequently, Qurayshite speech, which is a pure dialect, must in turn be considered as fully incarnating the linguistic norm of the Ar-abs.[68] The philologists attempted to support this dogmatic syllogism with economic and religious explanations. According to Jāhiz (d. 255/868), the great merchant city of Arabia enjoyed a clear and pure language precisely because it was the major religious and economic center for the Arabs. He supposed it to have learned from the Bedouin tribes that frequented it their finest expressions, their most striking words, and their most perfect phraseology. Meccan speech was thus thought to incarnate the Arab lan-guage at its highest point, which was a rich synthesis of the contributions of all the finest dialects of Arabia.[69]

---

al-Baghdādī). Until the end of his life, he was solicited by collators of Arabic poetry who traveled to Egypt to profit from his talents as a "transmitter." Medieval linguists claim that he said: "To learn about language from the Bedouins is like learning about the prophetic Tradition from the jurists": Azharī, *Tahdhīb al-Lugha*, 1:4.

67. The Qur'an speaks of itself as "a Revelation . . . in the perspicuous Arabic tongue" (26:192, 195). The idea that the Qur'an was revealed in Arabic returns in fifteen other passages. Experts in dogmatics made the inimitability of the Qur'an a literary proof of its divine revelation.

68. Ibn Khaldūn echoes this vulgate when he writes: "The (linguistic) habit of the Mudar became corrupt when they came into contact with non-Arabs. . . . The dialect of the Quraysh was the most correct and purest Arabic dialect, because the Quraysh were on all sides far removed from the lands of the non-Arabs. Next came (the tribes) around the Quraysh, the Thaqīf, the Hudhayl, the Khuzā'ah, the Banū Kinānah, the Ghatafān, the Banū Asad, and the Banūn Tamīm. The Rabī'ah, the Lakhm, the Judhām, the Ghassān, the 'Iyād, the Qudā'a, and the Arabs of the Yemen lived farther away from the Quraysh, and were (variously) neighbors of the Persians, the Byzantines, and the Abyssinians. Because they had contact with non-Arabs, their linguistic habit was not perfect. The Arabic dialects were used by Arab philologists as arguments for (linguistic) soundness or corruption according to the (degree of) remoteness (of the tribes speaking them) from the Quraysh": Ibn Khaldūn *Muqaddima*; trans. Vincent Monteil as *Discours sur l'histoire universelle*, 3 vols. (Beirut, 1967–68), 2nd ed., 3 vols. (Paris: Sindbad, 1978), 3:1266; quoted, slightly edited, from the English translation by Franz Rosenthal, *The Muqaddimah: An Introduction to History*, 3 vols. (New York: Pantheon, 1958), 3:343–44. For a critical bibliography of this theory, see Blachère, *Histoire de la littérature arabe*, 1:78.

69. Jāhiz, *Kitāb al-Amsār wa 'Ajā'ib al-Buldān*, ed. Charles Pellat, *Al-Mashriq* 60, no. 2 (March–April 1966): 169–205, esp. 177–78. Suyūtī falsely attributes this statement to Ibn Fāris (d. 395/1005): Suyūtī, *Al-Muzhir*, 1:128. Carl Brockelmann uses similar arguments to explain the appearance of the common language of Arabic poetry in the pre-Islamic age: "That language was constituted little by little; thanks to the unifying commerce that transhumance created . . .

Another thesis that circulated in the eighth century inscribes the Qur'anic revelation more broadly within the linguistic families of the Hejaz. According to a narration transmitted by the linguist and genealogist Abū 'Ubayda (d. 210?/825?), the Qur'an was revealed in seven tongues, five of which came from the region of Arabia stretching along the Red Sea between the Hejaz and Yemen that is known as Hawazān.[70] This is the land of the Sa'd and the Jashm, two tribal segments of the Bakr, the Nasr, and the Thaqīf. Abū 'Ubayda was of the opinion that the purest and clearest speech was that of the Banū Sa'd, because of a tradition that quotes the Prophet as saying, "I am the most eloquent of the Arabs because I am from Quraysh and I have been raised among the Banū Sa'd." Indeed, it has been attested that the infant Muhammad had a Sa'dite wet nurse. Abū 'Ubayda shares with his master Abū Amr ibn 'Alā the opinion that the most eloquent Arabs were those who lived on the Hawazān plateau, on the shores of the Red Sea between the Syrian Desert and Yemen.[71]

The Arab genealogists attached the dialects of these tribes to one linguistic family, that of the Mudar. It was from them that the Qur'an borrowed its language, which explains the overabundance of excellence with which the linguists credited them. According to Abū 'Ubayda, the Book of God also drew on the speech of Yemen, which perhaps explains the trips that certain linguists took to the land of the queen of Sheba. Our Fārābī, too, went to Yemen. It was when he was settled in the locality of Zabīd that he composed his *Dictionary of the Arabic Language*.[72]

Among the tribes that Fārābī considered to possess great eloquence there were the Tamīm. In their case, his appreciation of their language is inscribed in a continuity that goes back to the origins of the Basra school. The master who founded that school, 'Amru ibn 'Alā', had stayed among the Tamīm to collect their speech. On one occasion he is even depicted, surrounded by his main students in his study circle, explaining to two of

---

and also [thanks to] the pilgrimages to religious centers such as Mecca, it derived its abundant vocabulary from a great number of dialects": *Encyclopédie de l'Islam*, 1:408.

70. Suyūtī, *Bughyat*, 2:294; 113. Although a great connoisseur of genealogies and of the deeds of the Arabs, Abū 'Ubayda is considered less competent regarding languages than his fellow student Asma'ī: ibid., 2:113.

71. Abū 'Ubayda spent a long time among the Hawāzin. On one occasion he tells Abū Hātim al-Sijistānī: "More than one among those who have knowledge among the Hawāzin whose father or grandfather knew the age of the *Jahiliyya* [the pre-Islamic period] have informed me that . . .": Suyūtī, *Al-Muzhir*, 2:316. The confederation of the Hawāzin included the tribes of the 'Amir ibn Sa'sa'a and the Thaqīf, with whom Abū 'Ubayda was bound by a pact of fraternity. The Hawāzim "rear guard" included the Jushām ibn Mu'āwiya ibn Bakr, the Nasr ibn Mu'āwiya ibn Bakr, and the Sa'd ibn Bakr.

72. Yāqūt, *Mu'jam al-Buldān*, 6:62.

his colleagues the linguistic differences between the speech of the tribes of the Hejaz and the Tamīm. The master much admired the latter's eloquence, as they had given the Arabs some of their greatest pre-Islamic and Islamic poets, including the eternal rivals, Jarīr and Farazdaq. The Basra master, who was not fond of modern poetry, made an exception only for Jarīr, precisely because he almost never left his native desert.

At the advent of Islam, the Tamīm, a fairly large confederation of tribes, occupied a vast territory that included the better part of eastern Arabia, almost all of the Nejd, a part of Yamāma, and part of Bahrain. They moved in transhumance toward the northeast, where the Asad—another tribe reputed for its eloquence—were their neighbors, up to the banks of the Euphrates. The Zayd and the 'Amr were the two principal segments of the Tamīm, and they may have provided the grammarians with the two personages of their casuistic exchanges. At the beginning of the tenth century—Fārābī's era—linguists still considered the Tamīm the repository of a great linguistic authenticity, and that reputation stood firm at the end of the century. At that time Jawharī (d. 398?/1007?), the author of an important lexicographical dictionary, lived for a while among the people of the Nedj. It is interesting to see that his method for working is the same as that of his eighth-century predecessors: "I asked a member of the Banū Tamīm of the Nedj who was drawing water from a well," he recounts, "putting my finger on the *nakhīs* [a pulley, here with an enlarged hole with a wedge to stabilize the rope] what sort of instrument it was. In reality, I wanted to check whether it was pronounced *nakhīs* or *nahīs*. He answered me: '*Nakhīs*.' I added, 'Doesn't the poet say [and here he cites the verse] *nahīs*?' He responded, 'I have never heard that from our ancestors.'"[73] What is interesting about this anecdote is that it dramatizes a question to which I will have occasion to return, which is the superiority of direct evidence over bookish knowledge. In writing, the two terms are differentiated only by a diacritic point that even the most careful copyist or scribe might omit.

What can we say about this geography of language? That in its consideration of Arabic eloquence it mingles dogmatic and historical considerations. When the second caliph of Islam, 'Umar (d. 23/644) says, "Only the young of Quraysh and of Thaqīf should read from our copies of the Qur'an," and when the third caliph, 'Uthmān (d. 35/656) adds, "Take dictation from the Qur'an from the Hudhayl and take a scribe from among the

73. Jawharī, *Al-Sihāb*, ed. Ahmad 'Abd al-Ghafūr 'Attār (Cairo: Dār al-Kitāb al-'Arabī, 1956), 2:970.

Thaqīf," the two men are referring both to a dogmatic principle and to a historical one: the speech of those two tribes was closer than all others to the language in which God revealed the Qur'an to Muhammad. But when Fārabī declares that the linguists of his epoch hesitate to approve of the speech of the people of Thaqīf and Tā'if "because of their mixing with the merchants of Yemen who live among them," he is making use of an explanatory principle of a sociohistorical type that makes the mingling of the inhabitants of those two commercial centers with foreign populations the source of the corruption of their speech. As early as the mid-eighth century, it was thought that there was nothing more to be learned from the speech of Medina, "the city of the Prophet." Asmaʿī, a great connoisseur of language, asserted: "I have stayed for some time in Medina: during my entire stay there, I found not a single piece of valid poetry. I encountered only faulty or forged pieces."[74] Be that as it may, Medina in the pre-Islamic *jāhiliyya* never had great poets capable of exalting its talents for eloquence. Nor did Mecca have a great poet before ʿUmar ibn Abī Rabīʿa (d. 93/711)—hence, before the coming of Islam. How could its inhabitants, the Quraysh, be considered the possessors of a pure and correct language? "What proof do we have of the prestige that was attached, in the peninsula, to the Qurayshite dialect *before the coming of Islam?*"[75] None.

A Theory of the Stay in the Desert

The beginning of the tenth century marked the resurgence of a neo-Bedouinism that reestablished a connection with the past of the Basra school by putting a stay in the desert on the agenda for scientific reasons. This notion was backed by the leading philologists—Ibn Durayd (d. 321/933), Azharī (d. 370/980), Ibn al-Jinnī (d. 372/982), and Jawharī (d. 398?/1007?)—who, in imitation of their prestigious elders of the eighth century, flocked to the desert. At the same time that these scholars made sojourns in the desert, they collated dictionaries of the Arabic language counted among the most important that the Muslim world had known since Khalīl ibn Ahmad (d. 175/791). It was the latter to whom they all referred, to the point that their own methodology seems simply an a posteriori systematization of the experience of the "great transmitters" of the eighth century. In the brief note of introduction to his *Dictionary*, Jawharī restates this methodological position, reminding his reader that his three-point approach was

74. Yāqūt, *Irshād (Muʿjam al-Udabā)*, 6:110.
75. Blachère, *Histoire de la littérature arabe*, 1:76.

founded on "the acquisition [of language] by oral transmission [*riwāya*], its improvement by personal reflection [*dirāya*], and its use in oral exchange [*mushāfaha*] among true Arabs in their habitat in the desert."[76]

Still, for a definition of the tasks and methods of lexicography, we have to wait for Azharī and the most programmatic account ever written. To recall his itinerary briefly: Born in Herat, in what is now Afghanistan, he received a solid formation in his native city, studying with his maternal uncle in particular. He then determined to travel to Iraq. Wishing to satisfy the religious obligation of the pilgrimage first, he went in 924 to Mecca and Medina. On the way back from there, however, he was taken prisoner in Iraq in the "desert of Basra," where Bedouin tribes allied to the Qarmatians were sowing terror. In the introduction to his dictionary he describes this painful experience in full detail, not so much to arouse pity for his fate as to recall how, totally unexpectedly, he had occasion to join the school of the desert:

> I was sorely tried by the kidnaping in the year in which the Qarmatians at-
> tacked the pilgrims at Habīr [a locality on the road to Mecca]. The people
> who took me under their yoke were Bedouins, for the most part from
> Hawazān. At Habīr they were joined by several groups of Tamīm and Asad
> [from central Arabia]. These people were used to living in the desert, and by
> seeking out places watered by the rain where they could gather plants and
> frequenting water holes, they lived on the beasts from which they drew their
> nourishment. As true Bedouins of the desert, they spoke a language nearly
> devoid of solecisms or abominable terms. I remained in their hands for a long
> time. In the winter we camped in the Dahnā,[77] and in the springtime in the
> Sammān,[78] without counting our taking water in the two Sitārs.[79] I profited
> much from the conversations and discussions that I had with them, to the

---

76. Jawharī, *Al-Sihāh*, 1:33. On that lexicographer, see Régis Blachère, "Al-Gawharī et sa place dans l'évolution de la lexicographie arabe," in Blachère, *Analecta*, 21–28.

77. It is not known whether Azharī is speaking of the "large tract of country in the Arabian desert, forming part of the territory belonging to the tribe of Tamīm" that bore that name, or the dune region situated in the territory of the Banu Sa'd in the "desert of Basra": Ibn Khallikān, *Wafayāt al-Aʿyān*, 4:336; *Ibn Khallikān's Biographical Dictionary*, 4 vols. (Paris, 1842–71), "Azhari, Abu Mansūr al-," 3:50.

78. This may be either a plateau that Ibn Khallikān situates on the border of the Dahna' (mentioned above) or a sandy place situated nine days march from Basra. It was probably the second of these.

79. Two rivers in the territory of the Banū Sa'd said to be in the desert of Basra.

point of learning a considerable number of terms and narratives. Most of these figure prominently in my dictionary.[80]

Azharī does not relate his extraordinary adventure in the desert with the simple aim of presenting an anecdote. Quite the contrary, he uses it as the thread that attaches his approach to the prestigious transmitters of Basra in the eighth century. In the method that he recommends, investigation in the desert in contact with Bedouins "of the clearest and most correct speech" is placed first among his three practical sources; he states that "all that the great scholars have been able to write in their books cannot replace direct evidence [*mushāhada*] or substitute for an acquired experience and familiarity." The acquisition of linguistic information by oral transmission from masters in the discipline came only second, after which came reading and meditation on the masterworks, "such as the *Kitāb al-ʿAyn* attributed to Khalīl ibn Ahmad, then the books written in our own times."

Among the works of his contemporaries that Azharī disparages, there is a "Complement" (*Takmila*) to the *Kitāb al-ʿAyn* composed by Bushtī (d. 348/959), a philologist from the region of Bukhara. Azharī speaks of him at length. The book seems to him to present all the faults he is campaigning against. Bushtī relies on works that he has read without having received transmission of their contents through known and recognized masters. The author has no "audition" (*samāʿ*) with a qualified master. In order to justify or minimize this lack, he has thought it appropriate to base what he says on famous precedents that, in his eyes, authorize license. He cites Abū Turāb and Qutaybī as two illustrious predecessors who did as much. Azharī concedes that the two men have no "audition" for all of the books that they cite, but he adds immediately that they had masters "worthy of trust" (*thiqa*) from whom they learned their trade. Abū Turāb, for example, frequented "for years" Abū Saʿīd the Blind and "listened to a number of books of his." After that he traveled to Herat, in Afghanistan, where he listened to Shamr ibn Hamdawayh, who, in his youth, had attended the seminar of Ibn al-Aʿrabī (d. 231/845) in Kufa and studied "some of his books" with him, "without counting all that he had learned from the Bedouins of clear and correct speech and retained from their mouths." Azharī comments:

80. Azharī, *Tahdhīb al-Lugha*, 1:7.

If Abū Turāb cites men whom he has not seen or heard, one can tolerate it
and say to oneself that after all he must have memorized what he had read in
books, backed up by a sure "audition." In this case, the statements of those
whom he has not seen come only to reinforce those that he has heard from
others, somewhat like the traditionist scholars who, when a prophetic tradition in a particular chapter seems to them authentic because it has been
transmitted to them by relaters worthy of trust who have received it from
other, equally trustworthy relators, they follow it and use it as a support, then
add to it narratives that they have collected by the authorization of transmission [ijāza].[81]

Here Azharī assimilates the philologists' work of collection to that of
the traditionists. It is indeed true that both were faced with the same
problems when it was a question of collecting and critiquing the materials
that they had gathered (narratives, poems, and so forth). This was something that Asmaʿī (d. 213/828) and the great scholars of his epoch already
knew, particularly since some of them were also traditionists.[82] One narrative of which Asmaʿī is the protagonist illustrates this principle. Rabaʿī
(d. 329/940) states that he received it from his master, Mubarrad (d. 280/
893), who had heard it from a disciple of the Basra scholar. This student
relates that he was with his master when a group of men of letters from
Khurasan arrived at his doorstep. One of them, thinking to flatter the philologist, told him that he was held in high esteem in his far-off homeland.
Proudly puffing out his chest, Asmaʿī responded: "What excuse would I
have if my knowledge [ʿilm] were not worthy! Setting aside the ulemas, the
jurists, and the traditionists, and counting only the poets of pure language
whom I have known, there is So-and-So, So-and-So [and so on for a list of
some forty names]. From them have I heard and from them have I memorized. They possessed only what is authentic. How could my ʿilm not be
worthy? Do you know anyone who has gathered together as many sources
of transmission [riwāya]?"

The philologist ʿAskarī, grasping the theoretical implications of this
narration, notes at the beginning of the tenth century: "Asmaʿī makes
much here of the number of his transmissions [riwāya] concerning the science of poetry and language" because he believed that "the ʿilm is valid by

81. Ibid., 1:34.
82. Among these were Nadr ibn Shumayl (d. 203/818), Abū ʿUbayda (d. 210?/825?), and, before
them, Hammād ibn Salma (d. 167/783), to remain within the context of Basra. On these authors,
see Suyūṭī, Bughyat, 2:316–17 (for the first) and 2:294 (for the second); see Anbārī, Nuzhat, 1:96 (for
the third).

the auricular path and by reception from the mouth of men."[83] Asmaʿī is in fact credited with having proclaimed the primary rule of linguistic investigation, given in the form of an injunction: "It is just to transmit linguistic knowledge [*ʿilm*] in the name of the one who delivers it."[84]

The transmitter taken by the collector of linguistic materials as an authority was considered to be something like a witness.[85] By that same token, he must be credible, but in order for it to be credible, he must be *thiqa*, or "worthy of trust." The idea of bona fides was an invention of the jurists that the traditionists took over. It was already familiar to the linguists of the generation of Sībawayh (d. 180?/796?),[86] and it was the basis for the rule laid down by Ibn Fāris (d. 395/1005) that "language is taken by 'audition' [*samāʿ*] of *thiqa* transmitters."[87] Clearly, these are criteria that belong to the traditionist methodology. An example of their application is furnished by Abū al-Faraj of Isfahan (d. 356/967) in his *Book of Songs*, a vast anthology that the Middle Ages considered the "archive of the Arabs."[88] The material presented is surrounded with all the necessary guarantees, and systematically preceded by a "chain of guarantors." With the same stubbornness as an experienced traditionist, Abū al-Faraj offers his reader all of the various paths by which that information has come to him, with the result that one piece of information may have two, three, or four different chains of transmission.

83. Rabaʿī, *Al-Muntaqā min Akhbār al-Asmaʿī*, b–j. It should be noted, in passing, that the linguists, like the traditionists, use the term *ʿilm* in a metonymic manner to designate "their" discipline and not "science" in general. When they have a strategic interest in presenting their knowledge as *ʿilm*, the representatives of the other disciplines do the same.

84. Yāqūt, *Irshād (Muʿjam al-Udabāʾ)*, 1:81. Thanks to the irony of fate, the important anthology of Bedouin poetry composed by Asmaʿī, although he was considered one of the greatest transmitters of his time, met with only relative success, due to the small quantity of "rare words" that it contained and to the contractions he introduced into the chains of transmission of the poetic pieces given in it: Qiftī, *Inbāh*, 2:203.

85. There is a nuance here that should be kept in mind: juridical theory distinguishes between the legal witness (*shāhid*) and the informer (*mukhbir*). A blind man, for example, can be a dependable informer even though he cannot be a witness. On the one hand, his "testimony" enters into the elaboration of the law; on the other, it is excluded. This insoluble contradiction is a constituent part of Islamic juridical logic.

86. Suyūṭī, *Al-Muzhir*, 1:90; Dhahabī, *Siyar*, 9:496.

87. Abū Husayn Ahmad ibn Fāris, *Al-Sāhibī fī Fiqh Lughah al-ʿArab fī kalāmihā* (Beirut: Maktabat al-Maʿārif, 1993); repeated in Suyūṭī, *Al-Muzhir*, 1:87. The rule was in fact adopted by all the secular disciplines. For an example of its application in the domains of philosophy and medicine, see Ibn Abī Usaybiʿa, *ʿUyūn al-Anbāʾ fī Tabaqāt al-Atibbā* (Cairo, 1886; reprint, Beirut, 1965), 1:84–85.

88. Ibn Khaldūn writes: "There exists no book comparable to it, as far as we know": Ibn Khaldūn, *Muqaddima*, 3:1264; Rosenthal translation, 3:341.

Just as this method led its initiators to disappointments, it entangled the linguists in inextricable problems from which their discipline never recovered. "The erudite man of the ninth century," Régis Blachère rightly observes, "is backed into a desperate solution: a certain poem or narrative is receivable because a certain authoritative scholar or group of scholars held it to be authentic. Other [works], to the contrary, are dubious or unreceivable because those same authorities thought them suspect. A critique of the 'transmitters' is thus imperative for the erudite scholars, just as it was for the traditionists who serve them as a model."[89]

In order to justify his direct access to lexicographical reference works, and in the absence of a master, the author disputed by Azharī invokes the authority of the great masters of the early ninth century. Azharī seems to contest the legitimacy of this manner of access to knowledge, although elsewhere he seems to concede it to the prestigious elders mentioned by the man under accusation. That type of access to knowledge is called *wijāda*, a technical term, formed on the root *w.j.d.*, that can be rendered by "discovery" or by "invention," in the juridical sense of the word, as William Marçais suggests.[90] It speaks to the fact of acceding to a work without having had "audition" of it from a recognized master. Does Azharī contest the *wijāda*? What he says is contradictory: in one instance he rejects it, in another he recognizes it. It has in its favor the precedent of reputed linguistic scholars, however. In his book on Arab "Glorious Days," Abū 'Ubayda (d. 210?/825?), for example, says: "I have found in a writing in the possession of one of the sons of (my master) . . ." In reality, Azharī only objects to his adversary's *wijāda* because the man had not traveled to encounter "true" Bedouins and great masters. Hence, he places direct "audition" at the summit of the hierarchy of modes for the transmission of knowledge. All the great linguists concurred. In the classification established by one of them, "discovery" is the last of six listed modes for the acquisition of language, with "license" in fourth place.[91]

From Azharī's viewpoint, Abū Turāb—his adversary's most prominent authority—made a "voyage" that permitted him to frequent masters worthy of trust; he is thus irreproachable even when he uses books without having had a direct reading of their authors or qualified transmitters. But

89. Blachère, *Histoire de la littérature arabe*, 1:124.

90. Nawawī, *Le Taqrīb de en-Nawawi*, trans. William Marçais (Paris: Imprimerie Nationale, 1902).

91. Suyūtī, *Al-Muzhir*, 1:87–103. The others are "2nd: the reading of the disciple before the master; 3rd: hearing the reading of a third party before the master; and 5th: correspondence."

if one has had no direct "audition" of known and recognized masters, how can all knowledge be founded on what is nothing but a liberty taken? Azharī reproaches his adversary for doing just that.

Curiously, he addresses no criticism to "license" (*ijāza*). Admitting this mode of transmission is not something to be taken for granted. Many scholars rejected it because of the threat it represented to the voyage as a principle of knowledge. It was against their elders that reputed linguists such as Ibn Durayd (d. 321/933), Ibn al-Anbārī (d. 327/939), and Azharī (d. 370/980)—in imitation of great names in the religious sciences of the ninth century—defended its legitimacy. It is interesting to note that one of the defenders of this method validates it by an appeal to a prophetic precedent: "The Prophet wrote letters to kings transmitted orally by his emissaries. That oral transmission took its (proper) rank instead of and in place of his word and his discourse. Similarly he consigned in writing in a scripta [*saḥīfa*] regulations concerning taxes and the price of blood. Subsequently, people transmitted the content of this by taking authority from him. This could only be done by way of the 'delivery' [*munāwala*] of that writ or by 'license' [*ijāza*]. All of this supports the validity of the *ijāza*."[92]

Once again, we are invited to note the degree to which the secular sciences—in particular, those that had language as their object—continued to rely, in their debates, on the knowledge elaborated by the traditionists and their allies in the late eighth century. But if the doctrine of audition was bent by those who associated with it new modes for acquiring knowledge, no one contested the excellence of contact with a master, and hence travel.

Azharī reasserts his methodological positions when he turns to Qutaybī, whom his adversary had used as a refuge and justification. As a proof of the fame and reputation of this master, Azharī repeats his prestigious intellectual genealogy, one that attaches him to the Basra school through some of its most renowned members. How, Azharī exclaims indignantly, can anyone legitimately compare himself to such a man if he "knows only his village"? Who can say if the copies of the works at hand are not faulty? Or the meaning given to their content is not faulty as well? Like a pitiless prosecuting attorney, Azharī picks out disqualifying examples from his adversary's book to show his incompetence.

92. Ibid., 1:98. The author cited is Anbārī.

Among other things, he seizes on the term *'unna*, which the author of the first dictionary of Arabic philology, the *Kitāb al-'Ayn*, renders—citing a verse taken from A'shā (d. 82/701)—as *hadīra*, "a living hedge made of branches," but which the *Complement* explains as "cords hung up on which meat is put to dry." This allows him to administer the proof of his adversary's ineptitude:

> What Khalīl ibn Ahmad says is correct, if indeed it should be he who said it [thus implying that there is doubt of his authorship of the *Kitāb al-'Ayn*, attributed to him].[93] I have seen *hadīra* made of *arfaj*, a sort of spiny tree that grows on the plains, and of *rimth*, a type of tree of the tamaris family, placed as shoulder-high walls. Camels are enclosed within these to protect them from the cold from the north. I have seen the Bedouins call them *'unna* and place them as windbreaks. When they are dry, the Bedouins slaughter some camels, cut them up, and stretch out their quarters of meat on them to dry. I really do not see where the author of the *Complement* got the meaning that he gives to it. Perhaps he saw the needy on the pilgrimage to Mecca hang the meat of sacrificed animals to dry on cords and it came to his mind to explain A'shā's verse in this manner. *If he had seen the Bedouins in their desert*, he would have known that the *'unna* is a windbreak [*hadīra*] made of branches.

Not only has the incriminated linguist no "audition" by a recognized master; he has not traveled in the desert to see with his own eyes the object he refers to. Because he had seen something else that bore the same name, he was led into error. The man seems to Azharī a dubious lexicographer on the levels of both hearing and *autopsia*. How can one be a linguist when one has not *heard* from authorized mouths the knowledge one is presenting, and when one has not *seen* what one is talking about? In both cases, the accused has failed to make the voyage a principle of knowledge. He has been satisfied with a "nonauthorized" reading of books.

Leaving aside the major question of *autopsia* with the promise to return to it later, let us follow Azharī's indictment. In light of all the faults that Azharī attributes to him, the accused appears to be the very personification of the weaknesses of the method that Azharī denounces, in his introduction, as detrimental to the linguist's true work, which is, above

---

93. On Khalīl ibn Ahmad, a great Iraqi philologist of the eighth century, see Mahdī Makhzūmī, *Al-Khalīl Ibn Ahmad al-Farahdi: A'māluhu wa Manhajahu* (Baghdad: Wizarat al-Ma'aarif, 1960).

all, investigation. The man has not traveled, has not met illustrious masters, and has not lived in the desert. How could he legitimately claim to write a treatise on language? When the linguist arrived in Baghdad from Nishapur, he was in fact asked whether he had sojourned in the desert. He thought he could satisfy his interlocutors by saying that he had lived among the Bedouin Arabs who lived between Busht—his homeland—and Tūs.[94] This was exactly the reproach that had been leveled at Layth ibn Nasr. When his master Khalīl ibn Ahmad dictated the *Kitāb al-ʿAyn* to him, he asked him to complete it by continuing the inquiry that he himself had undertaken among the Bedouins. This he did. But instead of going to inquire in the "desert of the Arabs," he went among the sedentary Bedouins of his own native land, Khurasan, whose speech was not as pure as that of their compatriots who lived in the original desert, because "they had mixed with non-Arabs."[95] Thus, his detractors claimed, he made many mistakes.

Azharī was the last of the great linguists of the tenth century to have studied in the school of the desert. When he and Jawharī theorized about a sojourn among the Bedouins as a basic act in linguistic inquiry, they were in fact systemizing a phenomenon that was no longer a novelty. To be sure, the linguists of the tenth century gave it a new impetus, but after them it functioned in the memory of the discipline only as an act firmly attached to a prestigious past. The sojourn in the desert lost consistency, fallen victim to presuppositions underlying much of the linguist's work. As time went by, the desert no longer seemed the conservatory of the Arabic language, nor were the Bedouins seen as its depository. As with the anthropology of Bronislaw Malinkowski and his dream of exotic societies living in autarchy far from a devastating contact with "civilization," the sojourn in the desert metamorphosed into a lazy and nostalgic gesture that was no longer possible because of the Bedouins themselves. Corrupted by mixing with peasants, city dwellers, and non-Arabs, the inhabitants of the desert eventually brought on the irremediable loss of their linguistic paradise. In that case, what was the point of traveling to collect a language that had lost its authenticity?[96]

---

94. Yāqūt, *Irshād (Muʿjam al-Udabāʾ)*, 2:65.

95. Qiftī, *Inbāh*, 3:42.

96. This is precisely what Ibn Khaldūn was objecting to in the fourteenth century when he wrote: "No attention should be paid to the nonsensical talk of certain professional grammarians who are not capable of understanding the situation correctly and who think that eloquence no longer exists and that the Arabic language is corrupt. They draw this conclusion from the

In the centuries that followed, there was always a philologist or a lexicographer who would go stay in the desert, as in the good old days. These
trips seem to have lasted until the twelfth century. The grammarian Abū
al-Karam of Baghdad (d. 500/1106)—who spoke Arabic—and the philologist and Qurʾan exegete Zamakhsharī (d. 538/1143)—a Persian-speaking
native of Iran—are perhaps the two last representatives of this linguistic
current. The first of these men traveled to the Hejaz and to Yemen and
"inquired among the Bedouins *whose language he supposed to be* pure and
clear," his biographer notes with evident scepticism. The second chose
to leave his native Khwārizm to go live in the Hejaz, where he stayed long
enough to have "the wind of the desert and the perfume of the watering
places of the authentic Bedouin Arabs blow on his language."[97]

In the twelfth century, was there any need to go into the desert to fab-
ricate the "clear and pure" (*fusʾḥā*) Arabic language? Certainly not. Locked
up in books, the *fusʾḥā* had for some time been functioning as a closed system. There was no longer any need to travel to forge it, and even less need
to acquire it. The treatises that contained it circulated from one end of
Islam to the other. It no longer had its former power of attraction, though.
Once the language of empire, it was now no more than a provincial language that had to come to terms with other languages, Persian and Turkish
in particular. Nor was its cultural prestige the same: after the tenth century,
great monuments of literature had been written in Persian.[98] Politically
defeated and culturally diminished, Arabic nonetheless continues to con-
serve its status of a dogmatic idiom or, to put it differently, its status as
the language of Islam. With what qualifications? Both as the language of
Revelation and as the nearly exclusive linguistic framework of elaboration
for the basic books of all the elements that make up Islam. The various
religious tendencies, medieval and modern, have continued to live, doc-
trinally, on that inheritance.

At the origin of this hermeneutic situation there lies the connection
between ethnolinguistic inquiries that take the desert as their field of investigation and the vast and dual movement of the collection of traditions

---

corruption of the vowel endings [*iʾrāb*], the rules for which are their [particular] subject of study.
But such a statement is inspired by both partisan attitude and lack of ability": Ibn Khaldūn,
Muqaddima, 3:1268; Rosenthal translation, 3:345.

97. Qiftī, *Inbāh*, 3:257, 266. For a study devoted to Zamakhsharī's linguistic theories, see Fādil
Sālih Samarrāʾī, *Al-Dirāsāt al-Nahwiyya waʾl-Lughawiyya ʿinda al-Zamakhsharī* (Baghdad: Dār
al-Nadhir, 1970).

98. For a recent work on this question, see Richard G. Hovannisian and Georges Sabagh, *The
Persian Presence in the Islamic World* (Cambridge: Cambridge University Press, 1998).

(*ḥadīth*), on the one hand, and the gathering of materials related to the biography of the Prophet and to Islam (*sīra*), on the other. Like panels of a triptych, these three dogmatic endeavors were created with the unified aim of consolidating the canonical community of Muslims, thanks to "delivering the meaning of the scriptures and their application."[99]

99. Mohammed Arkoun, *La pensée arabe* (Paris: Presses Universitaires de France, 1975), 29. Nothing indicates this dogmatic nature of the *fusḥā* language better than the rule developed by Kisā'ī (d. 207/822), which states that "the *Sunna*—Islamic Tradition—is the judge of the language, but the contrary is not true": Ajūrī, *Ḥikāyāt 'an al-Shāfi'ī*, MS no. 3823, Asadiyya Library, Damascus, fol. 49a. It would be a mistake, in such conditions, to think that the *Lisān al-'Arab* (the great dictionary of the Arabic language worked out in the late thirteenth century) is a simple lexicographical tool. Its author, Ibn Manẓūr (d. 711/1312) says himself that what he was aiming at in its composition was "the conservation of the foundations of [the] prophetic language": *Lisān al-'Arab*, 1:8–9. By giving primacy to the Qur'an and to prophetic Tradition in the conception of his entries, he intended to establish an explicit connection with the "Sources of the Law" as they had been defined by Shāfi'ī at the end of the eighth century.

3

THE PRICE OF TRAVEL

When a medieval man of letters reproaches a colleague for not having had great masters, not having traveled, and not referring to books duly validated by "auditions," it is clear that he is blaming him for setting himself up as an authority. That accusation had disastrous effects on the professional credibility of the person so accused. It was a rule that whoever depended only on himself in reality was dependent on his own ignorance. Defying that rule was seen as an attack on the intellectual institution of filiation and its chief guarantee, the master. Thus, every time that someone infringed on that rule, he threatened the symbolic order of transmission. Warnings and conjurations periodically reminded scholars not to split off independently. This faith in the system was often reiterated in prefatory remarks in their works. Open the *Dictiones* of Qālī (d. 356/966), and we see the author starting off his text with praise of "science" (*'ilm*) and assurances that he will conform to the rules of its acquisition.[1] This philologist judges it necessary to remind his reader that he has known great masters and that, in order to approach them, he willingly

---

1. "When I saw that science was the most precious of merchandises, I understood that searching for it was the best form of commerce. Therefore I expatriated myself in order to assimilate it by transmission [*riwāya*] and deepen it by reasoning [*dirāya*] by assiduously frequenting a number of masters. After which I devoted myself to its collection and busied my mind with its memorization [*ḥifz*]. Having left my land with a firm and decided step, I plowed through vast uninhabited spaces, crossed agitated seas, climbed high peaks at the risk of my life and what I hold most dear": Abū 'Alī Qālī, *Amālī*, 3 vols. (Cairo: Dār al-Kutub al-Misrīyah, 1324 AH/1926), 1:3–4.

took on the trying experience of exile and, even more, of traveling at the peril of his life. One might think that the purpose of this sort of discourse was uniquely to flatter the author's ego, but that would be to forget that it was, first and foremost, a way to claim the basic right to speak with authority. In these terms, the voyage becomes coin, a means of exchange that serves to pay back a debt.[2] Because the social and economic history of the voyage is apparently intimately connected with its intellectual status, that history should be able to be told in terms of price.

Financing a Voyage

Travel was expensive. It involved paying for food, clothing, a room, transport by sea and a mount on land, paper, and books, without counting the incidental expenses that inevitably crop up.

The "searchers" (*tālib*) who took off on the roads to knowledge often did so as they were emerging from adolescence. At that age men were still dependent on their families, which, according to the expression that was used, "dowered" them.[3] Muhammad ibn Kathīr (d. 310/922), for example, was endowed by his parents in this manner. At each of the major stops of his itinerary he received sums of money sent from his native Tabaristan. One day, when the money was late in arriving, he was obliged to sell his clothing to pay for food.[4] His compatriot, the famous historian and exegete Tabarī (d. 310/922), who began traveling at a very young age, also received payments from his parents in each of the cities he reached. Given that he traveled the Muslim world from east to west, including Egypt,[5] he saw a good deal of the world. Because he was dependent on his family, he too had the experience of having to wait for his money to arrive. "One day," he recalls, "the subsidy that my father granted me was late in getting to me, [and] my need obliged me to remove the sleeves of my tunic and sell them."[6]

2. This figure of speech can be found in medieval literate discourse: Muslim scholars often compare "knowledge" with merchandise (*bidāʿa*), its acquisition to a commercial exchange (*tijāra*), and its domain to a market (*sūq*).

3. The word *jihāz* is also used for a bride's trousseau, a sign of its strong connotation of dependence.

4. Subkī, *Tabaqāt al-Sāhfiʿiyyah*, ed. Mahmūd Muhammad al-Tanāhī Al-Tānjī and Abd al-Fattāh Muhammad Al-Hilw, 4 vols. (Cairo: ʿĪsā al-Bābī al-Halabī, 1964), 1:653.

5. On the travels of this important doctor of Islam, see Claude Gilliot, "La formation intellectuelle de Tabarī," *Journal asiatique*, vol. 276, nos. 3–4 (1988): 203–44.

6. Khatīb al-Baghdādī, *Tārīkh Baghdād*, 14 vols. (Cairo, 1931), 2:164; also in Yāqūt, *Irshād al-Arīb ilā Maʿrifat al-Adīb (Muʿjam al-Udabāʾ)*, ed. David Samuel Margoliouth (1913–29); ed. Ihsān ʿAbbās, 7 vols. (Beirut: Dār al-Gharb al-Islāmī, 1993), 6:46; and Dhahabī, *Siyar Aʿlām al-Nubalāʾ*,

Those sleeves have an entire history that belongs as much to the realm of clothing styles as to that of literate culture.[7]

It might also happen that the would-be scholar would inherit a large fortune that permitted him to realize his dreams. The linguist Abū Isḥāq al-Ḥarbī (d. 285/898) was one of those happy few. He spent the money that he inherited on study. Born in Merv, in Khurasan, he settled in Iraq. One day he was reported to have received two entire camel loads of "Khurasanian paper,"[8] sent to him from his native land. A lover of books, he used enormous quantities of paper and ink. It was said that his house contained twelve thousand "notebooks" (*juz'*) filled with notes on philology and traditions. When someone asked him how he had brought together "so many books," he responded angrily, "With my flesh and my blood! With my flesh and my blood!"[9] This means that even when someone was lucky enough to be sheltered from pecuniary worries, travel remained a painful trial that was paid for with "flesh and blood."

If the father of a young scholar was himself a man of letters or a merchant, he might have his son accompany him on his peregrinations. Abū Bakr al-Sijistānī (d. 316/928) traveled under the tutelary shadow of his father, the great traditionist from Sijistan, Abū Dāwud (d. 275/888), to Khurasan, Persia, the Hejaz, Iraq, Syria, and Egypt.[10] Similarly, Abū al-'Abbās of Nishapur (d. 340/951) traveled with his father, a bookseller and paper seller, in 878, when he was fourteen years old. Together they went

---

ed. Shu'ayb al-Arna'ūṭī et al., 25 vols. (Beirut: Mu'assasat al-Risālah, 1982–83), 14:276. There are many examples of young men of letters whose families helped them to pursue their studies. One known case is that of the Andalusian Abū 'Abd Allāh ibn Qallās (d. 337/948), who was "equipped" by his father in 898: Khushānī, *Akhbār al-Fuqahā'*; in Spanish translation as *Ajbar al-fuqaha wa-al-muhadditin: Historia de los alfaquies y tradicionistas de Al-Andalus*, ed. Maria Luisa Avila and Luis Molinas (Madrid: Consejo Superior de Investigaciones Científicas, 1992), 177. Another is that of the famous traditionist Abū Ya'lā Mawṣilī (d. 307/919), who traveled extensively and at a young age thanks to the "great care" that first his father and then his maternal uncle lavished on him: Dhahabī, *Siyar*, 14:174.

7. It is known that, beginning in the ninth century, one sleeve—in general the right one—was larger than the other and served to hold the books that the man of letters carried with him.

8. On this type of paper, see Ibn al-Nadīm, *Fihrist*, ed. Riḍā al-Māzindarānī (Beirut: Dār al-Masīrah, 1988), 35; trans. Bayard Dodge as *The Fihrist of al-Nadīm: A Tenth-Century Survey of Muslim Culture*, 2 vols. (New York: Columbia University Press, 1970). See also Johannes Pedersen, *The Arabic Book*, trans. Geoffrey French, ed. Robert Hillenbrand (Princeton: Princeton University Press, 1984), 62–63; and Ḥabīb al-Zayyāt, "Suhuf al-Kibāba wa Sinā'at al-Waraq fī al-Islām," *Al-Mashriq*, October–December 1954, 225–29.

9. Qiftī, *Inbāh al-Ruwwāt*, ed. Muhammad Abū al-Faḍl Ibrāhīm, 3 vols. (Cairo: al-Hayah al-Miṣrīya al-'Ammah lil Kutub, 1981), 1:158.

10. Dhahabī, *Siyar*, 13:224.

to Isfahan, Kufa, Baghdad, Raqqa, Mecca, Ashqelon, Damascus, Tarsus, and Fustāt.[11]

A "searcher" could also finance his voyage of study through commerce. At that time, the routes that led to knowledge were also those that led to fortune. Scholars and merchants, attracted by the bigger cities, traveled in the same caravans and stopped at the same caravansaries. Like many traditionists who sought contact with the great doctors of Yemen,[12] Sufyān al-Thawrī (d. 161/777), later the founder of a school of law, often went to that part of the Arabian Peninsula. After acquiring a business in the region (perhaps at Aden) managed by "Yemenite brothers," he returned there on a yearly basis.[13] His pupil ʿAbd Allāh ibn al-Mubārak (d. 181/797) was perhaps the greatest scholar-traveler of his age. Born into a wealthy family in Merv, he more than once traveled in Yemen, Egypt, Syria, the Hejaz, and Iraq. He is reported to have spent on his travels large sums earned from a large business venture run by a manager.[14] His biographers report that when his father gave him fifty thousand gold dinars to set up a commercial company, he spent them to finance his search for knowledge.[15]

There were in fact a number of men of letters from Khurasan who combined learning and business in their itineraries. Khārija ibn Musʿab, a student of Abū Hanīfa (d. 150/767), is estimated to have spent some one hundred thousand silver dirhems on his studies.[16] His compatriot Hishām ibn ʿUbayd Allāh of Rayy (d. 221/835) is supposed to have spent some seven hundred thousand silver dirhems in the course of voyages that took him to Khurasan, Iraq, the Hejaz, and Yemen. In his travels he searched out more that one thousand seven hundred masters, a record rarely equaled.[17] In like fashion, Abū ʿAbd Allāh Dhuhalī (d. 258/871), called "the memorizer of Khurasan," earned his title by making three trips that took him to Iraq, Syria, Egypt, the Hejaz, and Yemen, during which he is reported to have

11. Dhahabī, *Kitāb Tadhkirat al-huffādh*, 3rd ed., 2 vols. (Hyderabad: Dairatu L-Maàrif-il-Osmana, 1955), 3:860. At an earlier date ʿAbd al-Rahmān, the son of the famous Abū Hātim al-Rāzī (d. 277/890), had traveled with his father in 868–69, when he was fifteen: Dhahabī, *Siyar*, 13:262.

12. Would-be scholars went to Yemen to hear famous traditionists such as Abū ʿAbd al-Rahmān Tāwus (d. 106/725) and his son ʿAbd-Allāh, Muʿīn ibn Zāʾida, or Maʿmar ibn Rāshid (d. 153/770), an Iraqi from Basra who had moved to Yemen.

13. Ibn Saʿd, *Tabaqāt*, ed. Karl Vilhelm Zetterstéen (Leiden, 1909), 6:258.

14. Muwaffaq, *Manāqib al-imām al-Aʿzam Abī Hanīfa*, 2 vols. (Hyderabad: Dāʾirat al-Maʿārif al-Nizāmīyah, 1903), 2:179.

15. al-Qādī ʿIyād, *Tartīb al-Madārik*, ed. Ahmad B. Mahmūd, 5 vols. (Beirut: Maktabat all-Hayāh, 1967–68), 1:301.

16. Muwaffaq, *Manāqib Abī Hanīfa*, 2:236.

17. Dhahabī, *Siyar*, 10:447; Kutubī, *ʿUyūn al-Tawārīkh: Wa-fihi min sanat 219H ilā 250 H* (Beirut: Dār al-Thaqafah, 1996), 8, no. 65.

spent one hundred and fifty thousand silver dirhems.[18] Although he was born in Baghdad, Muhammad ibn Nasr of Merv (d. 294/906) grew up in Khurasan and could boast of having made two voyages. During the second of these, in 873, he settled in Nishapur. He prospered there, developing a business that an associate managed for him while he, we are told, busied himself "with science and with devotion." In 888 he settled definitively in Samarkand, while his associate in Nishapur continued to make his business there thrive.[19]

Spending enormous amounts of money on their intellectual formation was not unique to men of letters from the Silk Road, however. Egyptians, Iraqis, and Andalusians did as much. One Egyptian reported to be wealthy, Ibn Qāsim (d. 191/806), who had trained in the juridical school of Medina and was one of its principal theorists, made a dozen trips to the Hejaz, spending some one hundred and twenty thousand gold dinars, his biographers tell us.[20] The Iraqi 'Alī ibn 'Āsim of Wāsit (d. 201/816) received nearly one hundred thousand gold dinars from his family to support his studies. A narrative shows him leaving Wāsit to go to Kufa with four thousand gold dinars in his pocket.[21] Yahyā ibn 'Umar (d. 283/896), an Andalusian, spent a more modest six thousand gold dinars to go first to Kairouan, then to Fustāt, in search of instruction.[22]

How dependable are these figures cited in the biographical dictionaries, one after the other, as records worthy of note? They may have only a rhetorical value. Still, it is a temptation to interpret them, in their excess, as sacrificial expenses consented to in order to give honor to the 'ilm, the scientia islamica. The biggest spenders were often the traditionists. Their expenses are in conformity with the respect accorded to their professional activity, which was understood as both intellectual work and a beneficent gesture of thanksgiving. Some risked their lives for it, willingly sacrificing themselves as combatants in the jihad at the frontiers of Islam. Why should not the wealthier among them risk their fortunes? It is worth recalling that the 'ilm they sought was a soteriological knowledge.

Nonetheless, secular considerations were not absent from these frenetic expenditures. We see wealthy men of letters indulging in ruinous

18. Khatīb al-Baghdādī, Tarīkh Baghdād, 3:417; Dhahabī, Kitāb Tadhkirat al-huffādh, 1:531; Sāhilī, Tabaqāt 'Ulamā' al-Hadī, ed. Ibrahīm al-Zaybaq, 2 vols. (Beirut: Mu'assasat al-Risāla, 1989), 2:211.
19. Dhahabī, Siyar, 13:436; Sāhilī, Tabaqāt, 2:362; Subkī, Tabaqāt, 2:247.
20. Dhahabī, Siyar, 11:121.
21. Khatīb al-Baghdādī, Tarīkh Baghdād, 11:447, 453.
22. Dhahabī, Siyar, 13:463.

spending in order to forge a reputation for themselves, for in this milieu, not all money spent went for studies. One might even speak of a redistribution of wealth. 'Abd Allāh ibn al-Mubārak (d. 181/797), a rich eternal itinerant, offers an example of an openhanded generosity of the sort.[23] The *Rihla* of Pseudo-Shāfi'ī, a tenth-century work, is shot through with this ideology of redistribution.[24]

Not all men of letters who traveled belonged to the wealthier classes of society. Far from it. Families did not always have the means to finance the studies of their sons, and the most highly motivated among the young did not wait to gather together the material resources that would permit them to go off on costly learning expeditions. Either out of a taste for adventure or out of a determination to get ahead in the world socially, they traveled on foot. In this milieu many in fact did so. The biographical dictionaries record some of these champions of endurance. Abū Hātim al-Rāzī (d. 277/890), who began traveling at the age of fifteen, was one of these. The account of his tribulations is exceptional enough in the ninth century to justify quoting it at some length:

> The first time that I traveled, I did so for seven years. I walked over a thousand parasangs,[25] after which I stopped counting. On leaving Bahrain I walked all the way to Egypt, from where I left on foot [for Syria]: [I went] from Ramla to Damascus, from Damascus to Antioch, from Antioch to Tartūs, and from there I returned to Homs to go to Raqqa and take the boat for Iraq. I did all of that when I was not yet twenty years old. . . . In 829 I remained in Basra for eight months; in order to eat I had to sell my clothes, one piece after another up to the last. With a companion I continued, in spite of everything, to do the tour of the masters. One day, when my companion had left me, I found nothing to satisfy my hunger but water. The next day, when he returned to fetch me, I followed him to the course, even hungrier. By the end of the day I was so devoured by hunger that I couldn't take it any more. Thus, the following morning, when he came to find me as usual, I could not prevent myself from admitting to him, "I have no more strength to accompany you." He asked me why, and I answered, "I cannot hide it from you any more: I haven't eaten anything for two days. He said to me, "I have two dinars left on me: one of them

---

23. One man of letters who met him while he was traveling was impressed by the provisions transported by his personal caravan, which included a large quantity of cloth, including fine stuffs from Khurasan, and two packages of roast chicken, all of it destined for the traditionists who accompanied him or whom he visited: see ibid., 8:410.

24. Shāfi'ī, *Rihla*, MS no. 9787 (microfilm no. 6137), Zāhriyya, Damascus.

25. The parasang (or *farsakh*) was roughly 5.7 kilometers.

is for you." I took the dinar from him and we left Basra. . . . One day when we had left Medina, we went to Jār to take the boat.[26] But the wind, which blew in the wrong direction, was not propitious for navigation. We waited there for three months. Our patience exhausted, we decided to pursue our route by land. We walked for several days, until we had exhausted our provisions of food and water. We walked for an entire day without eating or drinking, then a second day, and a third. By the evening of the third day we were so exhausted that we collapsed on the ground. The next day we continued on our route with difficulty. There were three of us: myself, a sheikh from Khurasan, and Abū Zuhayr from Merv. The sheikh was the first to fall exhausted from having walked too long. As we picked him up, we realized that he had lost consciousness. We left him where he fell and continued on our way. A parasang farther on, I collapsed in turn. My companion told me later that he continued to walk on alone until when he saw a ship anchoring in the distance. With the help of a piece of clothing, he signaled to its occupants, who came to his aid and gave him something to drink. [Once rescued,] he said to them, "Come give aid to my two companions." [As for me], I remember that a man moistened my face with water, then gave me something to drink. [The sailors] then rescued the sheikh. They treated us so well that we stayed with them for several days, until we had regained our strength.[27]

They were in fact to need that strength as they pursued their way to Fustāt, in Egypt.

Aside from the obstacles that all men of letters faced when they traveled, this narrative speaks poignantly to the privations and hardships of all sorts that awaited those who journeyed in search of learning without means and in precarious conditions. One traveler from Cordoba, Baqī ibn Mukhlad (d. 276/889), who "roamed the East and the West" in search of prophetic traditions, was one of these. As he was fond of repeating, "All the masters to whom I have traveled, I went to on foot." Having experienced the greatest privations in the course of his wanderings, he was proud to remind anyone willing to listen to him that he knew of no other man who had lived on nothing but cabbage leaves during his quest for knowledge.[28] Hunger was the daily lot of most traveling men of letters. Bukhārī (d. 256/869), a famous collator of prophetic traditions whose reputation has survived over the centuries, could have said the same. One of his traveling

---

26. Jār is on the Red Sea near Djeddah, a day and a night by foot from Mecca.

27. Ibn Abī Hātim, *Kitāb al-Jarh wa al-taʿdīl*, 9 vols. (Beirut: Dār al-Kitub al-ʿIlmiyah, 1952), 1:363–65.

28. Dhahabī, *Kitāb Tadhkirat al-huffādh*, 1:630.

companions relates that in Basra, "we were busy writing down traditions when we realized that we had not seen him for several days. When we went to look for him, we found him in his room half-naked [because] he had sold all that he possessed. To get him out of this fix, we took up a collection to offer him a few dirhems and get him some clothes."[29] How many times had this Bukhara traditionist known hunger, given that he began to travel at the age of fifteen?

Hunger assailed men of letters in the solitude of their bare rooms or on the endless road. When Abū Bakr al-Sijistānī (d. 316/928) made "the grand tour [tawāf] to the east and to the west," arriving in Kufa around 883, he is reported not to have had more than one single dirhem in his pockets. But he made judicious use of it by buying thirty mudd [one Iraqi mudd was equivalent to two pounds] of broad beans and eating one mudd's worth per day.[30] His compatriot Muhammad ibn Dāwud of Nishapur (d. 342/953) was less fortunate when he arrived in Iraq. He found Basra gripped by a dreadful famine. For forty days all he could find to eat was an unsubstantial bread locally called raghīf. When stricken with hunger pangs, he recited the surah Yā-Sīn, which Muslims consider "the heart of the Qur'an": "A Sign for them is the earth that is dead: We do give it life, and produce grain therefrom, of which you do eat. And We produce therein orchards with date-palms and vines, and We cause springs to gush forth therein: That they may enjoy the fruits of this (artistry): it was not their hands that made this: will they not then give thanks?" (36:33–35). But Ya-Sin is also the surah recited as a prayer for the dead and at wakes! Our traveler had endured infinite hardships after leaving his native city in 906. His wanderings continued until 948, taking him to Herat, Rayy, and Nasā (in Khurasan); to Jurjān on the Caspian Sea; to Ahwāz, Basra, and Baghdad

29. Subkī, Tabaqāt, 2:217. When, in 795–96, Ahmad ibn Hanbal (d. 241/855) decided to set off on his first study voyage, he was only an adolescent of sixteen. An indefatigable walker, he hiked through Iraq, Syria, the Hejaz, and Yemen. Born in extremely modest circumstances, he lacked the means to travel in decent conditions. One day in Kufa he felt his poverty as an injustice. He was unable to travel with fellow students who had decided to go to Rayyān to meet with an eminent traditionist. "Ah! If only I had had fifty dirhems!" he sighed long after. Being forced to walk determined his choice of voyages. One of his compatriots met him in Mecca in such a piteous state that he was worried. The young traditionist was exhausted and at the end of his strength. He had come from Yemen and had walked so long that his feet were cracked. In order to eat he had sold his sandals. As misfortune never arrives alone, the house of the woman he lodged with had been burgled by thieves, who had carried off his few possessions. Fellow students took up a collection in order to offer him clothing: Ibn 'Asākir, Tārīkh madinat Dimashq, ed. 'Alī Shīrī, 40 vols. (Beirut: Dār al-Fikr, 1995–96), 2:31–41.

30. Khatīb al-Baghdādī, Tārīkh Baghdād, 3:65–66; Sāhilī, Tabaqāt, 2:486.

in Iraq; to Damascus and Mosul in Syria, to Fustāt in Egypt; and to Mecca and Medina in the Hejaz. Forty years on the road.[31] He was lucky to have returned alive. Many did not do so, leaving their bodies on the rocky roads that split the steppes and the deserts.

Considering their quest for *'ilm* as an apostolate, at times religious men of letters lost their sense of reality. Dazzled by their desire to collect the greatest number of bits of knowledge, they hardly had set foot in one place when they were already thinking of another that they had not yet visited and that awaited them. Torn between the two, they crowded their daily agenda to excess. One young man of letters from Khurasan who went to Fustāt in 875–76 declared that he and his companions were forced to work day and night: "We were in Egypt for seven months, during which time we did not once eat a hot meal. Our days were given over to the frequentation of study circles; our nights to copying books and comparing our copies among ourselves." This young man reports one anecdote that gives a clear account of the feverish atmosphere that reigned in the small groups of students. After setting off one morning with one of his companions to the house of a master whose teaching they were following, they learned that the master was ill. But as they passed by the fish market on their way back to their lodgings, a fine piece of fish attracted their attention. They decided to buy it. But they hardly had time to return to the room that they shared when it was time to go attend another seminar, so they did not have time to fry the fish. They left it and ran to the mosque where the session was taking place. The fish stayed there, forgotten for several days, and only when it rotted and its smell bothered our students did they remember it. What to do? Throw it away? Out of the question: it had cost too much. They finally decided to cook it and eat it. The young man of letters draws a moral from this tale: "One cannot search for knowledge and pay attention to the well-being of one's body."[32] By the time he told this story, the young man was a veteran traveler: he made three voyages in his lifetime. Like him, a student in Baghdad in the late tenth century who was totally devoted to his studies forgot about the letters that his parents had sent him from Rayy. When he got around to reading them, he learned of the death, some time before, of a member of his family, as well as "other news, one item more disagreeable than the other, and which would have worried his mind." There is a moral in this tale as well, but this time it is his

---

31. Khatīb al-Baghdādī, *Tarīkh Baghdād*, 5:265–66; Dhahabī, *Siyar*, 15:420–21.
32. Dhahabī, *Siyar*, 13:265.

biographer who draws it: "If the searcher had read his mail at the proper time, he may have been turned away from study."[33]

Anecdotes like these serve more general functions. They signify that as they traveled, men of letters were often out of touch with the world around them. One of the characteristics of the voyage—the long voyage in particular—was that the traveler was dead to his kin because he was (at least for the moment) freed from his usual constraints of family and social obligations. One example of this social solitude comes from the late ninth century. It shows a young man of letters wearing himself out copying manuscripts by night. Tired of remaining seated so long in front of his manuscripts, he gets up and leaves his room to stretch his legs. Late at night he takes the time to admire the scintillating spectacle of the starry sky. He says his dawn prayer and goes to the place of business of a merchant he knows. He finds the man in his shop, hunched over his account books. The morning visitor salutes the man and glances at the account book, which immediately give him a feeling of strangeness and disquietude. It is dated Saturday! "Isn't it Friday?" he asks. The merchant smiles and answers, "I see that you were not at the Friday prayer."[34] How could he have been at the Great Mosque when, for two nights and a day, he had not stopped writing? All of that time had passed without his being aware of it. This tale can of course be seen as simply an edifying exemplum, but because it has found a place in a biographical dictionary of men of letters it presents a mode of being characteristic of men of study.

Men of letters often remembered their nighttime studies as a traumatic experience. Writing at night by a flickering oil lamp, when the day had been spent listening to masters speaking in their study circles, was in itself a trial of endurance. If we add that when they traveled, the majority of men of letters did not eat their fill or get enough sleep, we can imagine stress turning into a nightmare. Abū Yūsuf al-Fasawī (d. 277/890) knew what he was talking about when he said:

> At the time of my quest for learning, I arrived in a city where my visit coincided with that of a great master. In order to hear him I prolonged my stay there. I was far from my country [Persia] and my means of subsistence had begun to diminish. So as not to waste my time I applied myself to working ceaselessly, by night copying his books, by day reciting before him what I had written down the night before. One night I was seated, busy copying a

33. Qiftī, *Inbāh*, 2:70.
34. Dhahabī, *Siyar*, 13:190.

manuscript, when my vision became cloudy. No longer able to see either the lamp or the walls of my room, I began to weep over the distance that separated me from my family and over what was going to escape me in the way of knowledge. I wept so much that evening that I was exhausted. Stretching out on my side, I dozed off. It was thus that I saw the Prophet [in a dream], who called out to me and asked me cordially why I was crying. I answered him: "O Prophet of God! I have lost my eyesight, and my heart is gripped by the idea that the study of your Tradition [*Sunna*] is going to escape me. I weep also because of the distance that keeps me far from my land." After having listened to me, he asked me to approach him, and he passed his hand over my eyes. It seemed to me that at that moment he was reciting incomprehensible words. When I awoke [in the middle of the night], I noted happily that I had recovered my sight. I immediately went back to my copies and moved closer to the lamp to continue to write.

Copying the books of masters from whom one wanted to receive an "authorized reading" was done at night after retiring to the solitude of one's room with a candle or an oil lamp. The daytime was given over to attending study circles and to auditions. Consequently, it was looked at with disapproval to switch these tasks and do during the daytime what one should do at night. The world of traveling men of letters was subject to strong controls. Although pressure was moral, the future reputation of each man depended on his compliance. Post mortem disapproval might follow any deviation. This happened to an Andalusian named Ibn Habīb (d. 238/852). Recriminations pursued him back to Andalusia, spread by a man of letters returned from the East who claimed to have heard in Cairo that his compatriot had taken the books of a great local authority and had copied them.[35] When his fellow students asked him how he had acquired these books, he answered that he had gotten them from their author, who had authorized him to transmit them in his name. When those same fellow students went to the master to complain that he had shown favoritism to one of their number, they soon realized that the Andalusian had misled them. The author was in fact astonished to learn that he had been part of a form of transmission of works that he disapproved of. In fact,

---

35. The local authority in question was Asad ibn Mūsā (d. 212/827). On his importance in Egyptian culture of his time, see Raif Georges Khoury, '*Abd-Allāh ibn Lahī'a, 97–174/715–790: Juge et grand maître de l'école égyptienne* (Wiesbaden: Harrassowitz, 1986), 134ff. Khoury has edited a collection of his ascetic exempla: *Kitab az-Zuhd*, ed Raif Georges Khoury, new ed. (Wiesbaden: Harrassowitz, 1976).

the Andalusian had simply borrowed the books, which he had received no authorization to transmit.

This compromising tale is noted in the biographical works of Muslim Spain[36] and the East,[37] as well as in the dictionaries of the Malikite school of jurisprudence.[38] The case of Ibn Habīb was known throughout the Muslim world because it had become the symbol of a danger to the institution of the voyage. Thanks to this tale, we can see that the tension between the *ijāza* (something like a "certificate of transmission" for a given work delivered by its author or by a master who guaranteed the reading of it), the *wijāda* (the aim of which was to study a book in certain conditions in the absence of any guarantor), and the *rihla* (the "voyage" made in order to meet with internationally recognized masters) could turn into open conflict.

Paying a Personal Price

At the same time that they lived through the voyage as a trying experience, the men of letters whom we encounter in the present work sublimated its constraints as inherent signs of a male ideal, the principal components of which were virility, endurance, abstinence, voluntary privation, and a spirit of sacrifice. To return to the traditionist Abū Yūsuf al-Fasawī (d. 277/890), whom we left hunched over his writing desk: That evening he was wearing himself out, late at night, copying manuscripts until he could no longer see. A black veil fell over his eyes. That sort of accident was frequent in the world of medieval higher education. It often happened that men of letters, trapped in the web of a tormented life, lost their sight. It would be difficult not to ruin your eyesight if you spent years copying or correcting by night what you had noted down during the day. How could such men not wear themselves out, with no restorative sleep to give back vitality and energy to frail, malnourished bodies? Trouble with eyesight was something of a professional malady in this milieu. It led both to infirmity and ruined careers. We can understand Fasawī's distress as he faced the terrible drama of an unending night. All medieval men of letters were aware of this threat but played down its dangers. They thought that if they wanted to be among the best, they needed to take health risks. Bukhārī

36. Ibn al-Faradī, *Tārīkh 'Ulamā' al-Andalus*, ed. Ibrāhīm Ibyārī, 2 vols. (Cairo: Dār al-Kutub al-Islāmīyah, 1983), 1:271.

37. Dhahabī, *Siyar*, 12:106.

38. 'Iyād, *Tartīb*, 3:37.

(d. 256/869) very probably thought this to be true.[39] As one of his study companions reported, during his years of study he would wake up "fifteen or twenty" times in one night, "get out a fire brick, make a fire, and light a lamp," then spread out his notebooks to verify traditions that puzzled him.[40] The traditionist himself explains at length the conditions in which he nearly lost his eyesight because of long nocturnal hours spent in copying and verification. We learn that his troubles with his vision began when he was in Khurasan, but it was also there that he met a man who taught him how to care for his eyes.

The men of letters who traveled were not without some medical knowledge. We shall see in chapter 7 how an entire science of travel medicine arose toward the end of the second century of Islam. The treatment suggested to Bukhārī was to shave his head and cover his head with a hibiscus essence.[41] He attests that the remedy was efficacious, given that the symptoms disappeared as soon as he applied it. His compatriot from Merv, Hārūn ibn Ma'rūf (d. 231/845), was less lucky. His biographer tells us that he lost his sight permanently because of his continual "consultation of books." He interpreted the misfortune that befell him in Baghdad, far from his home, as divine punishment. In a dream he was told, "The one who shows more consideration for Tradition than for the Qur'an is soon or later punished," and he explains," I thought my blindness was the consequence of that choice."[42]

The young men whose itineraries we have just outlined often led a paroxysmal life. Without always really seeking it or leaving themselves open to it (as was the case with the mystics), the extreme life was forced on them as an experience of limits from which they emerged either fortified or broken. But at what price? Ahmad ibn Hanbal (d. 241/855), the famous Iraqi traditionist, often said, "We have acquired knowledge in humiliation." He knew what he was talking about. A man of quite modest origins, he

39. Bukhārī, a determined traveler and the best known of the collators of Islamic traditions of all ages, made two voyages in Syria and in Egypt, two in Mesopotamia, and several in Iraq, where he stayed four times in Basra and more than seven times in Baghdad, without counting the six years he spent in the Hejaz. On his return home, he died not far from Samarkand, after a cabal orchestrated against him by the traditionists of Khurasan: Khatīb al-Baghdādī, *Tarīkh Baghdād*, 2:13; Dhahabī, *Siyar*, 12:407.

40. Khatīb al-Baghdādī, *Tarīkh Baghdād*, 2:13.

41. Shāfi'ī had another remedy based on bits of liver, but of what animal is not known. He first tested it on someone whose eyesight had diminished and found that it gave the man sharper vision: Bayhaqī, *Manāqib al-Shāfi'ī*, ed. Ahmad Saqr, 2 vols. (Cairo: Makhabat Dār al-Turāth, 1971), 2:122; Dhahabī, *Siyar*, 10:56.

42. Dhahabī, *Siyar*, 11:130.

suffered to become a recognized man of letters. An indefatigable walker, he made the trip to Syria and "two or three" pilgrimages to Mecca on foot. He was familiar with fatigue, hardship, and exhaustion. At Kufa, to where he had gone to attend the study circle of Sufyān ibn 'Uyayna (d. 198/813), he fainted in the vestibule of the master's crowded house. This was in 799, and to go from Baghdad to Kufa the young Ahmad had traveled on foot.

In Yemen, at the house of 'Abd al-Razzāq (d. 211?/826?), one of the great authorities of the *hadīth* of his age,[43] Ahmad ibn Hanbal met a man of letters from Khurasan, Ibn Rahawayh (d. 238/852), who would also be called to a prestigious career as a traditionist. Their arrival coincided with one of the two legal holidays of Islam. At the collective prayer organized on that occasion, the two young men were so distracted that they forgot to recite a customary *takbīr* to the glory of Allah. The prayer ended, the master wanted to hear their reasons, and they had none, or at least no legal ones. They had simply been preoccupied by thinking about where they were going to start in their local quest for learning. To the point of forgetting to glorify God![44] This was not the first or the last time that Ahmad would fail to fulfill his ritual obligations correctly. On another occasion, while he was directing the prayers of a group of fellow men of letters, even though he was traveling, he was judged guilty of a "negligence." Interrogated about this "omission," he pleaded his feeble state of health: he had not eaten his fill for several days, he explained.[45] Later Ahmad ibn Hanbal, trained to endurance, wrote a book praising asceticism.

Faithful to a agonistic conception of the quest for knowledge, the men of letters whom we have encountered made a daily combat of their life of studies. But the tribute to be paid was so demanding that, as soon as one of their number thought that he had acquitted himself in a worthy manner, another, who had paid that tribute before him, reminded him that his satisfaction was derisory. In the early tenth century, young men come from "distant horizons" to listen to a highly reputed scholar of Nasā in Khurasan learned that lesson when they least expected it. This is how one of these young men, who later had a great career as a jurist, reports the scene:

43. His contemporaries thought that, after the age of the Prophet, no scholar was more sought after than he: Ibn Khallikān, *Wafayāt al-A'yān*, 8 vols. (Cairo, 1948); ed. Insān 'Abbās, 8 vols. (Beirut: Dār Thāqāfa, 1968–72), 3:216; trans. William MacGuckin, baron Slane, as *Ibn Khallikān's Biographical Dictionary*. 4 vols. (Paris, 1842–71).
44. Dhahabī, *Siyar*, 11:193.
45. Ibid., 11:194.

We were in the house of my master when some young people of good family arrived. They had made a long journey with the sole aim of listening to him. Addressing them, the master said: "Listen to what I have to say to you before beginning your study! We have learned that you were the children of affluent people who moved far from their homeland. Do not think for a minute that you can get out of [your obligations] so easily, thinking that you have paid heavy dues in the name of knowledge. I shall tell you what I myself endured during my quest for learning. After leaving my homeland, in my wanderings I met [at Fustāt] in Egypt a group of young men of letters. Together we frequented the circle of an old master who was at the time considered to be the greatest in rank in science. Every day he dictated to us, with parsimony, a few traditions, so that as time passed with him our means of subsistence began to shrink. In order to live, we were obliged to sell our clothes. We suffered from hunger to the point that our empty innards became twisted and folded up against one another. In our weakened condition, we could not move about freely. Circumstances forced us to drop the veil of modesty and reserve. But none of us dared to take the first step. We decided then to draw straws to see who would go stretch out his hand to bring us back something to eat. By designating me, chance threw me into perplexity. To get out of my difficulty, I prostrated myself twice and began to call on God. I had not ended my invocation when a servant coming from the palace entered the mosque.

Saved! Our young man was not to be subjected to the humiliation of begging. Divine intervention decided otherwise. Unfortunately, miracles were rare, and similar situations were many. Not all the men of letters in a desperate material situation had the unheard-of luck to have their prayers answered by heaven. Those who made long voyages because they had the means to do so were to count themselves lucky to endure the difficulties and the fatigue in conditions that were, all in all, more comfortable than those of their less well endowed fellow searchers. Therefore, the master reminded his young and wealthy visitors, do not let yourselves be dizzied by what you think to be an exploit.

Wealthy young men searching for knowledge were a small minority. The bulk of searchers knew discomfort and privations of all sorts on a daily basis. When the old master in Khurasan spoke to his visitors, he was reminding all of his students of the extent to which the voyage is an activity engendered by suffering. Darīmī (d. 255/868), who came from far-off Samarkand to study in the central lands of Islam, was one of the first collators of traditions to note down a *hadīth* to that effect. In it, the founder of Islam makes travel "a part of suffering" precisely because it puts the traveler under the grip of privation and brings him "lack of sleep, water, and food."[46]

In their moments of distress traveling men of letters often recalled the contents of the fear-inspiring prophetic dictum associating travel with suffering, and their descriptions of their own peregrinations seldom depart from its topoi. Almost all of them invoke the same literary clichés in one form or another, with the result that they all seem much the same and inspire a certain ennui. They all recall how "men of letters endure the greatest difficulties traveling in far-off lands, regard fatigue and lassitude with disdain, defy relaxing their focus and weakness, ruin themselves by expenditures, [and] put their lives in peril through landscapes that inspire fear."[47] When Ibn Abī Hātim of Rayy (d. 327/938) writes a substantial biography of his father, a famous traditionist, he speaks of the difficulties that the older man encountered during his voyages in a chapter entitled "Of What My Father Endured during His Quest for Knowledge because of Adversity."[48] Commonplaces dot the description of the exploits of a man who was, incontestably, a peerless walker. Nothing is missing, neither hunger nor thirst, neither the perils of the sea nor the dangers of the road. Later, in the tenth century, these markers of the exploit and of endurance lent some of their literary clichés to fiction.[49]

Elements of the voyage were sublimated and organized into a discourse (of which the soliloquy of the old master in Khurasan quoted above is an example) for both internal and external use. Internally, its function is to celebrate endurance, renunciation, patience, courage, modesty, and other expressions of virility as values that make up an authentic *asceticism*—that is, a discipline of life that a man imposes on himself in order to attain the "summits of knowledge" and to conform to its ethic. Externally, it presents

---

46. Dārimī, *Sunan*, 2 vols. (Beirut: Dār Ihyā' al-Sunna al-Nabawāyah, 1975), 2:286. Lines by the poet and erudite Buhturī (d. 284/897) echo this tradition: "If the vicissitudes of time crush you with their ills / put on the garb of distance and expatriation! / But know that suffering is a part of the Voyage / and say, 'My God, direct my feet toward inhabited lands!'": Tha'ālibī, *Al-Tamthīl wa al-Muhādarah*, ed. 'Abd al-Fattāh Muhammad Hulw (Tunis: al-Dār al-'Arabīyah lil-Kitāb, 1983), 400.

47. Khatīb al-Baghdādī, *Tarīkh Baghdād*, 2:52–53; 4:354.

48. Ibn Abī Hātim, *Kitāb al-Jarh wa al-ta 'dīl*, 1363.

49. In the *Séances* of Hamadhānī, the hero interrogates a young man "in a certain place of exile" and asks him: "By what road have you reached science?" The young man responds, "I have been searching for it, and I have found it difficult of access. . . . In order to get to it, I have had to take the wilds for my bed and stone for my pillow; I have had to chase away lassitude, surmount danger, take recourse in sleepless nights, embrace voyage as my companion": Hamadhānī, *Maqāmāt (séances)*; selections in French translation by Régis Blachère and Pierre Masnou (Paris: Klincksieck, 1957), 109.

itself as a message aimed at magnifying science and its legitimate holders. This self-celebration can be better appreciated when we think that for a long time, most of the great medieval men of letters were non-Arabs, freedmen, or clients. Given that such men had taken the Arabic language and culture, the religion of the Arabs, and the authorized interpretation of that religion as a means for emerging out of their condition and rising, both in society and in statutory terms, it is normal they should make an exhibition of their difficulties and their disillusionments as so many titles for consideration as "uncommon" men. There is in this message both the self-reference of the savant elite through exaltation and an affirmation of the self within a Stoic morality of effort and challenge.[50] This is alluded to by the philologist Abū 'Ubayda (d. 210?/825?), the son of a Christian slave in Herat, who tells his Baghdad students, "There are among you some who stay with me for scarcely five or six months and then start to say, 'I have remained too long!' "[51]

The ideology of endurance went halfway to dietetics and medicine, imposing on men of letters the type of body they should strive for. In the habitus invented by scholars of the eighth and ninth centuries, the body ought to be fat free, for they thought it impossible to have an alert mind, a lively intelligence, and a good memory along with a large, rotund body. The quest for knowledge was, precisely, a way for the body to thin down.

In the mind of these men of letters, obesity soon became a defect and an obese individual was seen as an imbecile. This is at least the opinion of Shāfi'ī (d. 204/819)—a great traveler[52]—who claimed not to have known any fat man who had succeeded in his studies, with the exception of one of his Iraqi masters. Asked for his reasons, he responded that the sage has only two choices: he either worries about his life in the beyond or concentrates on life here below. In either case, "fat and affliction are mutually exclusive." The jurist was alluding to a theory of character that views the fat man as thoughtless, closer to stupidity than to intelligence, to soft

---

50. Such a person "is bound also many a time to be laughed at and to be in disrepute, and to put up with joking and buffoonery as he struggles with might and main against his ignorance and overthrows it": Plutarch, "On Listening to Lectures," in *Moralia*, trans. Frank Cole Babbitt, Loeb Classical Library (Cambridge MA: Harvard University Press; London: William Heinemann, 1960), 1:255; trans. Pierre Maréchaux as *Comment écouter* (Paris: Payot & Rivages, 1995), 65. We have had occasion to see the extent to which the theme of humiliation (*dhill, dhull*) is present in the medieval conquest of knowledge.

51. Khaṭīb al-Baghdādī, *Tarīkh Baghdād*, 12:407; Dhahabī, *Siyar*, 12:496.

52. Shāfi'ī is credited with the first known complete travel narrative. We have several manuscript copies of this text and a poor edition that was falsely attributed to him but that is in reality a tenth-century work.

compliance than to vivacity, to indolence than to agility. Obedient to his own theory, Shāfiʿī conceived of an entire dietetics for himself, the principal rules for which have come down to us thanks to one of his associates. The master confided to him at Fustāt that in sixteen years he had only eaten his fill once. Then, regretting his voracity, he immediately put his finger down his throat and vomited the meal. "Why?" his disciple asked. His answer was: "Because satiety makes the body heavy, hardens the heart, softens sagacity, attracts sleep, and weakens piety."[53] Renouncing the pleasures of the body in order to better enjoy those of the mind was an ideal of Stoic resonance to which scholarly Islamic culture eventually aspired.

Terminus

Like the Stoics, most of the men of letters whom we have met here condemn "useless" voyages, by which they mean those made for pleasure or for glory.[54] Because it was, first and foremost, a literary practice, the *rihla*-voyage was—and had to be—undertaken with gravity and humility, given that acting to conquer knowledge was equivalent to acting to acquire virtue. This means that for some time the abolition of the voyage was feared as "an attack against Islamic knowledge." Hence the exemplary—in both senses of the term—nature of the condemnation of Ibn Habīb, which we have seen above.

53. Fakhr al-Dīn Rāzī, *Manāqib al-Imām al-Shāfiʿī*, ed. Ahmad Hijazī Ahmad Saqqa (Cairo: Maktabat al-Kulliyat al-Azharīyah, 1986), 106; Ibn ʿAsākir, *Tārīkh madinat Dimashq*, 15:12; Abū Nuʿaym, *Hilyat al-Awliyāʾ*, 10 vols. (Cairo: Maktabat al-Khānjī, 1932–38), new ed., 10 vols. (Beirut: Dār al-Kitāb al-Arabī, 1967–68), 9:127; selections trans. Muhammad Al-Akoli as *The Beauty of the Righteous and Ranks of the Elite* (Philadelphia: Pearl, 1995); Dhahabī, *Siyar*, 10:36. In the same era a doctor in Medina, greeting one of his Iraqi colleagues, Wakiʿ ibn al-Jarrāh of Kufa (d. 194/809), asks his companion, "What is all that fat on you, O ascete of Iraq?" The Hanafite doctor responds, "It is because of my joy for Islam!": Dhahabī, *Siyar*, 10:36. Wakiʿ was the author of *Book of Asceticism: Kitāb al-Zuhd*, ed. ʿAbd al-Rahmān ʿAbd al-Jabbār Faryawāʿī (Medina: Maktabat al-Dār, 1984).

54. On the concept of the voyage among the Stoics, see especially Seneca, *Letters to Lucilius* 1.1 and 1.2, 13.17, and 28.1–5; trans. Marie-Ange Jourdan-Gueyer as *Lettres à Lucilius: 1 à 29 (Livres I–III)* (Paris: Flammarion, 1992). Among many condemnations of the dilettante man of letters in Islam, one early tenth-century example states: "Instead of a voyage in search of science, it is a voyage of pleasure that he is taking": Hakīm al-Tirmidhī, *Tabāʾiʿ al-Nufūs*, ed. Ahmad ʿAbd all-Rahīm Sāyih and Sayyid al-Jumaylī (Cairo: al-Maktab al-Thaqāfī, 1989), 49; trans. Bernd Radtke and John O'Kane in *The Concept of Sainthood in Early Islamic Mysticism: Two Works by al-Hakīm al-Tirmidhī* (Richmond, UK: Curzon, 1996). For a number of examples in the tenth and eleventh centuries, see Ignaz Goldziher, *Muhammedanische Studien*, 2 vols. (Halle: Niemeyer, 1889–90); trans. Léon Bercher as *Études sur la tradition islamique: Extraites du tome II des Muhammadanische Studien* (Paris: Adrien-Maisonneuve, 1952), 223–30; trans. C. R. Barber and S. M. Stern as *Muslim Studies: Muhammedanische Studien*, 2 vols. (London: George Allen & Unwin, 1967).

But the *rihla*, which was not the only medieval way of conquering knowledge, had to compete with other modes of appropriation. The most important of these were, incontestably, the *ijāza* and the *wijāda*. *Rihla, ijāza,* and *wijāda*, the three principal internal institutions of intellectual life within Islam, correspond to three different, and even rival, modalities for the transmission of knowledge.[55]

Ijāza, Ignaz Goldziher quite rightly writes, constitutes, both from the point of view of its normal formation and from that of its aberrations, "something specific to Muslim society and without analogy in any other milieu."[56] Normally, the term refers to a sort of diploma that attests that its holder has successfully achieved, under the authority of a recognized master, an attentive and faultless reading of a particular work. In reality, it often appears to be a replacement for a long, difficult, and costly voyage. Men of letters who thought it impossible to undertake long trips or who, having taken them, were unable to stay long enough near the master whom they had gone to see to take learning from his mouth had to content themselves with copying the books that such a master taught or else with buying them, then submitting them to him so as to obtain "authorization" to diffuse them in his name, just as if they had undergone an "audition" with him. Until the ninth century, an acceptable *ijāza* required the physical presence of the "auditioned" person. Later centuries had a more liberal interpretation. Not all medieval doctors viewed the *ijāza* as a legitimate mode for the transmission of knowledge, however. Such major authorities of the tenth century as Abū Dharr al-Harawī (d. 434/1042) and the great ʿAbbāsid judge Mawardī (d. 450/1058) stated that "if the *ijāza* were valid, the voyage would be useless."[57] It was in that period that the *ijāza* gradually began to replace the voyage. It found a number of partisans who wrote works in its favor.[58] The door was thus open to one of the most aberrant modes for the transmission of knowledge in medieval Islam: the

55. On the transmission of knowledge in Islam, see especially Georges Vajda, *La transmission du savoir en Islam (VIIIe–XVIIIe siècles)* (London: Variorum, 1983); Jonathan Berkey, *The Transmission of Knowledge in Medieval Cairo: A Social History of Islamic Education* (Princeton: Princeton University Press, 1992); Michael Chamberlain, *Knowledge and Social Practice in Medieval Damascus (1190–1350)* (Cambridge: Cambridge University Press, 1994); and Nicole Grandin and Marc Gaborieau, eds., *Madrasa: La transmission du savoir dans le monde musulman* (Paris: Éditions Arguments, 1997). For a comparison between Islam and the West, see Georges Makdisi, *The Rise of Colleges: Institutions of Learning in Islam and the West* (Edinburgh: Edinburgh University Press, 1981).

56. Goldziher, *Études sur la tradition islamique,* 232. On the *ijāza,* see also ʿAbd Allāh Fayyād, *Al-Ijāzat al-ʿIlmīya ʿinda al-Muslimīn* (Baghdad: Matbaʿat al-Irshād, 1967).

57. Ibn Salāh, *Muqaddima,* ed. ʿĀʾisha ʿAbd al-Rahmān (Cairo: Wizārat al-Thaqāfah, 1974).

58. In this manner an Andalusian, Walīd ibn Bakr of Saragossa (d. 392/1001), wrote an entire book to defend the practice: see Goldziher, *Études sur la tradition islamique,* 235.

ijāza in absentia. It was even approved by traditionists as scrupulous as Khatīb al-Baghdādī (d. 463/1070): "As a consequence of this concept, we have been able to ascertain that all of our masters conferred the *ijāza* on absent children, without worrying about their age and without making sure that they possessed a sufficient degree of discernment. To tell the truth, we have not been able to verify whether they gave the *ijāza* to children not yet born, even though by going that far one would by no means break the rules of analogy."[59]

From that point on, the greatest doctrinal authorities of Islam would deliver or receive an *ijāza* delivered in absentia.[60] By permitting contact at long distance, epistolary exchanges also detracted from the prestige of the voyage.

And what about the *wijāda*? That literary practice, which consisted in becoming acquainted with a book without the mediation of a master, seems to have been as old as the voyage. From the start, it elicited serious reservations, but it finally came to be admitted as a legitimate means of acquiring and transmitting knowledge. A doctor in Basra who died in the 720s stood at the center of debate. His opinions are contradictory, however: one offers a solution of toleration; another, a firm condemnation.[61] Those opinions may perhaps have been invented around the beginning of the ninth century and credited to a prestigious intellectual personality from the past. As is known, this was an ancient practice that Islam had inherited. It consists in quoting a master from past times—"*magister dixit*," the Pythagorians said—to make him say what today's thinkers were saying. Thus, whether one wanted to defend the *wijāda* or reject it, there were two authoritative arguments available. The Basra doctor probably said yes to one student and no to another. It is interesting to note that the rejection was motivated by the rule stating that audition of any book must be made "before someone sure [*thiqa*]."[62] As we have seen, in this milieu,

59. Khatib al-Baghdādī, *Taqyīd al-ʿilm*, ed. Yusuf ʿIshsh (Damascus, 1949); quoted in Goldziher, *Études sur la tradition islamique*, 235. We have discovered that the same Khatīb al-Baghdādī devoted an entire text to the question of the *ijāza* given to someone who is absent or does not exist: see Khatīb al-Baghdādī, *Risāla fī Hukm al-Ijāza lil-Majhūl waʾl-Maʿdūm* (Ahmad III, 23/624), microfilm no. 269, Hadīth, Maʿhad a-Makhtūtāt al-ʿArabiyya (Institut Arabe des Manuscrits), Cairo.

60. The judge ʿIyād (d. 544/1149) recalls that "the *ijāza* in absentia was validated by the majority of the moderns": al-Qādī ʿIyād, *Al-Ilmāʾ ilā Maʿrifat Usūl ar-riwāya*, ed. Sayyid Ahmad Saqr (Cairo, 1970), 104.

61. Ibn Saʿd, *Tabaqāt*, 7:251; Ibn ʿAsākir, *Tārīkh madinat Dimashq*, 9:163b; Dhahabī, *Siyar*, 4:473–75.

62. This doctor, whose name was Ibn Sirīn (d. 110/728), inherited the solution named for him from one of his masters, who is reported to have recommended that all of his own books be

that "sureness" had a juridical status: it made testimony before a judge acceptable. At least in part, "audition" can be compared to juridical testimony, or *shahāda*.[63]

With the coming of the 'Abbāsids, the *wijāda* divided scholars. Before they died, some buried or destroyed their books by water or by fire out of fear of the danger it presented.[64] They feared "nonauthorized" readings because, as they warned, it would take only one negligent or incompetent copyist to twist the content of the book he was working on.[65] Mālik ibn Anas (d. 179/795), the great Meccan authority in questions of law and traditions, was one of these. But it was in the name of the principle of the voyage that he condemned the practice. In his opinion, the men of letters who agreed to this procedure were seeking "to load up": "They want to gather up a maximum [number of books] in a minimum time [spent with their authors or transmitters]."[66] Only two generations later, the *wijāda* won the approval of well-known men of letters, however. One of these, Ahmad ibn Hanbal (d. 241/855), was a prolific collector of traditions and an indefatigable traveler.[67] After him, his son and successor used the *wijāda* as well, but he seems to have used it only to utilize the vast documentary material left by his father. One of the conditions for validation of the *wijāda* was in fact that the name of the person who had copied the book in question had to be known.

erased at his death: 'Abd al-Razzāq, *al-Musannaf*, ed. Habīb al-Rahmān al-A'zamī (Karachi, 1972), 5:301.

63. Tirmidhī, *Jāmi'*, with the commentary of Abū Bakr ibn al-'Arabī, 12 vols. (Cairo: 1931); Dhahabī, *Kitāb Tadhkirat al-huffādh*, 1:123.

64. There are many examples in Khatīb al-Baghdādī, *Taqyīd al-'Ilm*, 49–58.

65. This is what Jāhiz (d. 255/868) was complaining about when he wrote: "The book falls into the hands of another copyist who reiterates the stratagem of the first. Thus, the work will continue to circulate among 'criminal' hands, subjected to the whim of accidents that denature it more and more until it contains characteristic errors, pure and simple lies": Jāhiz, *Tahdhīb Kitāb al-Hayawān*, ed. 'Abd al-Salām Muhammad Hārūn, 7 vols. (Cairo: Matkabat al-Khanjī, 1938–45); selections trans. Lakhdar Souami as *Le Cadi et la mouche: Anthologie du Livre des animaux* (Paris: Sinbad, 1988), 161.

66. Ibn Abī Abū Zayd al-Qayrawānī, *Kitab al-Jāmi' fī al-Sunan*, ed. Muhammad Abu-Ajfan and 'Uthman Batikh (Beirut: Muassasat al-Risalah; Tunis: al-Maktabah al-'Atiqah, 1985), 152. That jurist is credited with inventing the parallel between the long and difficult career of the doctor of Islam and that of his Christian counterpart, progressively climbing the ladder of the ecclesiastical hierarchy during a long life: Khatīb al-Baghdādī, *Al-Kifāya fī 'ilm al-Riwāya* (Beirut: Dār al-Kitāb al-'Arabī, 1985), 317; 'Iyād, *Al-Ilmā'*, 95.

67. During a stay at Kufa (still a young student, it is true) he attempted in every way possible to procure the *Summa* of Sufyān al-Thawrī (d. 161/777). He finally did obtain it, and he copied it without "audition": Dhahabī, *Siyar*, 11:190.

After the ninth century, the *wijāda* had the same fate as the *ijāza*. Eventually it became part of medieval intellectual mores, and few men of letters worried about the dangers that preceding generations had seen in it.[68] Its champions were often the same men who backed the *ijāza*. Khaṭīb al-Baghdādī (d. 463/1070) was one of these. In explanation of the conditions in which he himself had used the procedure, he states: "There is no difference between the fact of receiving books by testamentary prescription or buying them from a man at his death [*sic!*]. But it is acceptable to transmit the contents only by means of *wijāda*. This is what the men of science that we have known have always done. Otherwise, the acquirer can do nothing, unless he has already received them by *ijāza*. In that case, he is permitted to transmit the content of these books as if it were a part of his 'auditions.' It is only on that condition that it is acceptable to transmit the contents of books with the mention, 'So-and-So has informed us' or 'So-and-So has transmitted to us.'"[69]

The way thus lay open to all sorts of freer interpretations. Disillusioned, the polygraph Dhahabī (d. 748/1347) noted unhappily that by his time, "the acquisition of knowledge from the mouth of men had much diminished." It was the end of the voyage, he noted sadly. Or at least it was the end of a certain conception of the voyage as it had prevailed in the 'Abbāsid age. Indeed, in that polymath's times, the *rihla* no longer drew its pertinence from an epistemological context. It subsisted simply as a more or less massive fact in the realm of cultural sociology.

68. Dhahabī, *Siyar*, 11:486.
69. Khaṭīb al-Baghdādī, *Al-Kifāya*, 352–53.

·☾ 4 ☽·

AUTOPSY OF A GAZE

The men of letters whom we have encountered thus far traveled in order, they said, to "take science" from other, greater, and more prestigious men of letters than they, in the name of the institution characteristic of transmission by hearing in Islam: the *samāʿ*. Thanks to the polemic among tenth-century linguists, discussed in chapter 2, about whether or not someone could claim to be an acknowledged expert in the Arabic language without having stayed among Bedouins living in semiautarchy in the desert, presumed to be the guardians of that language, we have seen that in the Muslim Middle Ages listening was not the only access to truth. The accusations that the protagonists of this debate made against those who had not traveled to observe with their own eyes what they were talking about introduce a second mode, *ʿiyān*, or direct observation.

From its very beginnings, Islam considered the eye to be a source of knowledge. The Prophet himself is credited with the statement that "a fact related is not worth as much as a fact ascertained." The jurists of the classical age adopted that adage, making it a normative rule that established the primacy of the eye over the ear. From the viewpoint of Muslim law, the witness is someone who knows primarily because he has seen.

How, and in what circumstances, did Muhammad state what was in fact already a rule? According to the specialists in dogmatics, it was through a personal effort to interpret the episode in the Qurʾan of Moses and the golden calf. Moses, who learns from God that in his absence the people of Israel have become idolaters, withholds the tablets of the Law. But when he sees the idol with his own eyes, he no longer doubts the report and throws the tablets to the ground and shatters them. Commenting on this scene, one mid-ninth-century man of letters recalls that the Qur'an also develops the idea of the superiority of sight over hearing in the biblical episode in which Abraham says to God, "My Lord! Show me how You give life to the dead." When the Lord responds, "Do you not then believe?" Abraham adds, "Yes! but to satisfy my own understanding" (Qur'an 2:260). Paraphrasing the rejoinder of the Hebrew prophet, the commentator proposes that this rejoinder be read to say, "Yes, but it is so that my heart be made tranquil by the certitude of visual verification." The eye, he concludes, brings "the most noble certitude." But he agrees with the jurists and theologians that there is another sort of certitude that comes immediately after "the certitude of visual verification," which is acquired by hearing.[1]

In the name of that dogmatic superiority of sight over hearing, the Mu'tazilite theologians, with their Aristotelian rationalism, mocked the traditionists for having used insufficient discernment in their transmission of all sorts of traditions that the theologians considered unlikely. When ninth-century traditionists reported, for example, that the Prophet said, speaking of the year 100 of the Hegira (718 CE), "On that day there will be no living soul left on the earth," the prediction was visibly wrong, their critics claimed, "given that we are in the middle of the third century of the Hegira and there are now many more men than there were then."[2] Moreover, when the traditionists quoted the Prophet as saying, "If the Qur'an were placed in a skin then thrown into the fire, it would not burn,"[3] they were clearly in error because "one can at times see copies of the Qur'an burn or undergo the same vicissitudes as other objects or books."

As specialists of "transmission," the traditionists always found it difficult to respond to this sort of objection. On the other hand, the master theologians of "speculative reason" did not always totally reject Tradition. Rather, they were interested in purifying the corpus and rationalizing it by pruning away incoherent bits and ridding it of the jumble of fabulous and incongruous tales that encumbered it. Thus, the Mu'tazilite theologians were not hostile in principle to the paradigm of hearing to which an entire array of endogamous disciplines in formation in the late eighth

1. Ibn Qutayba, *Mukhtalaf al-Hadīth* (Cairo: Maktabat al-Kullīyat al-Azharīyah, 1966); trans. Gérard Lecomte as *Le traité de divergence du Hadīth d'Ibn Kutayba (m. 276/889)* (Damascus: Institut Français, 1962), 109.

2. Ibid.; Lecomte translation, 111.

3. Ibid.; Lecomte translation, 223–24.

century—exegesis of the Qur'an, the study of traditions, law, philology, poetic criticism, history—were affiliated.[4]

Although the ninth century dealt a serious blow to this paradigm by authorizing direct access to books without the mediation of a master, stretching the rule did not go so far as to permit questioning the genealogical principle of the transmission of knowledge. Not even Jāhiz (d. 255/868), who is considered one of the most determined medieval defenders of direct access to the book, went so far as to contest it. Rationalistic though he was, his brief in favor of books contains no rejection of transmission by way of hearing. The latter was circumscribed, to be sure, but never denied. He observes, "Man possesses knowledge only on the condition of having registered in his memory a considerable amount of information by way of hearing." He adds, however, that his library "has a content richer than what is gathered by simple listening."[5] I might note in passing that when Jāhiz was active, what we call "reading books" was expressed as "looking at" or "seeing in" books, given the absence of a magisterial authority to guarantee their content. Moreover, the process took place *silently*, using the eyes only.

This affirmation of sight as the source of knowledge was to blossom in the new scientific disciplines—medicine and astronomy, for example— that developed thanks in particular to the translation of the Greek corpus.

It was without a doubt a major event in the scientific history of Islam when, by order of caliph al-Ma'mūn (r. 813–33), astronomers who had created a group of verified tables (*zīj*) called *Zīj Ma'mūnī* or *Mumtahan* made observations in the desert of Sinjar and in the region of Diyār Rabī'a, which were completed by others made in Baghdad and Damascus.[6] To be sure, sight, as a sense-based source of knowledge, had not been absent from Arabo-Islamic culture before the translation of the Greek corpus,

4. In that age, to say that one did not believe what one saw was dangerous from both the dogmatic point of view and the political one. Such a declaration of principle in fact attacked Revelation just as much as it did community harmony. Anyone who made such a statement would be doubly condemned for *zandaqa*—that is, for both "unbelief" and "rebellion"—as Ibn Qutayba recalls: ibid., 290. On this question, see Georges Vadja, "Les Zindīqs en pays d'Islam au début de la période 'abbāside," *Revista degli Studi Orientali* 17 (1937): 173–229, esp. 200–201.

5. Jāhiz, *Tahdhīb Kitāb al-Hayawān*, ed. 'Abd al-Salām Muhammad Hārūn, 7 vols. (Cairo: Maktabat al-Khanjī, 1938–45); selections trans. Lakhdar Souami as *Le Cadi et la mouche: Anthologie du Livre des animaux* (Paris: Sinbad, 1988), 162.

6. Mas'ūdī, *Murūj al-Dhahab*; trans. Charles Barbier de Meynard and Abel Payet de Courteille as *Les priaries d'or*, 9 vols. (Paris: Imprimerie Impériale, 1861–1917); that translation reviewed and corrected by Charles Pellat, 5 vols. (Paris: Société Asiatique, 1962, 1989, 1997), 1:76. Qiftī recalls that these observations were made during the three years 830, 831, and 832: Qiftī, *Ibn al-Qiftī's Tārīkh al-hukamā*, ed. Julius Lippert (Leipzig: Dieterisch'sche Verlagsbuchhandlung, 1903), 359.

but it was thanks to Greek philosophy that visual knowledge was endowed with a clear epistemological status. The linguists, for example, made good use of their sight when they traveled through the desert to collect notes on poetry, language, habitat, animals, and geographical relief. But because they were reliant on what they heard from Bedouin informants, they went into the desert to learn about the linguistic usages of its inhabitants, not their ways of life. They concentrated on interrogating the Bedouins, listening to their responses, and transcribing what they said. Faithful to the method of the traditionists, they thought of themselves more as transmitters of the ancient language, poetry, and tales than as observers and analysts of Bedouin life. If they happened to use their eyes in their work as collectors—and some of them even composed descriptions of the Arabian Peninsula—the fact remains that when they described a region, an oasis, or a tribe, their observations were channeled through their motivations and their methods of transmission. It is significant that when Ibn Kalbī (d. 206/821), a renowned Iraqi genealogist and prose writer, composed a monograph on horses and another on Arabs in high places, he conceived of both studies as genealogical research.

Nothing illustrates the idea that most linguists had of their knowledge better than an anecdote concerning Asma'ī (d. 213/828) and his colleague Abū 'Ubayda (d. 210?/825?), both eminent representatives of the philological school of Basra. As they appear in this tale, they have been summoned by an 'Abbāsid vizier to discuss works about horses that each man has just composed. Following custom of the salons of the time, the two scholars are called upon to speak on the respective merits of their books. In order to differentiate between them, the vizier puts them to a test, asking each one to describe, in visual terms, the anatomy of his own horse, naming all of its parts. Embarrassed, Abū 'Ubayda declares that he is not a veterinarian and states that "everything contained in my book I have taken from the Bedouins."[7] He defends himself—and legitimately so—for not being a specialist in animal anatomy. His habitus is the product of the belles lettres literary code (*Adab*) of his epoch. Marshall Hodgson explains the mind-set that the *Adab* inculcated in its practitioners: "The learning of the adīb, whatever the field, was never clearly distinguished from his concern with belles-lettres. When the adīb studied 'biology,' for instance, he was

---

7. Anbārī, *Nuzhat al-Albāb fī Tabaqāt al-Udabā'*, ed. Muhammad Abū al-Fadi Ibrāhīm (Cairo: Dār nahdaf Misr., 1967), 120; Suyūtī, *Bughyat al-Wu'āh fī Tabaqāt al-Lughawīyīn*, ed. Muhammed Abū Ibrāhīm, 2 vols. (Cairo: Matba'at 'Īsā al-Bābī al-Halabī, 1964–65), 2:133.

not so much interested in learning the structure of organisms as in finding out all the strange things that could be said of them."[8]

Abū 'Ubayda's colleague, Asma'ī, played his hand more cleverly: he managed to give the name of every part of the horse and to attest it by a quotation drawn from Arabian antiquity. This procedure also reflects the genre of the *Adab* to the extent that, in composing his *Book of Horses*, his objective was not so much to produce a work of zoology as it was to gather together all the linguistic and poetic material available about horses. Like his colleague, he was operating as a philologist and a compiler of archaic language. That he proved himself more expert than his adversary does not alter the way he approached the composition of his work. His knowledge of animals[9] adds no more meaning to the philological aim of his work than Abū 'Ubayda's ignorance detracted from his.

It is not surprising that Asma'ī should have stated the golden rule of philology that the compiler must give his linguistic material "in the name of him who had transmitted it to him." That rule attaches philology to the paradigm of hearing. Like his colleague, who protested that he was no veterinarian, Asma'ī conceived of his profession no differently from that of a compiler of traditions. Where should we look in order to understand how sight came to govern knowledge? Since studying the effects of *autopsia* on the whole of Islamic culture in the Middle Ages is out of the question, I shall limit my remarks to a study of the question on a more limited scale, concentrating on one particular domain of knowledge—geography—that provides a good example of the epistemological revolution that sight operated in the classical Islamic *episteme*.

The Eye of the Popeyed Man

Jāhiz (d. 255/868), "the popeyed man," is among those who played an essential role in Islam in promoting sight to the dignity of a positive tool for knowledge. His *Book of the Round and the Square* is a genuine plea for a knowledge liberated from the dictatorship of the principle of tradition.[10]

---

8. Marshall G. S. Hodgson, *The Venture of Islam: Conscience and History in a World Civilization*, 3 vols. (Chicago: University of Chicago Press, 1974), 1:453–54.

9. It appears that it won Asma'ī nomination to a high post in the 'Abbāsid imperial postal system.

10. This epistle (which had a wide circulation during its author's lifetime) reached as far as Andalusia, where it was followed by Jāhiz's treatise on rhetoric, *Al-Bayān wa'l-Tabyīn*. ed. 'Abd al-Salām Muhammad Hārūn, 4 vols. (Cairo: Maktabat al-Khānjī, 1968). Many men of letters

Although the epistle had a known addressee, it could just as easily have
been addressed to a Shiite as to a Sunnite. In Shiite dogmatics, a tradition reputed to be sure, transmitted by guarantors of irreproachable reputation, and that went back, without a break, to their imams, was more
probative than the immediate perception of the senses. Struck with the
seal of the infallibility of their authors, the transmitted sayings guarantee
an absolute certitude that the senses, exposed to appearance and illusion,
cannot offer.[11] The Sunnite traditionists were also not far from thinking
that a tradition is probative when it goes back to the Prophet through
an uninterrupted chain of trustworthy guarantors. The epistle might even
have been addressed to a prose writer. In fact, it begins with an appeal to
anyone who is "little versed in the tradition, without experience, attached
to books rather than to reality, and who draws no difference between the
unexamined opinion of the inexperienced man and the attentive observation of the scrupulous researcher."[12] For instance, scholars collected verse
and composed narratives about the traditions centering on extraordinarily
long-lived figures in the pre-Islamic era.[13] Jāhiz declares that there is no effective proof and no decisive evidence to validate such tales of men with an
extraordinarily long life. What should be done with these stories? Reject
them? Things were not that simple, "given the verisimilitude of the events

discussed this work: Ibn Qutayba, *Mukhtalaf al-Hadīth*, is in part a critique of it from a Sunnite
and traditionist point of view. In the *Hawāmil wa-al-Shawāmil*, the other great questionnaire of
the Middle Ages, the questions that Tawhīdī (d. 414/1023) posed to Miskawayh (d. 421/1030) follow the indications laid out in Jāhiz's epistle. He tells us that a certain Ahmad ibn 'Abd'l Wahhāb
wrote an entire work to respond to his questions: Tawhīdī, *Hawāmil wa-al-Shawāmil* (Beirut:
Dār al-Kutub al-'Ilmīyah, 2001), 320, 327. Similarly, Abū al-Hasan 'Alī ibn 'Abd' al-'Azīz al-Jurjānī
wrote a brief work entitled *Responses to the Questions of the Book of the Square and the* Round,
mentioned in the *Thimār al-Qulūb* of Abū Mansūr al-Tha'ālibī (d. 429/1037): *Thimār al-Qulūb*, ed.
Muhammad Abū al-Fadl Ibrāhīm (Cairo: Dār Nahdat Misr Lil-tab' wa al-Nashr, 1965).

11. Ignaz Goldziher, *Vorlesungen über den Islam* (1910); trans. Félix Arin as *Le dogme et la loi
de l'Islam: Histoire du développement dogmatique et juridique de la religion musulmane* (Paris: Geuthner, 1958, 1973), 178; trans. Andras and Ruth Hamori as *Introduction to Islamic Theology and Law*
(Princeton: Princeton University Press, 1981). On the question of the *hadīth* of the imams, see
Mohammad Alī Amir-Moezzi, "Remarques sur les critères de l'authenticité du *hadīth* et l'autorité
du juriste dans la chi'isme imamite," *Studia Islamica* 85 (1997): 5–40. Amir-Moezzi furnishes an
abundant and useful bibliography.

12. Jāhiz, *Kitāb al-Tarbī' wa-l-Tadwīr*, ed. Charles Pellat (Damascus: Institut François de
Damas, 1955); trans. Maurice Adad as *Le livre du carré et du rond*, *Arabica* 13, no. 3 (1966): 268–94,
esp. 274.

13. In this connection, the poet Zuhayr ibn Janab supposedly lived for 450 years, and his
grandfather for 650; Durayd ibn Simnah, one of the heroes of the Antar cycle, was 450 years
of age at the time at which the *Sīrat 'Antar* is set. He was reported to have lived long enough to
have known the epoch of the Prophet. Philologists and historians include in this category of
mu'ammarūn people who lived as long as 120 or 150 years.

related." To declare them truthful was no easier, "since they bear no indication permitting [us] to consider them so." What was left was doubt,
which, according to Jāhiz, was the only methodological attitude to adopt
in like circumstances.[14] By doubting the existence of the long-lived figures
of the pre-Islamic era, Jāhiz dealt a blow not only to the relaters of ancient
tales,[15] but also to the traditionists.[16] Still, the age believed firmly in their
existence. Even in Jāhiz's lifetime, people referred to one man supposed to
be 320 years old.[17] We know the name of another macrobiotic figure who
died in 938 and claimed that he did not need to furnish chains of transmission to attest the authenticity of his traditions because he had known 'Alī
(d. 40/661), the fourth caliph of Islam, personally![18]

Jāhiz's method was not limited to arming the mind with doubt. As a
consequence, if the case of the macrobiotic figures gave him an opportunity to exercise doubt, the case of giants—whose existence was attested
in Arabic antiquity by those same prose writers and philologists—led
him to apply the standard of ocular proof. Here he openly denounces the
argument of genealogical proof as a lie and a fraud. Jāhiz simply does not

14. This methodological doubt—which often extends into existential doubt—runs through
the "scientific" works of Jāhiz. He writes in his *Book of Animals*, "Know, after what I have just related, how to localize the cases and situations in which doubt is obligatory so that, in function of
these contexts, you will learn to determine certitude, as well as the places and situations in which
it is necessary. Learn by yourself to know what is dubious. If that leads only to an apprenticeship
in the suspension of judgment preceding confirmation, it would already be an indispensable attitude": Jāhiz, *Tahdhīb Kitāb al-Hayawān*; Souami translation, 74.

15. The Iraqi prose writers Hishām al-Kalbī (d. 206/824) and Haytham ibn 'Adī (d. 207/822),
both of whom were born in Kufa, wrote the first monographs on the *mu'ammarūn*: Ibn al-Nadīm,
Fihrist, ed. Ridā al-Māzindarānī (Beirut: Dār al Masīrah, 1988); trans. Bayard Dodge as *The Fihrist
of al-Nadim: A Tenth-Century Survey of Muslim Culture*, 2 vols. (New York: Columbia University
Press, 1970).

16. On the insertion of these persons in the chains of transmission of the traditionists, see
G. H. A. Juynboll, "The Rôle of *mu'ammarūn* in the Early Development of the *Isnād*," *Wiener
Zeitschrift für die Kunde des Morgenlandes* 81 (1991): 155–75; reprinted in Juynboll, *Studies on the
Origins and Uses of Islamic Hadīth* (Brookfield, VT: Variorum, 1996), no. 7.

17. Although he was quite critical of Jāhiz, Ibn Qutayba does little but repeat his arguments
when he writes: "God has given us matter for reflection with the vestiges that [the ancient
peoples] have left on earth and the citadels that they constructed, the passages that they dug in
the heart of the mountains, and the steps that they cut. In this domain, the difference of propor-
tion is the same as between the duration of their life and ours: it is the same for their stature": Ibn
Qutayba, *Mukhtalaf al-Hadīth*, 314. That did not stop the same Ibn Qutayba from echoing the
reports of *mu'ammarūn* in his *al-Ma'ārif* (Beirut: Dār al-Kutub al-Ilmīyah, 2003), 271ff.

18. Ignaz Goldziher, *Muhammedanische Studien*, 2 vols. (Halle: Niemeyer, 1889–90); trans.
Léon Bercher as *Études sur la tradition islamique: Extraites du tome II des Muhammadanische Studien*
(Paris: Adrien-Maisonneuve, 1952), 210–13; trans. C. R. Barber and S. M. Stern as *Muslim Studies:
Muhammedanische Studien*, 2 vols. (London: George Allen & Unwin, 1967). There are a number of
examples in Juynboll, "The Rôle of *mu'ammarūn*."

believe in the existence of giants. "The weight, immense height, and bulk" of these mastodonic personages seem to him just as fantastic as the outlandish age of the macrobiots. But in this case, he can denounce belief in them more openly because he has tangible proofs from his own experience of direct observation:

> The argument against the lies of their authors is ready at hand; the proof that will establish the indigence of their minds is manifest: these are, for example, *the observations that we have* made about the size of nobles' swords, of the knights' lances, of the royal crowns conserved in the Kaaba, [and] the narrowness of their doors [and] the limited height of the stairs in their prehistoric palaces and their ancient cities. This is also demonstrated by the sarcophagi that served them as a burial place, the doors of their tombs in the bowels of the earth or at the summit of their mountains, their storage pits, and the height at which they placed their lamps in their temples, meeting places, and game rooms in relation to the tops of their heads.[19]

Nonetheless, Jāhiz has to restrain his enthusiasm in this administration of ocular proof. When faced with a revealed truth, he concedes that the extraordinary corpulence of the 'Adites is real, because it is attested by the Qur'an.[20] But all the other gigantic figures who inhabit the mythical tales of Arabian antiquity were pure invention, emerging straight out of the credulous imagination of men. Credulity is what aliments mythical interpretations of all sorts. Like the traditionists, the prose writers peddled chimeras on the faith of oral traditions. In considering the natural phenomenon of the tides, Jāhiz notes that the traditionists had long burdened its comprehension with pseudobiblical explanations. He asks what opinion the addressee of his epistle holds of their flux and reflux. Does he think that the phenomenon can be explained by "an angel who lowers and raises his foot"? If that is the case, he notes ironically, "perhaps the ruler of

---

19. Jāhiz, *Kitāb al-Tarbī'*, 44. Jāhiz returns several times in his works to the importance of material traces. In *Of the Serious and the Joking*, an epistle addressed to the vizier Muhammad ibn 'Abd al-Malik al-Zayyāt, he reminds his dedicatee, in the form of a quotation attributed to an "ancient" (read, a Greek philosopher), that "material indications are more solid than the witness of men, unless there is in the piece of information an [external] indication and unless the testimony is accompanied by a proof, because the indication does not lie and does not disguise, nor does it add or modify, whereas the witness of men is not so invulnerable, nothing guaranteeing it from corruption, to the extent to which that is possible": Jāhiz, *Quatre essais*, trans. Charles Vidal, 2 vols. (Cairo: Institut Français d'Archéologie Orientale du Caire, 1976–79), 1:108.

20. The 'Adites have been identified as a people of southern Arabia who were destroyed by Allah because they refused to listen to the teachings of their prophet, Hud: Qur'an 54:18–22.

the celestial sphere is an angel." And while we are at it, why not think that
thunder is "the voice of an angel scolding"? Anyone who believes this non-
sense is probably a devotee of common opinion and sheer twaddle. Jāhiz
states that he believes his interlocutor to be above such fairy tales. "Are
we to abandon philosophy and adopt the opinion of the orthodox mass, or
shall we tell ourselves that the flux and the reflux are the very effect of at-
tractive forces when [the moon] attracts and when it repels?" He prompts
his addressee's answer, suggesting a possible rational answer in the guise of
a false question: "What do you think of the opinion of those who declare
that there is a relation between the moon and the water and that, among
all the stars, it is the most like to fire by its nature, and that the flux and
reflux are determined by the attraction and repulsion that it exerts on the
water?" Jāhiz adopts the theory that he outlines in his question, since he
reminds his correspondent that instead of being a pseudoexplanation of a
religious nature, it is the result of experience and assiduous observation:
"It has been observed at [each one of the] mansions [of the moon] and
during the course of its successive revolutions; those who take an interest
in the flux and reflux know this."[21] With such rational arguments, how
could anyone deny ocular testimony and substitute rumor for it? Jāhiz expresses his astonishment: "I have seen people hold out against the truth
when it is acquired by deduction; I have never seen anyone resist it when
it results from direct observation."[22]

This does not mean that Jāhiz believed that ocular testimony was infal-
lible. He was not a sensualist, and his empiricism was not absolute. Like
Aristotle, he thought that knowledge gained through the senses must be
placed under the authority of reason, our only tool for the validation of
our comprehension of the sensible world: "The eyes can make a mistake
and the senses can lie."[23] These have to be subjected to the judgment of a
superior authority with the power of *tabayyun*,[24] a term designating clear
vision of things. How, in fact, can one turn his eyes away from his bad

21. Jāhiz, *Kitāb al-Tarbī'*, 308.
22. Ibid., 182.
23. Jāhiz returns to this idea in his *Book of Animals*: see *Tahdhīb Kitāb al-Hayawān*; Souami
translation, 77.
24. *Tabayyun* (lucidity) joins *'iyān* (direct observation) and *shakk* (doubt) as key concepts in
Jāhizian epistemology. The theme returns on several occasions in the *Book of Animals*, in which
Jāhiz adopts the remarks of Ibn Jahm the Barmecide, a secretary to the enlightened caliph
Ma'mūn: "I am extremely envious of the fate of the perplexed man who returns to certitude,
because any man whom perplexity has detached from his certitude must have but one object of
desire: to seek a clear vision of things [*tabayyun*]. One is always happy to reconquer the object of
his desires": Jāhiz, *Tahdhīb Kitāb al-Hayawān*; Souami translation, 75.

penchants (lack of experience, error, illusion, etc.), if not by considering that "the true and clear vision of things is the prerogative of reason"? It is thus the task of reason to hold the reins of sense and to be the ultimate criterion by which to judge errors of the senses.

This positive appreciation of the role of sight is not founded on any systematic disqualification of hearing or what has been learned by hearing. Jāhiz's conception of *autopsia* does not reject oral evidence when it presents guarantees that authenticate what it offers.[25] He states this clearly to his correspondent in the form of a reminder: "You already know that a piece of information [*khabar*]—whose origin is authentic and which has been transmitted rightly—indicates the truth just as well as direct observation [*'iyān*] and is as satisfactory as an oral statement coming directly to the ear."[26] But an item of the sort would not enjoy the same epistemological status as one credited to ocular testimony, which is defined as qualitatively superior to any other form of sense evidence. This is because, for Jāhiz, only sight was capable of explaining the "how" of things. Let the reader be warned: "There is no vexation with direct observation, no gloomy talk of 'necessity,' and no pensive halt before arriving at certainty."[27]

A Geographer in His Study

In his edition of the Arabic text of Jāhiz's *Book of the Round and the Square*, Charles Pellat rightly reminds us that if that work is to be understood, it needs the *Book of Animals*. The contrary is also true: one needs a good grasp of the meaning of the *Book of the Round* for a full grasp of the spirit of the *Book of Animals*. Not only does the latter deepen the "Greco-Arabian" (the term is Jāhiz's) theoretical framework offered in the *Book of the Round*; it is also a response to its list of questions—questions of capital importance constructed, as Pellat writes, around "the most delicate problems posed to the awareness of a Muslim rationalist of the ninth century." One example is Aristotle's treatment of cross-breeding among certain animal species (wolves and tigers) with female dogs, a topic that Jāhiz examines

---

25. Thus, in the *Book of Animals* Jāhiz cites his master: "Nazzām—and we have never doubted the information that he offered as evidence—told me that he had been present at the following scene": Jāhiz, *Tahdhīb Kitāb al-Hayawān*; Souami translation, 269.

26. In his *Tahdhīb Kitāb al-Hayawān* Jāhiz recalls (230) that he composed an epistle entitled *The Traditions (akhbār) and the Conditions of Their Validity*. It is perhaps this epistle that Charles Pellat has translated as "Les nations civilisés et les croyances religieuses," *Journal asiatique* (1968).

27. Jāhiz, *Kitāb al-Tarbī'*, 168.

critically in his *Book of Animals*. He uses the same method to examine this theory that he did to examine the belief in extralong life spans in the *Book of the Round*:

> We have just reproduced the statements of the Author of the *Logic*. We find it dificult to believe that a man like him could for so long have attached his name to the reports that he puts into his books—reports not validated by being put to the test and not confirmed by scholars. As it happens, in order to know whether his theses are well founded, we have only his own affirmations! As for the poets who, in their productions, have evoked the lycaon and the protelid, one looks in vain for any proof in their poems that would shore up their affirmations concerning these heterogeneous reproductions. We have reproduced these allegations as they stand, abstaining from bringing our own evidence, given that we possess no probative arguments to validate them.[28]

His severe criticism of Aristotle should not lead us to forget that Jāhiz himself operates by Aristotelian procedures. The Greek philosopher had spoken out with great vehemence against an attitude that, even when it remained faithful to logical rigor, turned its back on sense experience, relying on reasoning alone. To Aristotle's eyes, the ultimate aim of scientific reflection consists in discovering "what appears always and fundamentally in conformity with sensation."[29] He takes it for granted that agreement with the objective facts lies at the base of all positive knowledge and is its ultimate result. In the name of that agreement, he is brought to rejecting an explanation furnished by Empedocles and Democritus on the cause of sterility in mules because it seems to him not to take sense experience into account.[30] Similarly, his penchant for experimentation leads Aristotle to temper his own ingenuity. When he offers his personal ideas about the reproduction of bees (the queens engender queens and worker bees, and the latter engender the drones), he presents them as working hypotheses not yet confirmed by sufficient observation: "This, then, appears to be the state of affairs with regard to the generation of bees, so far as theory can take us, supplemented by what are thought to be the facts about their behaviour. But the facts have not been sufficiently ascertained; and if at

28. Jāhiz, *Tahdhīb Kitāb al-Hayawān*; Souami translation, 211.

29. Louis Bourgey, *Observation et expérience chez Aristote* (Paris: Vrin, 1955), 43.

30. Aristotle, *On the Generation of Animals*, 2.8.747a 34–b 10; trans. A. L. Peck, Loeb Classical Library (London: William Heinemann; Cambridge, MA: Harvard University Press, 1943), 248–49; trans. Pierre Louis as *De la génération des animaux* (Paris: Belles Lettres, 1966).

any future time they are ascertained, then credence must be given to the
direct evidence of the senses more than to theory,—and to theories too
provided that the results which they show agree with what is observed."[31]
But Aristotle, who was no sensualist, did not trust the senses any more
than Jāhiz did. Before the latter, he had posited that the senses are suscep-
tible to being fooled. It is clear in his *De generatione et corruptione* that sensation and truth can stand opposed to each other.[32] By granting sensation
and the knowledge that results from it only relative importance, he assigns
to critical reflection the task of subjecting the immediate appearance of
things to examination in order to gain access to their reality. When Jāhiz
recommends acting on the basis of a similar protocol in order to reach
knowledge of the sensible world, is he for one minute aware that he is an
Aristotelian?

Whereas Aristotle hesitates between the primacy of the eye (which he
defends in the *Metaphysics* 280a 25) and that of touch (which he defends
in *On the Soul* 2.9.421a, and 3.1.42b–435a), Jāhiz incontestably favors sight
above all the other senses. Sight lies behind his distrust of oral evidence.
His reticence regarding hearing covers the entire gamut, and he attacks
bookish learning just as much as oral traditions. When he speaks about
how sand snakes give birth, he emphasizes information that has come to
him through several sources of transmission, just like the traditionists, for
whom a multiplicity of chains of transmission for a given piece of information, which means different channels, was a criterion of guaranteed
authenticity. Nonetheless, Jāhiz questions this particular piece of information on the basis of criteria established in the *Book of the Round*: "Ibn
Abī'l-'Ajūz claimed in my presence that the serpents of the sands give
birth [to their young live]. The same information was communicated to
me by Muhammad ibn Ayyūb Ja'far, who had it himself from his father,
and also by Fadl ibn Is'hāq ibn Sulaymān. If that information goes back to
the latter, it cannot be anything but authentic, for he was a well of knowledge. In depending always on that chain of transmitters [*isnād*], some have
claimed that when wild sheep give birth, a viper is found in the birth sack.
Others claim . . ."[33]

Then, turning to the reader, Jāhiz warns against such information transmitted with known and recognized chains of guarantors to assure its au-

31. Aristotle, *On the Generation of Animals*, 3.10, 760; Peck translation, 344–47.
32. Aristotle, *De generatione et corruptione*, 1.3, 318b 27–33; trans. Charles Mugler as *De la génération et de la corruption* (Paris: Belles Lettres, 1961); trans. C. J. F. Williams as *Aristotle's De generatione et corruptione* (Oxford: Clarendon Press; New York: Oxford University Press, 1982).
33. Jāhiz, *Tahdhīb Kitāb al-Hayawān*; Souami translation, 78.

thenticity: "I have not transcribed these items in order for you to ratify them; but these are traditions [*riwāya*] that I wanted to have you hear. I want neither to ratify them nor challenge them. But may your heart lean rather toward rejection!"[34]

After hesitation, rejection. Feigned hesitation is an exercise in style. Given that Jāhiz classifies secondhand information as a mode of enunciation expressed as a depreciating "X has claimed that . . . ," he has already questioned its transmitter's credibility. That a person above suspicion transmits an item does not always suffice to guarantee its veracity. After having dealt with men of letters whose honorable reputation could not easily be doubted, Jāhiz turns toward the testimony of lesser persons and judges it unworthy to be accepted even when introduced by the more authoritative "I have seen." Common mortals lack clairvoyance, given their insufficient familiarity with the exercise of reason. This makes their testimony more aleatory. Certain social categories require greater caution than others: sailors and Bedouins, for example. Jāhiz rejects the testimony of the first of these because, he claims, "these are people who do not reflect on the ultimate meaning of what they say and do not consider the ethical value of their acts."[35] Without rejecting the testimony of the Bedouins a priori, Jāhiz nonetheless states that they are often undependable: "The Bedouins say that in the summer, after a light rainstorm, a truffle buried in the ground is partially transformed into a viper. When I related this to him, a chief of the Tayy tribe claimed that he had once seen an enormous truffle that attracted his attention. While he was contemplating it, he noticed that it moved. He tore it out of the ground: it was a viper. This is the sort of tale that I heard from the mouths of Bedouins, to the point that I pray God to protect me from all sin when I transmit such traditions."[36]

In his exigent attitude toward ocular experience, Jāhiz rejoins Aristotle, to the extent that he thought it insufficient to have observed with one's eyes in order for testimony to be valid. The examination of reason is also required. "The eyes make mistakes and the senses lie" was the lesson of the *Book of the Round* and the *Book of Animals*.[37]

And what about the *Book of Capital Cities*, Jāhiz's other major work? What connections are there between it and his two earlier books? Concerning geography, there is a clear continuity with the *Book of Animals*. A

---

34. Ibid., 340.

35. Ibid., 328.

36. Ibid., 347–48.

37. In a passage of the *Hayawān* Jāhiz goes so far as to recommend to the reader: "Do not follow what your eyes show you, but what reason shows you": ibid., 77.

monograph similar to the one by Ahwāz is already contained in the *Book of Animals*.[38] The same could be said of other geographical topics, such as a theory of climates or the relationship between man and his milieu.

Muslim geography owes a debt to Jāhiz's *Book of Capital Cities* in more ways than one, but as an heir to ancient Greece, it certainly did not wait for Jāhiz. Jāhiz himself was not even a geographer. What he brought to geography was a possible formation around a paradigm that, unlike mathematical and astronomical geography,[39] bore within it the making of a human geography. It is understandable that the initiators of human geography welcomed the *Book of Capital Cities*. Jāhiz proposed a break with "scientific" geography in several ways. First, he suggested that the voyage be inserted within an anthropology of the gaze that made ocular experience an essential tool for the production of positive knowledge, a theme that we have already encountered in both the *Book of the Round* and the *Book of Animals*. Second, he sketched out a framework of interpretation of the relationship between man, society, and the ecological milieu (a framework he had already worked out in the *Book of Animals*). Third, he proposed literary motifs for the new field of geography under construction.

A paradoxical work, the *Book of Capital Cities* was written by a man who had done little or no traveling. In it, direct experience of countries is in fact weak, if not null. The tenth-century artisans of the human geography were quick to point this out. But at the same time that they criticized the author, they praised the book as an admirable work, or at least as sufficiently worthy of interest to be copiously quoted, plagiarized, and recast in other forms. The encyclopedist Mas'ūdī is one of these. He states: "Jāhiz claims that the Indus comes from the Nile, and he gives as proof of this the existence of crocodiles in the latter. I do not know where he got such an argument. He advanced that thesis in his *Book of Capital Cities and*

38. Jāhiz, *Tahdhīb Kitāb al-Hayawān*, 4:140–43. This monograph does not appear in the Souami translation. It is reproduced by Ibn al-Faqīh al-Hamadhānī in his *Kitāb al-Buldān: Al-Hamadhānī's Geographie der arabischen Halbinsel*, ed. D. H. Müller (Leiden, 1891); selections trans. Henri Massé as *Abrégé du Livre des pays* (Damascus: Institut Français de Damas, 1973); by Tha'ālibī in his *Latā'if*; trans. C. E. Bosworth as *The Latā'if al-ma'arif of Tha'alibi: The Book of Curious and Entertaining Information* (Edinburgh: Edinburgh University Press, 1968); and by Yāqūt in his *Mu'jam al-Buldān*, ed. Ferdinand Wüstenfeld, 7 vols. (Leipzig, 1855–73; reprint, 6 vols. in 11 pts., Frankfurt: Institute for the History of Arabic-Islamic Science, 1944), 1:286, where he cites Hamadhānī.

39. For Muslim geographers Ptolemy was the major representative of that "scientific" geography. But Ptolemy himself carried forward an ancient tradition of "scientific" geography that placed the discipline side by side with mathematics and astronomy. On these relations, see Germaine Aujac, *Claude Ptolémée, astronome, astrologue, géographe: Connaissance et représentation du monde habité* (Paris: CTHS, 1933, 1997).

the Marvels of Various Lands. It is an excellent work, although the man has not navigated or traveled enough to know the realms and the cities."[40]

Ibn Hawqal was admiring as well, praising Jāhiz's book as "a precious work, which establishes his competence on the subject of the metropolis."[41] He cites the work twice in *The Configuration of the Earth*. The first time, he is describing the Bihistūn, a peak in the Jebel region. The second time is in his chapter on Transoxiana, when he appeals to Jāhiz's aesthetic tastes: "According to Abū 'Uthmān [Jāhiz], the neutral color of the fields, in the middle of a green vegetation, offers a charming picture. From this point of view, Transoxiana possesses incommensurable good fortune and is eminently favored."[42] Not everyone agreed: Muqaddasī criticized the *Book of Capital Cities* and reproached it for giving little specific information.[43] Still, his criticism was aimed less at the content than at the form. It was the extreme condensation that the Palestinian geographer disliked. He did not refrain from borrowing certain of the book's literary themes, however. Beyond what is explicitly given as borrowed, the shadow of Jāhiz can be seen in such observations as "By the taste of the water, the color, the high water level, and the presence of crocodiles in it, [the Indus] is like the Nile."[44]

Did Jāhiz travel or not? The question has preoccupied modern scholars, who tend to think that the ninth-century polymath made few voyages.

---

40. Mas'ūdī, *Murūj al-Dhahab*; Barbier de Meynard and Paret de Courteille translation, 1:84–85. This was an ancient error, traces of which can be found in Herodotus, who writes: "But as to Asia, most of it was discovered by Darius. There is a river Indus, which of all rivers comes second in producing crocodiles. Darius, desiring to know where this Indus issues into the sea, sent ships. . . . Voyaging over the sea westwards, they came in the thirtieth month to that place whence the Egyptian king sent the Phoenicians": *Herodotus in Four Volumes*, trans. A. D. Godley, Loeb Classical Library (Cambridge MA: Harvard University Press, 1920, 1990), par. 44, vol. 2, pp. 242–45.

41. Ibn Hawqal, *Kitāb Sūrat al-Ard*, ed. Johannes Hendrik Kramers (Leiden, 1939); trans. Johannes Hendrik Kramers and Gaston Wiet as *Configuration de la terre*, 2 vols. (Paris: Maisonneuve et Larose, 1964), 2:363.

42. Ibid.; Kramers and Wiet translation, 2:455.

43. "The *Kitāb al-Amsār* (*The Book of Capital Cities*) of al-Jāhiz is a small work, and the book of Ibn al-Faqīh (the *Book of Lands*) is along the same lines as it, though containing more trifling matter and stories. They excuse themselves for this by claiming that what they have introduced into their books they have done, so that the reader may find some relief, should he be bored." Another variant of the manuscript reads: "There are also al-Jāhiz and Ibn Khurradādhbih: their works are very much abridged, and nothing of much utility is to be derived from them": Muqaddasī, *Ahsan al-Taqāsīm fī Ma'rifat al-Aqālīm*, ed. M. J. de Goeje (Leiden: Brill, 1906); selections trans. André Miquel as *Ahsan al-Taqāsīm fī Ma'rifat al-Aqālīm: La meilleure répartition pour la connaissance des provinces* (Damascus: Institut Français de Damas, 1963), 16; trans. Basil Anthony Collins, reviewed by Muhammad Hamid al-Tai, as *The Best Divisions for Knowledge of the Regions* (Reading UK: Garnet, 1994); quoted from Collins translation, 5, 4–5.

44. Ibid.; Miquel translation, 64; Collins translation, 24.

That Jāhiz traveled little distinguishes him from his contemporaries and confers on him the title of having been a top-level intellectual figure who made no known genuine *rihla*, or long-distance voyage in quest of knowledge. But, on the other hand, just because he made no significant *rihla* does not means that he never traveled. He mentions travel in two places in the *Book of Animals*. In the first he states, "Despite my many voyages in the desert and the lands, in the desert regions of the Arabian Peninsula, the Byzantine Empire, Syria, Upper Mesopotamia, and other countries, I do not know . . ."[45] On a second occasion he recalls visiting the mosque of Damascus "when the route to that city was opened."[46] If some day an integral version of the *Book of Capital Cities* is found, we may know more about Jāhiz's wanderings, but the version available to us now is unfortunately incomplete. The passages alluded to by Mas'ūdī and Ibn Hawqal, for example, do not appear in it. I might nonetheless note that, despite its amputations, the available version of the *Book of Capital Cities* permits us to see that certain monographs are placed under the sign of *autopsia*. His piece on the Iraqi city of Hira is punctuated by at least four appearances of "I have seen," without counting many other terms that belong to the lexical and semantic field of vision: "I have also *seen* Hira the white [city]. Among all the houses that I have *observed* there, only the one of 'Awn the Christian is worth mentioning. I have *seen* the land that lies between it and the *qasaba* [administrative center] of Kufa and I have *examined* its color. I have *noted* that it was of a powdery grey tending toward black, and that it enclosed many small stones rough to the touch. Hira is a city in which it gets very cold in the winter. But in the summer the inhabitants take down the curtains in their houses for fear that the heat will set them on fire."[47]

This passage provides later geographers with a model of discursive organization of descriptive knowledge acquired by direct observation. Jāhiz delivers it to them along with his principle of explication that not only is the monograph founded on direct observations, but it is also presented as a global description of the city, apprehended within its ecological environ-

45. In another passage noted by Charles Pellat, Jāhiz is quoted as saying, "I have seen the big cities, the ones that are famous for the perfection and the solidity of their construction, in Syria, in the Byzantine Empire, and in other lands, but I have never seen a city . . . more beautiful . . . than Baghdad": Khatīb al-Baghdādī, *Tārīkh Baghdād*, 14 vols. (Cairo, 1931), 1:77; quoted in Charles Pellat, *Études sur l'histoire socio-culturelle de l'Islam (VIIe–XVe s.)* (London: Variorum, 1976), 61.
46. Jāhiz, *Tahdhīb Kitāb al-Hayawān*; Souami translation, 182.
47. Jāhiz, *Kitāb al-Amsār wa 'Ajā'ib al-Buldān*, ed. Charles Pellat, *Al-Mashriq* 60, no. 2 (March–April 1966): 169–205, esp. 202–3.

ment. The role of description might pass unnoticed if we fail to see it in relation to Jāhiz's theory of man's adaptation—and in fact, the adaptation of all living creatures—to the natural environment. Already in the monograph on Ahwāz, Jāhiz used a similar explanation applied to a comprehension of changes affecting innate qualities that he had observed among certain peoples—the Hashimites from Medina—and that he attributes to the influence of the local ecosystem.[48] Once again, we see the *Book of Capital Cities* in dialogue with the *Book of Animals* when it explains that "in the basaltic lands of the Banū Sulaym, humans, ferocious beasts, domestic animals, birds, insects, everything looks black," or that "the nature of the climate of the Turkish territories puts its mark on the camels, horses, and all wild animals who live there."[49]

Along with content that is fully worthy of tenth-century geography, the *Book of Capital Cities* supplies other passages that singularly resemble the habits of the traditionists and the prose writers. The monograph on Basra, where Jāhiz was born and died, for example, contains nothing that is anything like direct observation. Worse, it is written in the style of the *maḥāsin*, a rhetorical procedure in which Jāhiz excelled, which consists in praising the fine qualities of the subject treated. The principal authority cited, Madā'inī (d. 240/854) was, precisely, a prose writer. To avoid any hasty judgment concerning this monograph, it could be argued that it has come down to us in fragments. Yāqūt, the thirteenth-century bio-bibliographer, knew the work and gives passages from it in his *Dictionary of the Lands* that do not figure in the published manuscript.[50] That does not detract from the fact that, judged by the standards of tenth-century geography—already in operation in the monographs on Hira and on Ahwāz—the description of Basra piles up outworn clichés one after another.

In its mixture of different registers, the *Book of Capital Cities* is disconcerting, despite its filiation with the *Book of Animals*. To be sure, the latter also offers abundant quotations from Madā'inī and other transmitters of tales, ancient and modern. But it by no means bulges with traditions, although they might be more numerous if they did not work counter to Jāhiz's theoretical and methodological framework. We have seen him developing his principle of methodical doubt, a principle stated in the *Book of the Round* and reasserted in the *Book of Animals*. The utilization of

48. Ibid., 187.
49. Jāhiz, *Tahdhīb Kitāb al-Hayawān*; Souami translation, 239.
50. Yāqūt, *Mu'jam al-Buldān*, 2:467; 1:439.

oral traditions does not, a priori and in itself, contradict Jāhiz's postulates, and we know that he did not reject all oral information, irrespective of its source. The use that he makes of it, however, including in the *Book of Capital Cities*, does not derive from that of the traditionists and the prose writers. In his chapter on the attachment of humans, animals, and birds to their "homeland,"[51] there is a cascade of traditions, but they are used to reinforce a line of argumentation that gives ample space to the exercise of the senses and reason. To be persuaded of this, all we need do is compare this chapter to passages in the *Book of Animals* in which Jāhiz speaks of the attachment of living beings to their territories.[52] Jāhiz's utilization of traditions has nothing in common with the doxological usage that the traditionists and the prose writers make of them. André Miquel speaks to this point when he stresses that, in Jāhiz, "tradition never intervenes in itself, but rather in function of the demands of the context: [it is] presented not in itself, as an indispensable piece of the culture, but in the overall framework of the illustration of a phenomenon, essential, therefore, in virtue not of its given, but for its demonstrative capacity."[53] What difference does it make, under these conditions, if, in defense of the objective principle of the voyage, Jāhiz appeals to arguments drawn from the Qur'an? It simply emphasizes the religious credit with which the gesture is surrounded. So much the better if the Qur'an makes the act of movement superior to immobility! This simply illustrates the voyage in its positive aspect of activity that enlarges the scope of reason through experience (*tajriba*), inspection (*ikhtibār*), and choice (*ikhtiyār*) inherent in it.[54] The voyage as experience was the organizing principle of Muslim geography of the tenth century; it adopted as its own Jāhiz's principle that "the mind nourished by experience has no limit" and agreed that "the human mind is perfected only by voyages, the knowledge of lands, and the frequentation of people of all social conditions."[55]

51. Jāhiz, *Kitāb al-Amsār*, 171–74.

52. Jāhiz, *Tahdhīb Kitāb al-Hayawān*, 3:227, 258–59. See also the epistle on love of the homeland in Jāhiz, *Rasā'il al-Jāhiz*, ed. 'Abd al-Salām Muhammad Hārūn, 4 vols. (Cairo: Maktabat al-Khānjī, 1964), 2:388ff.

53. André Miquel, *La géographie humaine du monde musulman jusqu'au milieu du 11e siècle*, 4 vols. (Paris: Mouton, 1967–), 1:58.

54. Jāhiz, *Kitāb al-Amsār*, 173.

55. Jāhiz, quoted in Mahmūd ibn 'Umar Zamakhsharī, *Al-Muhādarāt wa-al-Muhāwarāt*, MS no. 6865, Zāhiriyya, Damascus, fol. 54a.

The Experience of the Voyage

When Mas'ūdī criticizes the *Book of Capital Cities*—a book that in other
ways he finds admirable—he does so in the name of the principle of the
voyage. His reservations are aimed less at the work itself, however, than
at its author, whom he reproaches for having traveled little or not at all,
and thus for having subordinated his descriptions of the lands and cities
that he evokes to evidence supplied by others. Mas'ūdī wants true geographical knowledge to draw its substance, first and foremost, from the
geographer's own visual experience. The more a geographer traveled, the
greater and the surer was his grasp of the *oikoumene*. If Jāhiz had visited
India and seen the Ganges, and if he had visited Egypt and observed the
Nile, he would not have given the two rivers a common source under the
pretext that they both had crocodiles. He would have known that "the Indus rises from well-known sources situated in the high country of the Sind,
on the territory of Kanodj, a dependency of the kingdom of Biruza, the
Kashmir regions, the Kandahar, and the Thakka, and that it then enters
into the Multan, where it is given the name of Mihran." Where knowledge
demanded direct observation, Jāhiz had been content either with a false
analogy deduced from the existence of crocodiles in the two rivers, or with
information drawn from whimsical sources.[56]

Mas'ūdī could legitimately correct the errors of his compatriot Jāhiz
(they were both Iraqi and had lived in Baghdad) because he himself had
traveled extensively. He had journeyed as far as India to the east and
Andalusia to the west, north as far as the Caspian Sea and south as far
as Zanzibar. He used his vast travel experience and his exemplary erudition to write a monumental *Universal History*, lost today but present in
a condensed version in his famous *Golden Prairies*. Aside from revealing
his extensive travel experience, *Prairies* is a striking work as much for the
bulimic eclecticism of its author as for his ample erudition and his match-
less spirit of curiosity, qualities that inspired Carra de Vaux to paint his
portrait:

56. In Jāhiz's day, there was a firm belief that the two rivers had the same source. His contemporary Ibrāhīm ibn Fazārūn, who had traveled in India, had learned from its inhabitants that
"the Mihran and the Nile have the same source [*sic*]": Ibn Abī Usaybi'a, *'Uyūn al-Anbā' fi Tabaqāt
al-Atibbā'* (Cairo, 1886; reprint, Beirut, 1965). That representation is also tied to the belief that
the rivers of paradise all rose at the same point, a belief also shared by Christians in the Middle
Ages: Jean de Joinville, *Histoire de Saint Louis*, ed. Natalis de Wailly (Paris, 1874), 103–5; quoted in
Jacques Le Goff, *Saint Louis* (Paris: Gallimard, 1996), 555–56.

His mind is open to all the systems, from the philosophies of the legendary sages to the multiple doctrines of the sects of his own time. A historian of religions, he extended his research far: he knew about Mazdaism, Sabaenism, and Buddhism, and he possessed abundant information on Christians and Jews. In the course of his voyage he personally questioned the doctors and savants of various nations, Jews, Persians, Christians, Kurds, and Qarmations; he conversed or argued with them, bringing to these interviews as much affability as curiosity, as much intelligence as little fanaticism . . . and it is not without astonishment that one sees him combine with the Muslim faith that taste for scientific investigation and that ease in commerce with infidels.[57]

If we remember how deeply Mas'ūdī had imbibed Hellenistic culture, comparison with his compatriot Jāhiz is unavoidable. Both men were incarnations of the traits of the great minds of the Middle Ages: a spirit of openness and an insatiable desire to embrace everything. That Mas'ūdī placed his own work, at least in part, under the sign of adventure is indicative of his great curiosity. That he opens the work with praise of the voyage is a way of declaring the virtues of *autopsia*. Far from functioning as a literary theme typical of the genre of the *Adab*—which appears to be the case with Ibn al-Faqīh, for example[58]—this praise goes beyond simple ornament. It is emphasized as a self-reference with a function of address: it presents a man who knows what he is talking about because he has traveled much. This direct address is amplified by the swarm of enunciations implying the voyage scattered through the text: "I have seen in the city of Istakhr in the Fārs . . ."; "I have seen, in the year 324, at Tiberias . . ."; "When we traveled through the land (of the Kurds) . . ."; "We traveled through the lands of Fārs, Kermān, and Sijistan, both in their cold parts and in their hot zones, and we have seen that . . .". As modalities of truth telling, all of these manifestations of "I have seen," "I have noted," "I have observed" function to establish the necessary ties between vision and persuasion and to attest to the truth of the narration:

> This is what I have seen in India, in the region of Cambay, famous for the noisy sandals that are made there, and in neighboring cities such as Sandan and Sufara. I was thus in Cambay in the year 915–16, when a brahmin named

Bānyā reigned there in the name of Ballaharà, the sovereign of Mankir. This Bānyā was very interested in discussions with the Muslims and the sectarians of other religions who arrived in his country. The city of Cambay is situated on a deep gulf, larger than the Nile, the Tigris, or the Euphrates, whose banks are covered with towns, sharecrop farms, cultivated fields, and gardens planted with coconut palms, and between these gardens and these waters, peacocks, parrots, and other sorts of Indian birds. Between the city and the sea that forms this bay, there is a bit less than two days [of travel]. However, the incoming tide is so strong that one can easily distinguish the sand that lies beneath it, and that only a little water remains in the very middle of the gulf. I saw a dog lying on the sand that the water had left dry and that resembled a desert; suddenly the flux [of the incoming tide] coming from the open water, advanced like racing horses; the dog, sensing [the danger], began to run with all his force to escape the water and get to dry land inaccessible to the tide, but the rapid and impetuous flow reached him in his race and submerged him.[59]

In this description of the incoming tide Mas'ūdī displays an admirable quality of writing and sense of detail. If seeing is an art, describing what one sees incontestably requires as much as if not more talent. Mas'ūdī does not let the language spontaneously dictate its own rules of organization to him. To the contrary, he uses a writing strategy that breathes life and emotion into his narration. By dramatizing a natural phenomenon—here the desperate race of a dog against the onrushing water—the narration transforms the incoming tide into a spectacle for the reader. Even if this is a narrative technique put to the service of observation, that fact is worthy of note. Once again, Mas'ūdī's methods recall those of Jāhiz.

The two men are also alike in the explanation that they give of the tides. Like his elder, Mas'ūdī rejects mythical interpretations and adopts a scientific theory espoused by the philosopher Kindī (d. 260?/874), the author of a treatise on the seas in which the tide is explained by the movement of the winds and the stars.[60] Jāhiz, without citing his source, offers

59. Mas'ūdī, *Murūj al-Dhahab*; Barbier de Meynard and Payet de Courteille translation, 1:102.

60. "The displacement of the waters of the sea, in these two directions, north and south, is [precisely] what is called flux and reflux; [for] it is to be remarked that what is flux in the south is reflux in the north, and that what is flux in the north is reflux in the south. When the moon happens to meet one of the planets during one of its displacements, the two actions coming to corroborate each other mutually, the heat increases and the flow of air intensifies, which brings on a violent rolling of the waters of the sea toward the coast opposed to the one where the sun is to be found. This opinion that the sea follows the movement of the winds is that of Kindī and of Ahmad ibn Tayyib al-Sarakhsī": Ibid., 1:102.

a similar explanation in his *Book of the Round*. Mas'ūdī's source is Sarakhsī (d. 286/899), a disciple of the philosopher who was the presumed author of "a fine work on routes and kingdoms, seas and rivers, [and] the histories of various lands."[61] The explanation places the tenth-century encyclopedist in the wake of Jāhiz. Like his illustrious predecessor, Mas'ūdī read deeply in the Greek authors (Ptolemy, Aristotle, Galen, and more) and their Muslim imitators.

Mas'ūdī had at least read Aristotle's *Metaphysics* and his *Generation of Animals*, two treatises that nourished Jāhiz's reflection. It is hardly surprising that, like his compatriot, Mas'ūdī should plead the cause of "what one can see with one's own eyes, by direct experience." The suspicion with which he regards certain informants is also typical of Jāhiz. Sailors, he states, report facts to which they claim to be "ocular witnesses," but he sets himself at a quite visible distance from their statements. With him, writers begin to doubt informers who "claim that . . ." How to distinguish the good grain from the chaff in what they say? Mas'ūdī gives no clear answer to that question, but when he uses "his effort of personal interpretation [*ijtihād*]" to validate certain reports, invalidate others, and treat still others warily, his method becomes evident. For him, the *ijtihād* is a hermeneutic procedure that allows him to subject statements to rational criteria of judgment. As he states,

> I have remarked that the navigators of Sīrāf and the Oman who sail the seas of China, India, the Sind, Zanzibar, Yemen, Qulzum [the Red Sea] and Abyssinia furnish information about the Indian Ocean that differs, for the most part, from that given by the philosophers and the other [scholars], according to whom we have indicated the dimensions and the surface area of the seas; they even claim that in certain places the immensity of the waters has no limit. I have made the same observation in the Mediterranean [inquiring among] captains of warships and commercial vessels, commanders and officers, and those who are charged with the organization of the military marine. . . . All of them exaggerate the length and breadth of the Mediterranean, [and] the number of its gulfs and ramifications.[62]

61. The book is entitled *Kitāb al-Masālik wa-al-Mamālik*. On its author, who was first a preceptor then a counselor of the caliph Mu'tadad, see Qiftī, *Tārīkh al-hukamā*, 77, where his name is given as Ahmad ibn Muhammad Sarakhsī.

62. Mas'ūdī, *Murūj al-Dhahab*; Barbier de Meynard and Peyet de Courteille translation, 1:92.

This "verity" is confirmed by a Syrian ship's captain, a man known as "the [seaman] best informed about the Mediterranean and the oldest." His experience and age, but also his intelligence and skill, made him an informant who could be trusted and a man listened to by the seafaring people who sought his advice. Everything combined to make him a witness worthy of confidence, including his many campaigns in the service of the struggle against the infidel. In presenting him, Mas'ūdī defines the criteria for the selection of the perfect ocular witness: age, experience, intelligence. To these objective criteria he adds others of a moral and religious nature. Together they define the legal condition of a man who is as prestigious as he is endowed with the aura of a champion of God's combat.

Mas'ūdī solicits witnesses as trustworthy as this captain, citing their names and painstakingly noting the date on which he met them. Others are drowned in the anonymity of the multitude. Why cite the names of persons who "say they have observed" or "claim that"? This is the case of certain sailors from Oman who claim that in the Gulf of Aden waves as high as enormous mountains never break as waves do in other seas. How could anyone confirm or deny this sort of information? When he can do so, Mas'ūdī subjects statements to his own reason or his experience as a traveler. To confirm the gravity of the dangers that await in the Gulf of Aden and the Sea of Zanzibar, he cites his own experience:

> The Sirafians also make this crossing, and I have myself navigated on that sea, leaving from Sinjār, the capital of Oman, in the company of several Sirafian sailors, among others M. and D., who perished in that sea with his crew. My last crossing from the island [of Zanzibar] to Oman goes back to 916. I was on board a ship belonging to Ah. and Ab., both brothers of Ad. Those two persons later perished, body and goods, in that sea. . . . I have of course navigated on many seas, the China Sea, the Mediterranean, the Caspian, the Red Sea, and the Sea of Yemen, [and] I have run dangers without number, but I know of no [waters] more perilous than the Sea of Zanzibar.[63]

Even prophetic traditions were subjected to examination. Mas'ūdī knew all of the fables that the traditionists had transmitted about the tides, in which they appear as a supernatural phenomenon. In his approach to the question, we can see him operating in two ways: one of these uses rational methods and treats these traditions as "marvelous narratives invented

63. Ibid., 1:94.

after the fact" that spring from the "imagination of the traditionists"; the other applies internal criticism to them, attempting to decode the chains of transmission by which such tales had been handed down. The result was the same, one examination reinforcing the other.

As with Jāhiz, Mas'ūdī does not go so far in his investigative method as to reject the very principle of Tradition. His method consists uniquely in disqualifying certain traditions and validating others. Adhering to the method of the traditionists themselves, Mas'ūdī's first criterion of judgment (like that of Jāhiz before him) is to inspect the guarantees presented in their chains of transmission. In his critique of the marvelous traditions connected with the tides, Mas'ūdī declares: "The things that we have just recounted are neither absolutely impossible nor obligatory, but rather enter into the category of what is possible and admissible, for they are transmitted only by isolated individuals and do not bear the mark of those traditions that have been transmitted by an uninterrupted chain of informants and enjoy a great renown, so that their transmission imposes their adoption and makes them obligatory in both theory and practice."[64]

In attacking "isolated traditions" (āhād) not attested by convergent chains of reporters, Mas'ūdī places himself in a long line of critics of traditionist methodology that goes back to Abū Hanīfa (d. 150/767). The latter, a native of Kufa and a man considered one of Islam's most renowned jurists and known as the founder of a school of law that still exists, favored rejecting traditions of that type, even when the probity of the transmitter was beyond question.[65]

Nonetheless, in his critique of traditions, Mas'ūdī does not limit himself to an internal examination of their genealogy of transmission. For him, it is not enough that a hadīth enters into the category of renowned traditions for it to be acceptable. It must have one additional quality: "When traditions of that sort are accompanied by proofs that demonstrate their truth, one must accept them with submission." He dares go no farther: "One must conform to the narrations contained in scripture and put them into practice, because God imposes it on us when He says: 'Take what the

64. Ibid., 1:111.

65. Ibn 'Abd al-Barr, al-Intiqā fi fadā'il a'imma al-thalāthah (Cairo: Maktabat al-Qudsī, 1931), 149–50. Debate between the partisans of the āhād and its opponents continued throughout the dogmatic life of the Middle Ages. The polemic between the Andalusian Ibn Hazm (d. 456/1064) and his compatriot Abū al-Walīd al-Bājī (d. 494/1100), a champion of the āhād, is perhaps the last high point in this doctrinal conflict, which was settled in favor of the traditionists. See 'Abd al-Majid Turki, Polémiques entre Ibn Hazm et Bāgī sur les principes de la loi musulmane: Essai sur la littérature zāhirite et la finalité mālikite (Algiers: Études et documents, 1973).

Messenger assigns to you, and deny yourselves that which he withholds from you.'"[66]

Thus far we have been speaking of Mas'ūdī as a geographer, but he was really a historian—a historian with strong geographical preoccupations.[67] That his works combine geographical topics with history is a decided novelty on the intellectual scene in tenth-century Islam. This was a tradition well anchored in Greek culture from Herodotus to Ephorus and Polybius, where it not only reserved a prominent place for *autopsia*, but also led historians to take an interest in geography, without slighting their primary vocation. Mas'ūdī embraces that tradition thanks to his own intellectual experience, a quality that won him the admiration of great medieval historians such as Ibn Khaldūn, whose admiration for Mas'ūdī led him to take him as a model. He praises Mas'ūdī for having made "extensive travels in various countries," and in his introduction to the *Muqaddima* he expresses his regret for being unable to paint an overall picture of the lands and the peoples, the customs and the religious beliefs as vast as that of his illustrious predecessor because he had not yet traveled to the East.[68] That the historian must not rely on oral testimony and book sources alone but also provide his works with his own direct observations was an idea familiar to medieval historians. Thus, the *History of the Viziers* by Sūlī (d. 335/946) was admired as a fine work because its author had actually seen many of the events that he wrote about. One Egyptian historian took on the task of correcting the errors of one of his colleagues and compatriots on the basis of his own observations. His intention was to base his historical research on the principle of *autopsia*, but in his description of a device to measure the water level of the Nile he made use of the observations of a foreigner, the Andalusian traveler Ibn Jubayr![69] Moreover, although he was writing in the fifteenth century, he used a twelfth-century source as if it were contemporary. It is true that proclaiming a program of truth is one thing and carrying it out is quite another.

66. Qur'an 59:7.

67. Mas'ūdī views history as the mother of all the sciences, and he writes in its praise the most enthusiastic defense left by any tenth-century Muslim: "It is to history that all science owes its development: philosophy draws its teachings from it, jurisprudence consults it, eloquence puts it to profit, the specialists in analogy rely on it, the authors of philosophic theses [cannot do without it] for their argumentation": Mas'ūdī, *Murūj al-Dhahab*; Barbier de Meynard and Payet de Courteille translation, 2:374.

68. Ibn Khaldhūn, *Muqaddima*; trans. Vincent Monteil as *Discours sur l'histoire universelle*, 3 vols. (Beirut, 1967–68); 2nd ed. rev., 3 vols. (Paris: Sindbad, 1978), 1:62; trans. Franz Rosenthal as *The Muqaddimah: An Introduction to History*, 3 vols. (New York: Pantheon, 1958), 1:65.

69. Franz Rosenthal, *A History of Muslim Historiography* (Leiden: Brill, 1952), 176.

A discrepancy between intentions and their realizations is characteristic of medieval works, but the gap between the two varies from one author to another. Thus, while he admires Mas'ūdī, Ibn Khaldūn reproaches him for having accepted and transmitted "absurdities," on the say-so of dubious informants: one of these was the claimed "Copper City" that an imaginary geography situated in the desert of Sijilmasa. "The desert of Sijilmasa has been crossed by travellers and guides. They have not come across any information about such a city." He notes about this fable, "There are many similar things."⁷⁰ Mas'ūdī was simply peddling "suspect narratives." He went farther, however, when he attributed certain of these to himself. Thus, when he introduces a description of funerary ceremonies customary at the court of the king of Ceylon with "This is what I have seen in Ceylon," he is simply lying, and the "I have seen" that signals that the item is to be believed is usurped. The unwary reader does not realize this, however: he cannot verify that the entire passage is borrowed, with certain formal modifications, from an anonymous *Relation of China and India* written a century earlier.⁷¹

Historians are in agreement that most of the voyages claimed by Mas'ūdī were authentic. The fact that this Iraqi globe-trotter plagiarized the *Relation* does not cast doubt on the credibility of all of the information that he claims to have drawn from his own observations. Why, then, did he neglect to mention his source here? The question is all the more troubling because in other cases he specifies, with ample detail, his borrowings from the works that he consulted. Could this have been an unfortunate intervention on the part of a copyist?⁷² One might also, and more seri-

70. Ibn Khaldhūn, *Muqaddima*; Monteil translation, 1:75; quoted from Rosenthal translation, slightly edited, 1:75, 76.

71. "In Ceylon, when the king dies, he is placed on a low cart.": anonymous, *Abbār as-Sin wa l-Hind*; ed. and trans. Jean Sauvaget as *Relation de la Chine et de l'Inde rédigée en 851* (Paris: Belles Lettres, 1948). 22. This is not the only example of Mas'ūdī borrowing from the *Relation*. Jean Sauvaget writes: "The similarity is so manifest and the common elements so numerous that some have not hesitated to claim that in reality the *Relation* formed a part of the second edition of the *Prairies d'or* or of the *Chronique du siècle* or some other work by Mas'ūdī": ibid., xxiv. It seems that Mas'ūdī had access to the *Relation* by the intermediary of the author of its Complement. We can in fact read in the *Prairies d'or*: "Mas'ūdī: says, 'Abū Zayd Muhammad ibn Yazīd of Sirāf, who was the cousin of Mazyad ibn Muhammad ibn Abrad ibn Bastāshā [?], the master of Sīrāf, is an eminent and distinguished man, [and he] told me in Basra, where he had settled after leaving Sīrāf in 915–16 . . .": Mas'ūdī, *Murūj al-Dhahab*; Barbier de Meynard and Payet de Courteille translation, 1:130.

72. This has been demonstrated by Nehemia Levtzion in the case of Ibn Hawqal, for example. He challenges the notion that the latter really crossed the Sahara. The work in question in fact contains statements such as "I saw a bill in Awdaghost certifying a debt owed to one of them (of the people of Sijilmasa) by one of the traders of Awdaghost who was himself of the people of

ously, challenge the medieval habitus of taking liberties with material that was not yet called the literary property of others. In this light, Mas'ūdī's undeclared borrowings would fall under the category of practices inherent in the style of the *Adab*, in which case plagiarizing was no more disapproved of than repeating unlikely stories.[73] Mas'ūdī's works display two rival models of the *Adab*: the rationalist, "open" manner, represented by Jāhiz (d. 255/868), and the rhetorical, "closed" manner of Ibn Qutayba (d. 276/889).

Mas'ūdī's assimilation of the Jahizian type of the *Adab*, in which ocular experience is an essential source of knowledge, nonetheless distances him from many of the "geographers" of his times. In the fragments that have come down to us of his *Precious Finery*, Ibn Rusteh, for example, writes with a straight face: "The narratives that I have inserted in this work on the other cities [other than Isfahan, his birthplace] come only from reports, at times true, at times fragile, or from legends, on which I have had to rely, trusting persons whose information would have to be rectified before accepting them." It is only when he speaks of Isfahan that he can write: "What I can say [about that city] is the fruit of my personal experience or of information on which it was impossible to embroider, because I was not content with only one witness."[74] In fact, the questionable statements found in Mas'ūdī's writings only prove that his works are inscribed within the cultural horizon of the *Adab* as a genre. To be sure, Mas'ūdī made the better choice between an *Adab* like the closed, enumerative, and bookish compilation of Ibn Qutayba and the version of Jāhiz, more open to curiosity about the world, more focused on comprehension, research, and experimentation, and in search of a synthesis (a synthesis forever renewed thanks, precisely, to the importance of the ocular experience). Admittedly, after Jāhiz had turned the *Adab* upside down with his paradigm

---

Sijilmasa." But Nevtzion believes that this is a copyist's error, or perhaps an extrapolation from something like "I saw a bill (or a cheque) of a debt owed by Muhammad ibn Abī Sa'dīn, written in Awadaghost": Nehemia Levtzion, "Ibn Hawqal, the Cheque and Awdaghost," *Journal of African History* 9 (1968): 223–33.

73. Jean Sauvaget rightly recalls that Mas'ūdī was not the only medieval author who plagiarized the *Relation*: "Many authors had no hesitation about exploiting it without saying a word, and among them there were estimable writers: Ibn al-Faqīh, Idrīsī, Quzwīnī, and epecially Mas'ūdī and Bīrūnī, [who are] as illustrious as they come": *Relation de la Chine et de l'Inde*, Sauvaget translation, xxviii.

74. Ibn Rusteh, *al-A'lāq al-Nafīsah*; trans. Gaston Wiet as *Les atours précieux* (Cairo: Société de Géographie d'Égypte, 1955), 175. André Miquel is mistaken when he poses the question of "whether he had traveled": Miquel, *La géographie humaine*, 1:193. Not only does Ibn Rusteh state that he had made a pilgrimage to Mecca, but he presents his description of Egypt as coming from his own experience: *A'lāq*; Wiet translation, 132–33.

of sight, Mas'ūdī was among those who subjected it to the revolution of
the voyage, even though he did not fully embrace all of its obligations. We
have to wait for the founders of human geography before an obligation of
travel became a rule.

A Clinical Look at Muslim Verismo

In Mas'ūdī's day, the urge to travel had inspired geography for a sufficiently long time that no one still wrote like Balādhurī (d. 279?/892?)—that
is, holding fast to the paradigm of hearing[75]—or like Ibn al-Faqīh[76]—who
carried on the *Adab* as it had been reduced to a system by Ibn Qutayba
(d. 276/889).[77] It was men such as Ya'qūbī, Muhallabī, Istakhrī, Ibn
Hawqal, and Muqqaddasī who helped to breathe life into the new geographical paradigm.

I shall follow three of these geographers—Ya'qūbī, Ibn Hawqal, and
Muqqaddasī—in my analysis of the major articulations of the invention
of geographical vision in the tenth century. Better than any others, their
works embody the ruptures made in geography that made the voyage a
principle of description. Ya'qūbī (d. 284/897) is credited with "the highest
honor for having understood that literature and travel were not two self-
contained worlds totally separate from one another."[78] A great traveler, it
seems that he left Iraq at a young age to go to Armenia. We next meet him
in Khurasan, at the court of the Tāhirids, then in India. After a return to
the central lands of Islam he was named a functionary in Egypt at a date
difficult to determine. It may have been while he was based there that he
traveled as far as the central Maghreb, where he frequented the court of
the Rustumids of Tahert in what is now Algeria. When he considers the
man's journeys and visits to 'Abbāsid and dissident principalities, Gaston
Wiet wonders whether he might have belonged to the "dangerous postal

75. Balādhurī's *Book of Conquests* opens with the words "Ahmad ibn Yahiā ibn Jābir has said:
'I have been informed by a group of specialists of traditions of the military action of the Prophet
and the [Muslim] wars of conquest, whose words I have followed and summarized": Balādhurī,
Kitāb Futūh al-Buldān, ed. M. J. de Goeje (Leiden, 1866). Each item is preceded by "So-and-So has
said" or "They have said."

76. Ibn al-Faqīh sets the tone for his *Book of Lands*, written around 903, in the introduction,
where he writes: "I have put into this work only the historic traditions, verses, citations, and
[exemplary] sayings that my memory has grasped and that I have been able to hear": Ibn al-Faqīh,
Kitāb al-Buldān; Massé translation, 3.

77. On the geographical conception of this polymath, see Miquel, *La géographie humaine*,
1:66–68.

78. Ibid., 1:101; Gérard Lecomte, *Ibn Qutayba, l'homme, son oeuvre, ses idées (mort en 276/889)*
(Damascus: Institut Français de Damas, 1965).

service."[79] Be that as it may, Ya'qūbī's book was written more for functionaries than for general readers. Addressing himself to representatives
of power, he writes soberly. He has none of the literary pretensions of the
great prose writers of the ninth century. But if he did not have the talent
of a great writer, neither did he have the faults of the *Adab* genre that appear in one of his contemporaries, who also wrote a *Book of Lands* but made
ample room in it for the marvelous and for traditional literary themes of
his times (such as the theme of exile). Nonetheless, unlike another high
functionary of the postal system, Ibn Khurdādhbeh, who wrote a work of
geography that relies exclusively on oral reports from voyagers and merchants, Ya'qūbī's book was written out of his own travel experience. This
in itself was an essential rupture with all the ways of doing geography that
had succeeded one another during the ninth century. For the first time in
Islam, there was a man who traveled in order to write a work of geography,
whose personal experience of the world is thus embedded in his work. He
states, in introduction to his *Book of Lands*: "In the flower of my young age,
at a time when I possessed a full acuity of mind and a great vitality and intelligence, I did my utmost to know the history of the world, as well as the
distances that separate one state from another. This penchant came to me
as a consequence of uninterrupted voyages that I made, beginning in my
childhood, and that long kept me far away from my native soil."[80]

When he emphasizes that his taste for history and geography had
launched him on the routes of the voyage at a very early age, Ya'qūbī is
giving us more than a biographical detail: he is setting up an instance of
the truth saying that permits him to speak more legitimately about the
lands that he has visited than someone who speaks of them without ever
having left home. This was undeniably an innovation in the field of human
knowledge in the Middle Ages. However, if there is hardly any doubt that
it brought on new things, it was nonetheless firmly anchored in the paradigm of hearing, with which it made no definitive break. By remaining,
at least in part, under the grip of the principle of Tradition, it was not far
from what the linguists were doing when they went into the desert to collect the pure language of the Bedouins from the mouths of its presumed
speakers. It is significant that Ya'qūbī, who tells us that he traveled to
write his *Book of Lands*, never declares that he did so in order to extend the
range of his ocular experience. Quite the contrary, he states that he traveled to meet other men who could give him information. Thus, Ya'qūbī's

79. Ya'qūbī, *Kitāb al-Buldān*; trans. Gaston Wiet as *Les pays* (Cairo, 1937), viii.
80. Ibid.; Wiet translation, 2.

conceptual tools lack the notion of the thing seen expressed in the ideas of *'iyān* and *mushāhada*. This means that some nuance is called for in a statement as decided as the following: "What triumphs with Ya'qūbī . . . is, as with his great successors, the attention given to direct observation [*'iyān*], explained and supported by a deep-rooted rationalism; in a word, the repudiation of the *Adab* as a system that explains culture, to the profit of investigation without any intermediary."[81] Ya'qūbī's own working method, as he details it in the introduction to his book, invites caution. He tells us himself that his method is not—at least in his explicit statement—to practice *autopsia*, but rather to interview witnesses from "far-off lands" so as to compare their reports and then verify them with "men worthy of confidence." Once information has been examined and verified, it can be written down. We are in the presence of a method that we have seen at work among traditionists, linguists, genealogists, and prose writers. But whereas those specialists compiled their items according to the archaic form of the tradition as narrative, Ya'qūbī organizes his oral sources—and this is an essential difference with the partisans of the paradigm of hearing—within the discursive framework of description. To be sure, the literary genre of the *Adab* had long made use of the procedures and resources of description. Ya'qūbī's descriptive strategy does not aim at a literary effect, however. Attentive to objectivity, its sole concern is to render an account according to a previously established questionnaire program in which nothing is left to chance. Tenth-century geography was to perceive the interest of such a questionnaire, arranged around a triple discourse blending political, social, and physical geography.

It is not because of any lack of knowledge that Ya'qūbī chose a model of writing so stripped down that it approaches enumeration, but rather by methodological choice. He possessed the culture of the *Adab*, but he refused to adopt its models and its themes. Similarly, he was well aware of the theory of climates of Greek geography, but he refused to organize his own description according to its categorizations. As a geographer of the Islamic empire, he made a deliberate choice of a plan of exposition dictated by political considerations, all of them focused on asserting (or reasserting) the 'Abbāsid primacy. This plan, which opens with his description of Baghdad, is divided into "four parts, according to the directions of the cardinal points."[82] Is it necessary to point this out? Despite appearances, dividing up geographical space has nothing spontaneous or

81. Miquel, *La géographie humaine*, 1:287.
82. Ya'qūbī, *Kitāb al-Buldān*, Wiet translation, 64.

fortuitous about it. The political considerations that governed his choice should not induce us to forget that he was reviving an ancient model of the representation of the inhabited world that rivaled that of the Greeks and that made Iraq the omphalos of the world. Consequently, there is no doubt that Yaʻqūbī had a good knowledge of the learned culture of his epoch. If we look to his works on historical subjects, we see that they show proof of his erudition.[83] The sole purpose of his spare writing style was to respond to the dual objective of presenting geographical learning as concrete knowledge and of satisfying the expectation of specific readers. The work of a functionary, the *Book of Lands* never forgets that is primarily addressed to other functionaries who need concrete and operational information. Of an administrative cast, it had immediate and utilitarian objectives. In the final analysis, it was concrete needs that determined its author's writing choices.

But the great maturity of Yaʻqūbī's writing style should not be used to hide inconsistencies in his method. Ocular witness and written proof are curiously absent, even though he makes use of direct observation and completes his information by using administrative and fiscal documents.[84] All of the constituent elements of what was to be the method of the tenth-century geographers are present in him. The voyage is there, and various means of investigation—ocular experience, oral witness, and the written document—are present as well. But the method has not yet blossomed into an explicit formulation. It has not yet achieved ways for thinking about itself. The task of effecting a total rupture between geography and the cultural system of the *Adab* and of deepening the epistemological revolution begun by Yaʻqūbī was to fall to others, in particular, to Istakhrī and Ibn Hawqal.[85]

I have opted to discuss only one of these two tenth-century geographers, Ibn Hawqal, because although that rupture is at work in Istakhrī, Ibn Hawqal, his heir, thought it through more completely. With Ibn Hawqal, geography became a science of the concrete and the geographer became an investigator motivated to do a "thorough study . . . of research

83. His knowledge of Greek culture must have been appreciable, given that he tells us that he had written a *History of the Greek Empire*: Yaʻqūbī, *Kitāb al-Buldān*, Wiet translation, 64.

84. Ibid., 325.

85. Yaʻqūbī's combination of geographical and historical themes is a sign of the methods of the *Adab*. He writes: "I have thus furnished the nomenclature of the capital cities, the military colonies, and the provinces. . . . One will find the distances that separate one country from another, one capital from another, *the name of the generals of the Muslim armies who have conquered one land or another, the date of that event, the year and season*, the total for land taxes, etc.": ibid., 3, my emphasis.

on conditions . . . and of the information gathered." In the introduction to his work, he emphasizes the "great diversity of observations and information." That diversity is all the richer in meaning because it is the harvest of "uninterrupted voyages."[86] Thanks to his "own research" and his "personal inquiries," Ibn Hawqal claims to describe, in each land he visits, each territory he travels through, "the veritable state of things" and "real situations." Because he conceives of geography as a concrete science, he places his inquiry under the sign of the real, which he appropriates by means of the voyage and the sense experience that travel implies. Of all the senses, he solicits sight in particular. He punctuates his narrative with continual references to his own actions, saying "I noted," "I established," "I gave," "I verified," "I collected." And because of his great "desire to render the description with success," he is extremely exacting, scrupulously collecting and compiling his materials. Unlike his predecessors, he wants to avoid becoming a prisoner of "the tales of informers or the lies of ignorant voyagers." He encourages his reader to use his own judgement so he will always "choose the truth."

The path that he invites the reader to take is not really new, however, because the book is inscribed—as its title recalls—in the tradition of the "configuration of the land" type of geography that emerged from the Greek heritage and that an impressive movement of translation, begun in the late eighth century, had made accessible in Arabic. But because Ibn Hawqal himself had not started down his road of servile imitation, he invites the reader to admire his innovations. Although he does not inventory all his ruptures with the conception of geography of Balkhī and his school,[87] he tells how he enriched cartographic geography:

> I have summarily noted the figures for distances, furnished an adequate
> description of cities, without omitting the other indispensable details. . . . I
> have clearly given the name of the places in each region treated, shown the
> junction lines of the border portions, indicated the dimensions of each canton
> with its configuration. . . . I have given precise information on the district [and
> about] the placement of each town in relation to the nearest locality. . . . Thus,

86. "I began these voyages by leaving Baghdad on Thursday 7 Ramadan of the year 331 [15 May 943]. . . . I was at the time in the prime and the freshness of age, in the flower and the inebriation of youth, with a remarkable capital of vigor and energy": Ibn Hawqal, *Kitāb Sūrat al-Ard*; Kramers and Wiet translation, 3.

87. On these ruptures, see Miquel, *La géographie humaine*, 1:293–94; and J. H. Kramers, "La question Balhī-Istarī-Ibn Hawkal et l'*Atlas de l'Islam*," *Analecta Orientalia* 10 (1932): 9–30, reprinted in the series Islamic Geography, ed. Fuat Sezgin, no. 31 (1992), 326–47.

whoever uses this map will have a clear idea of the placement, the situation, and the topography of each region, as well as of the thorough study that I have made of its disposition and its configuration.[88]

Better than in the geography of the "configuration of the land" of the school of Balkhī, with Ibn Hawqal the spectacle of the world can be stated and read on two mutually supportive levels, one cartographic, the other narrative. While one of these represents the inhabited world iconically, the other relates it in the form of a narrative. How does Ibn Hawqal eliminate the epistemological obstacle that had confronted Balkhīan geography? Essentially by firmly attaching it to the principle of the voyage. Because the voyage becomes an empirical mode of investigation, it guides the collection of information—a store of information that is necessarily considerable, given the project that it is destined to serve—but also its verification and rectification. Once that information has been collected and confirmed, it is organized, thus gaining in coherence and rationalization. Cartography, in return, draws profit from this collection of information by having available more ample and richer material. But because Ibn Hawqal refuses to be satisfied with a schematic representation, he moves in the direction of the only discursive framework truly capable of responding to the program of truth of an empirical geography: explanatory discourse of a descriptive sort.

The new geography emancipated itself from mathematics and astronomy because it was determined to be resolutely empirical. For that reason, it required that its specialists cover vast spaces. That might take years, at times decades, of investigation, which placed geographical learning in the long term. Scholars estimate that Ibn Hawqal worked more than twenty years at the writing of his work, but we know that he began to travel in 943 and that his book reached its definitive form around 988, which means that we should think of a longer period. And if we recall that his *Configuration of the Land* is itself presented as a corrected and completed edition of the *Book of Itineraries* of Istakhrī (whom Ibn Hawqal may have met in 951), we will have to stretch our calculation even farther.

Like Istakhrī and Ibn Hawqal, Muqaddasī was to pay a heavy tribute of time. He waited until he had reached the age of forty and had stopped traveling to compose his work. With Muqaddasī human geography reaches its maturity, a maturity that unfortunately was never equaled. Although he brought nothing new to what Istakhrī and Ibn Hawqal had already

88. Ibn Hawqal, *Kitāb Sūrat al-Ard*; 2.

accomplished, his art consisted in rigorously thinking through the bases of the new discipline.

Muqaddasī makes use of architectonic images to describe his methodology. He conceives of his work as an edifice seated on "firm foundations" and supported by "powerful pillars." But if the armature of his book gives it solidity and cohesion, it includes other elements that, although erratic, are no less necessary to the whole. The most solid part of this building—the foundation and bearing walls—is made up of the facts that the geographer has "witnessed and understood, learned and noted." Muqaddasī states, "Thus have I raised the building, and established its columns and pillars." He is so vehement in his assertion of the heuristic value of *autopsia* that he seems ready to think himself the only geographer to have made judicious use of ocular evidence. When he proclaims loudly that "there is not a single region I have not visited," it is to give credit to the idea that nearly all of his detractors have been lazy, contenting themselves with auricular information alone. A man sure of his entitlement, he describes for his reader the troubles that he has endured in order to put his work on a new base:

> I have been given thirty-six names, by which I have been called and addressed . . . all this on account of the various countries in which I have lived, and the many places I visited. Nothing remains of what befalls travellers that did not fall to my lot, barring only begging, and the commission of grievous sin. I . . . consumed *harīsa* with the Sūfis, *tharīd* (broth) with the cenobites, and *'asīda* [flour, butter, and honey pudding] with seamen. I was ejected in the night from mosques, have wandered in the steppes, gone astray in the deserts; at times I have been scrupulously abstinent, while again, at other times, have openly eaten forbidden foods. I have associated with the devotees of Jabal Lubnān (Mount Lebanon), also been on intimate terms with those in power. . . . A number of times I was close to drowning, and our caravans have been robbed on the highway. . . . I have kept company on the road with the licentious, and sold goods in the marketplaces. I have been confined in prison, and accused as a spy; I have myself witnessed the warrings of the Romaeans in warships, and the striking of bells in the night [at Christian meetings]. I have bound books for profit, bought water at high prices; have traveled in litters and on horseback; trudged in the hot sandstorms, and the snows. . . . I have made the Pilgrimage, and lived in the dependency of the mosque; I have fought in raids, when doing service at frontier posts. . . . I have had dire experience of pickpockets, and seen firsthand the artifices of scoundrels. Miscreants have hounded me, the envious opposed me, I have been slandered before

the rulers. I have entered the baths of Tabariyya and the fortresses of Persia; I have witnessed the Festival of al-Fawwāra (the Fountain) and the Feast of Barbārah [celebrated December 4], also visited the Well of Budhāʿah, the castle of Jacob, and his villages.[89]

One might think that Muqaddasī is using rhetorical resources just to dazzle the reader, but what he says is not pure boasting. His entire work bears witness to a vast travel experience, which gives his work its picturesque aspect and a scintillating brilliance. No other description of Muslim geography attains the same degree of density in its picture of social life as it was actually lived. That a geographer-traveler's narrative was able to embrace so strongly and so happily the social reality that it describes can perhaps be ascribed to the degree of maturity reached by the discipline itself, which unfortunately would soon reach saturation, incapable of renewal by exploring other possibilities. Muqaddasī's personality came into play as well. Among all of the geographers of his era, he was incontestably the one who best took on the role of the complete voyager. If, as Claude Lévi-Strauss points out, "a journey occurs simultaneously in space, in time and in the social hierarchy,"[90] then Muqaddasī was just as much an explorer of space and time as a social climber. Those three types of displacement, coupled with a consummate skill for observation, allowed his curiosity regarding humankind to find satisfaction and full development. The procedures he uses are not always the ones approved by morality. Duplicity, lying, cheating, imposture—all means were good. A magician of social infiltration, Muqaddasī pierced secrets. His habit of picking up data on the sly from those whom he targeted as a way to observe things "from the inside" amounts to espionage, a technique for which he may have been prepared by his clandestine activities as a missionary, a propagandist, and an Ismaili conspirator. The most dependable subterfuge, in such circumstances, is to change identity as often as necessary and to pass for someone else. A mocking impostor, Muqaddasī accumulates his adventures like fantastic mininovels.[91] Harīrī (d. 516/1122) was to use similarly hilarious situations

89. Muqaddasī, *Ahsan al-Taqāsīm*; Collins translation, 3, 45–46.

90. Claude Lévi-Strauss, *Tristes tropiques* (Paris: Plon, 1955), 94; quoted from *Tristes Tropiques*, trans. John and Doreen Weightman (New York: Atheneum, 1974), 85.

91. Relating how he managed to fool the mystics of the town of Sūs by passing himself off as one of them, Muqaddasī writes: "When I approached them they did not doubt that I was a Sūfī, and received me with welcome and greeting, sat me down amongst them, and began questioning me. They then sent a man who brought some food, but I refrained from eating as I had not associated with this sect before that time. So they began to wonder at my abstention, and my refraining from their practices. I wished then that I had associated with this creed, and thus would have

to fill out the portrait of the famous hero-adventurer of his *Séances*.[92] But Muqaddasī did not always get out of his scrapes so easily. One day when he was accused of heterodoxy in Isfahan, he was nearly lynched by an angry mob stirred up by an ascetic.[93] He quite understandably observes: "There is a vast difference between the author who has endured these realities and one who, comfortably installed (at home), composes his work according to hearsay."[94]

Muqaddasī introduces a broad-based attack on his predecessors, whom he accuses of practicing a lazy geography based on hearsay, with the phrase "Evocation (or mention) of what I have lived as an adventure (*asbāb*)." In his translation of this chapter, André Miquel quite justly tightens the periphrase with the more suggestive phrase "*choses vues*" (things seen). What is important to note in this chapter is that the term *sabab*, which Muqaddasī uses to speak of the "elements" or the "components" of his geography, is precisely the same term by which he designates the things that he has seen and the situations that he has lived through. No other statement is needed to show that the voyage, more than a means for collecting information, was for him a methodological tool. His slogan could well have been "Without inquiry, no right to speak," for inquiry governs the status of the geographer just as much as it does that of geography. Because the geographer is by definition a voyager, and even a globe-trotter, geography does not hesitate to borrow its writing models from the travel narrative.

---

known their rituals and learned their truths. But I said to myself, 'This is your opportunity, for this is a place in which you are unknown.' Thereupon I opened up to them, and put off the mask of diffidence from my face; then sometimes I would converse with them, other times I would scream with them, then again I would read them the poems. And I used to go out with them to the cells, and attend their convocations, until, by God, they began to trust me, as did the people of the town to the extent I had never intended. I became famous there, visitors sought me out; clothing and purse were brought to me, and I took them and paid them for them completely on the spot, because I was rich. . . . They used to think that I was becoming ascetic. So people began to stroke my clothes (for a blessing), and proclaim an account of me, saying, 'We have never, never, seen a *faqīr* (Sūfī mendicant) more deserving than this man.' The result was that when I had learned their secrets, and found out what I wanted to from them, I fled them in the calm of the night. By morning I had put a long distance between us. Then when I was in al-Basra one day wearing my (Sūfī) clothing, my slave following behind me, a man of the Sūfīs saw me, and stopped and stared at me, apparently struck at the recognition. But I passed him as if I did not know him." Muqaddasī, *Aḥsan al-Taqāsīm*, 415; Collins translation, 368–69.

92. Abdel Fattah Kilito, *Les séances: Récits et codes culturels chez Hamadhānī et Harīrī* (Paris: Sindbad, 1983).

93. Muqaddasī, *Aḥsan al-Taqāsīm*, 399; Collins translation, 354.

94. Ibid.; Miquel translation, 114.

However, to the extent that the work aimed at being comprehensive, the personal involvement of the geographer did not derive, as it does in the travel genre, uniquely from the desire to give a literary translation of a singular experience, but rather from the functional work of *autopsia*, conceived as a heuristic means for producing positive knowledge. This is why, if the work of Muqaddasī is saturated with narrative marks of the voyage, those marks are strewn there, above all, as traces charged primarily with expressing the author's insistence on telling things as they are. Their grip is just as firm on the discursive strategy as it is on the mode of exposition. Muqaddasī warns his reader: "My reporting on those elements which I specified in my introduction will vary in completeness from one region to another, and will be uneven in its scope; for I relate only what I know absolutely. This science is not such that proceeds by analogy, or is always uniform; rather it may be fully attained only by observation and enquiry."[95]

Muqaddasī's argument in favor of *autopsia* is not exclusive, however. He does not go beyond the assertion of the positive quality of sight as a privileged tool for the land geographer. For the geographer knows that (except for making all more stringent logical inquiry impossible) ocular testimony cannot disqualify other sources of information. Given that the chosen method consists in operating with territorial units as vast as they are varied, how, from an objective viewpoint, could anyone embrace them by means of sight alone? If he wants to avoid aporia, the geographer is obliged to take into account the efficacy of other types of testimony. Two such sources of information seem to Muqaddasī unavoidable: hearing and the written word. He recalls this when he writes: "This book of ours, then, falls into three parts: first, what I myself have witnessed; second, what I have heard from persons worthy of confidence; and third, what I have found in books devoted to this subject, and other than this." This enumeration bears the marks of a discrimination among these "elements." Its order, which is epistemological, assigns to each of them a different place in the process of producing geographical knowledge.

After ocular testimony, Muqaddasī views oral inquiry as a second mode of investigation for his geography. But, in order to admit its validity, he imposes on it conditions so drastic that he restricts its field of application, which is simply a way of reasserting the subordination of the oral tradition to *autopsia*: "For that on which they [reliable informants] agreed, I accepted as authentic: that on which they differed, I rejected. Whenever it

95. Ibid., 19–20; Collins translation, 6.

was necessary that I myself should go to a place and make inquiries there,
I did so; whatever I found unsatisfactory, and that my reasoning would
not accept I have ascribed to the person who related it, or I have simply
written, 'it has been asserted.' I have supplemented my work, too, with
materials I came across in the royal archives (khazā'in)."[96]

Statements such as this singularly distance their author from the
method of the traditionists, to the extent that the oral material collected
does not claim to be authoritative in some exclusionary fashion, either in
itself or by its conditions of transmission alone. In order to deserve to be
trustworthy, each piece of information must be expressed and compared
with others. In order to accomplish that verification, Muqaddasī did not
wait for potential informants to come to him in their wanderings. He
sought them out himself, taking long voyages to do so. In 987, he was in
Mecca in the hope of encountering Andalusian pilgrims capable of helping him confirm details in his chapter on Spain.

But if Muqaddasī was capable of being offensive when it was a question of secular narratives, he was much more circumspect when it came
to religious ones. This prudence did not go so far as to make him accept
all of the rules set down by the traditionists, however. In fact, his attitude
was that of their sworn enemy, the great Iraqi jurist of the eighth century,
Abū Hanīfa (d. 150/767), for whom Muqaddasī displayed the greatest attachment, to the point of adopting his hermeneutic techniques of a "personal effort of interpretation" (ra'y), a "personal appreciation" (istihsān),
and "established usage" (ta'āruf). Like Abū Hanīfa, Muqaddasī admitted
prophetic traditions only if they had several chains of transmission guaranteeing their prominence. He rejected traditions that the traditionists
called "unilateral" (āhād) and accepted as valid even though they had been
transmitted by one line alone, as we have seen Mas'ūdī do. Muqaddasī's
criticism of the traditionists' method often reached the point of personal
hostility:

> One day I was in the mosque in Wāsit, when I saw a man there around whom
> a crowd of people had gathered. I approached the group and heard him
> declare: "So and so has related to us that he learned from so and so that the
> Prophet—God's peace and blessings be upon him—said that God would draw
> Mu'āwiya close to him on the Day of the Resurrection, and would seat him
> by His side. He would anoint him with His own hands, and display him to
> mankind as He would a bride." So said I to him: "Why should that be? Is it be-

96. Ibid., 11–12; Collins translation, 3.

cause he waged war with 'Alī? May God be pleased with Mu'āwiya, but you are
a liar, you misguided one." At this the man exclaimed: "Seize this unbeliever."
The crowd moved towards me, but one of the learned men there recognized
me, and restrained them.[97]

Still, just like the most intransigent of his predecessors, Muqaddasī
could not resist the temptation to borrow from the traditionists their
definition of the informant (or the transmitter) as a "person worthy of
trust" (*thiqa*). Like certain of them, he had his favorites. His Shiite sensibility made him prefer the traditions that went back to the caliph 'Alī or
concerned him, to the point of relaxing his vigilance.[98] His sympathy for
Abū Hanīfa was based on that Iraqi jurist's pro-'Alī stance. This penchant
could perhaps be interpreted as a consequence of Muqaddasī's missionary
work for 'Alī's legitimism.

Muqaddasī boasts that there is no princely library that he has not frequented. The books that he had been able to consult there and the archives and documents to which he had gained access form his third source
of information. As with oral testimony, recourse to the written word did
not disqualify travel. Everywhere that Muqaddasī went in the Muslim
world, he made a point of visiting the private or princely libraries that were
opened to him. At Basra he completed his documentation in the library
founded by a secretary of state converted to rationalist Mu'tazilitism.[99]
That scribe's collection of books was so big that he enjoyed an international
reputation. It was the first of its kind, in Islam, to be set up as a private
foundation (*waqf*).[100] Thanks to his status as a public servant, his library
functioned as an institution for the public good, and its holdings and the
buildings containing them were inalienable. This confirms Muqaddasī's
statement that "subsidies were accorded to all those who went there and
applied themselves there to reading or transcribing works."[101] These subsidies were stipulated by the charter of the pious foundation. It is possible

97. Ibid., 127; Collins translation, 114–15.

98. Ibid.; Miquel translation, 108, for example.

99. Muqaddasī calls him Abū 'Alī ibn Sīwār al-Kātib; Ibn al-Nadīm says he was Abū al-Qāsim
al-Bistī. When he was writing his *Catalogue* (in 987–88), Ibn al-Nadīm knew the man only by reputation: "We will ask after that man and his books," he declares, "and we will reach his doorstep, if
God is willing": Ibn al-Nadīm, *Fihrist*, 139.

100. Youssef Eche, *Les bibliothèques arabes publiques et semi-publiques in Mésopotamie, en Syrie et
en Égypte au Moyen Âge* (Damascus: Institut Français de Damas, 1967), 100–101. According to Olga
Pinto, the library was burned by the Bedouins in 1090: Olga Pinto, "Le biblioteche degli Arabi
nell'età degli Abbassidi," *La Bibliofilia* 30 (1900): 139–65, esp. 151, cited by Eche.

101. Muqaddasī, *Ahsan al-Taqāsīm*, 413.

that as well as offering a roof and meals, this famous library also distributed paper, ink, and other supplies needed for transcription, as was the case with all similar institutions.

The other great library in which Muqaddasī worked on his book was the one that the Būyid ruler 'Adud al-Dawlah (r. 947–77) founded at Shirāz.[102] When that sovereign took the throne and made the Persian city his capital, he had his library fitted into one wing of the new palace that he had constructed. Muqaddasī has left us an admiring description of the internal architecture and organization of the library.[103] Richer than that of the Mu'tazilite doctor of Basra, this library was impressive both for its 360 rooms and for its collection of rare manuscripts.[104] Still, the Būyid sovereign had to admit that a secretary had beaten him in the race to found a great public library: "It is a work of public welfare in which we have been anticipated," he admitted regretfully.[105]

Besides frequenting the libraries of Iraq and Fārs, Muqaddasī consulted the holdings of at least two large libraries in Khurasan, one at Nishapur and the other at Rayy. The first was the work of the Sāmānid sovereigns, the second of the Būyid vizier Ibn 'Abbād (d. 385/995). We know little about the Sāmānid library, but we know that Ibn 'Abbād's library held several thousand works, to judge from the ten registers in which its holdings were listed. A sophisticated man of letters and an enlightened vizier, Ibn 'Abbād had the taste and the means to collect the most important works of his age. What is more, he was so attached to his library that when the Sāmānid prince Nūh ibn Mansūr (r. 943–54) invited him to move to his court as his vizier, he declined the offer, stating that he could not leave all of his belongings behind him at Rayy, and that if he moved, it would take a hundred camels just to transport his books.[106] Still in Sāmānid territory, Muqaddasī adds to the libraries that he had known another in far-off Bukhara, in Transoxiana, but he gives no details.

What did our geographer-voyager read in these libraries? First of all, the books of geography written by his predecessors: Jāhiz, Ibn Khurdādhbeh,

102. Ibid., 451; Collins translation, 396–97.

103. Ibid., 449; Collins translation, 396–97.

104. On this library, whose director was Ibn al-Buwwāb, one of the most famous calligraphers of the Middle Ages, see Johannes Pedersen, *The Arabic Book*, trans. Geoffrey French, ed. Robert Hillenbrand (Princeton: Princeton University Press, 1984), 123–24.

105. Ibn Athīr, *al-Kāmil fī al-tārikh*, 12 vols. (Beirut: al-Tibā'a wa'l-Nashr, 1982), 10:122; cited in Eche, *Les bibliothèques arabes*, 101.

106. When Mahmūd of Ghazna took over Rayy in 1029, in defense of orthodoxy he had the "heretical" books of this library burned and took the rest of the books to increase the holdings of his own library: see Pedersen, *The Arabic Book*, 122; Eche, *Les bibliothèques arabes*, 324.

Abū Zayd of Balkh, Abū 'Abd-Allāh al-Jayhānī, Ibn al-Faqīh of Hamadān, Istakhrī. This is the reading list of the great voyagers, almost all of whom traveled in the books of their predecessors. "After scrutiny of the archives and the books," Muqaddasī also consulted a number of maps, which he took it upon himself to complete: "As for the maps in which we have portrayed the countries, we made every effort to ensure their correctness, having carefully studied a number of drawings. Of these, one drawing I found in the library of the ruler of al-Mashriq, done on a sheet of paper in the form of a square, though on this I did not depend. Another drawing I came across, done on a piece of linen, was . . . also at Naysābūr, and square in shape. I saw, too, the drawings which Ibrāhīm al-Fārisī [Istakhrī] made, and these, coming closer to the facts, may be relied upon."[107]

Not only did our geographer pursue his investigations in the princely archives and the libraries, but he also completed his information with other documents. He makes a note of "registers" (perhaps portulans?) that he saw in the hands of seafaring men in the Persian Gulf and the Arabian Sea, stating, "From these sources I took copious notes of essential information, after I had studied them and evaluated them; and this I compared with the maps I have referred to."[108]

Muqaddasī's passion for books and written documents was shared by many of his predecessors. One of these, Mas'ūdī, displays it in his work as an insistence on rigor in his search for information. Among the books to which he had access, some were forbidden, circulated clandestinely by political agitators. He tells us: "I have seen . . . in the house of a freedman of the house of 'Umayya, a learned man of letters who belongs to the sect of the 'Uthmāniyya, a book of about three hundred leaves entitled *The Book of the Proofs of the Imamate of the Umayyads and of Their Many Merits.*" This was a work whose possessor would run a risk of condemnation before the 'Abbāsid courts. Other works were important because they contained valuable archival documents. Mas'ūdī recounts:

I have seen, in the city of Istakhr, in the house of a noble Persian family, a large book that contained the histories of the kings of Persia and of their reigns and the monuments that they raised, items that I have found in no other Persian books, neither in the *Khudāy Nāmuh*, nor in the *Āyīn-Nāmuh*, nor in the *Kuhan Nāmuh*, nor anywhere else. It pictures the kings of Persia, twenty-seven in number, of whom two are women. . . . The book that I saw

107. Muqaddasī, *Ahsan al-Taqāsīm*, 18; Collins translation, 6.
108. Ibid., 31; Collins translation, 10.

was written with the documents found in the treasury of the kings of Persia, and [it was] completed in the middle of [the reign of] Jumāda II [d. 113/731]. It was translated [into Arabic] for [the Umayyad caliph] Hishām ibn 'Abd al-Malik [r. 724–743].[109]

I shall put aside the question of the written word for the moment and return to it later.

Muqaddasī, Strabo, and Greek Science

According to André Miquel, the great merit of Muqaddasī was to have brought to its height a process begun almost a century earlier: the liberation of Muslim geography from its Greek attachments. But, Miquel continues, just as Muqaddasī's geography broke its connection to the Greek heritage, as if in compensation, it returned to the lesson of Strabo, the most illustrious of the descriptive geographers of antiquity. When Muslim geography arose under the caliph al-Ma'mūn (r. 813–33) thanks to Arabic translations of the works of Ptolemy and Marinus of Tyre, it was unacquainted with Strabo's works. When Muqaddasī encountered Strabo, he did so "through his own sources." For Miquel, the convergence of thought between the two men lies in their use of an imperial framework as a significant spatial unit and their desire to produce a "composite" work addressed to an enlightened but non-"specialized" readership and offer it the most widely known results of bookish erudition along with the results of the author's personal observation.[110]

The assertion that Muqaddasī's geography connects with that of Strabo is based on a misunderstanding. Not that the analogies that have been noted between the two works are false, but they are risky when taken at face value, as if they were of the same epistemological order. The misunderstanding resides, precisely, in the erroneous idea that the two geographers operated with the same presuppositions. They thought and wrote in two quite dissimilar cultural and cognitive contexts.

109. Mas'ūdī, *Kitāb al-Inbāh wa'l-Ishrāf*; trans. Bernard, baron Carra de Vaux as *Le livre de l'avertissement* (Paris, 1896), 151.

110. Miquel, *La géographie humaine*, 1:270–71. See also Germaine Aujac, *Strabon et la science de son temps* (Paris: Belles Lettres, 1966); Germaine Aujac, *La géographie dans le monde antique* (Paris: Presses Universitaires de France, 1975); Paul Pédech, *La géographie des Grecs* (Paris: Presses Universitaires de France, 1976); Claude Nicolet, *L'inventaire du monde: Géographie et politique aux origines de l'Empire romain* (Paris: Fayard, 1988); and François Hartog, *Mémoire d'Ulysse: Récits sur la frontière en Grèce ancienne* (Paris: Gallimard, 1996); trans. Janet Lloyd as *Memories of Ulysses: Frontier Tales from Ancient Greece* (Chicago: University of Chicago Press, 2001).

It is in fact difficult to comprehend what Strabo's intentions were if one does not know that he was disputing the validity of what might be called the mathematization of the world in the manner of Eratosthenes. Strabo himself speaks of that astronomer, mathematician, and philosopher as thinking he must make "a complete revision of the early geographical map"[111] around 245, about when Ptolemy III called him to be director of the Library of Alexandria. That project had been based on information gleaned from Alexander the Great's expedition and on the theorems of Euclidian geometry. Striving to make geography a scientific discipline allied to geometry, Eratosthenes attempted to give the *oikoumene* as precise a representation as possible. With an aim of that sort, the map could only operate as a "geometrical dispositive."[112] It was an approach to space that necessarily led to rejecting the Homeric representation of the world. It is as if he were saying, "Space needs to be disenchanted. Homer is not a dependable informant; he did not see and did not know; he was a poet who made fables, an author of fiction, not a geographer."[113]

Does this mean that the *mythos* was just lies and fabrications? It was in reaction to its depreciation that Strabo was protesting, following Polybius. He insisted, first, that geography was not affiliated with geometry, but with philosophy, and second, that Homer was speaking the truth. At that point Strabo, in defense of Ulysses—the man who knows because he has seen, the admirer of Gallus ("one of our good friends") who had brought back from his expedition in Arabia Felix knowledge that was both new and unprecedented—moved to operate within the framework of a problematic that conceded primacy of method to the ear over the eye. He writes, "And he who claims that only those have knowledge who have actually seen abolishes the criterion of the sense of hearing, though this sense is much more important than sight for the purposes of science." Germaine Aujac, Strabo's editor and French translator, thinks that he was brought to a defense of the superiority of hearing over sight uniquely as a

111. Strabo, *Geography*, 2.1.2; trans. Germaine Aujac et al. as *Géographie*, 9 vols. in 10 pts. (Paris: Belles Lettres, 1966–96), 2:1, 2; quoted from *The Geography of Strabo*, trans. Horace Leonard Jones, 8 vols., Loeb Classical Library (Cambridge, MA: Harvard University Press; London: William Heinemann, 1960), 1:255.

112. Christian Jacob, "Fonction des cartes géographiques," in Marcel Detienne and Giorgio Camassa, eds., *Les savoirs de l'écriture: En Grèce ancienne* (Villeneuve d'Ascq: Presses Universitaires de Lille, 1992), 295. See also Christian Jacob, *L'empire des cartes: Approche théorique de la cartographie à travers l'histoire* (Paris: Albin Michel, 1992); trans. Tom Conley as *The Sovereign Map: Theoretical Approaches in Cartography through History*, ed. Edward H. Dahl (Chicago: University of Chicago Press, 2006).

113. This passage is based on Hartog, *Mémoire d'Ulysse*, 113.

way to excuse himself for having limited personal experience.[114] This argument is hardly persuasive, because it simply consists in accusing Strabo of laziness. To counter such an accusation, Strabo himself writes: "I have travelled westward from Armenia as far as the regions of Tyrrhenia opposite Sardinia, and southward from the Euxine Sea as far as the frontiers of Etheopia. And you could not find another person among the writers on geography who has travelled over much more of the distances just mentioned than I; indeed, those who have travelled more than I in the western regions have not covered as much ground in the east, and those who have travelled more in the eastern countries are behind me in the western; and the same holds true in regard to the regions towards the south and north."[115]

Given his emphasis on his own extensive travels, one would expect Strabo to defend *autopsia* as the method of his descriptive geography. Against all expectation, however, he launches into a defense of auricular testimony, in favor of which he pleads, not by default, but for its intrinsic qualities. His defense is based on a theory of knowledge in which hearing enjoys an undeniable superiority over sight. Thus, he works on the basis of a theoretical choice, not governed by contingencies connected with his life experience. This choice situates Strabo with the Epicureans, for whom hearing is the instrument the most apt to furnish information at a distance.[116]

What Strabo attempts to demonstrate is that scholars operate in the same way as the intelligence. Scholars combine the oral information that comes to them just as the intelligence rearranges concepts *on the basis of the senses*.[117] Reiterating the idea that all the senses work together to elaborate concepts, Strabo adds: "Our senses report the shape, colour, and size of an apple, and also its smell, feel, and flavour; and from all this the mind forms the concept of apple. So, too, even in the case of large figures, while the senses perceive only the parts, the mind forms a concept of the whole

114. Strabo, *Geography*; Aujac translation, 1:36; Strabo quoted from Jones translation, 1:453.

115. Ibid., 2.5.11; Jones translation, 1:451.

116. Lucretius, *De rerum natura*, 4.595–615; Marie Laffranque, "La vue et l'ouïe: Expérience, observation et utilisation des témoignages à l'époque hellénistique," *Revue philosophique* 153 (1963): 75–82.

117. Strabo, *Geography* 2.5.11; Jones translation, 1:451. Germaine Aujac's translation gives "à partir des sens" here; the translation by Amédée Tardieu, *Géographie de Strabon* (Paris, 1886–90), a "still valuable translation," according to Marie Laffranque, gives "l'intelligence combine les différentes idées d'après le témoignage des sens." The Jones translation states, "The mind forms its ideas from sense impressions": 1:451.

from what the senses have perceived." Sight, like the other senses, is fragmentary. A third instance, "intelligence," has to intervene to surmount the
scattered nature of sense perceptions. Comparing the geographer to the
military strategist, Strabo imagines the scholar using partial information
to put together all of the aspects of the *oikoumene* in the same way that a
general of an army on a campaign would mix and synthesize the scattered
information that reaches him: "Why, generals, too, though they do everything themselves, are not present everywhere, but they carry out successfully most of their measures through others, trusting the reports of messengers, and sending their orders around in conformity with the reports
they hear." Even though the geographer may travel, he cannot reconsti-
tute the inhabited world by himself. Like the general in the field, he has to
rely on others. The best center of operations is, precisely, a good library.[118]
In this manner, Strabo restates, and without ambiguity, his preference for
indirect information and action via an intermediary.

If we return to the Muslim Middle Ages, we can see that just such a
theory was attached to what I have called the paradigm of hearing. With
one exception: instead of excluding the voyage, "Islamic" listening insisted
on it. From the opening paragraphs of his great *Inquiry on India*, Bīrūnī
(d. 442/1050) declares that he is relying on both auricular and written knowledge. However, his work is far from being the product of a compiler cozily
settled in among his books. Curious about the world, Bīrūnī was not only
a great devourer of books—he knew many languages—but also a great devourer of space—he was a great voyager.

Although he did not neglect *autopsia*, Bīrūnī nonetheless preferred the
oral tradition and the written word. This was a methodological choice. He
knew that "*hearsay* does not equal *eye-witness*; for in the latter the eye of the
observer apprehends the substance of that which is observed, both in the
time when and the place where it exists." But he turned away from that
principle because, he adds, there is all that lies in the past and in the future, "which either has ceased to exist or has not yet come into existence,"

118. Strabo, *Geography*, 2.5.11; Jones translation, 1:451. This defense of books is only com-
prehensible if we take into account that Strabo's intent was to "then relate the history of the
city or of the world from its origins to the present time. Under those conditions, the historian
has greater need of other books and takes the library route. The role of inquiry (the *historie*)
diminishes and that of compilation grows: the historian has become a reader. Everyone agrees in
thinking that the facts are givens—they are there—[and] what is important resides in how they
are put to work : not *what* to say, but *how* to say it.": François Hartog, "Histoire," in *Vocabulaire
européen des philosophies: Dictionnaire des intraduisibles*, ed. Barbara Cassin (Paris: Le Robert, Seuil,
2004), 554–58.

which the eye is incapable of apprehending.[119] Such events, which give
probative force to the oral tradition and to books, also assert their operational efficacy. That does not mean, however, Bīrūnī quickly adds, that
one must treat oral and written tradition on the same level. Even if the
book is a part of the oral tradition, it is superior to it. It is, in fact, "what
is most sure." That is so true that, without the book, one could never truly
have any acquaintance with ancient societies. Like Strabo, Bīrūnī reasons
as a man of books, and like Muqaddasī, he defends the functions of both
the oral and the written word. This dual choice of method supposes that
the only way to know the culture of others is to put oneself to learning
language and studying their texts. This is just what Bīrūnī, a Muslim, did
in order to study Vedic India.

But if Bīrūnī closely resembled Strabo, he was more distant from
Muqaddasī. When Strabo says that the geographer trusts "as organs of
sense those who have seen or wandered over any region, no matter what,
some in this and some in that part of the earth,"[120] we see nothing here
of the method of Muqaddasī. Strabo's rule is more like that of the ninth-
century geographers. Because he grants sight a methodological superiority over the other senses, Muqaddasī makes the voyage a rule of conduct
that the geographer cannot easily ignore. Although that method allows
that one can, when necessary, substitute other forms of evidence for visual information, it does not tolerate abandonment of the voyage. When
the geographer cannot use his sight, he must, insofar as it proves possible,
make personal use of his hearing. It is only when the information sought
cannot be gathered directly that he can, according to certain specific criteria, appeal to indirect sources. Although the geographer should continue to keep his eyes riveted on Greco-Roman antiquity, he should turn
away from Strabo entirely and look to Herodotus to find a precedent for
Muqaddasī's methods.

It is known that Greek historiography owed much to Herodotus for
having introduced it to problems raised by sense-based knowledge and
by the question of alterity.[121] Unfortunately, he offers us no discourse on

119. Al-Bīrunī, *Tahqīq mā li'l-Hind*, ed. Edward C. Sachau (London, 1887); trans. Vincent-
Mansour Monteil as *Enquête sur l'Inde*, 39; quoted from *Alberuni's India: An Account of the Religion,
Philosophy, Literature, Geography, Chronology, Astronomy, Customs, Laws and Astrology of India about
AD 1030*, trans. Edward C. Sachau, 2 vols. (London, 1888), 1:3.
120. Strabo, *Geography*, 2.5.11; Jones translation 1:453.
121. Arnaldo Momigliano, "Greek Historiography," *History and Theory* 17, no. 1 (1978): 1–28;
reprinted as chapter 1 of his *Problèmes d'historiographie ancienne et moderne*, trans. Alain Tachet et al.
(Paris: Gallimard, 1983).

method, nor does he talk about his vast experience as a traveler. We would
search his text in vain for any methodological exposé on the heuristic value
of *autopsia*. It is only by analyzing how he organizes his discourse that the
place of *opsis* becomes clear. Certain figures and turns of phrase reflect his
discursive strategy, however. To pick one example, after describing what
he has seen in Egypt, Herodotus turns to his reader (or to his listener)
and warns him: "Thus far all I have said is the outcome of my own sight
and judgment and inquiry. Henceforth I will record Egyptian chronicles,
according to that which I have heard, adding thereto somewhat of what I
myself have seen."[122] Elsewhere, describing a labyrinth that the Egyptians
constructed, he writes: "I have myself seen it, and indeed no words can
tell its wonders; were all that Greeks have builded and wrought added together. . . . We ourselves viewed those [chambers] that are above ground,
and speak of what we have seen; of the underground chambers we were
only told; the Egyptian wardens would by no means show them, these being, they said, the burial vaults of the kings who first built this labyrinth,
and of the sacred crocodiles. Thus we can only speak from hearsay of the
lower chambers." As with the preceding example, he adds, "The upper we
saw for ourselves, and they are creations greater than human," which is
one way to place oral information under the control of sight.

The primacy of the eye over hearing is inscribed in the order of his narration. The traveler, in his role of narrator, begins by telling about what
he has seen, then what he has heard, and then passes on to the things for
which he cannot (or can no longer) say "I saw."[123] Although it is actual-
ized within the narrative, this affirmation of the primacy of the eye is not
presented as a methodological principle. The only time that it appears as
a proclamation, it is expressed as a speech act reported by Herodotus. In
order to persuade Gyges, one of his confidants, the king of Lydia says to
him: "I think, Gyges, that you do not believe what I tell you of the beauty
of my wife; men trust their ears less than their eyes; do you, then, so con-
trive that you may see her naked."[124]

The distinction between the testimony of the eyes and that of the ears
was not new in Greek culture. It can be found in Homer's *Odyssey*, when
Ulysses says to the bard Demodocus: "Well and truly dost thou sing of the
fate of the Achaeans, all that they wrought and suffered, and all the toils

---

122. Herodotus, 2.99; quoted from *Herodotus in Four Volumes*, 1:384–85. For what follows, see
Herodotus, 2.148; *Herodotus in Four Volumes*, 1:454–57.

123. François Hartog, *Le miroir d'Hérodote: Essai sur la représentation de l'autre* (Paris: Gallimard,
1980), 279.

124. Herodotus, 1.8; *Herodotus in Four Volumes*, 1:10–11.

they endured, as though haply thou hadst thyself been present, or hadst heard the tale from another."[125] Homer's thought found a perhaps proverbial form in Heraclitus, for whom "eyes are more accurate witnesses than the ears,"[126] a formula often compared with that of the apologist for the king of Lydia reported by Herodotus, to the point of raising confusion regarding its paternity. On the faith of that confusion Lucian, for example, attributed Heraclitus's formula to Herodotus. This amalgam might seem less regrettable if we consider that Lucian's "error" can be interpreted in a sense that would make the *opsis* less an affair of philosophers than of historians.[127] I am obliged to note that fragment 101 has come down to us as a quotation given by Polybius in his *History*.

With Thucydides, we arrive at a stripping down and a hardening of the methodological perspectives opened up by Herodotus.[128] Thucydides sets the question of the relation to the other outside the field of historical investigation, and he reinforces the coherence of Herodotus's criteria, to the point of declaring the impossibility of any history that is not contemporary. Concerning the events of the past, he writes, "It is difficult in such matters to credit any and every piece of testimony."[129] Stressing the role and the importance of *autopsia* in historical research, he declares that he will say nothing that he does not judge to be perfectly sure:

125. Homer, *The Odyssey*, 7. 491; quoted from the Loeb Classical Library edition in 2 vols., trans. A. T. Murray (Cambridge, MA: Harvard University Press; London: William Heinemann, 1960), 2:293. In her French translation of Herodotus Andrée Barguet gives a different slant to this passage: "When you sing so well the fate of the Achaeans, their ills, and their exploits, and all of their setbacks, did you see them with your own eyes or by the eyes of another?" Following Hannah Arendt, François Hartog comments on this passage in a text entitled "Premières figures de l'historien en Grèce: Historicité et histoire," in *Figures de l'intellectuel dans la Grèce antique*, ed. Nicole Loraux and Charles Miralès (Paris: Balin, 1998), 123–42.

126. Heraclitus, *Fragments*, 101a; quoted from Heracleitus, *On the Universe*, in *Hippocrates*, vol. 4, trans. W. H. S. Jones, Loeb Classical Library 15 (Cambridge, MA: Harvard University Press; London: William Heinemann, 1967), 474–75.

127. "The attribution to Herodotus is significative: he was the first to apply Heraclitus's thought to historiography": Guido Schepens, "Éphore sur la valeur de l'autopsie," *Ancient Society* 1 (1970): 163–82, esp. 166.

128. For a discussion of the norms of historical credibility in Herodotus and Thucydides, see Arnaldo Momigliano, "The Place of Herodotus in the History of Historiography," *History* 43 (1958); reprinted in Momigliano, *Studies in Historiography* (London: Weidenfeld & Nicolson, 1966), 127–42; in French translation as chapter 8 of Momigliano, *Problèmes d'historiographie ancienne et moderne*; and Marcel Detienne, *L'invention de la mythologie* (Paris: Gallimard, 1981, 1992), 87–122.

129. Thucydides, *History of the Peloponnesian Wars*, 1.20; trans. Charles Forster Smith, 4 vols., Loeb Classical Library (Cambridge, MA: Harvard University Press; London: William Heinemann, 1980), 1:29; trans. Jacqueline de Romilly as *La guerre du Péloponnèse* (Paris: Presses Universitaires de France, 1965).

But as to the facts of the occurrences of the [Peloponnesian] war, I have
thought it my duty to give them, not as ascertained from any chance informant nor as seemed to me probable, but only after investigating with the
greatest possible accuracy each detail, in the case both of the events in which
I myself participated and of those regarding which I got my information
from others. And the endeavour to ascertain these facts was a laborious task,
because those who were eye-witnesses of the several events did not give the
same reports about the same things, but reports varying according to their
championship of one side or the other, or according to their recollection.[130]

I have quoted Thucydides at some length on the difficulty of verifying his
sources because the passage is singularly similar to the one already cited in
which Muqaddasī explains the trouble he went to in order to complete his
verification of information he had received. In both cases, the primacy of
direct visual observation is reaffirmed and indirect evidence is criticized.

With Polybius's critique of Timaeus, we encounter another convergence with Muqaddasī in a theme that challenges those "who have never
traveled through the lands or visited the regions." One of Polybius's reproaches regarding his illustrious predecessors' method bears on Timaeus's "bookish" conception of historical knowledge.[131] As he himself states
in book 34 of his *History*, Timaeus lived for nearly fifty years in Athens
without budging out of the city; thus, he could not have acquired any "experience of active service in war or any personal acquaintance with places."
Polybius tells us that because Timaeus spent much time in the libraries,
where he acquired a vast "bookish" knowledge, he considered himself particularly well suited to be a historian. "But to believe, as Timaeus did, that
relying upon the mastery of material alone one can write well the history
of subsequent events is absolutely foolish, and is much as if a man who had
seen the works of ancient painters fancied himself to be a capable painter
and a master of that art."[132] Polybius reminds his reader that of the two
instruments of knowledge, sight and hearing, it is sight that Heraclitus
finds the most trustworthy, for "the eyes are more accurate witnesses
than the ears." Timaeus, however, had chosen the more agreeable but also
the less sure of those two means for gathering information, because "he

130. Ibid., 1.22; Smith translation, 1:39.
131. On these criticisms, see Marie Laffranque, "L'oeil et l'oreille: Polybe et les problèmes de
l'information en histoire à l'époque hellénistique," *Revue philosophique* 158 (1963): 75–82.
132. Polybius, *The Histories*, 12.25h, 25e; trans. W. R. Paton, 6 vols., Loeb Classical Library
(Cambridge, MA: Harvard University Press; London: William Heinemann, 1960), 4:381, 376–77;
trans. Denis Roussel as *Histoire* (Paris: Gallimard, 1970).

entirely avoids employing his eyes and prefers to employ his ears." Using his ears offered two ways to become informed. He ultimately chose hearsay: rather than worrying about gathering oral reports, he was content to dig in books. By that choice, Timaeus had opted for the lazier solution. Polybius adds that one can find all bookish information "without any danger or hardship" by taking the trouble to live in a "town rich in documents or to have a library near at hand." But in order to pursue personal inquiry, one must endure the greatest hardships and consent to ruinous expenditures. There follows a tirade that recalls Muqaddasī thundering against those who, "comfortably installed" at home, compose works based on hearsay or compilation. Polybius concurs that book knowledge is one of the three parts of historical research, but as Muqaddasī was to do for geography, he puts it in third place, after direct observation and oral report. The ideal, in his opinion, was to subordinate any veritable historical program to the dictum of Ephorus that "if we could be personally present at all transactions such knowledge would be far superior to any other."[133] We return to Thucydides' idea that the only veritable history is contemporary, an idea to which Polybius subscribes, against Timaeus. In the Hellenistic age, the spiritual heirs of Timaeus, in particular the prose writers of the Alexandria school, continued to turn their backs on *autopsia*. Through Timaeus, Polybius's criticisms may be aimed at them.

Are Polybius's complaints about Timaeus and his like a simple reassertion of the principle of the *autopsia*, as conceived by Herodotus and Thucydides? Put in these terms, the question supposes that those two fifth-century historians had the same conception of that principle. That is not the case, however. Whereas in Herodotus there is no rupture of principle between "knowing and hearing,"[134] for Thucydides the only veritable historical knowledge is directly procured by sight or procured indirectly by the intermediary of a visual witness: "Now, what need is there to speak about matters quite remote, whose only witnesses are the stories men hear rather than the eyes of those who will hear them told?"[135] There is in Herodotus a special inflection of the juridical meaning of the

---

133. Ibid., 12.27b, 12.25c,12.27.4, 27.7; Paton translation, 4:401, 376–77, 401, 403. Polybius also criticizes Ephorus for the way in which his *History* describes land battles: "Ephorus seems to me in dealing with war to have a certain notion of naval warfare, but he is entirely in the dark about battles on land": 12.25f; Paton translation, 4:379.

134. Hartog, *Le miroir d'Hérodote*, 282.

135. Thucydides, *History of the Peloponnesian Wars*, 1.73; Smith translation, 123.

istor, a term that establishes a clear superiority of the eye over the ear.[136] Although he notes the gap between the two, Herodotus does not go so far as to transgress the framework established by the juridical term. But by admitting only visual and/or oral proof, he rejects the idea of written proof. Thucydides does the same when he limits the means for proof. The question of writing as a norm that produces truth does not seem to be on the agenda in fifth-century Greece. Arnaldo Momigliano observes about Herodotus: "When he travelled to the East, he found any amount of written evidence, but he had not been trained to read it."[137] Momigliano (and after him François Hartog) attributes this exclusion of the written word to the orality proper to Greece of the fifth century. This was a world, Hartog tells us, marked by the absence of writing, "barely a world of the written word." Given that the context of the Hellenistic age was a good deal more marked by the presence of writing, its use was necessarily more socialized. We can observe, in fact, that in the age of Polybius historians tended to admit writing as a source of knowledge. Polybius, who does not go against that tendency, limits himself to defining the conditions under which, according to him, written statements should be admitted as proof. He assigns to writing a place that puts it in third position after visual proof and oral proof. By giving the written word an epistemological status, Polybius considerably enriches the method that he inherited from Herodotus and Thucydides. This is also what Muqaddasī did within the framework of the Muslim tenth century when he programmed the truth factor of his geography differentially, around the three sources—sight, hearing, and the written word—that constitute testimony. But where Polybius makes a concession to what he calls "bookish knowledge," Muqaddasī thinks in terms of the place and status of the written word. For him, the latter is not limited to the treasures in the libraries; it includes archival materials as well. Knowledge can thus be both bookish and archival. Muqaddasī shares

---

136. The *istor*, Émile Benveniste observes, is "a witness in so far as he 'knows,' but primarily in virtue of what he has *seen*": Émile Benveniste, *Le vocabulaire des institutions indo-européennes*, 2 vols. (Paris: Minuit, 1969), 2:173; quoted from *Indo-European Language and Society*, trans. Elizabeth Palmer (London: Faber, 1973), 440.

137. Momigliano, "The Place of Herodotus," in *Studies in Historiography*, 128; in *Problèmes d'historiographie ancienne et moderne*, 171. On the relationship between the written and the oral in ancient Greek historiography, see Bruno Gentili and Giovanni Carri, "Written and Oral Communication in Greek Historiographical Thought," in *Communication Arts in the Ancient World*, ed. Eric A. Havelock and Jackson P. Hershbell (New York: Hastings House, 1978), 137–55; and Rosalind Thomas, *Literacy and Orality in Ancient Greece* (Cambridge: Cambridge University Press, 1992).

his concern with archives with other geographers of his century, in particular, with Ibn Hawqal, who was capable of such observations as "I have scrutinized the contracts involving Palestine and the colony of Jordan in the epoch of Abū al-Misk Kafūr. The functionaries named by him in the years 948–50 and 959–60, under a land regime that was at times free and at times contractual, were [three names follow]"; or "I have scrutinized the figures for receipts from Syria . . . and what I have seen was communicated to me by the X bureau for the year 908 and the year 918, with all the chapters, including the rights of the Treasury and the additional taxes, without counting functionaries' salaries; these all amounted to 39 million dirhems."[138]

When Jāhiz observed, in the mid-ninth century, that "in past times precedence was given to the tongue over the calamus, to oral communication over written communication, [but] in our day, the interest of the word has shifted toward the hand and the advantages that it offers, the services that it renders, the needs that it satisfies,"[139] he was acknowledging the cultural revolution that had transformed Arabo-Islamic culture into a civilization of the book. Muqaddasī wrote his geography within the framework of that new urban culture familiar with the techniques of the written word. Many factors contributed to this new state of affairs: a monotheistic revelation and a scriptural tradition, a centralized and omnipresent administration, a flourishing intellectual activity in response to the need to decipher revelation, broadly democratic teaching, and the constitution of an extensive network of public and semipublic libraries, the first that were open to all comers. Given this context, it seems obvious that Muqaddasī should consult archives: an imperial power that masters the techniques of paper manufacturing cannot help but accumulate heaps of paper. Beyond its function as a technique in the hands of the power structure, the written word took on immense cognitive importance in that age, to the point that, as a geographer, Muqaddasī made it a fundamental tool for his apprehension and knowledge of the world.

This affirmation of the importance of the written word is troubled by Muqaddasī's relationship with orality, however. If we can believe François Hartog, "in order for there to be an archive, [there must be] people who write, and in order to utilize archives or work on the basis of archives, the written must, in one way or another, be privileged as more *true*, more *authentic*, more *sure* than the oral [although it is understood that writing

138. Ibn Haqwal, *Kitāb Sūrat al-Ard*; Kramers and Wiet translation, 1:176, 186.
139. Jāhiz, *Tahdhīb Kitāb al-Hayawān*; Souami translation, 157.

can lie]."[140] Muqaddasī was, without any doubt, a man of writing who belonged to a culture of the written. He was also a scholar skilled in working with archival material. But he concedes no predominance to the written. Like Polybius, Muqaddasī thinks that primacy rightfully belongs to sight, supplemented by hearing. It is difficult to explain an attitude such as this by the relative importance of orality in Islamic culture of Muqaddasī's day. The explanation would be quite evidently tautological, or at the least insufficient. We will have to seek elsewhere to make sense of how he resolves the tension between the oral and the written. We will have to seek, not in a supposed "lack" or "insufficiency" in society, but in its program of truth—that is, in its criteria of credibility and its procedures for stating what is true. Muqaddasī's attitude can only be explained if we know that he was acting in conformity with a legal model for access to the truth. His scientific protocol is based on a juridical conception of testimony.

Muslim jurists learned early on to distinguish between two types of testimony: ocular testimony (*shahādat ʿiyān*) and auricular testimony (*shahādat samāʿ*). They decided that the first was superior in fact and in law to the second in procedures to establish "certitude" (*yaqīn*). But they stipulated that, under certain conditions, auricular proof could take the place of ocular proof. In limiting the conditions under which testimony was acceptable, those same jurists declared that perfect testimony must be given orally. Thanks to some subsequent doctrinal accommodations, the majority of jurists came around to admitting written testimony (*shadāhat al-khutūt*). This shift in the earlier doctrine was the work of ʿAbbāsid jurists of the ninth century. The arrangements that it permitted consisted in making written proof a source of access to the truth, after direct observation and knowledge by hearsay. Muqaddasī constructed his conception of the truth as an inheritance from that juridical methodology. That concept was so deeply imbued with law that it demanded of its informants the same "honorability" (*ʿadāla*) that a Muslim judge expected of witnesses who appeared before him. Like a magistrate, the geographer felt free to examine his informants, accepting some and eliminating others. When he had doubts about their testimony and had no way to verify whether or not they were telling the truth, he gave their names and titles, shifting responsibility for what they say to them. Because *ʿadāla* was at once a juridical concept, a moral quality, and a social status, he gave the principal biographical facts for each of his informants.

140. Hartog, *Le miroir d'Hérodote*, 291, emphasis in original.

It is tempting to assign this conception of the establishment of proof to a hypothetical "restrictive literacy,"[141] given that it privileges the oral over the written and sight over hearing. To be persuaded that the contrary is true, we need only recall the high degree of technicality and sophistication of Muslim law and note that it is a written law. It contains a speech exercise that does not necessarily appertain to the world of orality. Nor to memory, which is the corollary of orality. In the age of Muqaddasī, there were a number of scholars who were hostile to writing and whose attitude cannot be explained by the sociocultural context in which they lived. That category of men of letters fits within the paradigm of living tradition. Far from discrediting them, their epoch granted them genuine admiration, and because it accepted several regimes of truth, it was open to the idea that speech was not an obstacle to the efficacity of the written.

So with whom can we compare Muqaddasī? With Herodotus? With Thucydides? With Polybius? They were historians; he was a geographer. They all did indeed have in common recourse to *autopsia* as a mode of scientific investigation. But their domains of application were not the same as his. Strabo was originally a historian, too. His major work is a history in forty-seven books constructed as a sequel to Polybius's history. We can understand why Strabo composed his *Geography* in the same spirit as his historical work: "After I had written my *Historical Sketches*, which have been useful, I suppose, for moral and political philosophy, I determined to write the present treatise also; for this work itself is based on the same plan, and is addressed to the same class of readers, and particularly to men of exalted stations in life."[142]

Thucydides determined to make history a science of the contemporary, limiting its field of investigation to the domains of the political, the institutional, and the military, as a way to rescue it from the temptation of blending with other intellectual disciplines. Everything that might resemble chorography or ethnography was eliminated. Where ethnography is concerned, one might say that Thucydides succeeded, but on the terrain of geography his strictures fell on deaf ears. History and geography had been mixed together in the Greek national tradition since the days of Hecateus of Miletus. Strabo cites as predecessors who had been led to an interest in geography because of their vocation as historians Ephorus and

141. Jack Goody, *The Domestication of the Savage Mind* (Cambridge: Cambridge University Press, 1977); trans. Jean Bazin and Alban Bensa as *La raison graphique: La domestication de la pensée sauvage* (Paris: Minuit, 1979). The French translators render the expression "restrictive literacy" by "littéralité restreinte."

142. Strabo, *Geography*, 1.1.23; Jones translation, 1:47.

Polybius, both of whom "have set forth the topography of the continents in separate parts of their general histories."[143]

Muqaddasī's work is completely free of the subordination of geography to history represented, in Islamic culture, by Mas'ūdī's *Golden Prairies*, but traces of which can be found in Ya'qūbī, the first Muslim geographer to make *autopsia* a principle of description.[144] Muqaddasī's book presents the double paradox that, although it is undeniably the heir to an entire Greco-Muslim tradition, it is also a realization that seems without equivalent in the Middle Ages.

143. Strabo, *Geography*,8.1.1; Jones translation, 4:3. Book 34 of Polybius's *Histories* is dedicated to a description of Europe.

144. Gaston Wiet tells us, in the introduction to his translation of Ya'qūbī, that before being a geographer, Ya'qūbī was "a historian who had to his credit a history of the Greek empire, a history of the conquest of North Africa, and a short work on the ancient peoples": Ya'qūbī, *Kitāb al-Buldān*; Wiet translation, ix–xi.

·☾ 5 ☽·

ATTAINING GOD

To return to the desert: We are at the end of the eighth century, and an Iraqi philologist who is making linguistic inquiries among the Bedouins is traveling through their arid land when he encounters a dying man by the side of the road. He tries to assist him in his last hour, but the young man seems unconscious. The linguist then recites the Witness of the faith in Allah for him, but the dying man, coming to, finds the strength to murmur: "You remind me of the name of God, whereas it is in him that I burn!" He was a mystic.

In an age in which specialists in philology, poetry, genealogy, and ancient tales took great pains to learn from the Bedouins, another emerging class of learned men in Islam also focused on the desert. These were mystics seeking a fundamental alterity in solitude. By walking in the traces of the "desert Fathers" these people—there were women as well as men among them—reestablished connection with an ancient myth. Why and how did they make a sojourn in the immensity of desert lands a means for getting closer to God? Under what conditions were they persuaded to do so? What experience—ritual and intellectual—did they eventually draw out of it? In an attempt to bring some elements of an answer to these questions, I hope to deepen understanding of the voyage as a literary practice in the pages that follow by examining the functions that ascetics and mystics assigned to the experience.[1]

---

1. For convenience, I shall speak of ascetics and mystics without specifying what set the two apart. For an analysis of their different profiles, see Leah Kinberg, "What Is Meant by *Zuhd*?"

The Theory of the Errant Life

To justify their departure for the "desert,"[2] the mystics invented a type of travel that was fundamentally different, in its nature and in its object, from the *rihla* that normally took travelers toward known and recognized places to meet masters who were themselves well known and recognized. Like those other learned men, the mystics used the *rihla* to get closer to their master thinkers. Unlike the scholars, however, the mystics soon felt its limitations; in particular, that it tended to lead to only one aspect of knowledge, its "appearance," or *dhāhir*. The mystics considered themselves the bearers of a sort of knowledge that reached beyond obvious causes to decipher the "hidden" (*bātin*), which explains their definition of mysticism as the "science of the within" (*'ilm al-bātin*). Going beyond appearances required the invention of a new form of travel, the *siyāha*, which they endowed with probative status by making it one of the principal instruments for deepening their mysterious knowledge of reality. As things worked out, however, the new practice was not radically different from other sorts of ritual travel, for although the wandering that it described was specifically intended to take the traveler everywhere and nowhere, that same traveler was enjoined to stay within the limits of the "abode of Islam." Hence its function was that of spiritualizing Islamic space.

The "vagabond saint" (*sā'ih*) is a familiar figure in the Qur'an, which defines it in different ways. But it was by meditating on the collective personage of the *sā'ihūn* in the Qur'an that ascetics and mystics forged their concept of the errant life. The *sā'ihūn*, cited among the nine categories of the sincere believers in God (Qur'an 9:112), have intrigued commentators, ancient and modern. Who were they? In his translation of the Qur'an, Ré-

---

Studia Islamica 61 (1985): 27–44; and Christopher Melchert, "The Transition from Asceticism to Mysticism in the Middle of the Ninth Century C.E.," *Studia Islamica* 83 (1996): 51–71.

2. The term "desert" has to be understood both in its geographical definition and in its broader sense as a solitary place that is uninhabited or nearly so. In this second sense, a mountain is also a "desert," as it was in an ancient representation in the Near East associating the two. "For the Babylonians, for example, the desert is one with the sparse plateau that rises by the depression formed by the Tigris and Euphrates rivers. Even today, the Arabs of Iraq and Syria call that plateau *djebel*, or mountain. The Bedouin who leaves a city by the river and goes into the desert will say that he is going to the *djebel*": Elena Cassin, "Le semblable et le différent: Babylone et Israël," in *Hommes et bêtes: Entretiens sur le racisme*, ed. Léon Poliakov, actes du colloque (Paris: Mouton, 1975), 115–27, esp. 115. When St. Anthony opts to leave for "the desert," he in fact goes to live in a mountain area and ends his days at the foot of Mount Kolzim (or Qulzum), near the Red Sea: Athanasius of Alexandria, *The Life of Antony*, trans. Tim Vivian and Apostolos N. Athanassakis with Rowan A. Greer (Kalamazoo: Cistercian Publications, 2003); trans. Benoît Lavaud as *Vie et conduite de notre père Saint Antoine* (Bégrolles en Mauges: Abbaye de Bellefontaine, 1979), chap. 11.

gis Blachère speaks of *"ceux qui glorifient"* (those who glorify) God. Perhaps less hesitantly, Denise Masson translates:*"ceux qui se livrent à des exercises de piété"* (those who devote themselves to pious exercises). Both translators avoid the philological content of the term and offer dogmatic interpretations. Similar translations, which dominate in exegesis of the Qur'an, load the term with a content that detaches it from other realities, notably, Christian ones. From a philological point of view, although the term *siyāha* covers all forms of wandering, historically it refers consistently to the lifestyle of hermits and monks.[3] From a sociological viewpoint, Muslims of the eighth and ninth centuries could not have been unaware that there were Christians living among them who practiced, in varying degrees, the exalted life with which wandering was associated.[4] Canonical exegesis dogmatically chooses to ignore all of these facts. In his commentary on the Qur'an, Tabarī (d. 310/922) applies great ingenuity to avoiding this issue. This major exegete and historian echoes interpretations that have the manifest aim of detaching the term from its connection with wandering. His dogmatic adjustments make *sā'ihūn* equivalent to *sā'imūn*, or "fasters." In support of this interpretation he cites an entire series of concordant traditions, one of which states, "The *siyāha* of that *umma* [community of Muslims] is fasting." Another states, unsurprisingly, that well before being known by Christians, "the *siyāha* was in use among the sons of Israel." It was precisely in order to avoid imitating writers on scripture whose prestige had declined that Tabarī amputated nearly all of its content from the term, leaving only fasting. Still, his ample exegesis (and this is its chief interest) permits us a glimpse of a meaning of *siyāha* that is less restrictive than the one he pleads ex cathedra. He places that definition in the mouth of an Iraqi traditionist of the eighth century, who declares, "Anyone who abandons food, drink, and carnal commerce with women is a *sā'ih*."[5] This broader interpretation is not centered exclusively on fasting. It adds

3. Penitents, monks, and nuns are mentioned in Arabian poetry (in Hutay'a, for example). When Muhammad speaks of *sā'ihūn*, "he has before his mind's eye the wandering monks of whom he must have seen many during his comings and goings before his prophetic call": Ignaz Goldziher, *Vorlesungen über den Islam*; trans. Félix Arin as *Le dogme et la loi de l'Islam: Histoire du développement dogmatique et juridique de la religion musulmane* (1910) (Paris: Geuthner, 1958, 1973), 122; quoted from the English translation by Andras and Ruth Hamori, *Introduction to Islamic Theology and Law* (Princeton: Princeton University Press, 1981), 130.

4. The most impressive evidence of this is that of a Syrian man of letters who lived in the late eighth and early ninth centuries. He is cited in Father Anastase, "Un document islamique sur le monachisme au IXe siècle," *Mashriq* 12 (1908): 883–92.

5. Tabarī, *Tafsīr*, ed. Mahmūd Muhammad Shākir, 14 vols. (Cairo: Dār al-Ma'rif, 1956), 14:505–6.

sexual abstinence, a requirement that is characteristic of the hermit's
mode of life. The door is thus open for *siyāha* to recover its full meaning. Although it is difficult to know exactly when mystical exegesis of
the Qur'an reconnected with the connotations of wandering contained
in the term, a statement credited to the great Shiite imam Ja'far al-Sādiq
(d. 148/765) hints at an answer to that question.[6] One of the ways to ensure
personal salvation that he preaches is to "wander from land to land" or at
least to "abandon one's carnal soul in desert solitudes."[7]

Ja'far al-Sādiq calls someone with a vocation to wander in God a
mushtāq, or "desiring one," because he is "a person who does not know how
to take pleasure in the savors of food and drink, who rejects the warmth
of the hearth, who refuses the company of men, who possesses no dwelling place, who inhabits no particular town, who wears no special clothing,
and who is not fixed in any one place." Embarked on his wandering, he
hopes for nothing but to get closer to the object of his desire. Like Moses
guiding his people through the desert, he too, in his mad race to God,
would like to say to him, "I hastened to You, O my Lord, to please You"
(Qur'an 20: 84).[8]

The Mosaic topos of the exile and the wandering in the desert connects
Ja'far's theme of making one's way toward God to traditions that go back
to the early eighth century.[9] It seems, however, that it was not until the
following century that Tustarī (d. 283/896), speaking of ways to approach
God, explicitly connected *siyāha* and *zuhd* (wandering and renunciation)
in his commentary on the Qur'an. An Iraqi theologian and mystic, Tustarī
describes wandering as the way he himself strengthened his renunciation
of the world.[10]

Without contradicting the official commentaries, mystical exegetes of
the Middle Ages followed the line laid down by Tustarī. Commenting on
Qur'an 9:112, Qushayrī (d. 465/1073), for example, first restates the idea
that the *sā'ihūn* were also *sa'imūn*, or fasters. But he restricts the sense of
sawm to that of abstinence in general. For him, *sa'imūn* were still "those

6. The exegesis attributed to Ja'far al-Sādiq played a major role in the elaboration of Muslim
mystic vocabulary: see Paul Nwyia, "Le *Tafsīr* mystique attribué à Ga'far Sādiq," *Mélanges de
l'Université Saint-Joseph* (Beirut), 43, fasc. 4 (1968): 181–230.
7. Ja'far al-Sādiq, *Misbāh al-Sharī'ah* (Beirut: Muassasat al-A'lamī lil-Matbu'āt, 1980), 110.
8. Ibid., 196.
9. This same theme appears in the *Tafsīr* also attributed to Ja'far al-Sādiq: see Nwyia, "Le
Tafsīr mystique," 196.
10. Tustarī, *Tafsīr al-Qur'ān al-adhīm* (Misr: Matba'at al-Sa'ādah, 1329 AH/1908), 106.

who abstain from seeing anyone other than God and who prohibit themselves from serving anyone but him." By reestablishing the *siyāha* as a
"wandering in search of God," this doctrinaire mystic gives a new definition in which the *sā'ihūn* are people who travel continually in search of
i'tibār (teaching) and *istibsār* (intuition).[11] By the first of these acts, they
learn and become imbued with exemplary observation of the world and
its "marvels." By the second, they become initiated into the intuitive faculty of penetrating beings and things and knowing them thoroughly. The
two concepts of *autopsia* represent the cognitive bases on which the *siyāha*
rests, making it a modality of the "description of the world."[12] *Basar*, the
root of the term *istibsār*, refers to the act of seeing things with one's own
eyes as well as penetrating them with one's intelligence. *Basīra* shapes "inner sight," which is "the faculty of penetrating things." If we know that
this is also another term for "proof" and for an "argument brought by the
witness," we can understand it in the light of the Islamic theory of testimony that, in principle, accords primacy to sight. By that same token,
we can better appreciate the importance that Sufism gives to the eye as a
source of knowledge.

   In fact, leafing through medieval mystical texts, one often encounters
the legal rule that states that "nothing is equal to an ascertained fact."[13]
The theory of the *siyāha* is gnoseologically founded on acceptance of that
dogmatic principle. Thus, ascetics frequently privileged the eye over the
ear. The young Bistamī (d. 260/874) was moved by his encounter with his
older countrywoman Fātima of Nishapur (d. 223/838) because, as he says,
"whatever the spiritual station I talked to her about, what she told me
about it came from a visual knowledge [*'iyān*]."[14] Similarly, a theoretician
of mysticism of the eleventh century recalled that, although those who
pursue mystical "science" are of three sorts, between one who speaks of
it out of personal experience and another whose knowledge comes from

   11. Qushayrī, *Latā'if al-Ishārāt*, ed. Ibrāhīm al-Basyūnī, 2 vols. (Cairo: Dār al-Kātib al-'Arabī,
1981), 2:67. Denis Gril recalls that for Ibn al-A'rabī, the *siyāha* consisted, precisely, in "traveling
over the land in order to practice meditation [*i'tibār*] and become closer to God)": Ibn al-'Arabī,
Kitāb al-Isfār 'an Natā'ij al-Asfār; in ed. and trans. Denis Gril as *Le dévoilement des effets du voyage*
(Paris: Éditions de l'Éclat, 1994), x.
   12. The term *istibsār* enters into a number of titles of medieval works of history and geography.
   13. See, for example, Sulamī, *Risālat al-Malāmatiyya*; trans. Roger Deladrière as *La lucidité
implacable: Èpître des hommes du blâme* (Paris: Actes Sud, 1991); and Ibn al-Qunfudh, *Uns al-Faqīr*,
ed. Muhammad al-Fāsī and Adūlf Fūr (Rabat: al-Markaz al-Jāmi'ī lil-Bahth al-'Ilmi, 1965).
   14. Ibn al-'Arabī, *Manāqib Dhū al-Nūn al-Misrī*; trans. Roger Deladrière as *La vie merveilleuse de
Dhū'l-Nūn l'Égyptien* (Paris: Sindbad, 1988), 236.

hearsay, there is room only for the imposture of someone who speaks neither out of experience nor from hearsay.[15] This superiority of direct observation over oral tradition was at work in the Egyptian Gnostic Dhū al-Nūn, the disciple of the Fātima of Nishapur mentioned above. Invited to comment on the edifying words put to music with a fine melody, he gave a description of paradise in which the Garden of Delights resounds with the sweet and charming voices of houris. To give full force to an evocation that, by definition, was based on hearsay, he added: "That is the savor that Tradition informs us of; what is there to say of what will be the savor of the vision!"[16] The enthusiasm of this Egyptian Gnostic clearly shows where his preferences lie. Without rejecting hearing as a source of knowledge, he favors the eye, which, in the context of his exclamation, offers an evident cognitive superiority. Favoring sight is, in fact, widespread among the great masters of Sufism. Hallāj (d. 309/922) says much the same in his *Garden of Knowledge*. He writes, aiming his criticism at "anthropomorphic" traditionists, "He who says, 'I know Him as He has described Himself (in the revelation!)—this means to let traditional authority suffice without (experiencing) direct confirmation."[17] Far from being content to adhere intellectually to the theory of the superiority of sight over the other sources of sense knowledge, the mystics strove to experience it personally. They made it an integral part of their errant life.[18]

15. Ansārī, *Manāzil Sālahīn*; trans. Serge de Beaurecueil as *Chemin de Dieu: Trois traités spirituels* (Paris: Sindbad, 1985; reprint, Paris: Actes Sud, 1997), 84.

16. Ibid., 153.

17. Louis Massignon, *La passion de Husayn ibn Mansūr Hallāj, martyr mystique de l'Islam*, 3 vols. (Paris: Gallimard, 1975), 3:341; trans. Herbert Mason as *The Passion of al-Hallāj: Mystic and Martyr of Islam*, 4 vols. (Princeton: Princeton University Press, 1982), 3:323. The short work in question, the *Bustān al-Ma'rifa*, is translated in this work in its entirety.

18. As did Hallāj, for example, in his celestial Ascension: "(4) 'When the stipulated time ran out for Moses,' he left his dear ones, for reality was going to take him for 'its own;' and in order to consummate this full gift of himself, he declared himself satisfied to go receive (indirect) information, given the lack of (direct) vision: so that there was a difference between him and 'the best of carnal creatures' (that is, Muhammad). He said: 'As for me, I will go obtain for you some information (on that fire down there).' (5) If the 'well-directed' thus contented himself with (indirect) information to start out on the road (to God), how could 'he who seeks his way' not be satisfied with a (direct) indication to set himself on his way?" Massignon, *La passion de Husayn ibn Mansūr Hallāj*, 3:309–10. Not all mystics spoke out against oral tradition, however. A Gnostic who was a contemporary of Hallāj and who was of the opinion that "certitude can be of three kinds" gives first place to oral tradition (*khabar*) or "the certitude of good tidings (from God)," second place to the probative sign (*dalāla*), or "the certitude of (divine) proofs," and only third place to direct observation (*mushāhada*), or "the certitude of witnessing (God)": Qushayrī, *al-Risālah*, ed. Ma'rūf Zurayq and 'Alī 'Abd al-Hamīd Baltah'jī (Beirut: Dār al-Jīl, 1990), 112; quoted from *Al-Qushayri's Epistle on Sufism: Al risala al-qushayriyya fi 'ilm al-tasawwuf* (Reading, UK: Garnet, 2007), 196.

The mystic voyage thus finds justification in a conception of nature that makes it a reservoir of symbols that elicit marvel from a contemplation of the world by scrutinizing the "signs" (*āyāt*) that guarantee its order and harmony. Meditation on those signs provides "lessons" and "teachings." The Qur'an, the principal initiator of this universal semiology, invites believers to consider that nothing that exists in nature is without significance: everything is a "great sign." This is why, when Abū Hafs of Nishapur (d. 265/879), the founder of the mystical school of "blame" (*malāma*), forbade his disciples to practice the *siyāḥa*,[19] his friend Hamdūn al-Qassār (d. 271/884) objected: "Has not God said: 'Have they thus not traveled the land and reflected?'"[20]

The idea of a nature saturated with symbols, in which someone able to see and read perspicaciously can decipher the signature of the divine power underlying beings and things,[21] brings Sufism singularly close to other arrangements of knowledge, in particular to the *'Ajā'ib*, an erudite literary genre that appeared in the ninth century.[22] The marvelous *'Ajā'ib* were defined by Carra de Vaux as "monuments, facts, beings such as those to be met with in geography and in history." Although it is not sure that these are real, "it is even less sure that they are false: they are above all

19. See Frederick de Jong and Colin H. Imber, "Malāmatiyya," in *Encyclopédie de l'Islam*, new ed. (Leiden: E. J. Brill; Paris: Maisonneuve et Larose, 1966), 4:217–22; and in *The Encyclopaedia of Islam*, new ed., ed. E. J. Van Donzel (Leiden: Brill, 1966), 6:223ff.

20. Sulamī, *Risālat al-Malāmatiyya*, 41. The divine question returns five or six times in the Qur'an, for example, in 30:9. Many citations from the Qur'an of this sort can be found in anonymous, *Adab al-Mulūk*, ed. Bernd Radtke (Beirut: Steiner, 1991).

21. Dhū al-Nūn (d. 245/859) relates: "I found myself in the cultivated countryside of the banks of the Nile. I stayed in the middle of the fields, and I saw a woman, of the black race, who approached a spike of grain. She rubbed it between her fingers, then threw it away and abandoned it, in tears. She cried out: 'You who are he who sowed it when it was still nothing in the earth as a dry seed, you who made it become a sprout, then who made it grow a stalk that rose up, and you have placed grain harmoniously disposed all around it . . . I am astonished that one [that is, nature] can disobey the one who holds such power.'": Ibn al-'Arabi, *Manāqib Dhū al-Nūn*; Deladrière translation, 267.

22. The Sufism of his epoch would willingly have accepted this remark of Jāhiz's: "If you note that an animal is not eager to help men, unable and resistant to giving him aid and assistance, or even very harmful, to the point that mounting a guard against them is necessary—this is the case of animals with claws or teeth such as vipers and wolves, or that have a stinger and are hairy, like scorpions, hornets, and wasps—then you must know that their utility resides in the fact that they constitute a trial, a calamity that God has prepared precisely to test the endurance and the patience of humans": Jāhiz: *Tahdhīb Kitāb al-Hayawān*, ed. 'Abd al-Salām Muhammad Hārūn (Cairo: Matkabat al-Khanjī, 1938–45); trans. Lakhdar Souami as *Le Cadi et la mouche: Anthologie du Livre des animaux* (Paris: Sinbad, 1988), 55. Medieval hagiography established a close connection between mysticism and the animal world.

difficult to confirm."[23] The fact that the marvelous operates on the terrain of ambiguity and metamorphosis creates a singular connection between mystic discourse and the *'Ajā'ib*. The two forms of knowledge have in common that they draw from the same Qur'anic, biblical, and rabbinic sources, and they aim at bringing a response to the essential tensions that confronted the people of past times. Both were thought to contribute to resolving the enigma of relations between the human and the divine, the visible and the invisible, the natural and the supernatural, the ordinary and the extraordinary, and the believable and the unbelievable. But whereas the cosmographers, geographers, and historians attempted to give enigma an objective interpretation and the moralists to give it a subjective content, the aim of the mystics was to experience it. In their wanderings they went to the ends of the world and of society to encounter its many figures and return with adequate answers.

The mystics were thus of two sorts: some preached vagabondage, and others, because they feared "going astray," stayed in one place. Some shared the convictions of Abū Hafs of Nishapur and others sided with his friend Hamdūn al-Qāssar. Still, with the exception of Hujwīri,[24] few specialists in doctrine took over the theory of the superiority of the "residents" (*muqīmūn*) over the travelers (*musāfirūn*). The "residents" seem to have been a minority in Sufism. Their sedentary status should not be taken too literally, however. For many of them, it was a snare, and their immersion in the crowd a cover-up. Under the appearance of a simulated presence, they in fact lived in a fundamental solitude that made them just as absent from the world as if they had been nomads. Those who experienced the *siyāha*—at least at the time of their initiation—formed the majority of the members of the "spiritual tribe." They found doctrinal support among theoreticians of the Baghdad school, such as Junayd (d. 298/910), for whom God, by exposing the saints "to ruin and exile" made them targets of the trial, and by subjecting them "to all ills" made them "taste an unmixed

23. Bernard, baron Carra de Vaux, introduction to anonymous, *Abrégé des merveilles* (Paris: Klincksieck, 1898), 18.

24. Hujwīri, who wrote in the mid-eleventh century, explains that the mystics who lived in one place in the "service of God" were superior to those who traveled through the land as pilgrims. The first did so in the interest of God, whereas the second did so in their own interest. This is why "the sign of research" can be found in the category of the travelers and "the sign of arrival" can be found in that of those who stayed put. Those who have found and have stayed in one place are necessarily superior to those who seek: Hujwīri, *Somme spirituelle: Kashf al-Mahjūb*, trans. Djamshid Mortazavi (Paris: Sindbad, 1988), 388; trans. Reynold A. Nicholson as *The Kashf al-Mahjub: The Oldest Persian Treatise on Sufism* (Leiden: Brill; London: Luzac, 1911, 1976).

death."[25] The anonymous tenth-century author of a manual of mysticism devotes an entire chapter to the question of the errant life, which he connects to the theory of *tawakkul*, or giving over everything into God's hands. "Entering into the solitudes, remaining alone in the deserts, and the endurance of hunger," he stresses, permit the "aspirant" to place his soul "in the hands of God" purified of all passions. "Taming one's passions," "practicing exile," "perfecting abandonment to God" are key notions in a progress toward God conceived as a "flight into the deserts and the mountains."[26] Following this anonymous writer, even the most moderate Sufi dogmatists found it obligatory to mention the *siyāha*. Abū Tālib al-Makkī (d. 386/996), who devoted a chapter of his manual of Sufism to the "rules of travel and its goals," insisted on the canonical motivations for seeking religious knowledge, on a sojourn at the frontiers of Islam, and on travel to religious sites, but he still found it necessary to devote a chapter to the errant life, which he connected with the theory of "abandonment to/in God."[27] Qushayrī (d. 465/1073) did the same in a chapter on "the rules of travel" entirely devoted to reasons for leaving home.[28] The idea that roving is a condition for access to holiness was a commonplace in Muslim mysticism of the time.

Topographical Writing

Tarīqa, in the technical language of Muslim mysticism, signifies spiritual action: the term includes the notions of "way," "road," and "method." But although mystical "ways" may be of several kinds, they all come down to two major ones: the "way of inebriation" (*tarīq al-shukr*) and the "way of sobriety" (*tarīq al-sahw*). Neophytes who join one group or the other are called *murīd*, or "aspirants to/in God." The term was universally accepted, but those to whom it was applied were called by various other names. The divine quest is presented as a route, an initiative, an itinerary, or an approach, and the aspirant in/to God is a *viator*: according to the case, a *sālik* who is making his way to God, a *sā'ir* who walks in the way of God, or a *wāsil* who has already reached the point of arrival in God. More globally, Muslim mysticism itself appears as a discourse of the voyage in which all means of travel are good to imagine. Its linguistic universe is so strongly

25. Junayd, *Rasā'il*; trans. Roger Deladrière as *Enseignement spirituel* (Paris: Sindbad, 1983), 147.
26. Anonymous, *Adab al-Mulūk*, 37, 59.
27. Abū Tālib al-Makkī, *Kitāb qūt al qulūb*, ed. 'Abd al-Qādir Ahmad 'Atá (Misr: Maktabat al-Qāhirah, 1964), 2:204–8.
28. Qushayrī, *al-Risāla*, 289; *Al-Qushayri's Epistle on Sufism*, 297.

marked by terms relating to walking, horseback riding, the cavalcade, and covering ground that it seems incapable of speaking any other language. This is why mystical writing unfolds like a topographical text that speaks in terms of routes, roads, stations, stages, and watering places. It establishes a close connection between the act of reading and the act of seeing, and, by that token, it gives to any mystical itinerary the aspect of a conduit to the vision of a place: the place in which the truth of him who speaks true because he has seen is declared and realized.

Although such terms as *ḥāl* (state) and *maqām* (station) had been part of the mystical lexicon since the mid-eighth century, the ascetics of Islam do not seem to have expressed their experience in terms of advancing on a route until around the beginning of the ninth century. Abū Sulaymān al-Dārānī (d. 211/826) was one of the first to use the language of the open road. That Iraqi mystic, who left his homeland to live in Syria,[29] seems to have developed a topographical theory of holiness in which those who arrive at God cannot retrace their steps. Because the route that takes them to God resembles no other route, the elect who are called upon to take it can neither take the "wrong road" nor turn back. The only person who can retrace his steps, Dārānī insists, is he who takes an ordinary road.[30] The road that leads to God, however, is not like the others: it is the way of election and of the choice of God. Thus, one who takes it can never go astray.

In Dārānī's day, Muslim mysticism still did not possess a language of its own. Not until the mid-ninth century did mystics compose works in which their experience was described as a systematic object. The most recurrent image is, precisely, that of physical advance, of following a route, of traversing a terrain. Dhū al-Nūn (d. 245/859) was perhaps one of the first mystics (and in Egypt, the first) to speak in rigorous terms of *aḥwāl*, or "states of mystical union," or of *maqāmāt*, or "stages or degrees of mystical union."[31] Although no treatise by this mystic has come down to us directly, fragments of his work are known to us, thanks to the wide circulation of the work in the Middle Ages. To judge by the remaining passages, Dhū al-Nūn was a subtle topographer.

29. Khaṭīb al-Baghdādī, *Tārīkh Baghdād*, 14 vols. (Cairo, 1931), 10:248–50; Ibn al-Mulaqqin, *Ṭabaqāt al-awliyā'*, ed. Nūr al-Dīn Shuraybah (Cairo: Maktabat al-Khānjī, 1973), 389–92.

30. Abū Nuʿaym, *Ḥilyat al-Awliyā'*, 10 vols. (Cairo: Maktabat al-Khānjī, 1932–38); new ed., 10 vols. (Beirut: Dār al-Kitāb al-Arabī, 1967–68), 11:261; selections trans. Muhammad Al-Akoli as *The Beauty of the Righteous and Ranks of the Elite* (Philadelphia: Pearl, 1995).

31. Dhahabī, *Siyar Aʿlām al-Nubalā'*, ed. Shuʿayb al-Arnaʾūṭī et al., 25 vols. (Beirut: Muʾassasat al-Risālah, 1982–83), 11:534.

While Dhū al-Nūn was teaching in Egypt at Fustāt, Muhāsibī (d. 243/
857) was teaching in Baghdad.[32] Like that of his colleague, Muhāsibī's
teaching bore the marks of topographical language. The title of one of
his major works illustrates this spatial conception of access to God, as it
speaks of the *qasd*, or "action to direct oneself or go toward," and the *rujū'*,
or "return" to God. The technical instrument for thinking about this approach to or return to God is *makām*, or "station."[33] This was a time in
which almost all attempts to impose system on the mystical experience
borrowed the verbal terms and the postures of the voyage. Among these
elaborations, that of Bistamī (d. 260/874) was perhaps the boldest and
the most innovative. It inaugurated new perspectives in the exploration
of the schemata of the voyage by taking inspiration from the Ascension
of the founder of Islam. In his evocation of Muhammad's Ascension, or
Night Journey (*isrā'*) and Ravishment (*mi'rāj*) that transported him first to
Jerusalem, then to heaven, where he was placed in the presence of God,
Bistamī, who said, "I have planted my tent near the Throne" after having
"traversed the deserts, reached the steppes, and crossed into the kingdom
of the Invisible,"[34] gave Sufism two new resources for speaking of travel:
ascension[35] and "Icarism."[36] Bistamī was banished from his native city for
declaring that he had experienced a *mi'rāj* like that of the Prophet.[37] But
whereas the journey of the Prophet, his model, ended happily ("He saw
him . . . beside the 'lote-tree beyond which none may pass'"), Bistamī's

32. Abū Nu'aym, *Hilyat al-Awliyā'*, 10:76–77.

33. Muhāsibī, *Al-Qasd wa-al-Ruj' ilā Allāh*, ed. 'Abd al-Qādir Ahmad 'Atā (Cairo: Dār al-
Turāth al-'Arabī, 1980).

34. Abū Nasr Sarrāj, *The Kitāb al-Luma'*, ed. Reynold Alleyne Nicholson, 2 vols. (Leiden: Brill;
London: Luzac, 1914), 1:391; 'Abd al-Rahmān Badawi, *Shatahāt al-Sūfiyya*, vol. 1, *Abū Yazīd Bistamī*;
trans. Abdelwahab Meddeb as *Les dits de Bistamī* (Paris: Fayard, 1989), 21.

35. On this saintly figure's ascension, see Louis Massignon, *Essai sur les origines du lexique technique de la mystique musulmane* (Paris: Geuthner, 1922; Vrin, 1968), 278. The most complete narrative of medieval Sufism to have come down to us is that of Ibn al-'Arabi, for a detailed study of
whom, see Michel Chodkiewicz, *Le sceau des saints: Prophétie et sainteté dans la doctrine d'Ibn 'Arabī*
(Paris: Gallimard, 1986), 181–221; and Claude Addas, *Ibn 'Arabī, ou, La quête du soufre rouge* (Paris:
Gallimard, 1989); trans. Peter Kingsley as *Quest for the Red Sulphur: The Life of Ibn 'Arabī* (Cambridge: Islamic Texts Society, 1993), 186–204. For a study of experimentation with ascension in
medieval Sufism in general, see Nadhīr El-Azma, "Some Notes on the Impact of the Story of the
Mi'rāj on Sufi Literature," *Muslim World* 43 (1973): 93–104. The dossier of ascension is also treated
in Mohammad Alī Amir-Moezzi, ed., *Le voyage initiatique en terre d'Islam* (Louvain: Peeters, 1996).

36. "I was changed into a bird whose body was unity and whose wings were duration. I continued to fly in the heavens of comment for ten years. I flew far, covering eight hundred thousand
times the distance between the Throne and the dust. I did not cease flying. . . . Then I flew
over . . .": Bistamī quoted in Badawi, *Shatahāt*; Meddeb translation, 1:125.

37. On his ascension, see M. Lory, "Le *Mi'rāj* d'Abū Yazīd Bistamī," in Amir-Moezzi, *Le voyage initiatique en terre d'Islam*, 223–38.

mi'rāj, which was founded on a meditation of Qur'an 53:1–18, ended tragically in a void: "I saw there the tree of unity . . . and I looked, and I knew that all of that was only enticement."[38] By deception or illusion (*khad'a*), the saint had been unable to see what the Prophet had seen. When, at a later date, Hallāj too spoke of his experience of ascension as a *mi'rāj*, he claimed that Bistamī's ecstasy was incomplete rather than a failure.[39]

Thinking of the mystical experience in topographical terms was a commonplace among Hallāj's contemporaries. He himself speaks of "distances traveled," of striding "among the mountains and the hills," and of the "saddles of those who will arrive together at the way station lodging." He conceives of the quest for God as progress along a road that he places, as did his master Junayd, under the sign of the trial "over a rough path, filled with obstacles that make its access difficult, scattered with perils and ambushes, and infested with brigands and cutthroats." Placed in the presence of so many impediments, few are the travelers on this road who arrive at their destination safe and sound. All of those whom God does not surround "with his science and his love" perish or lose their way. It is in order to ward off such dangers that Hallāj, acting as an expert guide, offers travel hints to "brothers" who already possess "a retinue, travel tools, and cleverness" and explains to them "how to make the crossing" without risking death.[40]

Most mystic dogmatists chose to play the guide. In his *Manāzil al-Qāsidīn*, Hakīm al-Tirmidhī (d. 320?/932?) poses as a "tracker" for whom the desert holds no secrets. Even his title indicates this, as *manzil* (plural, *manāzil*) means "1. Place where one stops, places foot on the earth, or makes a halt; 2. Hostelry, inn; 3. Station, stopping place on the road." As for *qāsid* (plural, *qāsidūn*), it is "he who goes, directs himself intentionally toward a point." Even before we open it, the treatise introduces us into the economy of travel by dramatizing, in two words, the voyage of a determined man who, in order to cross through the space between him and his destination, must travel by stages. In order to get where he wants to go, such a man has to take the time to go progressively through the stages

38. Bistamī quoted in Badawi, *Shatahāt*; Meddeb translation, 1:179.

39. In his edition of Hallāj's *Mi'rāj*, Louis Massignon states that he thinks Hallāj was alluding to Bistamī's experience when he stated: "Thus have I seen a bird (spiritual = a soul) among the birds (mystics), a bird with two wings,—he denied my glory (= my state of union), as he continued to soar, but he could not fly with me in the air of pre-eternity": Massignon, *La passion de Husayn ibn Mansūr Hallāj*, 3:318; quoted from Mason translation, 3:300.

40. Hallāj, *Kitāb al-Sayhūr*, my translation; in Massignon, *Essai sur les origines du lexique*, annexed texts, no. 28, p. 447.

of his itinerary, station after station. And to spare his mount, he must rest
at the way stations, halts, or hostelries that line his way. This itinerant
writing echoes other mystical writing traditions. Christian mysticism, for
example, had gone through a similar experience before Islam, as seen in
such treatises as the *Ladder of Divine Ascent* or *Heavenly Ladder* of St. John
Climacus, "the undisputed masterpiece of Byzantine spiritual guidance."[41]
There is no influence or anteriority here: it is characteristic of all mysticism that its writing, hence its reading, unfolds like an itinerary. The specific form chosen depends on the individual case. To remain with Christians and Muslims, it is a familiar fact that both groups used the literary
genres of the "ladder," the *via*, or "way," and the *itinerarium*.[42] If Christians
thoroughly explored the resources of the ascent image, Muslims preferred
those of the route.

Sufism as a Crossing of the Desert

To judge, speaking from the Christian experience, that Muslim mysticism
used the desert more as an illustrative theme than as an inspiration is inexact.[43] It is true that, until the mid-ninth century, ascetic masters did not
think of their experience in terms of crossing the desert.[44] It is no less true,
however, that after that date the idea took hold rapidly in almost all doctrinal writings. In the ninth century two men embodied the two contrary
tendencies: Dhū al-Nūn (d. 245/859), an Egyptian, and Bistamī (d. 260/874),
from Khurasan. For Dhū al-Nūn, who borrowed his vocabulary from the
geographers of his own time, authentic saints were not subjected to the
trial of the crossing of the desert. Because God had shown them the High

41. Peter Brown, *The Body and Society: Man, Woman, and Sexual Renunciation in Early Christianity* (New York: Columbia University Press, 1988), 237; in French translation as *Le renoncement à la
chair: Virginité, célibat et continence dans le christianisme primitif* (Paris: Gallimard, 1995), 293.

42. Concerning Christianity, see E. Bertaud and A. Rayez, "Échelle spirituelle," in *Dictionnaire
de spiritualité*, 17 vols. (Paris: Beauchesne, 1932, 1960), 4:62–86; and E. Bertaud, "Guides spirituels,"
Dictionnaire de spiritualité, 6:1154–70.

43. Roger Arnaldez, "The thème du désert dans la mystique musulmane: Thème d'inspiration
ou thème d'illustration?" in *Les mystiques du désert dans l'Islam, le judaïsme et le christianisme* (Gordes:
Abbaye de Sénanque, Association des amis de Sénanque, 1975), 89–96.

44. In a late narrative concerning Ibrāhīm ibn Ad'ham (d. 161/777), we hear that ascetic from
Balkh making repeated appeals to God for pardon in which he tells the deity that, if, in a moment
of weakness, he did not know what he was saying, it was because he had "lost his way" (*tihtu*) in
his love for him. The verb *tāha*, which expresses the idea of "wander," "go astray," "lose oneself,"
or "lose one's head," belongs within the vocabulary of the desert experience. Hence the name Tih
Banū Isra'īl (Place of Wandering of the Sons of Israel) given to the part of the desert where the
Jews wandered on their flight from Egypt: Ibn al-Mulaqqin, *Tabaqāt*, 7–8.

Road (*mahajja*), "they went through the valleys without passing through deserts." Led to their destination by a benevolent Guide who knew how to spare them the perils of the *mahlaka*, the "immense desert" that bore death in its name, they only took the *masālik*, sure, well-marked, and frequented routes.[45] Unlike Dhū al-Nūn, Bistamī makes the desert crossing a necessary stage in the path that leads to God. It is part of his own experience: "I have crossed the deserts and reached the steppes. I have traveled through the steppes and come to the kingdom of the invisible," he says in one stanza. But rather than a hostile place, the desert is peaceful and a place that one penetrates under the guidance of the divine injunction "Do not cite our words to just anyone, God says to his Friend. Forget them. Repeat them to the camels in the desert."[46] Although our fragmentary knowledge of the works of these two mystics makes it difficult to pursue this contrast, it can be said that when their followers elaborated their own doctrine of the desert, they looked more to Bistamī than to Dhū al-Nūn.

It is incontestably with Junayd (d. 298/910) that the image of the desert enters fully into the discursive economy of Sufism. The rhetorical and symbolic effects inherent in this figure present the mystical experience, from the start, as an experience of the desert. Describing to one of his disciples "the dangers of the spiritual way," Junayd uses the language of those who are familiar with the dangers and the incertitude of immense desert spaces. He describes setting off toward God as a venture as dangerous as crossing the Mafāza, the great Sahara that separates Persia from Khurasan. As the traveler plunges into the desert, the scattered landmarks that he has used as guides begin to fade, then to blend into the features of a terrain of unclear morphology. Advancing blindly, he goes through an "unknown space" and crosses a "boundless land." Clemency has given way to hostility; self-assurance to fear. He feels the first pangs of abandonment. Next comes despair: "It is then that there is no more access road for him who seeks, no more goal for him who wanders, no more salvation for him who flees." Every detour prompts a sacred terror. Every low spot leads to a fall that leaves him nowhere. "Who will save [him] from this situation? Who will help [him] escape from these perils?" The seeker for God can always console himself with still being alive after all the dangers he has endured. In order to persuade himself of this, he only has to think

---

45. Abū Nuʿaym, *Hilyat al-Awliyāʾ*, 10:338. Dhū al-Nūn's conception here was followed by one of his Palestinian disciples, Tāhir al-Maqdisī, who adopts the idea that there are no "deserts" (*mafāwiz*) that present an obstacle to the seeker for God in his quest, for "the route that leads to him is wide open": Ibid., 10:317.

46. Bistamī quoted in Badawi, *Shatahāt*; Meddeb translation, 1:124, 37.

of the many who have failed. "How many men who plunged into this enterprise have been carried away? How many presumptuous men have been overturned, their souls having been led to perdition under the effect of a deceitful illusion, and having thus hastened their end?" This is where Junayd ends his description of the fearful forced march toward God. He can say no more without unveiling mysteries. He excuses himself for having been able to offer only a "partial description" of the "perilous desert." That description itself is only an "allusion" to a science about which he will not speak: "To unveil that science would be impossible, what is more, because the one who finds himself in the desert is as if he no longer existed."[47] At the borderline between the human and the desert, the burning theater of his experience, the traveler toward God has no words left to relate his crossing.

Hallāj was among those of Junayd's entourage who saw the desert as a great obstacle to their successful initiation: "And it is then the rocks," he declaims in one of his stanzas, "and then the plain, then the desert, and the river; then the flood, then the dessication. And it is the inebriation, then the sobering up." In Hallāj's solitudes, as in Junayd's desert, losing one's way is a constant threat to those who dare to venture into them: "It would be good to have you take pity on the one whose heart is gripped in the bird's two claws: infatuated, bewildered, a wild man, he flees from one desert to another; he wanders without knowing where."[48] Hallāj calls this man who staggers on, lost, the "expatriate" (gharīb). In order to attain "spiritual reality," he is subjected to a harsh trial. Although "the roads giving access [to that reality] are narrow, and one encounters on them fires that shoot up next to deserts that sink," he is obliged to follow them. As a traveler, the expatriate knows, however, that he must prepare for his "departure for the desert" and for confronting "aloneness," "maceration," "captivity," and "beating the flint that gives no fire." He also knows that he must "pay attention, be astonished, reflect, be patient, give his opinion, detach himself, choose a method" and, above all, "take a guide." Only after "having finished the crossing of the desert"—the "desert of the science of spiritual realities"—can he "embrace it as a whole." He is aided in his mortal crossing by the reassuring image of one eminent exile, Moses, represented as a model of a contemplative man seeking union with God.[49]

47. Junayd, Rasā'il; Deladrière translation, 66–67.

48. Hallāj, Akhbar al-Hallaj: Recueil d'oraisons et d'exhortations du martyr mystique de l'Islam Husayn ibn Mansur Hallaj, ed. and trans. Louis Massignon and Paul Kraus, 3rd ed. (Paris: Vrin, 1975), Dīwān, poems III, 45, and IV, 46.

49. Massignon, La passion de Husayn ibn Mansūr Hallāj, 3:314.

The desert of Hakīm al-Tirmidhī (d. 320?/932?) was just as dangerous as those of Hallāj and his master, Junayd, if not more so. For the "Sage of Tirmidh," the traveler who succumbs to his carnal soul in the combat that he is carrying on with it is lamentably projected into "the deserts of stupefaction," where he collapses, prey to isolation and the sense of solitude brought on by "the emptiness of the desert." Stigmatized in his soul and his flesh, he is overwhelmed by the unbearable experience of what the Qur'an calls the *mudtarr*. At bay, he must take up the burden of a man in distress who, gnawed by expectations and incertitude, cannot decide whether to continue or turn back. In desperation he cries out to God to save him from himself by helping him to purify his soul. And as in Qur'an 27:62, he who "listens to the (soul) distressed (the *mudtarr*) when it calls on Him" responds to his appeal.[50] It is God's duty to succor the "needy man who has exhausted his rations, [lost] his baggage, and remains, in a state of stupor, in desert lands not knowing what path to follow."[51] Did not the Law permit those "lost in the desert" to eat the flesh of animals that had not been ritually slaughtered?[52]

That theory is illustrated in Hakīm al-Tirmidhī's account of his own conversion. In this autobiographical passage (one of the first of the genre) he tells how, at the age of twenty-eight, he left home to go study in Iraq, after making the pilgrimage to Mecca. Far from home, he was seized by a spiritual crisis that precipitated his return to his hometown in Nishapur. What were conditions like as he crossed the Mafāza, the great desert between Persia and Khurasan? His *Autobiography* does not say. What it does

50. In his French translation of the Qur'an, Régis Blachère translates the word *mudtarr* as "besogneux" (needful). Denise Masson translates it as "malheureux" (unfortunate one), which seems to me to correspond better to Tirmidhī's intentions here. See Régis Blachère, *Le Coran*, 3 vols. (Paris: Maisonneuve, 1947–60); and Denise Masson, *Le Coran* (Paris: Gallimard, 1967).

51. Hakīm al-Tirmidhī, *Kitab Sīrat al-Awliyā*, in *Drei Schriften des Theosophen von Tirmid: Thalathat musannafāt lil-Hakīm al-Tirmidhī*, ed. Bernd Radtke, 2 vols. (Beirut: Arabisch-Deutsche Ausg., 1992–), 15. Hakīm al-Tirmidhī returns to the question of the *mudtarr* in his famous *Kitāb Khatm al-Awliyā*: Hakīm al-Tirmidhī, *Khatm al-Awliyā.*, ed. 'Uthman Yahyá (Beirut: al-Matbatah al-Kāthūlīkīya, 1965).

52. The theosopher seems to have borrowed his theme of the *mudtarr* from one of the great mystics of Nishapur, Abū Hafs the Blacksmith (d. 265/879), whom we have already encountered, the reputed founder of the mystical way of the Malāmatiyyah, the "movement of blame" that asserted that the ascetic must never seek out consideration, so as to devote himself uniquely and humbly to the love of God. He states that one should never ask anything of God unless he finds himself in a situation of the *mudtarr*, with "a broken heart and a feeling of powerlessness." This applies only to those who can find no way out of their troubles by themselves, "neither in God nor among men": Sulamī, *Risālat al-Malāmatiyya*; Deladrière translation, 88.

say is that this return was neither planned nor even desired. Hakīm al-Tirmidhī was obliged to go through the most overwhelming moment of his life and come to terms with it alone. He had no master, no companion to advise him and guide him in the "Way." Not because he had not tried. After some vain investigations, it was in the form of a book, he tells us, that the word of "People of Knowledge" rang in his ears. Thanks to this manual and its instructions on how to strengthen the heart, he pursued his initiation. To one side, he had a guidebook; to the other, the desert. "My heart," he writes, "took pleasure in retirement and in desert places, and I circulated ceaselessly among ruins and tombs." A book cannot wholly replace a master, however, and the neophyte long sought "trustworthy beings" who alone could help him advance in the way of God. Alas, "this was in vain." He nonetheless continued to wander among "the ruins and the desert places" on his own. Until the day when the skies opened up for him in a "spiritual illumination." One evening, exhausted and dazed, he lost consciousness. In a dream he saw rise up before him an immense desert that, he declares, "I did not know" and in which a grand council of wise men was taking place. Not far off, there was a nuptial chamber. A voice murmured in his ear: "You will be taken before the Lord." He drew aside the veils (of the bridal bed?) and went in, and was instantly submerged in reverent fear. Although the chamber contained nothing—no being, no image—he intuited that he was before God. This was confirmed later by the chamberlain charged with guarding the chamber. His ecstasy was a success: the young Tirmidhī felt the Way open up to him. With an admirable obstinacy, he remained in the desert solitudes until the day when the master of truth that he yearned to meet came along to help him complete an initiation that he had begun alone. For a long time he had only the book and the desert, two masters whose answers were uncertain. Of the two, it was, paradoxically, the desert that turned out to be the better guide. After several unsuccessful attempts, it opened up to him the path that he had so desperately sought.[53] This is why Tirmidhī's *Autobiography* makes the desert more than simply the background for the mystical experience. Instead, it has the status of a highly important personage. A Sufi adage says that the neophyte must be in the hands of his master like a dead body in the hands of the person who washes it. This experience of ritual death imbues mystical

53. Hakīm al-Tirmidhī. *Khatm al-Awliyā*; selections in French translation in ʿUthman Yahyā, *Le Kitāb Khatm al-Awliyā d'Al-Hakīm al-Tirmidhī* (dissertation, École Pratique des Hautes Études, 1976), 30–31.

representations of the desert. We have already seen Junayd associate death with the desert and stress its importance.

What is in Junayd and his disciple Hallāj just an obstacle to be surmounted (and in Hakīm al-Tirmidhī an obstacle that might easily lead to failure) becomes in Nifarrī (d. 354/965), another mystic from Khurasan, an extreme image of loss. In his *Book of Spiritual Addresses*, God says to someone who is seeking him: "Seek not the shadow of the desert: for in My vision there is neither brightening nor shadow. The desert is the stage of two men: of him who associates other gods with Me, and of him who is veiled from Me. The desert is everything that is other than I."[54] This divine warning makes the desert a dead-end path that leads nowhere, not a stage to be gone through or an obstacle to be surmounted. Nifarrī's desert is more deceitful that Tirmidhī's; it is a world of mirages and illusions. His negativity is also more radical, because the desert is a space of error and false belief. Only outcasts plunge into it.

For the Baghdad school, the desert is a place that raises shivers only because it is the way that leads to God. In the Khurasanian mystical tendency represented by Nifarrī, it is above all a place of failure. In both instances, however, it appears as an image worth contemplating, in the one case as the happy outcome of a necessarily difficult but successful quest, in the other case the unhappy outcome of that same quest. That is, the two tendencies join in referring to a mystical school of writing in which crossing the desert shows the truth or the untruth of a place. That type of writing has the particular characteristic of being composed of places or, better, of a succession of pictures showing what cannot be said. Because it claims to express the unspeakable, it unfolds like a visual writing in which saying is showing and reading is seeing. This recalls, but in a totally different epistemological context, the habits of the geographers, whose language the mystics borrowed. In order to represent the domain of Islam, Muslim geographers in effect adopted a discursive strategy that consisted in telling about space in the form of itineraries. That way of appropriating space gave rise to an entire literary genre of "itineraries" (*masālik*), which are to Muslim culture—which never took well to the sea—what the long sea voyage was to Greek culture. It may also explain how the two forms of writing, the mystical and the geographical, come together on the principle of *autopsia*.

---

54. Niffarī, *Mukhātabāt*, 35:190; trans. Arthur John Arberry as *The Mawāqif and Mukhātabāt of Muhammad ibn 'Abbi 'l-Jabbār al-Niffarī* (Cairo: Maktabat al-Mutannabī, 198?).

The Voyage to Syria

It is a known fact that religious symbolism makes certain places predestined for attention more than others. Because it tends to establish a strong connection between space and the sacred, it ends up, every time, spiritualizing geography and using it in support of its semiology. This leads to "holy places" and other "sacred spaces" that add a particularly visual sense to scripture. The expression "holy place" first appeared in Christianity in the fourth century (hence somewhat late) to designate places in which the events of the New and Old Testaments had taken place.[55] As an heir to that spiritual geography, Islam chose Syria and Palestine as its land of the elect.[56] When Muslim asceticism in turn made that same region one of its great destinations, it took over its biblical prestige, expressed, as early as the eighth century, in the dual theme of exile and of a meritorious sojourn in that blessed place. First saturated with meaning in the Jewish context, then in the Christian, that part of the Near East was stamped with the seal of Islam. There is a story that illustrates the point to which Islam considered the region exemplary. When the caliph al-Ma'mūn (r. 813–33) came to inspect the fortresses on the Syrian-Byzantine frontier, he asked to meet the holy men of Hims.[57] At the time the city had the reputation, throughout the Muslim world, of sheltering a particular class of friends of God. These were the men that the caliph wanted to see. An entire group of ritual figures were presented to him, among them a man who did not look like much, but who was described to the caliph as an extraordinary being: "This man counts among the *abdāl*; if we are visited by a misfortune, we solicit him, he invokes God, and immediately we have relief; if we are stricken by drought, we organize supererogatory prayers, we turn to him,

55. On this point, see the texts brought together and edited by Pierre Maraval under the title *Récits des premiers pèlerins chrétiens au Proche-Orient (IVe–VIIe siècle)* (Paris: Cerf, 1996).

56. This was the Shām of Muslim geographers of the Middle Ages; it designated what is now Syria, Lebanon, Palestine, Israel, and Jordan. The "titles of glory" (*fadā'il*) of this province of Islam are displayed in such works as 'Ali ibn Muhammad Raba'i, *Fadā'il al-Shām wa-Dimashq*, ed. Salah al-Din Munajjid (Damascus: al-Majma' al-'Ilmī al-'Arabi-Minashq, 1951); and Ibn Abī al-Hawl, *Fadā'il al-Shām*, ed. Salah as-Din Munajjid (Damascus). Certain of these works are dedicated to specific places, as is Muhammad ibn Nāsir ad-Dīn al-Sawwāy, *Risālat Shann al-Ghāra fī Fadl Ziyārat al-Maghāra*, MS no. 4391, Zāhiriyya, Damascus.

57. In the ninth century Hims (or Homs, later Edesa), could boast several *abdāl*, such as the ascetic and traditionist Yahiā ibn 'Uthmān (d. 255/868): Dhahabī, *Siyar*, 12:307. According to a tradition transmitted by Fudayl ibn Fudāla, among the *abdāl* who lived in Syria there were twenty-five living in Hims, thirteen in Damascus, and two in Bīsān: Ibn 'Asākir, *Tārīkh madinat Dimashq*, ed. 'Alī Shīrī., 40 vols. (Beirut: Dār al-Fikr, 1995–96), 1:63.

he prays to God, and immediately it begins to rain."[58] This edifying story contains one of the reasons for which Syria was considered holy and its land became the home of the *abdāl*, or "substitute" saints. Even a century earlier, 'Abd-Allah ibn al-Mubārak (d. 181/797), a famous Khurasanian jurist and traditionist, claimed that he knew four such men of God, two of whom lived in Syria.[59]

A representative of primitive asceticism, 'Abd-Allah ibn al-Mubārak published the first traditions concerning this class of saints. One of these presents the caliph 'Alī rebuking an Iraqi soldier during the battle of Siffīn because he has heard the man cursing the Syrian rebels. The caliph reminds the man that it is not good to insult the Syrians because among them there are pious men who reject the fratricidal divisions that are tearing Muslims society apart. Those good men were, precisely, the *abdāl*.[60] In another tradition, attributed to the Prophet, the founder of Islam states that "there will always be in my community *seven* [saints] whose prayers will be answered whenever they invoke God: by them you will be rescued and by them you will know abundance." The holy man presented to the caliph al-Ma'mūn is credited with just such powers. The function of intercession was amplified by other traditions that arose in the ninth century and that attributed to a society of hidden saints (of which the *abdāl* were simply a working part) great cosmic powers. The functioning of the universe depended on them. Without them, it would collapse.[61] Traditionists such as Ahmad ibn Hanbal (d. 241/855) and mystics such as Tustarī took it on themselves to flesh out the physiognomy of this council of saints on whom the fate of the physical world depended. Ibn Hanbal published a tradition in which a man in the early eighth century had a dream in which

---

58. Ibn 'Asākir, *Tārīkh madinat Dimashq*, 5:33; Dhahabī, *Siyar*, 12:340.

59. Dhahabī, *Siyar*, 8:425.

60. This tradition was also transmitted by Nu'aym ibn Hammād (d. 220/844), the disciple and countryman of Ibn al-Mubārak: Nu'aym ibn Hammād, *Kitāb al-Fitan*, ed. Suhayl Zakkār (Mecca: al-Maktabah al-Trjārīyah, 1991), 108.

61. Even in the mid-ninth century, the more scrupulous of the traditionists considered these traditions to be false: this is the case in particular of Ahmad ibn Hanbal, *Musnad*, ed. Ahmad Muhammad Shākir, 15 vols. (Cairo: Dār al-Ma'ārif, 1946–56), 5:322; followed by Ibn 'Asākir, *Tārīkh madinat Dimashq*, 1:67; Ibn al-Salāh, *Fatāwā* (Cairo: Maktabat ibn Taymīyah), 1:183; and Ibn al-Bayda', *Tamyyīz*, 4. Among these traditionists, the first who gave credit to this tradition was Haytham ibn Kulayb al-Shāshī (d. 335/946), *Musnad* (Medina: Maktabat al-'Ulum wa-al-Hikam, 1989), 3:182; followed by Haythamī, *Majma' al-Zawā'id* (Beirut: Dār al-Kitab, 1967), 10:62–63. The mystics, who had an interest in promoting such traditions, validated them at the end of the ninth century. The oldest source seems to have been Hakīm al-Tirmidhī, *Nawādir* (Beirut: Dār Sādir, 1972), reprint of (Istanbul, 1876) 69, 70, 110; followed by Abū Nu'aym, *Akhbār Isbahān*, ed. Sven Dedering as *Geschichte isbahāns [von] Abū Nu'aim*, 2 vols. (Leiden: Brill, 1931), 1:180.

he saw the Prophet, who told him that the *abdāl* dwelled in Syria.[62] When Tustarī was asked who these "substitute" saints were, he replied: "They are called so because they are capable of modifying their states and removing their body from physical laws." They incessantly passed "from one state to another" or "from one stage of [divine] knowledge to another." They drew both their name and their principle of continuity from their powers of change and permutation (*badal*). As soon as one of them died, he was immediately replaced by another. Tustarī adds that there are forty of them, and that they form the base of a spiritual pyramid, the heart of which is occupied by a synod of seven "pious ones" or "pillars" (*awtād*) and the summit by the "pole" (*qutb*) around whom the "wheel" turns.[63]

Even before being the place of residence of a special category of the elect of God, Syria was a blessed land. Jerusalem was the third of the Islamic holy places, after Mecca and Medina.[64] From the start, Islam recognized the religious prestige of the city. In order to dispute the Holy City with Jews and Christians, the Prophet went so far as to orient canonical prayer in its direction, but changed his mind. He also thought that communication with heaven was more propitious in Jerusalem than anywhere else. According to Tradition, the founder of Islam made his Ascension (*mi'rāj*) from the later site of the Dome of the Rock.

In the Middle Ages, once Islam had brought Jerusalem into the category of the sacred,[65] ascetics and pilgrims flocked en masse to within its walls. Many of these men and women made a rather long stay there (several months or several years) as "neighbors of God" (*mujāwir*), a devotional practice current in Mecca from the mid-eighth century. When Nāsir-ī Khusrū arrived in Jerusalem as a pilgrim in mid-April 1046, he was impressed by

---

62. Ibn Hanbal, *Kitāb al-Zuhd*, ed. Muhammad Jalāl Sharaf, 2 vols. (Iskandarīyah: Dār al-Fikr al-Jāmī'ī, 1980–84), 305.

63. Tustarī, *Tafsīr*, 46.

64. For a description of travelers to the Holy City, see John Wilkinson, *Jerusalem Pilgrimage, 1099–1185* (London: Hakluyt Society, 1988); F. E. Peters, ed., *Jerusalem: The Holy City in the Eyes of Chroniclers, Visitors, Pilgrims, and Prophets from the Days of Abraham to the Beginning of the Modern Times* (Princeton: Princeton University Press, 1985); "Multiple Jérusalem: Jérusalem terrestre, jérusalem céleste," special issue, *Dédale*, nos. 3 and 4 (1996); and Aryeh Graboïs, *Le pèlerin occidental en Terre sainte au Moyen Âge* (Brussels: De Boeck Université, 1998). For a comparative study of Jewish, Christian, and Muslim pilgrims to Jerusalem in the modern age, see Lucette Valensi, "Anthropologie comparée des pratiques de dévotion: Le pèlerinage en Terre sainte au temps des Ottomans," in *Urbanité arabe: Hommage à Bernard Lepetit*, ed. Jocelyne Dakhlia (Paris: Sindbad; Arles: Actes Sud, 1998), 117–32.

65. For an account of this recuperation on the architectural level, see Oleg Grabar, *The Formation of Islamic Art* (New Haven: Yale University Press, 1973, 1987); trans. Yves Thoraval as *La formation de l'art islamique* (Paris: Flammarion, 1987), 72–92.

the "great concourse of *mujāwir* and worshipers" attached to the sanctuary of the Rock.[66] Here *mujāwara* had connotations of expectation. The "very level" open space called Sahīra visible in the distance on emerging from the mosque occupies an important place in Islamic eschatology. Traditions tells that it is there that the resurrection and the Last Judgment will take place.[67] "That belief," Nāsir-ī Khusrū observes, "attracts a crowd of people to Jerusalem from all corners of the world, who come there to end their days and to find themselves close to the place designated by God."[68] Men and women who aspired to Islamic sainthood wanted to be right there at the appointed time. They came in such numbers that nearby, at the edge of the Sahīra, there is a vast cemetery filled with the tombs of saints who were the objects of a cult in the Middle Ages that continues to this day.[69] The pious persons buried there had come from all quarters to end their days as "neighbors of Allah." According to a tradition reported by Wahb ibn Munabbih, a major figure in the introduction of biblical narratives into Islamic culture, "the inhabitants of Jerusalem are the neighbors of God, and God has the duty not to torment his neighbors."[70] It is above them that "the gate to heaven" will open.

Muslim asceticism adopted Syria's vocation for holiness quite early on.[71] Several traditions that exhorted the faithful to travel to Syria are attested in the eighth century. One of these, noted by 'Abd Allāh ibn al-Mubārak (d. 181/797), quotes one of the Companions of the Prophet as saying, "A time will come in which all true believers will go to Syria."[72] Another tra-

---

66. Nāsir-ī Khusrū, *Safar Namèh: Relation du voyage de Nassiri Khosrau en Syrie, en Palestine, en Egypte, en Arabie et en Perse pendant les années de l'Hégire 437–444 (1035–1042)*, ed. and trans. Charles Henri August Schefer (Paris, 1881; reprint, Frankfurt am Main: Institute for the History of Arab-Islamic Science, 1994), 82; ed. and trans. Wheeler M. Thackston as *Nasir-i Khusrav's Book of Travels* (Costa Mesa, CA: Mazda, 2001).

67. Ibn al-Faqīh al-Hamadhānī, *Kitāb al-Buldān: Al-Hamadhānī's Geographie der arabischen Halbinsel*, ed. D. H. Müller (Leiden, 1891); trans. Henri Massé as *Abrégé du Livre des pays* (Damascus: Institut Français de Damas, 1973), 117.

68. Nāsir-ī Khusrū. *Safar Namèh*, 68.

69. In the Valley of Jehoshaphat, which circled the city to the east and to the south, "many virtuous men and women" were buried in the Jewish cemetery visited by Rabbi Jacob in the 1240s: see "Multiple Jérusalem," 140.

70. Ibn al-Faqīh, *Kitāb al-Buldān*, 119.

71. The eschatalogical and hagiologic reasons for this were joined by war-related motivations that will be examined in the following chapter. The frontier marches of Missīssa, Tarsus, Edessa, and Antioch attracted religious men of letters from all parts of the Muslim world, to the point that, by the eighth century, their *ribāt* were not only fortresses but international centers of study and meditation.

72. 'Abd Allāh ibn al-Mubārak, *Kitāb al-Jihād*, ed. Nazīh Hammād (Cairo: Majma' al-Buhūth al-Islāmīyah, 1978), 156. Hākim al-Nīsābūrī considered this tradition to be "authentic," according to the criteria of Bukhārī and Muslim (although neither of these transmitted it): Hākim

dition collected in the ninth century has the Prophet saying, "You will emigrate near the place where Abraham emigrated."[73] Similar traditions seem to have accompanied the sojourn in Syria as a spiritual journey in the ascetic circles of Iraq and Khurasan even before the mid-eighth century. This may explain the voluntary exile of Ibrāhīm ibn Ad'ham (d. 161/777). Born in Balkh, he took his training in Iraq, from where he left to live in Syria.[74]

Ibrāhīm ibn Ad'ham lived out his austere life in northern Syria. Liberated from attachments to the world, he often repeated to those who came to him in his solitude that God, who has given nothing to the "poor" in this world, expects nothing from them in the next world.[75] What could be demanded from beings who had broken the better part of their ties with society and taken on a savage state so as to dedicate themselves entirely to God?

When Ibrāhīm ibn Ad'ham journeyed to the *ribāt* of Missīsa or Tarsus, on the Syrian-Byzantine frontier, he found there a community of learned men, come from various regions of the Muslim world to lead a life of meditation, study, or holy warfare in those strongholds. Many volunteers of the jihad—several groups of them by the mid-eighth century—were ascetics. Some of these were made up of people from Khurasan. In one of these Ibrāhīm met a young compatriot, Shaqīq of Balkh (d. 194/809), who was to become his companion. The account of the meeting of the two men shows Shaqīq surrounded by "young Syrians interrogating him about mystical states and stations." We also know of other men who went, like Ibrāhīm, to seek "the lawful" in Syria. "For thirty years, all of them ate nothing but lawful food";[76] another is described as a seeker of the "pure lawful"; a third is given as a "tough believer."[77] A fourth was reputed to be a *nāsik*, continually engaged in devotions of the cult of God.[78]

---

al-Nīsābūrī, *Al-Mustadrak ʿala al-Sahīhayn*, ed. Yūsuf ʿAbd al-Rahmān Marʿashī (Beirut: Dā al-Ma ʿfah, 1986), 1:301. It also appears in Ibn ʿAsākir, *Tārīkh madinat Dimashq*, 1:301.

73. Ibn al-Faqīh, *Kitāb al-Buldān*; Massé translation, 116.

74. "When I began my wandering [*siyāha*]," he relates, "I had been in Iraq. I had lived there for some time, but I did not find there the licit [*halāl*] life that I was seeking. I then asked a sheikh where I could find lawfulness. He answered me: in Syria. I went to a city called the Victorious but that in reality was called Missīsa. I remained there for some time, but without finding there the lawfulness to which I aspired. I again asked a sheikh where I could find the life that I was seeking; that man indicated Tarsus to me and told me: 'You will find there a life in conformity with what you seek and much piety'": Ibn ʿAsākir, *Tārīkh madinat Dimashq*, 2:172.

75. Ibid., 2:182.

76. Abū Nuʿaym, *Hilyat al-Awliyāʾ*, 9:319.

77. Ibn Hajar al-ʿAsqalānī, *Lisān al-Mizān* (Beirut: Dār all-Fikr, 1986), 10:72.

78. Ibid., 3:149.

In the narratives that describe the ascetics who flocked to Syria we can trace the development, in the mid-eighth century, of a durable form of organization of Muslim mysticism: a master surrounded by disciples who lead a life of meditation and abstinence under his guidance. Nineteenth-century scholarship attributed that errant life to the influence of Syrian hermits. Although more recent scholars (Louis Massignon, for one) have challenged that interpretation, it nonetheless continues to serve as an explanation, on the local level, for the anchoritic life in Islam.[79] Most of the first ascetics in Syria were outsiders from Iraq, Khurasan, or Egypt, but some were from Syria itself. The earliest arrivals were Iraqi, the majority of them from the Basra school, but there were also some from Kufa. Interestingly, the first two great ascetics from Khurasan known to have been in Syria in the mid-eighth century were associated with those two schools. The first Iraqi to arrive in Syria after choosing renunciation, a man known as "the Ascetic,"[80] belonged to the elite ideologico-combatant sector of the *qurrā'*, which took its name from psalmody and from meditation on Revelation in the Qur'an.[81] Banished from his homeland for having preached a spirituality contrary to religious legalism, he was placed in supervised residence in Damascus. Little is known of this man of piety, except that he preached an asceticism turned toward examination of conscience (*muhāsaba*), obligatory chastity, and the practice of vegetarianism. Other accusations, such as claiming that he was "in the example of Abraham," were added later. That was quite enough to make the political authorities condemn him to exile. Another man sent into exile by the same caliph was the prestigious Abū Dharr al-Ghifārī (d. 31/651), one of the few Companions of the Prophet to have followed the path of asceticism.

In Damascus the Ascetic is reported to have become friends with another eminent figure in nascent Muslim asceticism, the learned Ka'b al-Ahbār (d. 32/652). A converted Jew and the transcriber of many biblical and rabbinic parables, he held the Ascetic in such high esteem that he called him "rāhib al-umma" (monk of Islam). In Syria the Ascetic continued to follow the same monastic life that he had led in Iraq, spending

79. Denis Gril, "Les débuts du soufisme," in *Les voies d'Allah: Les ordres mystiques dans l'Islam des origines à aujourd'hui*, ed. Alexandre Popovic and Gilles Veinstein (Paris: Fayard, 1996), 33.

80. This man was 'Amir ibn 'Abd al-Qays.

81. These "reader-reciters of the Qur'an" played a major role in the Great Discord that shook Islam between 656 and 661. On this elite, see Hichem Djaït, *La grande discorde: Religion et politique dans l'Islam des origines* (Paris: Gallimard, 1989), 125–37. For other names that should be added to the list of the pious and the scrupulous *qurrā'* of Basra who took a vow of poverty given in Massignon, *Essai sur les origines du lexique*, see Ibn 'Asākir, *Tārīkh madinat Dimashq*, 26:22.

more of his time on the heights of Mount Qāsyūn than in Damascus. Several traditions note that he was in contact there with Christian hermits. One of these shows him, in the solitudes of the Bādiyat, making the acquaintance of a Christian monk, who asks him what he is doing in such an isolated and dangerous spot. When the Ascetic responds that he is there by order of the government, the hermit rejoins, "A community of which you are the worst subject is an excellent community indeed."[82] We owe this story to Mālik ibn Dīnār (d. 128/745), one of the principal disciples of Hasan al-Basrī (d. 110/728), a major figure in Iraqi asceticism. The fact that Hasan had relations with the Ascetic may explain how and why, in Mālik's entourage, the trip to Syria had become the end result of all successful asceticism. Did Hasan himself make the trip to Syria? We do not know. We do know that another of his disciples, 'Abd al-Wāhid ibn Zayd (d. 177/793), was one of the principal promoters of this sort of voyage. The medieval biographers associate his stay in Syria with two encounters, one with a "fool of God," the other with a monk from whom he retained the lesson of a Jesus who preached exile. The account of the meeting of the two anchorites given by Qutham the Ascetic quotes 'Abd al-Wāhid as saying to him:

> I was descending from the Darāya when I saw an anchorite monk chained to one of the tombs of the cemetery of the hamlet. I was afraid of him, to the point of being shaken by a great fear. When I asked him if he were a djinn or a human, he answered me, "How can you be afraid of anyone else than God? I am only a lost man whose sins have brought him down and who has fled them in God. I am not a djinn but a vain man!" I added, "Who keeps you company?" He responded, "The wild solitude!" Then I asked him, "What do you eat?" He answered, "The fruits of the trees and the plants of the earth!" I said, "Do you like and do you desire the company of men?" He answered, "I fled their company and I removed myself from their society!" When I finally asked him, "Are you in the way of Islam?" he responded, "I do not know what Islam is; I only know that Jesus recommended isolation to us when people sink into corruption."[83]

---

82. Ibn 'Asākir, *Tārīkh madinat Dimashq*, 26:28.

83. Ibid., 37:219. In another version of this story the Christian declares, "Hunger is my seasoning, fear [of God] is my emblem, work is my clothing, my feet are my mount, the moon is my lantern, the sun is my fire, and the grasses that the beasts nibble are my subsistence. I spend my nights [and my days] in deprivation, and yet no one is as rich as I": Abū Nu'aym, *Hilyat al-Awliyā'*, 2:137.

If it is difficult to know whether all of these narrations reflect some real
occurrence transfigured into exemplary conduct, there is no mistaking the
meaning that they took on for ninth-century mysticism: they gave it inspiration and justification. The image sketched out in this exemplum of Jesus
as a personification of exile worked at a deep level in the field of mystical
representations, where it functioned, along with the image of Moses, to
encourage identification with them. Throughout the Middle Ages, the
pairing of Jesus and Moses embodied the two essential acts—exile and
the errant life—around which mysticism organized detachment from
the world. A number of biblical forgeries presented the "Fathers of the
Desert" in terms of their image. Charged with establishing wandering as a
mode for approaching God, Moses is told by God to be like "the solitary
bird who flies over the desert lands" or to "wander over the earth meditating and taking heed" to the point of wearing out his shoes and breaking his
traveler's staff. Described as a prophet of renunciation, Jesus is presented
as an embodiment of the figure of the exile.[84] All those who walk in his
traces, one tradition of the late eighth century insists, will become "the
beings the most dear to God," and it adds, "Blessed are the exiles." Who
are these exiles? "Those who flee with their religion who, on the day of
the Last Judgment, will be regrouped with Jesus at their head," was the
response of the Prophet of Islam.[85]

Abū Muslim al-Khulānī (d. 62/681) is very probably the first ascetic of
Islam whose hagiographic cycle associates hope with the Christ-related
theme of flight from the world. In one narrative in this cycle, which resembles others from the Christian hermit tradition, an anchorite describes
him at his death as a "companion of Jesus, the son of Mary."[86] It may not
be surprising to learn that this ascetic of Yemenite origin, who converted
to Islam around 640, had lived in Darāya, where, in fact, he was buried

84. Ibn Abī Shaybah, *Musannaf*, ed. 'Abd'l-Khāliq al-Afghānī, 5 vols. (Hyderabad, 1967); ed.
Kamāl Y. Al-Hūt, 7 vols. (Beirut: Dār all-Tāj,1989), 7:65.

85. Ibn Hanbal, *Kitāb al-Zuhd*, 170. There is a variant in Ibn Kathīr, *Al-Bidāya wa'l-Nihāya*,
14 vols. (Cairo: Matba'āt al-Sa'ādah, 1932–39), 2:96, in which Hasan al-Basrī (d. 110/728) states: "Jesus
is the 'head'[ra's] of those who renounce, on the day of the Last Judgment." He then adds, "Those
who flee with their sins [dhunāb] will regroup around him on the day of the Last Judgment." One
ninth-century source dedicated to Christian monasticism in Syria says of Jesus that "he perfected
renunciation of the world and made it beloved of all": Anastase, "Un document islamique sur le
monachisme au IXe siècle," 891. The "Islamic" parables attributed to Jesus are collected together
in Miguel Asín Palacios, *Logia et agrapha Domini Jesu apud moslamicos scriptores asceticos praesertim
usitata*, 2 vols. (Paris: Firmin Didot, 1916–29).

86. Ibn 'Asākir, *Tārīkh madinat Dimashq*, 9:22a; Dhahabī, *Siyar*, 9:13. On this ascetic, see also
Ibn Sa'd, *Tabaqāt*, ed. Karl Vilhelm Zetterstéen (Leiden, 1909), 7:448; and Abū Nu'aym, *Hilyat
al-Awliyā'*, 2:22.

after dying of wounds suffered in combat against the Byzantine forces. In the following generation there were other learned men who were influenced by asceticism. One was Abū Qilāba (d. 105?/723?), who left Basra to go settle in that village not far from Damascus, thus providing a tenuous link that indicates that the installation of 'Abd al-Wāhid ibn Zayd and his disciples there was part of an established tradition.

At the time, the population of Darāya was not exclusively Muslim. Christians must have been fairly numerous, given that there is word of a church there in the mid-eighth century.[87] This would also explain the presence of Christian anchorites in the outlying areas. Living in cells hollowed out of the mountainsides, these monks may have influenced the choice of Darāya on the part of the Basra ascetics. At the death of 'Abd al-Wāhid ibn Zayd, one of his disciples (also from Basra) continued his teaching, taking the name of Darānī from the locality.[88] Although it cannot be proven, it is probable that the presence of leading representatives of the ascetic school of Basra led to the creation of a monastery on the model of the one at 'Abbādān, a monastery-*ribāt* situated on the Persian Gulf that had been had been fortified by one of the disciples of Hasan al-Basrī and that, from its founding, had welcomed ascetics from Basra and Kufa.[89] Darānī stayed there for some time, and Louis Massignon believes that his master reorganized what he calls the "cenobitic agglomeration" of 'Abbādān.[90]

After Darāya, two other cities in Palestine, Jerusalem and Ramla, attracted ascetics from Iraq and Khurasan in the eighth century. Jerusalem, already a privileged place for students of scripture, offered nascent asceticism opportunities in dogmatics and hagiography. It was considered as important as Mecca, for example, and it was thought to be the place of residence of Khadir, a legendary personage looked to as a spiritual guide,[91]

87. Ibn 'Asākir, *Tārīkh madinat Dimashq*, 26:67.

88. Khatīb al-Baghdādī, *Tārīkh Baghdād*, 10:248–50.

89. Yāqūt, *Mu'jam al-Buldān*, ed. Ferdinand Wüstenfeld, 7 vols. (Leipzig, 1855–73; reprint, 6 vols. in 11 pts., Frankfurt: Institute for the History of Arabic-Islamic Science, 1994), 4:74.

90. Massignon, *Essai sur les origines du lexique*, 214.

91. On this personage, see Louis Massignon, "Élie et son rôle transhistorique: Khadariya en Islam" (1955), reprinted in Massignon, *Opera minora*, ed. Youkim Moubarac (Paris: Presses Universitaires de France, 1969), 142–61; and Hassan Elboudrari, "Entre le symbolique et l'historique: Khadir im-mémorial," *Studia Islamica* 76 (1992): 25–39. One of the oldest and most complete pseudobiblical narratives concerning Khadir is the *Kitāb Bad' al-Khalq* of 'Umārah ibn Wathīmah al-Fārisī (d. 289/902): *Les légendes prophétiques dans l'Islam depuis le Ier jusqu'au IIIe siècle de l'Hégire: Kitāb Bad' al-Khalq wa Qisas al-Anbiyā*, ed. Raif Georges Khoury (Wiesbaden: Harrassowitz, 1978), 1–23. That author states that Elias resides in "the mountains of the East," and Khadir in the "mountains of the West." But every year, the two immortals meet in Jerusalem, from where they

two qualifications that may explain the choice of the Karrāmiyya to establish one of the main centers of their congregation in Jerusalem.⁹² Ramla was, above all, a center for ascetics from Kufa. According to Massignon, one of these founded a monastery there in 767 on the model of the *ribāt* of 'Abbādān.⁹³ With the formation of mystical circles and monasteries in these centers in Syria and Palestine, Syria enlarged its vocation as a land that welcomed the study of Sufism.

At Darāya, Darānī, surrounded by Syrian and Iraqi disciples, professed an approach to God founded on renunciation of the world and self-annihilation: "The best proof of proximity to God," he taught, "is when he examines your heart [and sees] that you want no one, in this world and in the next, outside of him." Darānī calls this total renunciation of everything that is not God *zuhd*. It is, along with fear, the key to the door to the beyond and the "foundation of all things in this world and in the other." The elect live it in this world as a "punishment" while waiting to rejoin their Lover and take delectation in the joys of his vision.

Judging Darānī 's teachings not quite orthodox, the local doctors leagued together against him and obtained his expulsion from Syria. But the master mystic had already prepared for his succession. He could count, in particular, on Ibn Abī Hawārī (d. 246/860), a disciple from Kufa. But this underestimated the disapproving local opposition. Already irritated, the ulemas of Damascus orchestrated a new intrigue against the disciple, whom they accused of preaching the superiority of the saints over the prophets. Although they did not manage to have him condemned, they did succeed in having him expelled. Like his master, Ibn Abī Hawārī went to live in Mecca as a "neighbor of God," and according to some sources, he ended his days there. According to others, he obtained permission to return to Syria and carry on the teaching of his master, which had in fact continued uninterrupted thanks to another disciple who was both effective and discreet.⁹⁴

---

depart in pilgrimage to Mecca. In one variant Jerusalem is given as the place of residence of Khidr or Khadir.

92. On this mystical sect, see C. E. Bosworth, "Karrāmiyya," in *Encyclopédie de l'Islam*, new ed. (1966), 6:694a; and in *The Encyclopaedia of Islam*, new ed. (1966), 6:667.

93. Massignon, *Essai sur les origines du lexique*, 234.

94. Ibn Abī Hātim, *Kitāb al-Jarh wa al-ta'dīl*, 9 vols. (Beirut: Dār al-Kitub al-'Ilmiyah, 1952), 2:47; Abū Nu'aym, *Hilyat al-Awliyā'*, 10:50; Sulamī, *Tabaqāt al-Sūfiyah*, ed. Nūr al-Dīn Shuraybah (Cairo: Dār al-Kitāb al-'Arabī, 1953), 98, 102; Dhahabī, *Siyar*, 12:93. The greatest Iraqi ascetics of the age contracted *suhba* (initiatic fellowship) with the principal disciples of Darānī or traveled as pilgrims in the mountains of Syria and Lebanon. Representatives of the school of Baghdad as important as Nūrī (d. 295/907) and Abū Turāb al-Nakhshabī were among these. Others returned to

In Syria Ibn Abī Hawārī had been married to a woman of saintly reputation. She was buried near Jerusalem, in the Kidron Valley, where she was
the object of a cult throughout the Middle Ages.[95] She is not the only female who appears in this ascetic milieu: the sources mention many women
who embraced an ascetic vocation in Syria. Darānī 's entourage included
several saintly females who, not content to remain in the background,
took on functions in the initiation process. Unfortunately, they remain
anonymous.[96] Darānī speaks of their positive presence:

> As I was walking one day on the road to Jerusalem, I saw a woman wearing a
> robe of rough cloth and, on her head, a woolen scarf. She was seated, bowed
> over with her head between her knees, and weeping. I approached her and
> said to her, "What makes you weep, young woman?" She answered, "How can
> one not weep, O Abū Sulaymān, when I love his encounter?" I said, "So whom
> do you love?" She responded, "Does the lover love anything else than meeting
> the Loved One?" I said, "And who, then is your Loved One?" She answered,
> "The One who knows the invisible." I said, "What should one do to love him?"
> She responded, "If you succeed in purifying your soul of its faults and if your
> spirit wanders in the kingdom of the heavens, you will know how to arrive
> at the love of the Loved One." I said, "In what state are [lovers] found?" She
> answered, "Their bodies are thin, their complexion is changed, their eyes are

Iraq, and still others made a name for themselves where they were. Among those who remained,
the most important was certainly Ibn al-Jallā (d. 306/918), a mystic who left Bagdhad to settle in
Damascus, probably during the time he spent wandering in Syria, following the example of his
two masters, Nūrī and Abū Turāb. Ibn al-Jallā embodied Baghdad myticism in more than one
way: it was a family tradition, as his father had been a disciple of Bishr al-Ḥāfī (d. 227/841) and had
known Maʿrūf al-Karkhī (d. 200/815). Ibn al-Jallā's contemporaries included Ibrāhīm al-Qassār
(d. 326/937), an ascetic born in Raqqa, in Mesopotamia, who died at a very old age and whom
Sulamī considered to be "one of the most eminent sheikhs of Syria." For a long list of ascetics who
came to the region, see Michael David Bonner, *Aristocratic Violence and Holy War: Studies in the
Jihad and the Arab-Byzantine Frontier* (New Haven: American Oriental Society, 1996), 157–83.

95. She may have been buried in Damascus, however. On this female mystic, Rābiʿa of
Basra, see Dhahabī, *Siyar*, 8:258; and Ibn al-Mulaqqin, *Tabaqāt*, 408. She is not to be confused
with another, older Iraqi female mystic, Rābiʿa al-ʿAdawiyya (d. 185?/802?), whose tomb and
maqām Harawī mentions in 1173: Harawī al-Mawsilī, *Kitāb al-Ishrārat ilā Maʿrifat al-Ziyārāt*; trans.
Janine Sourdel-Thomine in *Guide des lieux de pèlerinage* (Damascus: Institut Français de Damas,
1952, 1957), 68. For a discussion of the two Rābiʿas as legendary figures, see Julian Baldick, "The
Legend of Rābiʿa of Basra: Christian Antecedents, Muslim Counterparts," *Religion* 20 (1990):
233–47.

96. Michel Chodkiewicz has noted the extent to which medieval hagiographic dictionaries
crush female saints under the veil of anonymity: see Michel Chodkiewicz, "La sainteté féminine
dans l'hagiographie islamique," in *Saints orientaux*, ed. Denise Aigle (Paris: De Boccard, 1995),
99–115. See also Ruth Roded, *Women in Islamic Biographical Collections: From Ibn Saʿd to Who's Who*
(Boulder, CO: Lynne Rienner, 1994), a work that I have been unable to consult.

tearful, their hearts beat fast, their souls are split open, and their tongues, from much remembrance of their Loved One, are [full of] ease and abundance." I said, "Where does all the wisdom with which you express yourself come from?" She answered, "It is not a thing that comes with age, O Abū Sulaymān!" I said, "How did it come to you?" She responded, "By purity of attachment [or affection] and by good conduct." [Then, having recited verses of love], she rose up, and while I watched her moving away, she slipped between two mountains.[97]

If we can believe the late medieval sources, Darānī remained faithful to the concept of love that the anonymous saintly woman teaches in this passage.[98] When that Iraqi mystic arrived in Syria, another saintly woman, Fātima of Nishapur (d. 223/838), left Khurasan to go, like so many of her pious compatriots, to live in Mecca as a "neighbor of God." The little that we know of her is that Bistāmī knew her and sincerely admired her. During a pilgrimage to Mecca the Egyptian mystic, Dhū al-Nūn (d. 245/859) met her and traveled with her as master and disciple, going several times to Syria. On her deathbed in Jerusalem, she gave her pupil final instructions: "Persist in sincerity, and fight your carnal soul by works."[99]

In Jerusalem, but also in the nearby mountains, Dhū al-Nūn met a number of female saints. One brief but striking encounter with a "Lost One" was a revelation to him. He states, "I looked to see where the voice was coming from, and I found myself in the presence of a woman. She was dressed in a sort of woolen tunic and wore a black horsehair veil. She seemed worn out by her efforts, exhausted by sorrow, emptied of her substance by love, and wounded to death by spiritual emotions." Dhū al-Nūn had just enough time to learn arcane secrets from her, but he was powerless to help her and she died in his arms, still nameless. He was to learn her identity later, however, when her life was summarized in one sentence: "For twenty years people thought she was mad, [but] it was only the desire for her lord that killed her."[100] After having situated sainthood among women, the "mystic fable" associates it with madness and the fabulous. Sainthood takes on the appearance of madness because in the gap between the visible and the invisible, it reflects the great tension between the "inner" (bātin) and the "outer" (dhāhir).

97. Ibn al-Mulaqqin, Tabaqāt, 391–92.
98. Qushayrī, al-Risālah, 20.
99. Ibn al-ʿArabī, Manāqib Dhū al-Nūn, 236–37.
100. Ibid., 276.

Medieval hagiographic texts regarding Dhū al-Nūn shows him encountering other "madmen" in Syria. In the Lukkām Mountains he solicits the company of one of them. Searching for the man, he meets a group of ascetics who tell him that the "gnostic" whom he wants to see is in reality a madman. When Dhū al-Nūn asks what sort of folly has stricken the man, he is told that most of the time he is distracted: when spoken to he does not answer, and when he does answer no one understands him, at which point he begins to lament, lacerate himself, and beat himself. Instead of being dissuaded by this portrait, Dhū al-Nūn is even more eager to admire the saint concealed behind these acts. After a difficult climb, he finally finds himself at the head of a valley, where he meets a thin young man with yellowed, sunburnt skin, who asks him why he is so eager to meet the man. When Dhū al-Nūn asks him about the supposed madman, the young hermit responds, "The Madman is the name they have given me." Dhū al-Nūn wants to know everything about the man and why he embraced the hermit's life, but his only answer is, "It is my love for him that made me wander, and it is the intense emotion that he makes me feel that has made me a solitary."[101]

In the Lukkām Mountains, where he seems to have stayed for some time, Dhū al-Nūn met a number of hermits, women, young men, and old men. Some lived in a hut, like one old woman blinded from weeping; others in grottoes.[102] While making his way through the mountains, the Egyptian mystic tells us (and the principle of *autopsia* obliges) that he stopped in a wooded valley draped in a mantle of green to "admire the beauty of the flowers, the green grass of the pastures, the tender chirping of the birds in the copses, the murmur of water running over pebbles, the coming and going of the beasts around the watering places, the sound of the wind rushing through the branches of the trees,"[103] when a sad and tremulous voice reached him. He followed the sound, which led him to the entrance of the grotto of a female anchorite.[104] She may have been one of the "substitute"

101. Ibid., 273–74. An example of this type of meeting also figures in Abū Nuʿaym, *Hilyat al-Awliyāʾ*, 10:340.

102. Junayd credits Abū Shuʿayb al-Birāthī with being the first Baghdad mystic to have used a grotto as his place of meditation: Abū Nuʿaym, *Hilyat al-Awliyāʾ*, 10:325. On the great ritual prestige of these men of God living in grottoes in the early tenth century, see Tanūkhī, *Nishwār al-Muhādarāh*; selections trans. Youssef Seddik as *Brins de chicane: La vie quotidienne à Bagdad au Xe siècle* (Arles: Actes Sud-Sindbad, 1999), 89–91.

103. When he broke a tree branch in these same mountains, Abū al-Khayr al-Aqtaʿ, a mystic of the mid-tenth century, cut off his hand, which earned him the surname of Al-Aqtaʿ, or "the Amputated": Abū Nuʿaym, *Hilyat al-Awliyāʾ*, 10:378.

104. Ibid., 10:262–63. For another example of anchorites living in grottoes in the mountains of Syria, see ibid., 10:356.

saints (*abdāl*) who had chosen to live in the Lukkām Mountains, as one of Dhū al-Nūn's Palestinian disciples suggests. In these same mountains, that pupil had met a man who had revealed to him that his heart was sealed with that of Abraham, and that he was a rainmaker. He also confided that he lived there in the company of six other men. These were, of course, "the seven privileged ones among the *abdāl*" that the caliph al-Ma'mūn had heard of and wanted to meet, as we have seen.[105]

Like their Christian counterparts,[106] the Muslim ascetics used grottoes in Syria as retreats. Certain of these localities were surrounded with great biblical prestige. On the slopes of Mount Qāsyūn, a spur of the Anti-Lebanon Range overlooking Damascus, several such caves are thought to have been frequented by the prophets in biblical times. Abraham is supposed to have been buried in "a grotto that extended to great narrowness."[107] When the Andalusian Ibn Jubayr visited the place in 1184, a large mosque had been erected above the spot. He describes the building as "great and high," divided into many oratories "like high chambers dominating the countryside." It was there, Tradition states, that the "Friend of God" came to pray. A mile or so to the west, there is another biblical grotto, where Abel, assassinated by his brother Cain, is said to have left traces of blood "from approximately halfway up the mountain to the grotto," hence its name of the "Grotto of Blood." In that blessed place, an entire line of prophets, from Abraham to Moses, from Lot to Jesus, including Job, is supposed to have prayed.[108] When Ibn Jubayr visited it, the grotto was dominated by a "solidly built" oratory that had rooms and "conveniences for habitation." At the summit of the mountain a cavern named for Adam also had an oratory above it that was described as "a blessed place." Down the slope from the grotto, in the hollow of the mountain, there is a Grotto of Hunger where "seventy prophets starved to death."[109]

105. Ibid., 10:318. In another narrative, we see Tāhir leaving Ascalon in the direction of Gaza to search for these same *abdāl*: ibid., 319. See also Ibn Abī al-Dunyā, *Kitāb Sīrat al-Awliyā* (Beirut: Muassasat al-Kutub al-Thaqafīyah, 1993), 39–40. On the medieval belief that the Lukkām Mountains were the abode of these *abdāl*, see Ta'ālibī, *Thimār al-Qulūb*, ed. Muhammad Abū al-Fadī Ibrāhīm (Cairo: Dār Nahdat Misr Lil-tab' wa-al-Nashr, 1965), 232–33.

106. This was particularly true in Syria: for the ninth century, see the Arabic document published by Father Anastase under the title "Un document islamique sur le monachisme," 888. For another Syrian example in a Syrian source, see Ibn 'Asākir, *Tārīkh Baghdād*, 37:219.

107. Ibn Jubayr, *Riḥlat*, ed. M. J. de Goeje (Leiden, 1907); trans. Maurice Gaudefroy-Demombynes as *Voyages d'Ibn Jubayr*, 4 vols. (Paris: Geuthner, 1949–56), 3:316.

108. The "titles of glory" of this grotto are outlined in al-Sawwāy, *Risālat*.

109. There were forty prophets, according to Harawī, *Kitāb al-Ishrārat ilā Ma'rifat al-Ziyārāt*; Sourdel-Thomine translation, 26–27. On these grottoes, see Janine Sourdel-Thomine, "Pèleri-

An oratory was constructed there as well, as a sign of veneration. As is evident, the Andalusian traveler describes local mystical life as highly structured, and the monasteries (*ribāt*) as numerous.[110] He was seeing the end of a long historical process marked by the passage from the grotto as a symbol of the hermit's life to the establishment and spread of institutionalized and cenobitic forms of asceticism.[111]

When did the grotto give way to the oratory—that is, when did asceticism move from the hermit to the cenobite—in the mountains of Syria? The ninth-century sources are mute on the question.[112] A tenth-century geographer from Palestine mentions no oratory on Mount Qāsyūn in the Damascus region. In his description of the mountains of Lebanon, he observes only that "Muslim hermits have built themselves huts of straw and eat fruits." There is no mention of hermitages or oratories. This means that in the mid-tenth century, the ascetics continued to live in these mountains as they had in the age of Dhū al-Nūn. In all of the mountains in Syria, this geographer notes only two oratories: one on the mountain that dominates Tyre, the other on the Golan. He states that the population of the region and the local authorities paid an official visit to the first of these in mid-*sha'ban*. Were there hermits living there at the time? We do not know. We do know that in the Golan, which "faces Lebanon, towards Damascus [*sic*],"[113] the geographer met a master mystic in an oratory "with forty men dressed in garments of wool." The master and his companions lived there, subsisting on acorns softened by macerating them in water, mixed with a local wild barley.[114]

---

nages damascains," *Bulletin d'Études Orientales* 14 (1952–54): 65–85, esp. 70–71; and Louis Massignon, *Les Sept Dormants d'Éphèse (Ahi-al-Kahr) en Islam et en chrétienté*, 4 vols. (Paris: Geuthner, 1955–58), 87–88. The three revealed religions all frequented the cult sites at the grottoes. During his stay in the Holy Land between 1238 and 1244, Rabbi Jacob, the messenger of Rabbi Jechiel of Paris, visited some of these tombs. He writes in the account of his travels, "The grotto of Simeon the Just and his disciples is near Jerusalem, as well as that of the prophet Haggai. On the other side of Jerusalem lies the Grotto of the Lion, where there lie the bones of the just who were assassinated by the king of Greece for the saintliness of the name": Rabbi Jacob, cited in "Multiple Jérusalem," 141–42.

110. Ibn Jubayr, *Rihlat*, 3:330–31.

111. Abū Nu'aym, *Hilyat al-Awliyā'*, 10:386.

112. Ibn al-Faqīh, for example, states that Lebanon is "the mountain of the Sufi anchorites and saints," but that is all he says on the topic: *Kitāb al-Buldān*; Massé translation, 136–37.

113. André Miquel points out that Muqaddasī has the Golan Heights facing south.

114. Muqaddasī, *Ahsan al-Taqāsīm fī Ma'rifat al-Aqālīm*, ed. M. J. de Goeje (Leiden: Brill, 1906), 237–38; selections trans. André Miquel as *Ahsan al-Taqāsīm fī Ma'rifat al-Aqālīm: La meilleure répartition pour la connaissance des provinces* (Damascus: Institut Français de Damas, 1963);

Unlike their Christian counterparts, the first Muslim ascetics do not seem to have been particularly intent on founding hermitages (*sawma'a*) in the mountains or in the desert. In contrast, the sources are unanimous about the contacts established between the anchorites of the two religions. Thanks to their testimony, we have proof that, from the viewpoint of the religious history of Syria and Egypt, Muslim asceticism gave new force and vigor, in the eighth and ninth centuries, to a phenomenon that had reached its apogee in Christianity in the third to fourth centuries.[115] But although Muslims prolonged and broadened the action of the "Fathers of the Desert," they also departed from them, and their asceticism took on characteristics of its own. Given fundamental principles and dogmatic questions that differed from those of late antiquity, the forms and structures of the socio-religious framework of eastern Christianity had to be changed. Unlike its Christian counterpart, Muslim asceticism of the 'Abbāsid age was only weakly institutionalized. That form lasted until the early twelfth century, when it was replaced by a highly structured cenobitism (as observed and described by the Andalusian traveler Ibn Jubayr).[116] What arose was a sturdier institutional organization, the confraternity and its network.

As long as Muslim asceticism focused on the hermit's life, it continued to look to Christian monasticism as a model. Its more venturesome masters even made monasticism the object of their meditation. In the ninth century, the sources continue to show them consulting their Christian colleagues on questions of theology. A discussion like the one that Ibn Abī Hawārī had with a monk of the monastery of Harmala on the dual nature of Adam, whose body was of terrestrial clay and whose spirit of celestial light, made the rounds of mystic circles in Syria. When its general terms were reported to his master, Darānī, he approved of its tenor.[117] In other circumstances, it was Junayd, the master of the Baghdad school,

---

trans. Basil Anthony Collins, reviewed by Muhammad Hamid al-Tai, as *The Best Divisions for Knowledge of the Regions* (Reading, UK: Garnet, 1994), 172.

115. Here the two major figures are St. Pacomius (d. 346) and St. Anthony (d. 347), both of them in Egypt. On their works, see Peter A. Resch, *La doctrine ascétique des premiers maîtres égyptiens du quatrième siècle* (Paris: Beauchesne, 1931); and Paulin Ladeuze, *Étude sur le cénobitisme pakhomien pendant le IVe siècle et la première moitié du Ve* (Paris: Fontemoing; Louvain: Van Linthout, 1898).

116. On the early Muslim religious orders, see, in particular, Annemarie Schimmel, *The Mystical Dimensions of Islam* (Chapel Hill: University of North Carolina Press, 1975, 1990); trans. Albert Van Hoa as *Le Soufisme ou les dimensions mystiques de l'Islam* (Paris: Cerf, 1977, 1996), 304–21.

117. Ibid., 21.

whom we see on Mount Sinai,[118] surrounded by his disciples, discussing the techniques of ecstasy with a Christian hermit.[119] Earlier, Dhū al-Nūn had offered the example—inconceivable in later centuries—of a mystical initiation of a Muslim by a Christian. The report of this encounter merits a pause. Dhū al-Nūn states: "In the course of one of my voyages through Syria, I crossed a river that bore the name of River of Gold, and I passed near a village when my attention was attracted by a hermitage. I then cried out to the hermit who occupied it, 'Hermit! Answer me!' As he refused to respond to me, I cried again, 'You who are devoted to the Lord, answer me!' He then showed himself to me and asked me, 'What do you need and what do you want?' 'I want an edifying word from which I can draw profit.' 'Have you abandoned this world below?' 'Yes.'"[120]

The initiation lasted several days, during which the Christian mystic taught his Muslim pupil how to move closer to God in a process that combined asceticism, a vow of poverty, and vegetarianism. Faithful to that experience, the Egyptian mystic later defended in his own teaching the idea that the monastic life (*rahbāniyya*) is the highest expression of holiness. In Fustāt we find him explaining to a mystic from Basra that, among the "friends of God," there are "men whose heart shines under the effect of the light that emanates from certitude." Dhū al-Nūn calls these exceptional beings *ruhbān*, "monks among the greatest, kings among the worshipers, princes among the ascetics."[121] We would know more about the customs of the *rahbāniyya* in Islam if the *Book of Monks* of Burjulānī (d. 238/852) had come down to us.[122] That book offered a number of examples of contacts, connections, and exchanges between anchorites, Christian and Muslim—all things that later centuries tried to forget.

118. Harawī notes, at the end of the twelfth century, that in the Christian hermitages of Sinai "there is no lack of holy personages; anachorites and monks stay there": *Kitāb al-Ishrārat ilā Ma'rifat al-Ziyārāt*, 218.

119. Ibid., 68.

120. Ibn al-'Arabī, *Manāqib Dhū al-Nūn*, 346–48.

121. Abū Nu'aym, *Hilyat al-Awliyā'*, 10:371, with a variant in Ibn al-'Arabī, *Manāqib Dhū al-Nūn*, 270–71. When one of his disciples asks him what soul can bear the recommendations that he has made, Dhū al-Nūn responds, "A soul that is capable of enduring hunger and of affronting the shadows; a soul that has traded life here below for that of the beyond without stipulations or particular clauses; a soul that has taken on the *rahbāniyya* of disquietude": ibid., 10:356–57.

122. The *Book of Strangers* of the Iraqi Abū Bakr al-Ajūrī (d. 360/970), contains a citation of this book that is significative of this interpenetration: see Abū Bakr Ajūrī, *Kitāb al-Ghurabā'*, ed. Ramadān Ayyūb (Damascus: Dār as-Bashair, 1992), 65–69. On Burjulānī's lost book, see Massignon, *Essai sur les origines du lexique*, 72–73. See also A. J. Wensick, "Rahbāniyya," in *Encyclopédie de l'Islam*, new ed. (1966), 8:410–12; and in *The Encyclopaedia of Islam*, new ed. (1966), 8:396ff.

Entering into the Desert

Along with the mountain, the desert, in the strict sense of the term, was the major place for contact and communication with the divine. Like the mountain, it was to nature what the city was to culture. But more than that, it was the very negation of life. The strong image that the Middle Ages projected onto the desert is that of a mineral world penetrated with ideas of fear and of death. A symbol of vacuity, the desert was perceived less as empty than as absence, however. It is the absence of life, human life in particular, that gives the desert its anthropological density. The desert is always a deserted place. Because it is loaded with the memory of all those who have lived in it, an uninhabited house is never an empty house. It remains as full as if it were inhabited. The strangeness of the desert resides, precisely, in this gap between the empty and the full. Certainly, an empty space can be full only in a strange manner. The extraordinary slips into the hiatus that separates the normal and the strange. At that point, Muslim hagiography speaks of a "rupture in the normal course of things." It is that disquieting strangeness that the mystics went to look for in the desert, in order to defy it just as much as to appease it.

Ibrāhīm ibn Ad'ham (d. 161/777) was one of the first ascetics whom the sources show making the desert the site of a spiritual conversion. His hagiographic novel presents him as a young man from Balkh of princely origin given over to a voluptuous worldly life. One day when he was participating in a hunting party, a "voice" disturbed the life of ease that he was leading by whispering in his ear, "Is it for this that you were created? Is it for this that you were fated?" The young prince instantly abandoned his mount, removed his rich clothing, put on the rough woolen robe of a shepherd, and, as a sign of his rejection of the world to which he had belonged, "entered into the desert" with the objective of making a penitential pilgrimage to Mecca on foot. Like all pilgrims from Khurasan, he passed through Iraq, where he entered into contact with the schools of asceticism of Basra and Kufa. One exemplum shows him on the road of the Holy Places outside Kufa, where he meets a curious personage who introduces him to the "supreme Name." This is a sign that his peregrination was in reality a journey of initiation. When he encounters Khadir, Ibn Ad'ham learns from this mythological personage that the master who initiated him was none other that the prophet David, according to one variant, or his own eminent compatriot Dāwud of Balkh, according to another. Whether it had been the one or the other, the man revealed to him the great name of God "so that by its mystery he might make his heart firm, overcome his weaknesses, and soften his solitude."[123] Ibrāhīm of course transmits this experience in the desert to his disciples. An text shows one of them, "out of renunciation and divestment," making the pilgrimage to Mecca on foot from his native city of Herat, in what is now Afghanistan. One of his companions relates his experience in the desert in these terms:

> Ibrāhīm ibn Shībān said: Ibrāhīm ibn Bistanbih remained in the desert without eating or drinking, or even desiring anything at all. He said [to us]: "My soul made me believe that I had a high place with God. At that instant, a man called me on my right and said to me: 'O Ibrāhīm, how can you prejudge God in the secret of your being?' I turned toward him and answered him: 'Alas! That is indeed what I did.' He then said to me: 'Do you know how many days I have remained delivered over to abandonment [in the desert] without eating or drinking?' I said: 'God alone knows it.' He answered: 'Twenty-four days, during the course of which not the least thought like yours came to me, whereas if I swore, by his name, so that he would transform that tree into gold, he would do it.'" Ibrāhīm comments, "The beneficial appearance of that man was the cause of my awakening [tanbīh] and my return to my first state."[124]

This exemplum confirms the desert's dual function as a place of conversion and a place of initiation. Without conversion, wandering is unthinkable. It is emptied of its spiritual content. Any journey that is organized must, in principle, be an initiation. The desert is its paradigmatic space, to the extent that it is the cultural incarnation of the void. Under such conditions, there is no journey of initiation that is not one of trials and for which the desert could not serve as a metaphor. Similarly, there is no conversion that does not create a void within and around oneself.

Dhū al-Nūn is one of those who, in the early ninth century, underwent that dual experience of the desert. Following the steps of "The Desert Fathers: Anthony to John Climacus,"[125] he took the sandy solitudes of the Nile Delta as the site of his repentance. He relates: "One day I went out of Fustāt to go to a village. On my way, I stopped in a desert place [sahra]. I slept, and when I opened my eyes, I saw a blind lark fall from its nest.

123. Abū Nuʿaym, Hilyat al-Awliyāʾ, 10:44–45; Qushayrī, al-Risālah, 391–92.
124. Abū Nuʿaym, Hilyat al-Awliyāʾ, 10:43.
125. I am borrowing from Peter Brown the title of chapter 11 of his The Body and Society, 213–40. See also Antoine Guillaumont, "La conception du désert chez les moines d'Égypte," Revue de l'histoire des religions 188 (1975): 3–21; and, for an overall view of the monastic movement in Egypt, Otto F. A. Meinardus, Monks and Monasteries of the Egyptian Deserts (Cairo: American University in Cairo Press, 1961, 1989).

The ground split open at the shock, and out of the opening there came
two bowls, one of gold and the other of silver. In one there was sesame; in
the other, water. I ate from one and drank from the other until I said to
myself, "That is enough!" I repented my sins and settled at the gate [of the
Lord] until he admitted me."[126] After then, Dhū al-Nūn made wandering
a way of life. He traveled in Syria, Iraq, the Hejaz, Yemen, and even as
far as the Maghreb. His hagiographers offer many accounts of his experiences in the various deserts of the Middle East. Some of those experiences
take place in the desert of the Sinai, to which Muslims of the Middle Ages
gave the name Place of the Wandering of the Sons of Israel (Tih Banū
Isra'īl). It was there that he made the greatest number of encounters of
the third type. In one exemplum we see him making his way across the
Tih and meeting a man with "black curly" hair going in his same direction. Our gnostic was intrigued by his unexpected traveling companion,
whose ebony hair turned white every time he invoked the name of God.
He learned from the man that he was seized by a wandering fever: "If you
felt what I feel," the man told him, "you would be like me, in continual
wandering."[127] Thanks to this enlightened being, he discovered that "God
has creatures whose hearts leap up at the mention of him, just as the birds
fly up."[128] In another exemplum it is a young black woman whom he meets
in the Tih. Her eyes fixed on the sky, she seems "plunged into a total dis-
traction." She is less absent that she seems, however, for to his astonishment, she calls Dhū al-Nūn by name: "O man of little faith," she cries.
"God created spirits two thousand years before bodies. Then he made
them turn about the Throne; and those who knew each other then were in
harmony, whereas those who ignored one another were in disagreement.
It is during that round that my spirit knew yours."[129] In this attraction of
like and like we recognize one of the great Platonic themes, that of remi-
niscence, as discussed in the *Lysis*, and that Aristophanes makes fun of in
Banqueters.[130]

126. Sulamī, *Tabaqāt al-Sūfiyah*, 219; Qushayrī, *al-Risālah*, 433; variant in Dhahabī, *Siyar*, 11:534.
127. Abū Nu'aym, *Hilyat al-Awliyā'*, 10:368.
128. Ibid., 10:391.
129. Ibn al-'Arabī, *Manāqib Dhū al-Nūn*; Deladrière translation, 255–56.
130. Plato reminds Lysis that "yea, ever like and like together God doth draw": *Lysis*, 214a, in
Plato, vol. 5, *Lysis, Symposium, Gorgias*, trans. W. R. M. Lamb, Loeb Classical Library (Cambridge,
MA: Harvard University Press; London: William Heinemann, 1961), 41. Several ninth-century
sources mention the Platonic myth put into the mouth of Aristophanes. One of these is the first
treatise on profane love in Islam: Abū Bakr Muhammad ibn Dāwud, *Kitāb al-Zahra* (Chicago:
University of Chicago Press, 1932), 1:15., where it is rendered quite faithfully.

Other mystics are described as inhabiting the Place of the Wandering of the Sons of Israel. One of these wandered about the Sinai Peninsula for fifteen days without finding his route.[131] Another met there a young man "as beautiful as an ingot of silver," who was traveling "without provisions" to Mecca. As the mystic expressed his surprise at seeing the unknown young man traveling "without provisions, camel, or money," he answered, "How can the One who preserves the heavens and the earth be incapable of delivering me to Mecca without any provisions?"[132] thus giving the mystic a lesson in "abandonment to/in God." More cruelly, an Iraqi Sufi who lived in Egypt was desperate because he was unable to repress "a desire" of the heart. Unable to expiate his error, he wandered in the Tih, prey to despair. His companions, who had set off to find him, reached him as he lay dying in the shade of a dune. One of them had just enough time to hear him say, "Rise up! You are in the place of elevation of the Friends (of God)" before he expired.[133]

In the mid-ninth century, entering the desert was a move that received broad social support in Sufi circles. Those who never experienced the desert were perhaps in the minority. The most enthusiastic defenders of the practice did not hesitate to base their careers on it. We can see them traveling alone, in the company of their masters, or with companions. In that epoch, a sojourn in the desert found doctrinal justification in the theory of *tawakkul*, an attitude that consisted, essentially, in putting oneself in the hands of God, resigning and abandoning oneself to him—an attitude that Shaqīq of Balkh (d. 194/809), whom we have met traveling with one of his masters in the mountains of northern Syria, was one of the first to define.[134] Travel in desert lands (often "without viaticum")[135] to the peril of one's life soon became one of the major means for initiation into the *tawakkul*. One mystic of the Baghdad school tells of his experience thus:

One day when I had gone into the desert without provisions, a great misery grasped me. Walking along, I saw a halt in the distance. I was delighted, to the

131. Qushayrī, *al-Risālah*, 114.

132. Ibid., 181–82; *Al-Qushayri's Epistle on Sufism*, 196.

133. Qushayrī, *al-Risālah*, 309.

134. Ibn 'Asākir, *Tārīkh madinat Dimashq*, 13:138.

135. When Ibn al-Jallā (d. 306/918), an eminent Iraqi mystic settled in Syria whom we have already met, was asked, "What do you say about a man who enters into the desert without provisions"? he answered, "That is a task for the men of God." When pressed to answer the question "And if one of those men died there?" he answered (in a pastiche of a rule of law): "It is up to him who kills him to pay the debt of blood": Sulamī, *Tabaqāt al-Sūfiyah*, 178.

point of imagining that I was already there. But on reflection, I said to myself, "And if I were to find repose by putting myself into other hands than his?" I then decided to dig a hole in the sand and put myself in it until someone came along to get me out and lead me to the halt. After having dug my hole, I slipped into it up to my chest with great difficulty, scraping my skin. In the middle of the night, the inhabitants of the stage heard an "invisible interlocutor" [*hātif*] crying out: "O people of the halt, there is a man of God buried in the sand, go and help him!" Some villagers then came to get me out of my hole and take me to their village.[136]

In this anecdote the mystic actualizes a thought that his master has transmitted to him: "He who macerates his flesh sees his sins fall away from it, like the tree that sees its leaves fall."[137] The aphorism echoes a saying of Bistamī (d. 260/874), according to which the man of God who enters into the desert slips out of his "me," freeing himself from himself and from the world, "like a snake that gets rid of his skin."[138] The metamorphosis, a magic of the between, plays at the edges of life and death and chooses spaces that are themselves situated at the limits of the full and the empty. Once again, the desert appears as a spatial metaphor of total abnegation, a metaphor that reflects the way in which the mystic must fashion his own destiny as one of the elect. Without this, he has no powers: "The Signs and the miracles do not come to the saints without exercise or effort," a mystical treatise of the late ninth century proclaims.[139] What is the *mujāhada*, the combat against oneself, against one's passions, if not "the separation from the self and the joining with God."[140] Understandably, when all-powerful God turns his gaze away from the ascetic, it is in the name of his decomposed body that he states:

136. The man was Abū Saʿīd Karrāz (d. 286/899): see Qushayrī, *al-Risālah*, 171; and Ibn ʿAsākir, *Tārīkh madinat Dimashq*, 1:432. For another example of extreme mortification of the flesh on the part of Abū Saʿīd Karrāz, see Kalābādhī, *Kitāb al-Taʿarruf li-Madhhab ahl al-Tasawwuf*, ed. A. J. Arberry (Cairo: Maktabat al-Khānjī, 1933), 172.

137. Massignon, *Essai sur les origines du lexique*, 300.

138. Al-Bīrūnī, *Tahqīq mā liʾl-Hind*, ed. Edward C. Sachau (London, 1887); trans. Vincent Monteil as *Enquête sur l'Inde*; and trans. Edward C. Sachau as *Alberuni's India: An Account of the Religion, Philosophy, Liberature, Geography, Chronology, Astronomy, Customs, Laws and Astrology of India about AD 1030*, 2 vols. (London, 1888); cited in Massignon, *Essai sur les origines du lexique*, 276.

139. Abū Saʿīd Karrāz, *Kitāb al-Sidq*, 70; ed. and trans. A. J. Arberry as *The Book of Truthfulness (Kitab al-sidq)* (London: Oxford University Press, 1937).

140. Jaʿfar al-Sādiq; *Tafsīr*; Nwyia edition, 216. This same mystical commentary on the Qurʾan states (192): "It is by making a gift of one's blood [one's substance?] that the faithful attains the lands of his lover and approaches his master."

My tears, I have exhausted them; my eyelids, I have made them bleed.
My body, I have worn it out; my heart, I have consumed it.
My eyes, Lord, with which I saw the world, I have made them blind![141]

To claim that the desert served the mystics of Islam only as a decorous
background for their spiritual anecdotes is to be deaf to all of this wealth
of experience.

Society and Its Obverse

In one of the oldest narrations concerning Khadir, a pseudobiblical personage taken as a spiritual guide by medieval mysticism, we see him respond to the call of God by abandoning the palace of the king, his father,
to go live in retirement with his wife. One day God, who created him and
who chose Khadir to adore him "on the tops of the mountains in the company of the wild beasts," "in the bottom of the valleys with the land animals," and "on the shores of the seas," orders him to break with his wife,
his last attachment to society. God wants him to be alone, enclosed in a
solitude impermeable to the world of men. Then, after having renounced
living in society, broken the filial connections that attached him to his
father the king, and told the subjects of the kingdom that he would not be
their king, Khadir is subjected to the painful trial of separating from his
wife. He must repudiate the woman he loved just as he had repudiated the
world, thus radically cutting his last tie with humans. In return, God gives
him immortality, a castrated immortality, because it condemns him to live
in "the deserts, the wild valleys, and the seas."[142]

All candidates to sainthood are called to this trial of separation in one
way or another and follow its paradigmatic course. It is both the payment
for their renunciation of worldly life and the price to be paid in order to
enter into the company of God. Without breaking with their social world,
the saints cannot become "other." They must, at least temporarily, abandon the *uns* for the *wahsha*—that is, they must repudiate "social life," "living together," "sociability," and "commerce" with men in order to embrace
the "savage life," the "state of nature," and "solitude." The term *uns* refers

141. The theme of "because of you, Lord, I am sick" is a recognizable expression of the amo-
rous blackmail described by Roland Barthes in his *Fragments d'un discours amoureux* (Paris: Seuil,
1977); in English translation by Richard Howard (New York: Hill & Wang, 1978).

142. These details are borrowed from a ninth-century source: 'Umārah ibn Wathīmah al-
Fārisī, *Les légendes prophétiques dans l'Islam*.

to a world of humans (*insān* = man); *Wahsha* refers to the savage state and
animal nature (*wahsh* = beast, wild animal). The trial consists in renouncing
a false happiness within the group in order to seek the true happiness in
the "desert." By tearing oneself away from the *uns* of men, one enters into
the society of God. From the ninth century on, mystical languages uses
this term to indicate the "station" that ends the list of stages that must be
reached to gain admission into the divine intimacy.[143] Where could those
making their way toward God experience vacuity in order to free themselves from the plenitude of the world, if not in marginal and solitary
places? They had no choice but to break—at least symbolically—with all
the social figures of identity: the city, the family, class, status, and work.

How, at the frontiers of the visible and the invisible, could one continue
to be an inhabitant of the earth and yet claim to be celestial? Or, which
amounts to the same thing, how could one become an angel while being a
man or a woman? According to whether the question was to pull oneself
out of the "world" or out of the "dwelling place of the I," medieval mystics
of all tendencies were faced with the serious Platonic question of "imprisonment."[144] This theme, which arose in the mid-eighth century,[145] found
its full development in the tenth century, when mystics agreed that, in
order to "flee the world," one must escape not just one but several prisons.
The first is the world here below, where the friends of God are obliged to
remain for "a determined duration."[146] The second is the prison that keeps
the heart in the grip of profane desires. The third is the one that holds
the soul. As long as the soul remains in it, it lives, moaning and unhappy,
in the ardent desire for the celestial kingdom, by the side of the angels.
That imprisonment is also of a "determined duration." When the mystics

143. Abū Saʿīd Karrāz (d. 286/899), *Kitāb al-Sidq*, is one of the first treatises, among those that
have come down to us, in which one can find a systematic presentation of the Sufi experience. On
the *uns*, see 71–75.

144. For the reception of this notion by a great Muslim philosopher, see Charles Genequand,
"Platonism and Hermetism in al-Kindī's *Fī al-Nafs*," *Zeitschrift für Geschichte der Arabischen-
Islamischen Wissenschaft* 88, no. 4 (Frankfurt am Main, 1987): 1–18; and J. Jolivet, "La topographie
du salut d'après le Discours sur l'âme d'al-Kindī," in Amir-Moessi, *Le voyage initiatique en terre
d'Islam*, 149–58.

145. According to a tradition collected by ʿAbd Allāh ibn al-Mubārak (d. 181/797) and attributed to the Companion of the Prophet ʿAbd-Allah ibn ʿAmrū, "The world is the paradise of
the infidel and the prison of the believer; the believer, when his soul leaves his body, is like the
prisoner who, when he is given back his liberty, rolls on the ground and capers about": ʿAbd Allāh
ibn al-Mubārak, *Kitāb al-Zuhd wa-al Raqāʾiq*, ed. Habīburrahmā Aʿzamī (Beirut: Muhammad ʿAfīf
al-Zughbī, [1971?]), 211.

146. This theme is illustrated in medieval hagiography by the green bird or birds that accompany the saint to his final dwelling place. A prophetic tradition represents the souls of the elect in
the form of birds of that same color.

liberate themselves from it, they become "people of abandonment." But once they are stripped of their fleshly envelope, does this mean that they leave the universe of incarceration? No, certain thinkers respond, because they make the effort to escape from the prisons of worldliness in order to better submit themselves to God.[147] Yes, others say, to the extent "they attain the ranks of closeness to God," they shed the "carnal soul": such a man "has separated himself from his passion and presented himself as a bondsman before God." At that point his burden of fatigue and woes is lifted from him.[148]

147. Anonymous, *Adab al-Mulūk*, 22–23

148. Hakīm al-Tirmidhī, *Tabā'i' al-Nufūs*, ed. Ahmad 'Abd al-Rahīm Sāyih and Sayyid al-Jumaylī (Cairo: al-Maktab al-Thaqāfī, 1989), 75; quoted from the English translation by Bernd Radtke and John O'Kane in *The Concept of Sainthood in Early Islamic Mysticism: Two Works by al-Hakīm al-Tirmidhī* (Richmond, UK: Curzon, 1996), 234.

·⟨ 6 ⟩·

Going to the Borderlands

The Ulemas and Jihad

In 915 a group of Iraqi men of letters returned to Baghdad from the frontier borderlands of Theodosiopolis (Erzurum), in Armenia, where they had gone to fight against the infidel.[1] On its way the group was joined by a young man born in what is now Diyarbakir, in Turkey, who later had a brilliant career as a philologist. Everywhere it went, the group received a warm welcome from the population. In the imperial capital it was met by joyful crowds. The Kurdish student was sorely tempted to pass himself off as a member of the group so as to receive some of the honors showered on the others. He soon did so, taking on the identity of a man of letters and a soldier, a characteristic figure in medieval Islam.[2] His usurpation worked so well that from then on he was known as Qālī, a reference to the Arabic

1. On the frontier, see, in particular, Michael David Bonner, "The Naming of the Frontier: 'Awāsim, Thughūr, and the Arab Geographers," *Bulletin of the School of Oriental and African Studies* 57, no. 1 (1994): 17–24; Bonner, *Aristocratic Violence and Holy War: Studies in the Jihad and the Arab-Byzantine Frontier* (New Haven: American Oriental Society, 1996), chap. 5, "The *Thughūr* in History," 135–56; R. W. Brauer, "Boundaries and Frontiers in Medieval Muslim Geography," *Transactions of the American Philosophical Society* 85, no. 6 (1995), 12–15, 25–26 (on the question of the *thugūr*, or fortified towns, in particular); Jacqueline Chabbi, "Ribāt", in *Encyclopédie de l'Islam*, new ed. (Leiden: E. J. Brill; Paris: Maisonneuve et Larose, 1966), 8:510–15; and in *The Encyclopaedia of Islam*, new ed., ed. E. J. Van Donzel (Leiden: Brill, 1966), 8:493–506; and Agostino Pertusi, "Tra storia e leggenda: Akritai e ghazi sulla frontiera orientale di Bisanzo," in *Rapports du XIVe Congrès international des études byzantines*, 2nd theme, *Frontières et régions frontalières du VIIe au XIIe siècle* (Bucarest, 1971), 1:237–83.

2. Albrecht Noth, "Les 'ulamā' en qualité de guerriers." In *Saber religioso y poder político en el Islam*, actas del simposio internacional (Madrid: Agencia Española de Cooperación Internacional,

Qalīqalā, the name of the province from which his traveling companions
were returning.[3] What did his new but borrowed ritual prestige really do
for him? We do not know. All that we know is that, in the early ninth
century, the ideology of going to the frontier operated strongly enough
to affect a young man and to electrify crowds. It seemed to appeal both
to the elite and to provoke mass enthusiasm. Georges Bataille, the author
of *The Accursed Share* (*La part maudite*) would have attributed that ideology
to the warlike spirit of early Islam, but he would have been wrong, to the
extent that it was no older than the class of learned men who instigated it.
This glorification of combat was, in great part, the work of the traditionists of the preceding century.[4] Moreover, it arose in relation to the sort of
knowledge that they initiated.

It is clear that a sojourn at the frontier was the result of a ritualization
of knowledge. The phenomenon is not exclusive to Islam: other earlier or
contemporary cultures experienced it. This means that it was by inherit-
ing a tradition that Islamic knowledge was realized in virtuous practices.
It was able to engender models of behavior and to give full proof of its efficacy and its validity. In a more specifically internal manner, it drew from
its finalism—a finalism in essence soteriological—reasons for supporting
knowledge with exemplary practices. A stay at the frontier found a place
in dogma in Islam as a consequence of the larger articulation of intellectual practices within a social praxis. It conquered that place legitimately
by taking onto itself the *practical* function of bringing the earth closer to
the heavens.

The late eighth-century ideology of combat at the frontier was unable
to win over the founding masters, who, admittedly, had other things on
their minds, in particular, the defense of the *'ilm*, which they considered
just as important as ritual, if not more so. They may even have been hostile to it, given that they defended such principles as "A day of just and
right juridical consultation is worth more than a year of combat at the

1994), 175–95, esp. 175. This text continues Noth's important comparatist study of jihad and the
ribāt, Noth, *Heiliger Kreig und heiliger Kampf in Islam und Christentum* (Bonn: Röhrscheid, 1966).

3. Abū al-Hasan al-Qālī (d. 356/966) remained in Baghdad until 939–40; from there, he emigrated to Andalusia, where he ended his days in Cordoba: Qiftī, *Inbāh al-Ruwwāt*, ed. Muhammad
Abū al-Fadī Ibrāhīm, 3 vols. (Cairo: al-Hayah al-Misrīya al-'Ammah lil-Kutub, 1981), 1:217.

4. The enthusiasm for combat is part of a defensive jihad that had no relation to what was
at work in the wars of conquest of the first century of Islam. On this question, see the works of
Michael Bonner already cited; John Kelsay and James Turner Joynson, eds., *Just War and Jihad:
Historical and Theoretical Perspectives on War and Peace in Western and Islamic Traditions* (New York:
Greenwood, 1991); and Alfred Morabia, *Le Gihad dans l'Islam médiéval: Le "combat sacré" des origines
au XIIe siècle* (Paris: Albin Michel, 1993).

frontier."[5] One text aimed at asserting the excellence of knowledge over rituality describes one such man as a voyager who has reached many "horizons," but at no point does it say that the frontier was among his destinations. Nonetheless, the sources describe him as respectful of the jihad and of those to carried it on. One source shows him demanding of his future son-in-law a sizable marriage settlement that he planned to share out between "the *mujāhid* and the needy." This narrative, like others, shows that the early doctors sincerely venerated combat in God's name. But their interests lay elsewhere, in pleading the cause (not yet won) of literate practices such as the *rihla*-voyage as a quest for knowledge just as important as other devotional practices (if not more so). To illustrate that broadly felt need, Mak'hūl (d. 112/730), one of their major figures, traveled in Egypt and Syria, in Iraq, and in the Hejaz. But although he deliberately went to Syria to seek prophetic traditions concerning rules pertaining to war booty,[6] we do not know that he went to the military frontier. Like the other great men of letters of his epoch, his itineraries are free of all war experience, and he concentrated on working to lay the bases for Islamic knowledge.

Obviously, at the beginning of the eighth century, there were men of letters who were candidates for frontier combat, but they were few in

---

5. Dhahabī, *Siyar A'lām al-Nubalā'*, ed. Shu'ayb al-Arna'ūtī et al., 25 vols. (Beirut: Mu'assasat al-Risālah, 1982–83), 4:66. One thing should be kept in mind: before the term *djihād* became popularized, the word most utilized to designate combat at the frontier was *ghazw/ghazwa*, a term that lies behind the French word *razzia* and that means "military expedition," "campaign," "war," etc. The root *gh.z.w.* also enters into the historico-literary genre of the *Maghāzī*, which narrates the military deeds of the Prophet and his Companions. The anteriority of the word *ghazw* over that of *djihād* is by itself an indication that the ideology of combat at the frontier was a late development. On the medieval use of the term *ghazw*, see Françoise Micheau, "Les guerres arabo-byzantines vues par Yahya d'Antioche, chroniqueur arabe melkite du Ve/XIe siècle, "in *Eupsychia: Mélanges offerts à Hélène Ahrweiler*, 2 vols., Byzantina Sorbonensia (Paris: Publications de la Sorbonne, 1998), 2:541–55. On the question in general, see Patricia Crone, *Slaves on Horses: The Evolution of the Islamic Polity* (Cambridge: Cambridge University Press, 1980), 3–17; Martin Hinds, "Maghāzī,"in *Encyclopédie de l'Islam*, new ed. (Leiden: E. J. Brill; Paris: Maisonneuve et Larose, 1966), 5:1151–54; and in *The Encyclopaedia of Islam*, new ed. (1966), 5:1161–64; Hinds, "'Maghāzī' and 'Sira' in Early Islamic Scholarship," in *La vie du prophète Mahomet*, Colloque de Strasbourg (Paris: Presses Universitaires de France, 1983), 57–66; and John Wansbrough, *The Sectarian Milieu: Content and Composition of Islamic Salvation History* (Oxford: Oxford University Press, 1978), 71–87.

6. Abū Dāwud al-Sijistānī, *Jāmi' al-sahīh*, 9 vols. in 19 pts. (Baduz: Jam'iyat al-Maknaz al-Islāmī, 2000–2001), 1:274. There remains the enigma of why, at the end of the eighth century, several traditions regarding the jihad redacted by Muhammad ibn Hasan al-Shaybānī are attributed to Makhūl: see Shaybānī, *Kitāb al-Siyar al-Kabīr*, ed. Salāh al-Dīn al-Munajjid, with commentary by Muhammad ibn Ahmad al-Sarakhsī, 3 vols. (Cairo: Ma'had al-Makhtūtāt bi-Jāmi'at al-Duwal al-Arabīyah, 1957–60), 7, 27.

number.[7] Those whose names we do know are not major figures. Still, the situation was to change very fast. Not even two generations later, the most renowned scholars began to add a sojourn on the frontier to their list of achievements. Ibn 'Awn (d. 151/768), who was one of these, is described as an excellent horseman and a courageous fighter who did not shy from single combat.[8] He was born in Basra, a city that, thanks to its situation on the Persian Gulf, also offered its learned men opportunities for sea combat. Among a number of disciples, another of Basra's men of letters is described as a sailor-combatant who was killed in combat and buried on an island in the Indian Ocean.[9] The other great intellectual city of Iraq, Kufa, could also boast combatant-scholars. One of its doctors, Sufyān al-Thawrī (d. 161/777), the founder of a school of law, is of particular interest. One narrative shows him in Jerusalem, then doing a forty-day retreat at the *ribāt* of Ashqelon, in Palestine,[10] then returning to Mecca, where he settled to teach and live as a "neighbor of God."[11] His many disciples subscribed to what was becoming the ideology of the jihad.[12] Their engagement in the *mujāwara*, as "neighbors of God" in Mecca, does not seem to have precluded participation in the activities connected with the *murābata*, or sojourn at the frontier.[13]

It was above all in the circles of his disciples that the profile of the scholar-hero at the frontier takes on distinctive traits. A pupil of one of these men, Ahmad ibn Hanbal (d. 241/855), is representative of this type. The son of a frontier combatant who died a heroic death, he was the future founder of a school of traditions and of law associated with his name. When still a student, he expressed his support of the ideology of the jihad by making a trip from Baghdad to the Syrian frontier city of Tarsus on foot. Later, when he had become a specialist in prophetic exempla, he redacted many traditions praising combat, such as the one that recalled

7. One of these was 'Abd al-Rahmān ibn Hurmuz (d. 117/735), a doctor from Medina who left to settle in the *thagr* of Alexandria, where he ended his days: Ibn Sa'd, *Tabaqāt*, ed. Karl Vilhelm Zetterstéen (Leiden, 1909). All points on the frontier, fortified or not, but where invasion was feared, were called *thagr* (plural *thugūr*). There was also Abū Sa'īd ibn Kisān (d. 125/742), who is known to have fought on the Syrian-Byzantine frontier.

8. Dhahabī, *Kitāb Tadhkirat al-huffādh*, 3rd ed., 2 vols. (Hyderabad: Dairatu L-Ma'arif-il-Osmana, 1955), 1:157.

9. Ibn Sa'd, *Tabaqāt*, 7:277.

10. The *ribāt* was a religious and military institution, often fortified, installed at the frontier or in dangerous places such as the desert. See Chabbi, "Ribāt."

11. Khatīb al-Baghdādī, *Tārīkh Baghdād*, 14 vols. (Cairo, 1931), 13:470; Dhahabī, *Siyar*, 7:260.

12. One of these, Sufyān ibn 'Uyayna (d. 198/813), was the redactor of one of the first traditions justifying the *rihla*-voyage.

13. Dhahabī, *Siyar*, 10:157.

that "jihad is the monasticism of Islam."[14] He spread the notion that a stay on the frontier was a meritorious act. One of his pupils, originally from Khurasan, became known for his ardor in combat and his devotion to the frontier *ribāt*, to the point that he became known as "Ribātī." The governor of Khurasan took note of him and appointed him to a responsible position in the frontier institutions. The master was not happy that one of his disciples compromised himself with a prince, and when he received the young man in Baghdad, he admonished him in terms that left no doubt about his reprobation.[15] Nonetheless, his own younger son was named the judge of Tarsus, the most prestigious of the ninth-century borderlands,[16] a post he accepted only after his father's death. The master's leading student, Abū Bakr al-Murūdhī (d.275/888), best embodied the ideological tradition of the jihad in its full and scrupulous purity.[17] Born in Khwārizm, he settled definitively in Baghdad, where he made his career. One scene shows him leaving with a group of loyal companions for the Syrian-Byzantine frontier and being joined on the way, between Baghdad and Sāmārra, by a large group of spontaneous volunteers. He tried in vain to persuade this mass of people to go back home, but the crowd grew until it was estimated to have numbered several thousand. Some of the followers of this eminent traditionist were by no means unhappy with this success with the populace.[18] By the middle of the ninth century, the ideology of the jihad

14. Ahmad ibn Hanbal, *al-Musnad*, ed. Ahmad Muhammad Shākir, 15 vols. (Cairo: Dār al-Ma'ārif, 1946–56), *hadīth* nos. 11349 and 13306.The first to publish this tradition was Muhammad ibn al-Hasan al-Shaybānī (d. 189/804): *Kitāb al-Siyar al-Kabīr*, 23.

15. The master asked his disciple, "Is it necessary that one say, on the day of the Last Judgment, where is the Tāhiride and its partisans? It is up to you to see where you want to place your feet": Khatīb al-Baghdādī, *Tārīkh Baghdād*, 2:6; Ibn Abī Ya'la, *Tabaqāt al-Hanābila*, 2 vols. (Beirut: Dār al-Kutub al-'Ilmīyah, 1997), 1:45; Ibn Qudāmah al-Maqdisī, *Tabaqāt 'ulamā' al-hadīth*, 4 vols. (Beirut: Mu'assasat al-Risālah, 1989, 1996), 2:227. A longer version of this anecdote can be found in Sam'ānī, *Kitāb al-Ansāb*, ed. 'Abd al-Rahmān ibn Yahyā Mu'allimī, 3 vols. (Hyderabad: Matba'at Majlis Dairat, 1962–), 3:39.

16. Ibn Abī Ya'la, *Tabaqāt al-Hanābila*, 1:175.

17. Another son of Ahmad ibn Hanbal, 'Abd-Allah, also took trips to Tarsus: Dhahabī, *Siyar*, 14:130.

18. One member of his entourage turns to him and says, "Give praise to God, who has spread your science [*'ilm*]" The master, moved, breaks into tears and responds, "It is not my science, it is that of Ahmad ibn Hanbal!": Khatīb al-Baghdādī, *Tārīkh Baghdād*, 4:424; Dhahabī, *Siyar*, 13:175. At the time renowned traditionists often moved the masses, exhorting them to jihad by exciting their imaginations through heroic depictions of the frontier. One such man left Nishapur, his city of birth, to go to the Syrian borderland of Tarsus by way of Baghdad, and in the course of his interminable procession, he inspired many vocations to travel to the frontier, even from his starting place. When this military expedition arrived in Rayy, it gathered in new candidates for combat, and when they all got to Baghdad, the volunteers from Khurasan made such a strong impression on the inhabitants of that city of the caliphs that their procession became several thousands.

could count on solid popular support. Dogmatic expressions of the phenomenon were well established, along with hagiographic images of a sojourn at the frontier. Reinforced by a apparatus of doctrinal justification
(to which I shall return), the *murābata* now had its deeds, its heroes, and
its exempla.

An Ideology of Combat

The myth of the frontier, created in a traditionist milieu, found backing
within the framework of Tradition. The move for its justification seems to
have begun in the latter half of the eighth century. A papyrus roll from an
Egyptian judge who died in 790, 'Abd-Allāh ibn Lahī'a, held among Arabic
papyri at Heidelberg, offers an example of one of the earliest traditions
praising the jihad.[19] The text states that combat for God, which is a community duty by state prerogative, is *also* a voluntary act, freely consented
to and individual. It was perhaps in support of that tradition that the redactor went to the Syrian-Byzantine frontier.

The book credited to 'Abd-Allāh ibn al-Mubārak (d. 181/797) with the
significant title of *Book of the Jihad* is thought to date from that same epoch. As its title indicates, the book is wholly dedicated to praising and
justifying combat in God's name and service at the frontier. Its presumed
author was himself a frontier combatant. In the course of his many peregrinations he traveled in Egypt, where he met the author of the papyrus
roll. Modern scholars have challenged the attribution of this book to this
particular Khurasanian jurist and traditionist, but there are ways to verify
the attribution, at least in part. I am thinking, in particular, of the many
traditions that the presumed author received from a Basra master who
died in Yemen, where he had settled in 750. Those traditions have come
down to us independently through two compilations of traditions, one by
a Yemenite disciple of that same master, the other by a Khurasan native
who must have known his eminent compatriot in his youth. Beside these
two sources, there are others that attest that certain exempla and tradi-

---

When the group arrived in Tarsus, it had been on the road for nearly a year: Ibn 'Asākir, *Tārīkh
madinat Dimashq*, ed. 'Alī Shīrī, 40 vols. (Beirut: Dār al-Fikr, 1995–96), 2:352. On the role of "volunteers" for frontier combat, see R. Paret, "Mutatawwi'a," in *Encyclopédie de l'Islam*, new ed. (1966),
7:778; and in *The Encyclopaedia of Islam*, new ed., ed. E. J. Van Donzel (Leiden: Brill, 1966), 7:776;
and Bonner, *Aristocratic Violence and Holy War*, 151–53. Some men of letters from Khurasan were
mutatawwi'a from father to son, as was Abū Bakr Hamshādh (d. 349/960), mentioned in Sam'ānī,
Kitāb al-Ansāb, 4:275.

19. Raif Georges Khoury, *'Abd-Allāh ibn Lahī'a (97–174/715–790): Juge et grand maître de l'école
égyptienne* (Wiesbaden: Harrassowitz, 1986), annex 364, nos. 125–26; annex 285, no. 280.

tions that appear in the *Book of the Jihad* were in circulation in traditionist and mystic circles in the mid-ninth century. This does not accredit the attribution of the work in question to 'Abd-Allāh ibn al-Mubārak, but it at least leads us to think that the work was compiled, at the latest, at the end of the ninth century. For this reason, it merits our attention as an important old source.

The book is openly placed under the sign of a tension, as it attempts to decide which is more meritorious, combat at the frontier or pilgrimage (with its corollary of living in Mecca as a "neighbor of God"). It offers a large number of prophetic traditions in support of the superiority of service at the frontier over pilgrimage—which orthodoxy nonetheless considers to be one of the "five pillars" of religion for all who have the health and the means to accomplish it. Traditions favoring combat in God are often placed in the mouth of Companions of the Prophet, whom the eighth-century doctors consider to be their eponymous ancestors. One of them is made to say, "I would take more pleasure in receiving a whiplash 'in the way of Allah' than in making pilgrimage after pilgrimage"; another states, "A military expedition 'in the way of Allah' is preferable to fifty pilgrimages."[20] The literary exaggeration of these traditions should not mislead us. As Albrecht Noth recalls, the fact that these traditions plead in favor of the jihad does not mean that other acts of devotion are any less worthy. The comparison should be considered simply as indirect evidence on the connection between the jihad and other religious practices.[21] How far back do these traditions go? Although our means for knowing are limited, we are at least sure that the first tradition was set down in the corpus of two traditionists, one of whom died in 826, the other in 841,[22] which permits us to suppose that it was known by learned men of the late eighth century.

Pilgrimage, with which jihad is compared, leads directly to the medieval institution of living as a "neighbor of God," principally in Mecca. Are combat (*ghazw*) and being neighbors (*mujāwara*) opposed or complementary? To highlight the tension between *ghazw* and *mujāwara* the Muslim Middle Ages usually dramatized their terms in narrations and personified them through two doctors of contrasting opinions: 'Abd-Allāh ibn

20. 'Abd Allāh ibn al-Mubārak, *Kitāb al-Jihād,* ed. Nazīh Hammād (Cairo: Majma' al-Buhūth al-Islāmīyah, 1978), 172. These statements are followed by other traditions of similar import.

21. Noth, "Les 'ulamā,'" 181.

22. The first of these is 'Abd al-Razzāq, *al-Musannāf,* ed. Habīb al-Rahmān al-A'zamī (Karachi, 1972), 5:260; the second, Ibn Mansūr, *Sunan,* ed. Sa'īd ibn 'Abd Allah ibn Abd al-'Azīz Āl Humayd, 5 vols. (Riyadh: Dār al-Sunay'ī, 1993) 2–3:144.

al-Mubārak (d. 181/797) was represented as a champion of *ghazw*, and his compatriot and fellow disciple Fudayl ibn 'Iyād (d. 187/803) as a partisan of *mujāwara*.[23] 'Abd-Allāh is supposed to have protested against the quietist choice of his fellow disciple and called upon him to renounce it and embrace a militant career at the frontier. In the good tradition of warrior-poets, this champion of the faith is reported to have given his compatriot his opinion in a poem sent from Tarsus in 793:

> O devotee of the two sanctuaries, if you could see us, you would know that
>   your devotion is only a game.
> You tire out your mount in vain, while our horses exhaust themselves at war.
> You water your cheeks with tears while our necks are stained with our blood.
> For you the aromatic perfumes, for us the impetuous hoofs and gray powder.
> From messages that have been exchanged between us there springs a true
>   word, sincere, and that does not lie,
> But it is still not enough for us who breathe in the dust of the horses of God
>   and the smoke of sparkling braziers.[24]

The aim of this poem is to link Islamic knowledge with a militant praxis. The final line refers to a tradition that reappears in the *Book of Jihad*, which says that "never will the dust [raised by the mounts of warriors] in the 'way of Allah' be mixed with the smoke of hell in the throat of a believer."[25] This tradition figures in several ninth-century collections of *hadīth*.[26] Although the question of forgery has been raised, it has been attested that this work was conceived with the use of ancient materials. Consequently, there is no reason to think that the author of the *Book of the Jihad* did not know that tradition. What follows is less sure, and bears a whiff of arrangement. To thank the emissary who brought him this verse missive—and to tell his *mujāhid* friend that he was right—Fudayl sends him a tradition in which a Companion asks the Prophet to tell him by what pious action he might obtain "the retribution of the *mujāhid* walking in the way of God." The Prophet answers him that even by enduring all the suffering in the world one could never obtain the same merit as

---

23. We know that Fudayl had studied in Iraq and that he left to settle in Mecca, where he lived as a *mujāwir* until he died.

24. Harawī al-Mawsilī, *Kitāb al-Ishrārat ilā Ma'rifat al-Ziyārāt*; trans. Janine Sourdel-Thomine in *Guide des lieux de pèlerinage* (Damascus: Institut Français de Damas, 1952, 1957), 149.

25. 'Abd Allāh ibn al-Mubārak, *Kitāb al-Jihād*, 47.

26. Ahmad ibn Hanbal, *al-Musnad*, 2:256, 342, 441; Nāsā'ī, *Sunan*, ed. Abd'l-Fattāh Abū Ghadda (Beirut, 1986), 4:12.

combatants in God. This narration was edited by a twelfth-century biographer.[27] That it is of late date is attested by the fact that Khaṭīb al-Baghdādī (d.463/1070), for example, does not mention it in his dictionary of traditionists who frequented Baghdad.[28]

To tell the truth, however, the ancient sources give a quite different image. They show the "neighbor of God" showing enormous circumspection about going to the frontier. In one narration a ninth-century prose writer cites a man who had done all he could to get to the Syrian front at Tarsus but had been captured by the Byzantine forces and had abjured Islam.[29] This perhaps helps us to interpret his reported reaction on hearing of the death of Abū Isʾhāq al-Fazārī (d. 185/801), an eminent Iraqi jurist and a prominent figure at the frontier. The man is reported to have said that he often wanted to go to the Syrian borderland area of Missīsa, where Fazārī was living, not to "seek out the merits of a sojourn at the frontier," but to visit a former study companion.

These anecdotes hint at a dispute among the representatives and defenders of the two sorts of destinations of journeys. Tension between a trip to the frontier and a sojourn in Mecca was attested, we now know, even during the lifetimes of our two men. At the time, becoming a "neighbor of God" had already begun to attract learned men, including one famous traditionist of Kufa.[30] This transmitter of sacred narrations gathered about him a group of *mujāwir*, among them a known poet.[31] As a form of devotion it seems to have met with success only at the very end of the eighth

27. Ibn ʿAsākir, *Tārīkh madinat Dimashq*, 32:451.

28. Khaṭīb al-Baghdādī, *Tārīkh Baghdād*, 10:159, under "ʿAbd-Allah ibn Mubārak." Ibn Jawzī (d. 597/1200), who does not list them in his historical annals, does give them in his hagiographic dictionary: Ibn al-Jawzī, *al-Muntadham fī Tārīkh al-mulūk wa-al-ūmam*, ed. Muhammad ʿAbd al-Qādir ʿAtā and Mustafā ʿAbd al-Qādir ʿAtā, 19 vols. (Beirut: Dār al-Kutub al-ʿIlmīyah, 1992), 9:59, under "ʿAbd-Allah ibn Mubāk"; and Ibn al-Jawzī, *Kitāb Sifat al-Safwah*, 4 vols. (Hyderabad: Matbaʿat Dāʾirat al-Maʿārif al-ʿUthmānīyah, 1936–37), 4:140. They appear in Dhahabī (d. 748/1347), *Siyar*, 8:413.

29. Ibn Qutayba, *ʿUyūn al-akhbār*, 4 vols. (Cairo: al-Muʾassasah al-Misrīyah, 1964), 2:365; ed. F. S. Bodenheimer, trans. L. Kopf, as *The ʿUyūn al-Akhbār of ibn Quṭayba* (Paris: Académie International d'Histoire des Sciences, 1949); and cited in Chabbi, "Ribāt," in *Encyclopédie de l'Islam*, new ed. (1966), 5:514; and in *The Encyclopaedia of Islam*, new ed. (1966), 8:496.

30. This man was Sufyān ibn ʿUyayna (d. 198/813): see Khaṭīb al-Baghdādī, *Tārīkh Baghdād*, 5:185; Dhahabī, *Siyar*, 8:470. On the relationship between the two men, see Abū Nuʿaym, *Hilyat al-Awliyāʾ*, 10 vols. (Cairo: Maktabat al-Khānjī, 1932–38); new ed., 10 vols. (Beirut: Dār al-Kitāb al-Arabī, 1967–68), 8:114.

31. Abū Muhammad ibn al-Munādir (d. 198/813): see Abū Hiffān al-Mihzamī, *Akhbār Abī Nuwās*, ed. ʿAbd al-Sattār Ahmad Farrāj (Cairo: Dār Misr lil-Tibāʾah, [1953?]), 22. For an anecdote concerning Abū Nuwās in the study circle of Sufyān ibn ʿUyayna, see ibid., 120.

century, and it was not so much the traditionists as the ascetics who adopted it: fewer traditionists seem to have practiced the *mujāwara*.

According to Jacqueline Chabbi, writing in her entry for *The Encyclopaedia of Islam* under "Ribāt," the conflict between partisans of the ideology of the jihad and their adversaries set in opposition "those who, of quietist tendency, aspired to make *mugjāwara*" and "those who aspired to make *ribāt*," and she describes those who professed "the ideology of *djihād*" as "circles yet to be identified."[32] Even when couched in terms that suggest doubt, statements such as these suggest that partisans and adversaries of a sojourn at the frontier formed opposing camps. This is far from true. The tension between *murābata* and *mujārawa* cut through the same groups and the same milieus. At times it can be observed on the individual level in someone who participated in both the *ribāt* and the *mujāwara*. In 829, Abū 'Ubayd ibn Sallām (d. 224/838), a well-known philologist and traditionist, formerly a judge in the Syrian border area of Tarsus, made the pilgrimage to Mecca. After having fulfilled his religious duty, he prepared to return to Baghdad. The night before his departure, however, he had a dream that changed his plans. He saw the Prophet "seated on a rug and surrounded by chamberlains." When he tried to draw closer, he was prevented from doing so by the chamberlains: they did not want to allow someone who was preparing to leave the "House of God" to enter into contact with their master. When he awoke the next morning, the ex-judge decided to remain in the city of God, and he kept this promise to be a "neighbor" until his death.[33]

Mystics, too, celebrated the dual meritorious sojourns in Mecca and at the frontier. One major figure of the mystical school of Baghdad, Abū Sa'id Karrāz (d. 286/899), was among them. After peregrinations that took him to the outlying parts of Syria,[34] he settled as a *mujāwir* in Mecca, where he

---

32. Quoted from Jacqueline Chabbi, "Ribāt," in *Encyclopédie de l'Islam*, new ed. (1966); and in *The Encyclopaedia of Islam*, new ed. 1966, esp. 495.

33. Yāqūt, *Irshād al-Arīb ilā Ma'rifat al-Adīb (Mu'jam al-Udabā)*, ed. David Samuel Margoliouth (1913–29); ed. Ihsān 'Abbās, 7 vols. (Beirut: Dār al-Gharb al-Islāmī, 1993), 6:162. This is similar to what happened to the Iraqi traditionist Abū Bakr al-Ajūrī (d. 360/970). When he arrived in Mecca, he prayed to God that he could spend a year in the holy city as a *mujāwir*, and he immediately heard a voice from the beyond telling him that he must in fact spend thirty years there. He spent the rest of his life in Mecca: Ibn al-Jawzī, *al-Muntadham*, 7:55; Ibn Khallikān, *Wafayāt al-A'yān*, 8 vols. (Cairo, 1948); ed. Insān 'Abbās, 8 vols. (Beirut: Dār Thāqāfa, 1968–72), 4:623; Subkī, *Tabaqāt al-Shāfi'iyyah*, ed. Mahmūd Muhammad al-Tanāhī Al-Tānjī and Abd al-Fattāh Muhammad Al-Hilw, 4 vols. (Cairo: 'Īsā al-Bābī al-Halabī, 1964), 3:149.

34. In Ibn 'Asākir, *Tārīkh madinat Dimashq*, 1:428, a certain Abū Bakr of Tarsus praises him. Does this means that he was a *murābit*?

practiced both reflection and teaching. His stay in Mecca seems, in fact, to have been connected with his mystical experience. His biographers mention several times that he complained that "for twelve years" he had gone back and forth between Mecca and Medina in the hope of having a vision of God, but all in vain.[35] This search for a visual contact with God may have been the cause of his expulsion from Mecca.[36]

At the time, the *mujāwir* formed a heterogeneous and variable world. There were both temporary and permanent adherents. The temporaries were themselves of two sorts: those who came for a few weeks and those who spent one or several years before they returned home. At the end of the ninth century, their numbers grew to the point that the authorities in the holy city judged it necessary for them to have a sheikh.[37] The man who was named was a jurist and traditionist from Nishapur. One of his successors (and perhaps an immediate successor) was an ascetic from Basra, a member of the school of Baghdad. In 920, that role was taken by another Sufi who had arrived twenty years earlier from Nishapur.[38] The fragmentary data lead to two conclusions: the first is that the *mujāwir* of that epoch were recruited almost exclusively among Iraqis and Khurasanians; the second is that representatives of the mystical school of Baghdad were prominent among their leadership. The other regions of the Muslim world were hardly represented. Andalusians, for example, appear only in the tenth century.[39]

35. Ibid., 1:431.

36. Before this Baghdad mystic, another Iraqi mystic, established in Syria, had been the target of a similar measure. The object of rowdy comments on the part of the ulemas of Damascus, who had organized a cabal against him, he took refuge in Mecca, where he lived as a "neighbor of God": Ibn Abī Hātim, *Kitāb al-jarh wa al-ta ʾdīl*, 9 vols. (Beirut: Dār al-Kitub al-ʿIlmīyah, 1952), 2:47; Abū Nuʿaym, *Hilyat al-Awliyāʾ*, 10:50; Sulamī, *Tabaqāt al-Sūfiyah*, ed. Nūr al-Dīn Shuraybah (Cairo: Dār al-Kitāb al-ʿArabī, 1953), 98, 102; Dhahabī, *Siyar*, 12:93.

37. We do not know how many they were in this epoch. Nāsir-ī Khusrū, who stayed in the holy city between November 1050 and May 1051, states that there were "about five hundred" of them. Compared to the overall population, which he estimated at "about two thousand inhabitants," this was a sizable number: Nāsir-ī Khusrū, *Safar Namèh: Relation du voyage de Nassiri Khosrau en Syrie, en Palestine, en Egypte, en Arabie et en Perse pendant les années de l'Hégire 437–444 (1035–1042)*, ed. and trans. Charles Henri August Schefer (Paris, 1881; reprint, Frankfurt am Main: Institute for the History of Arab-Islamic Science, 1994), 206; ed. and trans. Wheeler M. Thackston as *Nasir-i Khusrav's Book of Travels* (Costa Mesa, CA: Mazda, 2001).

38. Abū Nuʿaym, *Hilyat al-Awliyāʾ*, 10:376; Sulamī, *Tabaqāt al-Sūfiyah*, 341. See the list of sheikhs given in Louis Massignon, *La passion de Husayn ibn Mansūr Hallāj, martyr mystique de l'Islam*, 3 vols. (Paris: Gallimard, 1975), 1:150n3.

39. Dominique Urvoy expresses the thesis that, aside from occasional exceptions, the ulemas of that part of the Muslim world (contrary to those of the eastern Muslim world) were not much involved in a frontier combat directed by the governing forces: Dominique Urvoy, "Sur l'évolution de la notion de Gihād dans l'Espagne musulmane," *Mélanges de la Casa Velázquez* 9

The presence of many *mujāwir* from Khurasan among the Iraqis, and later the Andalusians, goes against Chabbi's thesis that the opposition between *mujāwir* and *murābit* paralleled a division between "peoples of Arabia, i.e., of 'Irāk, against the Syrians, the Khurāsānians, and the westerners, Maghribīs and Spaniards."[40] As far as one can judge from the materials brought together here, the tension between the two descriptions of the journeyer spared neither individuals nor groups. Even an ideologue of the jihad such as 'Abd-Allāh ibn al-Mubārak did not escape that tension, for although his medieval biographers present him as a champion of the frontier, they also describe him as deeply attached to the pilgrimage to Mecca.

Jihad and Hagiography

Basing her remarks on a ninth-century biographer, Chabbi recalls in her *Encyclopaedia of Islam* article that at the time of 'Abd-Allah ibn al-Mubārak, "the idealization of figures of the frontier does not yet seem to have been greatly emphasized." Then, referring to a *hadīth* transmitted by a traditionist of the time, who states that "*djihād* is the monasticism . . . of Islam," she stresses that "later, however, warriors of the frontier were to be seen, in a manner simultaneously unreal and symbolic, as varieties of saints. . . . There was even talk of the presence on the frontier of *abdāl* . . . ascetic or pietistic persons who are regarded as intercessors and dispensers of *baraka*." This makes it understandable that, as she says several lines later, the expression "later" refers to the times of the biographical dictionaries for mystics who were writing about themselves after the eleventh century.[41]

(1973): 335–71. Pierre Guichard speaks of the "absence of emergence of a sensibility of the jihad in Andalusian culture of the twelfth century": Pierre Guichard, *Les musulmans de Valence et la Reconquête (XIe–XIIIe siècle)*, 2 vols. (Damascus: Institut Français de Damas, 1990), 1:100. For an opposing viewpoint, see Vincent Lagardère, *Les Almoravides: Le Djihād andalou (1106–1143)* (Paris: L'Harmattan, 1998). For the experience of one man at the frontier, see Carlos de la Puente, "Vivre et mourir pour Dieu: Oeuvre et héritage d'Abū 'Alī al-Sadafī (m. 514/1120)," *Studia Islamica* 88 (1998): 77–102. In the Maghreb, on the southern shores of the Mediterranean, there was less doubt about the importance of the engagement of men of letters at the frontier: Heinz Halm, *Reich des Mahdi*; trans. Michael Bonner as *The Empire of the Mahdi: The Rise of the Fatimids* (New York: Brill, 1996), "Ribāt and Jihād," 221–38. For the Maghreb, see also Georges Marçais, "Note sur les ribats en berbérie," in *Mélanges d'histoire et d'archéologie de l'Occident musulman*, 2 vols. (Alger: Imprimerie Officiel du Gouvernement Général de l'Algérie, 1957), 1:23–36.

40. Chabbi, "Ribāt," in *The Encyclopaedia of Islam*, 8:495.
41. Ibid., 8:498.

Put in these precise terms, these statements are inexact. The work of
exemplification and insinuation of the extraordinary by which the combatants of the frontier were transfigured is not a late phenomenon. It was
at work during the entire ninth century. Ibn Abī al-Dunyā (d. 281/894), a
man of letters close to mystical circles in Baghdad and a royal preceptor,
played an important role in the propagation and popularization of these
idealized images in a vast work wholly destined for a secular public and in
great part still accessible today. Nourished by the ideology of the jihad,
Ibn Abī al-Dunyā filled his books with exempla in praise of martyrdom.
A dying man, being covered with a cloth and prepared for ritual wash-
ing, pushes aside the cloth from his head and prays, "O my God, do not
let me die before according me the honor to combat in your way!" The
man in fact survives, only to die a martyr's death on the field of battle.[42]
In another anecdote it is the combatant's mount that seals his master's
saintliness.[43] This story seems to have had a broad diffusion, given that its
redactor cites the various chains of guarantors through whom it had come
down to him. An eleventh-century critic of traditions held all of those
chains to be authentic. That same critic, on the contrary, rejected the authenticity of another exemplum redacted by Ibn Abī al-Dunyā. One of
the chains that he cites was in fact challenged as early as the ninth century.
The narration that it is supposed to authenticate rests on the authority of
a traditionist from Jurjān, a frontier region of Transoxiana of the land of
the Turkoman Ghuzz people, passed on through a Syrian transmitter.[44] It
should be remembered that the traditionists who questioned the item did
so not because they had subjected it to a critique of its content or because
they denounced any incoherence or absurdity in it (like those whom they
accuse of forgery, they hold the miracles to be true), but rather because
it presented "weaknesses" in its chain of transmission. According to the
specialist in traditions Ibn Abī Hātim (d. 327/938), the man from Jurjān
was an "unknown."[45] To say of a transmitter that he is unknown destroys
the credibility of the narration transmitted in his name. Moreover, the

42. Ibn Abī al-Dunyā, *Man āsha baʿda al-mawt*, ed. ʿAbd Allāh Muhammad Darwīsh (Beirut:
Ālam al-Kitub, 1986), 20.
43. Ibid., 27–28. This exemplum is repeated in Ibn Abī Dunyā, *Kitāb Mujābī al-Daʿwah* (Beirut:
Muʾassasat al-Risālah, 1984), 49; and cited in Abū Bakr Bayhaqī, *Dalāʾil al-Nubuwwa*, ed. ʿAbd
al-Mutī Qalʿajī, 8 vols. (Beirut: Dār al-Kutub al-ʿIlmīyah, 1985), 6:49.
44. Ibn Abī Dunyā, *Man āsha baʿda al-mawt*, 31–32.
45. Ibn Abī Hātim, *Kitāb al-Jarh wa al-taʿdīl*, 3:413. See also Khatīb al-Baghdādī, *Tārīkh
Baghdād*, 8:366.

redactor himself is suspect in his faith for having failed to maintain probity. As for the transmitter whom the man from Jurjān cites, he was called
a liar by one critic of traditions who died in the mid-ninth century.[46] Similarly, Bukhārī (d. 256/869), who had dual status as a "neighbor of God"
and a man of the frontier, marked his traditions "reject."[47] That double
criticism on the part of authorities unanimously recognized by their peers
circumscribes the forgery to the early ninth century. That did not prevent the extraordinary narrative from continuing to circulate, or to find
respected redactors who diffused it again a century later.

If we can believe their chains of transmission, these exempla circulated
from one end of the Muslim East to the other; it was a condition of their
standardization. Ibn Abī al-Dunyā cites one that he transmits under the
authority of a traditionist from Merv via a chain of guarantors of his homeland. In this genealogy there figures a man famous for his exploits at the
frontier and known for being the ideologue of the jihad (we have already
encountered the *Book of the Jihad* attributed to him). Here the champion
of the faith is presented only as passing on the narrative, which he had obtained through a traditionist from Basra, who said that he had in turn gotten it from his Syrian transmitter-narrator through another, unidentified
man. There follows a story in which the combatants of an expedition into
Byzantine territory attack a city. In defense, the enemy responds with a
mangonel. A projectile catapulted by that engine of war hits one of them
in the leg, crushing his knees. The wounded man, who is from Medina, remains unconscious long enough for his companions to think him dead, but
then they hear him laugh out loud. They think him still alive, but he remains
in a coma. His companions despair to see him come back to life, when they
hear him sobbing and weeping salty tears. When the man comes to, he tells
of a superb vision of paradise that explains his contrasting emotions:

> I was transported to a chamber in topaz or in emerald and put into a bed.
> When I had been settled in there, I heard the clicking of jewels to my right.
> The woman who wore them appeared before me. Everything about her was
> so ravishing that I cannot tell which, of her appearance, her clothing, or her
> necklace, was the most beautiful. . . . When I had told her what had hap-

---

46. Ibrāhīm ibn Ya'qūb Jūzjānī, *Ahwāl al-Rijāl*, ed. Subhī al-Badrī Samarrā'ī (Beirut: Muassasat al-Risālah, 1985). In the course of his peregrinations, this Khurasanian made stays in the
thaghr of Syria.

47. Dhahabī, *Mīzān al-i'tidāl*, ed. 'Alī M. Al-Bajjāwī, 4 vols. (Cairo, 1963–64), 1:598.

pened to me, she burst out laughing and approached me and sat at my right.
I asked her who she was, and she answered me that her name was Khūd and
she was my wife. When I reached out to touch her, she said, "By your head
[don't be in such a hurry]! You will be among us by noon!" Just as she left me,
I heard another clicking of precious stones to my left, and another woman,
just as beautiful, appeared before me. She treated me in the same manner as
the preceding one. When I tried to come closer to her, she gave me the same
response. I then wept.[48]

The end of the story tells how at noon, at the hour at which the muez-
zin calls the faithful to prayer, the man from Medina bent down to one
side and passed away. Not to die—"Do not say of those who are slain in
the way of Allah: 'They are dead'" (Qur'an 2:154)—but to continue to live
surrounded by sensual houris who people, as "Companions pure and holy"
(Qur'an 4:57), his dazzling images of the martyrs' paradise.

After the author of the *Book of the Jihad*, other great heros of the
frontier appear in the hagiographic work of Ibn Abī al-Dunyā. Glancing
through the great dictionary of medieval mystics of Abū Nuʿaym of Isfahan (d. 430/1038), we can see that certain exempla come right out of the
works of our redactor. We cannot deny that these narratives date from the
ninth century, because we can check their spread in several overlapping
sources. Although it is true that ʿAbd-Allah ibn al-Mubārak, whom the
later hagiographers depict as a hero of the frontier, appears in the earlier
sources simply as the transmitter of a tradition praising the jihad, this was
already no longer the case with his contemporary and compatriot Ibrāhīm
ibn Adʾham, who is described as the central figure in at least one hagiographic novella involving a miracle at sea.[49] This example alone is enough
to defeat Chabbi's categorical judgment crediting the heroic stylization of
the combatants of the frontier to the fabulations of later hagiographers. A
tenth-century source shows the personage of Ibrāhīm ibn Adʾham already
fully elaborated. Indeed, in the collection of traditions that Ibn Manda
(d. 395/1004) compiled under his name, that mystic already appears as an
ideologue of the jihad and a hero of the frontier. Later biographers drew
their materials from this collection as well. For example, they borrowed
such traditions as the one that preaches the superiority of martyrdom at

48. Ibid., 1:37–38.
49. Ibn Abī al-Dunyā, *Kitāb Sīrat al-Awliyā* (Beirut: Muassasat al-Kutub al-Thaqafiyah,
1993), 35.

sea.[50] It states, "All the faults of the terrestrial martyr are pardoned, with the exception of his debts and deposits. For the martyr at sea, all is pardoned, including debts and deposits."[51]

Belief in the *abdāl*, great anonymous saints with cosmic functions who resided principally in the Lukkām Mountains, the mountainous barrier that forms a natural frontier between Syria and Byzantium, is a similar instance. Far from being a late invention, that belief was already widespread in traditionist circles in the early ninth century. The tradition (which we have already seen) that the caliph 'Alī (r. 656–61) told one of his soldiers not to insult the Syrians, who were rebelling against him, because among them there were saintly men known as *abdāl*, was known at least from the end of the eighth century. It can be found in the *Book of the Jihad* of 'Abd-Allāh ibn al-Mubārak, transmitted under the authority of two transmitters, one of whom died in 742, the other in 770. It is not impossible that he had direct connections with these two men. The biographers are in agreement in establishing direct master-student relations among them. Chabbi, however, contests that the *Book of the Jihad* is—even in part—the work of 'Abd-Allāh ibn al-Mubārak. Fortunately, we have a source that credits his transmission of this tradition: the *Corpus* of 'Abd al-Razzāq (d. 211?/826?), who includes it in the same chain of transmission that 'Abd-Allah ibn al-Mubārak gives.[52] The two men had been in personal contact with the same transmitter, who had been their master.

We have another indication that this tradition circulated in the ninth century in its republication by Ibn Abī al-Dunyā under the authority of a transmitter who had it from 'Abd al-Razzāq.[53] Ibn Abī al-Dunyā is also the redactor of another of the latter's traditions on the topic of the *abdāl*. It,

50. Ibn Manda, *Musnad Ibrāhīm ibn Adʿham*, ed. Majdī al-Sayyid Ibrāhīm (Cairo: Maktabat al-Qurʾān, 1988), 35. In the tenth century there was a traditionist by the name of 'Abd ibn Abid in the *ribāt* of Jawzanāwus, in Transoxiana, who taught the commentary of a work of traditions of the preceding century bearing on "the virtues of the *ribāt*." Moreover (and this is significant for our purposes) the same man is given as the transmitter of the *Book of the Jihad* of 'Abd-Allah ibn al-Mubārak, which he taught with a chain of transmission going back to the author, from whom he was separated only by five links: Samʿānī, *Kitāb al-Ansāb*, 4:126–27. If, what is more, this datum is placed in relation to the arrival of such students of 'Abd-Allah ibn al-Mubārak as the ascetic Ahmad ibn Tawba, "the Volunteer," we can see how the ideas of the great Khurasanian master were propagated in the *thagr* of Transoxiana: ibid. Samʿānī, *Kitāb al-Ansāb*, 4:362. All of these pieces of information, put together, accredit the attribution of the *Book of the Jihad* to 'Abd-Allah ibn al-Mubārak from the ninth century at least. This is enough to ruin Chabbi's line of argumentation.

51. Abū Nuʿaym, *Hilyat al-Awliyāʾ*, 8:50.

52. 'Abd al-Razzāq, *al-Musannāf*, *hadīth* no. 20455.

53. Ibn Abī al-Dunyā, *Kitāb Sīrat al-Awliyāʾ*, 30.

too, figures in the *Book of the Jihad*.[54] Consequently, there is no doubt concerning the circulation of belief in these "substitute saints" in traditionist
circles in the eighth century. What the ninth century did was to amplify
the belief and give it wider social resonance. In the new century people
wanted to know everything about these hidden saints and to give them
a physiognomy. This is how the questions raised in the *Book of the Round
and the Square*, by Jāhiz (d. 255/868), one of the two most significative ques-
tionnaires that have come down to us from the Middle Ages, should be
interpreted.[55] Jāhiz writes: "Tell me about the *abdāl*! Are they now at 'Irj
or at Bibīsān? Or have they been dispersed, as they were before? Tell me:
Are they all 'Arabized converts' or Arabs? Or are they all of 'mixed race'?
What did the 'Master of Antioch' do? Why were Salmān [the Persian]
and, after him Bilāl [the Abyssinian] instituted [as *abdāl*]? Who was [so
instituted] after them?"[56] The questions that Jāhiz asks are those of a man
who disputes a theory of holiness current in his day. Ibn Abī al-Dunyā
echoes them regarding a tradition for which he cites a traditionist of Kufa
who died in 813. The latter is reported as having heard one of his masters
in Medina say that when prophecy ceased (the founder of Islam is dogmatically considered to be "the seal of the prophets"), God substituted for
those messengers forty men of the nation of Muhammad, who were called
the "Substitutes." None of these was to die before having been replaced by
someone else. These exceptional beings drew their cosmic status of "pillars of the earth" from their collective function of intercession, a privilege
formerly enjoyed by the prophets.[57] Ahmad ibn Hanbal (d. 241/855) seems
to have been the earliest redactor of this tradition, which he considered,
however, "rejected" because of the presence in its chain of transmission of
a Basra scholar who adhered to the doctrine of free will.[58] All of this did

54. 'Abd-Allah ibn al-Mubārak, *Kitāb al-Jihād*, 156; 'Abd al-Razzāq, *al-Musannaf*, *hadīth*
no. 20457; Ibn Abī al-Dunyā, *Kitāb Sīrat al-Awliyā*, 30.

55. The other significant questionnaire is by Tawhīdī (d. 414/1023) and Miskawayh
(d. 421/1030): *Kitāb al-Tawābi' wa-al-Zawābi*, ed. Ahmad Amīn and Sayyid Ahmad Saqr (Cairo:
Lajnat al-Ta'līf wa-al-Tarjamah wa-al-Nashr, 1951).

56. Jāhiz, *Kitāb al-Tarbī' wa-al-Tadwīr*, ed. Charles Pellat (Damascus: Institut Français de
Damas, 1955), 28; trans. Maurice Adad as *Le livre du carré et du rond*, *Arabica* 13, no. 3 (1966):
268–94.

57. Ibn Abī al-Dunyā, *Kitāb Sīrat al-Awliyā*, 27.

58. Ahmad ibn Hanbal, *al-Musnad*, 5:322. In the ninth century the tradition was also rejected
by Abū Zur'a (d. 260/873). The *hadīth* was resurrected by such tenth-century traditionists as Abū
Sa'id al-Shādhī (d. 335/946): ibid., 3:124. In the following century it was authenticated by Haythamī
(d. 458/946), *Majma' al-Zawā'id* (Beirut: Dār al-Kitab, 1967), 10:52–63; and redacted by Abū
Nu'aym, *Akhbar isbahān*, for which see *Geschichte isbahāns [von] Abū Nu'aim*, ed. Sven Dedering,
2 vols. (Leiden: Brill, 1931), 1:180.

not prevent mystics of the latter half of the ninth century from adopting the theory of the "substitute saints."[59]

Placing the "substitute" saints in Syria was only in part connected with the myth of the frontier, however.[60] Still, although the tradition behind that placement appears in a work like the *Book of the Jihad*, it is because in the author's mind it was connected to his topic, which was frontier combat. This authorizes us to think that when that tradition recalls that God "pushes dangers far from the Muslims" thanks to the *abdāl*, it is referring to the dangers of external aggression. This is only one use of a tradition that authorizes other uses. In fact, parallel traditions—and there are others even in 'Abd-Allāh ibn al-Mubārak—correspond to another and much older belief that endowed Syria with great prestige as a biblical and eschatological land. As we have seen in the preceding chapter, many narrations circulating in the ninth century, notably within mystic circles, exhorted believers to go to that land of exile. More than the traditionists and the jurists, it was those mystics who, in effect, internalized the theme of "expatriation" and publicized it in several traditions at the end of the eighth century.[61] Submitting to this injunction with good grace, a large number of them settled in Syria. And although many of these lived in the Syrian-Byzantine mountain range of the Lukkām, not all of them were overly concerned about what was happening on the frontier. Those who, for one reason or another, were locally considered to be *abdāl* did not always forge their destiny as ritual personages by means of military activism.

To summarize: there is no doubt that the myth of the frontier was a reality in the late eighth century. Nor that the ascetics and the traditionists

59. Tustarī, *Tafsīr al-Qur'ān al-adhīm* (Misr: Matba'at al-Sa'ādah, 1329 AH/1908), 45–46. According to the author of this work, these were "the *mujāhid* in God," an expression that should be taken in a mystical sense, not a warlike one. See also Hakīm al-Tirmidhī, *Kitāb Sīrat al-Awliyā*, 122–23, and his response to a question put to him from Rayy on the identity of the *abdāl* in his *Jawab kitab min al-Rayy*, in Hakīm al-Tirmidhī, *Thalāthat musannafāt lil-Hakīm al-Tirmidhī*, ed. Bernd Radtke (Beirut: Dār al-Nashr, 1996), 175–76.

60. This idea occurs in Massignon, *La passion de Husayn ibn Mansūr Hallāj*, 1:66. See also André Miquel, *La géographie humaine du monde musulman jusqu'au milieu du IIe siècle*, 4 vols. (Paris: Mouton, 1967–), 4:38.

61. A trace of this can be found in the papyrus roll of the Egyptian judge 'Abd-Allah ibn Lahī'a (d. 174/790) published in Khoury, *'Abd-Allāh ibn Lahī'a*, 265, no. 135. His biographers describe him as a *ghāzi* on the Syrian-Byzantine frontier: Dhahabī, *Siyar*, 8:19. The papyrus roll includes several traditions on the eschatological prestige of Syria. They are placed in the mouth of Ka'b al-Ahbār, a Jew converted to Islam at the death of the Prophet: ibid., 291, no. 317; 303, no. 394; 293, no. 331. In the latter tradition, a Companion asks Ka'b what stops him from going to live in Medina, where the Prophet's tomb is located, and Ka'b responds, "I read in a revealed book that Syria is the treasure of God on earth."

who propagated that myth had often been to the front. What is less sure
is that any great numbers of learned men went to the frontier to fight and
seek martyrdom. In defending this thesis, Albrecht Noth and Michael
Bonner accredit the idea that all the men of letters of the classical and
medieval epochs who went to the frontier for a time did so "as warriors."
At the height of the movement, the scholars who were actual combatants
were limited in number. This weak involvement is perhaps explained by a
very simple fact: in order to make war, a man not only had to have a horse
and equipment adequate to the task, but he also had to have experience
in the handling of arms that not all men of letters had. They seem to have
resided at the frontier uniquely out of piety and study-related interests.
This is, for example, what emerges from the confidences of one such man
who died in 873. In the evening of his life he confided to his entourage
that, if his health had been less uncertain, he would willingly have given
away all that he possessed to go live in Tarsus or in some other spot on the
Syrian-Byzantine frontier. He wanted to end his days in a blessed place,
loaded with memories of his student years. There were fortified towns in
Syria that were important centers for the transmission of law, traditions,
and mysticism in the ninth century. An indefatigable journeyer, our aging
man of letters had stayed in them in the course of three voyages through
the central lands of Islam: in 828 (when he was only twenty years old), in
833 (when he was present at, but did not participate in, the taking of the
Square of the Pearl from the enemy), and in 844.[62]

Did learned men of the Muslim early Middle Ages go to the frontier
only out of religious fervor and an interest in studies?[63] After all, the great
intellectual and sacred centers were to be found in the central lands of the
domain of Islam. Why go to the frontier, if not to repel an external threat
by arms or at least conjure it away with words? By taking on a spiritual
content that gave it the same legitimacy as other forms of devotional and
study-related travel, the journey to the frontier acquired a dogmatic status. It became a founding deed. But, unlike the other forms of travel that
founded Islam in its religious, political, and linguistic centers, it instituted

---

62. Ibn Abī Hātim, *Kitāb al-Jarh wa al-taʿdīl*, 1:340–59. This globe-trotter relates that during
his second trip to the Syrian frontier, he left Tarsus to go to Homs, and then returned to Tarsus,
where, he notes, "There were still a few of the traditions of Abū Yaman that I had not heard; I
heard them, then I went to Bīsān, and from there to Raqq, where I went back up the Euphrates
to go to Baghdad": ibid., 1:359.

63. The *Kitāb Siyar al-Thughūr* of ʿUthmān ibn ʿAbd Allah Tarsūsī (d. 400/1010) shows the
point to which religious studies were intense in Tarsus: the Great Mosque of that frontier fortified city was the principal center of studies.

Islam at its margins. As a consequence, settling—permanently or temporarily—in the borderlands acquired the value of confirmation of oneself
in contrast to others. Residents of the frontier saw themselves as vigilant
defenders of Islam; as ulemas—which is to say, characteristic members of
the Islamic structure—they had the sense that they were working, at least
symbolically, to keep the dividing line between the self and others, not as a
line that divides, but as the frontier that circumscribes conformity.[64]

That dual function of consecration and conjuration gave the sojourn at
the frontier its ritual prestige. By giving it a normative content, jurists and
traditionists lent it enormous powers of sanctification. In doing so, they
stipulated that anyone who sojourned, out of piety, in a fortified town obtained—and without even having fought once—the status of martyr if he
should happen to die. Sublimated in this way, the frontier soon became a
formidable source of spiritual energy. As soon as its myth took shape, it
joined with the belief in "substitute saints" who, thanks to their location
at the frontier, served to guarantee the ineffable order of God lodged in
the "House of Islam."

64. I share the viewpoint of Mary Douglas here: she writes that the "idea of society" is a form
that "has its external boundaries, marginals, internal structure": Mary Douglas, *Purity and Danger:
An Analysis of Concepts of Pollution and Taboo* (New York: Praeger, 1966; Routledge, 2005), 144;
trans. Anne Guérin as *De la souillure: Essais sur les notions de pollution et de tabou* (Paris: Maspero,
1971), 130.

·◖ 7 ◗·

WRITING THE VOYAGE

Narrating an Absence

I s it true that the activity of travel, in the modern age, "evidently" involved the introduction of "motifs of the voyage and voyagers" into
Western literary and para-literary creation?[1] How could such a close link
between literature and the voyage have been established? Supposing it
to have been the case, how can we explain the fact that someone like La
Bruyère insisted, and with rigor, on the need to talk about his travels, while
speaking in mocking tones of "those people who out of restlessness or
curiosity embark on long journeys, who keep no diaries and write no descriptions, who carry no notebooks; who go to see things, and who either
don't see them or forget what they have seen; who are only anxious to look
at unfamiliar towers or steeples, and cross rivers that are not called Seine or
Loire; who leave their native land merely in order to return to it, who like
being away from home, and hope some day to be travelled men."[2] To tell
the truth, the great seventeenth-century writer could object to gratuitous

---

1. Hanna Dziechinska, "La noblesse polonaise aux XVIe et XVIIe siècles face au voyages," in
Voyager à la Renaissance, actes du colloque de Tours, 1983, ed. Jean Céard and Jean-Claude Margolin
(Paris: Maisonneuve et Larose, 1987), 193–201, esp. 197. Tzvetan Todorov has generalized this
empirical observation, stating that travel narratives seem to be as old as travel itself, if not older:
Todorov, *Les morales de l'histoire* (Paris: Hachette, 1997), 121; trans. Alyson Waters as *The Morals of
History* (Minneapolis: University of Minnesota Press, 1995).

2. Jean de La Bruyère, *Les caractères de Théophraste . . . avec Les caractères; ou, Les moeurs de ce siècle*,
trans. Robert Garapon (Paris: Garnier, 1962), "De la mode," 395; quoted from *Characters*, trans.
Jean Stewart (Baltimore: Penguin, 1970), 252.

vagabondage only because he linked travel and writing in a moralizing perspective. According to the neo-Stoic principles underlying his thought,
travel was intimately associated with both knowledge and the writing
from which knowledge derives its reason for being.[3]

What the French know as "Le Grand Siècle" was also the age in which
the Western genre of travel literature, while keeping its edifying purpose,
shifted from the sphere of knowledge to the domain of literature. There,
too, the combination was possible only because it found a reason for being
in the principle that one travels in order to write.[4]

In any event, a philosophical and/or aesthetic model of the world was
needed for the articulation between voyage and writing to be possible.
Without it, any transformation into literature remained problematic.

Where Islam is concerned, specialists have also posited a spontaneous
relation between the voyage and its narration. One writer states that the
transfer from oral narration and written narration is but a step, quickly
taken, and that the travel narrative arose "quite naturally."[5] In reality,
nothing in Islamic culture displays any such relationship. Despite the formidable experience that plucked the men of letters of Islam, en masse,
from their homes and propelled them to the edges of Islam's territories,
there is little, before the ninth century, that resembles a travel-related literary genre. This is not the first difference, however. When the traditionists set themselves to collecting traditions that justify travel, the voyage
was already almost a century old. We would have to wait another hundred years to see Muslim travelers bothering to write down their voyage

3. Francine-Dominique Liechtenhan, "Le voyagiste ou *peregrinationum scriptor*: Un homme
de métier à la fin du Grand Siècle," in *Écrire le voyage*, ed. György Tverdota (Paris: Presses de la
Sorbonne Nouvelle, 1994), 143–52, esp. p. 147. La Bruyère arrived at Stoicism via Justus Lipsius: On
the relationship between the two thinkers, see Jacqueline Lagrée, "Juste Lipse: Destins et Provi-
dence," in *Le Stoïcisme au XVIe et au XVIIe siècle: Le retour des philosophies antiques à l'âge classique*,
ed. Pierre-François Moreau (Paris: Albin Michel, 1999), 77–93. The English philosopher Francis
Bacon (who expressed astonishment that people should keep a journal when they travel by sea
and not when they travel by land) links travel, experience, and writing in a similarly moralizing
perspective: see Bacon, *Essayes; or, Counsels, Civil and Moral*; in French translation as *Essais de
morale et de politique* (1625); trans. Antoine de La Salle (1836; Paris: L'Arche, 1999), 78–82.
    4. This is even truer in the romantic nineteenth century, when "henceforth the narration
becomes the prime condition for the voyage instead of being its result or one of its possible consequences": Roland Le Huenen, "Qu'est-ce qu'un récit de voyage?" in *Les modèles du récit de voyage*,
Littérales 7 (Nanterre: Centre de recherches du Département de français de Paris X-Nanterre,
1990), 12. See also Michel Bideaux, "Le voyage littéraire: Genèse d'un genre," in *Modèles du récit de
voyage*, 179–98.
    5. Mahammed Hadj-Sadok, "Le genre 'Rih'la,'" *Bulletin des études arabes* 40 (1948): 196–206,
esp. 198.

or voyages. There were indeed narrations in the ninth century, but they circulated orally in the appropriate milieus. People were just beginning to write them down. The marriage between the voyage and writing was not yet on the agenda.

How could it have been that men of letters who traveled widely often did not think of putting their travel experiences in writing? The reason is that in their eyes, telling about it was not the prime condition for the trip. At the same time that it favored the rise of the voyage, what I have called the "paradigm of hearing" quite paradoxically proved an obstacle to both the emergence and the full development of the literary genre of the travel account. This is probably why the texts of the ninth-century writers on geographical topics still bear compromising signs of the cultures of listening and compilation. Rather than hiding the fact, those authors openly proclaimed their allegiance to the working methods of the prose writers and the traditionists. When one of them proclaims, "I have put into my work only the historical traditions, the verse, the citations, and the sayings that *my memory has grasped and that I have been able to hear*," it is clear that he is putting his entire faith in auricular testimony.[6]

If we except the experimental sciences (medicine, astronomy, mechanics, and so forth),[7] it is clear that in the ninth century, sight was still relatively undeveloped as a tool for description and knowledge. Geography, which had just begun to adopt it, allowed it to function as a principle of organization and explanation only in the following century. Is it just by chance that the travel narrative also found durable forms of writing only

6. Suhrāb expresses this idea in the introduction to his *Marvels of the Seven Climates*: "I have always liked to read the books of the predecessors [i.e., the Greeks] and have sought out all that they said concerning the configuration of the earth. . . . I have found all of that in books that take a long time to comment on and that are hard to utilize. Therefore it seemed to me preferable to summarize all those books in one book that will be easy to understand and that anyone can use who wants [to know about] the configuration of the earth": Suhrāb, *Kitāb 'Ajā'ib al-Aqālīm*, ed. Hans von Mzik (Leipzig, 1876; reprint, Leipzig: Harrassowitz, 1930), 5. A similar introduction appears in Is'hāq al-Zayyāt, *Dhikr al-Aqālim*, 57.

7. Even this domain of knowledge reserve surprises, however: Mas'ūdī reproduces an interesting debate among physicians sponsored by the caliph Wāthiq (r. 842–47), who asked them, "How can one acquire knowledge of medicine and the principles from which that science is drawn? Is it (by the testimony of) the senses? Or else by analogy and tradition? Is it perceived a priori by the intelligence or, to the contrary, does that science and its method rest on oral teaching, as several orthodox doctors claim?": Mas'ūdī, *Murūj al-Dhahab*; trans. Charles Barbier de Meynard and Abel Payet de Courteille as *Les prairies d'or*, 9 vols. (Paris: Imprimerie Impériale, 1861–1917; that translation reviewed and corrected by Charles Pellat, 5 vols. (Paris: Société Asiatique, 1962, 1989, 1997), 4:1168.

beginning with the tenth century? The coincidence between the two types of writing is worth keeping in mind.

When we examine the great men of letters who traveled in the ninth century, we see that their travel narratives circulated widely in the circles they were a part of. As word of them passed from one person to another, a chain of scholarly solidarity perpetuated oral memory of them. But the ninth century was also an epoch of the triumph of writing over orality and of the rise of the book in Islam. Oral travel narratives slowly gained a more literary form, borrowing their narrative conventions from the *khabar*.[8] Ibn Khuthayma (d. 243/857) included in his *Book of Science* fragments of the travel narrative of one of the first (if not the first) globe-trotting men of letters of Islam, Mak'hūl (d. 112/730). He obtained these fragments from one of the Syrian masters, who had them from a direct disciple of Makhūl, who had died in Syria.[9] Other travel accounts may have been collected under similar circumstances. Their transmission at times uses the same channels as family memoirs. The son of Ahmad ibn Hanbal (d. 241/855) included in his biography of his father whole portions of his travel notes.[10] Ibn Abī Hātim (d. 327/938) did the same, including in a biographical dictionary of men of letters the *rihla* of his father, a famous traditionist, in two chapters, one entitled "On What My Father Endured in the Way of Difficulties in the Course of His Quest for Knowledge," and the other, "On What Is Said about the *Rihla* of My Father."[11] One thing needs to be said: When the biographical and autobiographical genres began to develop in Islam, they opened up to travel narratives, which they adopted as the constituent topoi for their writing.[12] As is known, the same link

8. The *khabar* was a "narration," a "relation," an "information," or an oral tradition, usually secular, which was presented in a narrative form. For a narratological analysis of the *khabar*, see M. D. Beaumont, "Hard-Boiled: Narrative Discourse in Early Muslim Traditions," *Studia Islamica* 83 (1996): 5–32.

9. Ibn Khuthayma Zuhayr ibn Harb, *Kitāb al-'Ilm*, MS no. 3830, Zāhiriyya, Damascus, fol. 188b.

10. Sālih ibn Ahmad ibn Hanbal, *Sīrat al-Imām Ahmad ibn Hanbal*, 2 vols. (Alexandria: Mu'assasat Shabāb al-Jāmi'ah, 1981). On this biography, see Nimrod Hurvitz, "Biographies and Mild Asceticism," *Studia Islamica* 85 (1997): 41–66.

11. Ibn Abī Hātim, *Kitāb al-jarh wa al-ta'dīl*, 9 vols. (Beirut: Dār al-Kitub al-'Ilmīyah, 1952), 1:259–61, 263–66.

12. Biographical dictionaries in Andalusia show this clearly, from Khushānī, *Akhbār al-Fuqahā'*, ed. Maria Luisa Avila and Luis Molinas (Madrid: al-Majhlis al-Alā lil-Abhāth al-'Ilmīyah, 1992); through Ibn al-Faradī (d. 403/1013), *Tārīkh 'Ulamā' al-Andalus*, ed. Ibrāhīm Ibyārī (Cairo: Dār al-Kutub al-Islāmīyah, 1983); to Ibn Bashkuwāl (d. 578/1182), *Kitāb al-Sila*, 2 vols. (Cairo: Dār al-Misrīyah, 1966). For a study of one of the first travel *khabar* collected by Khushānī, see Manuela Marin, "*Rihla* e biografias de Ibn al-Qallās (m. 337/948)," in *Homenaje al Professor José Maria Forneas Besteiro* (Granada, 1994), 581–91. See also Luis Molina, "Lugares de destino de los viajeros anda-

between travel writing and the writing of biographies and autobiographies is confirmed in Western travel literature.

The voyage *khabar*—the form in which travel narratives, incidentally, came into the biographical genre in Islam—has a dual nature. In its principle of organization, it is a narrated and fragmentary discourse in which the author-transmitter is not confused with the narrator; as a form of narration, the *khabar* belongs to a sociocultural world in which the travelers who *talk* about their voyages feel no need to write about them. Not because they do not know how to do so, but because they have inherited a genealogical principle that structures all written productions as acts of reported language. Given these conditions, it seemed enough to the traveler-scholars that their peers know that they had a voyage to their credit and that the dictionaries in which their names would appear after their death relate some of the tales of their adventures that they had taken care to diffuse. One learned man of the tenth century who wanted to write a biography of his master tells, without surprise, of having discovered a *khabar* of a voyage the master had taken scribbled on "the back" (that is, on the title page) of a work of exegesis of the Qur'an.[13]

With this example, we enter into the making of travel narratives as they functioned within the framework of the *khabar*. A man of letters and an experienced traveler reports an episode from his peregrinations to another man of letters, who thinks it useful to jot it down on the margins of one of his books. A biographer, seeking material for a portrait of the first man, encounters this book and notes the episode in question. The *khabar*, originally an oral message, has become a written text the minute that the person who receives it, instead of simply remembering it, puts it down on paper. The text, now free to circulate independently of its mediators, thus lends itself to being used in all manner of written operations, not the least of which is being placed in the biography of the person who is both the hero of the tale and its source of emission. But if our traveler—in this case, Tabarānī (d. 360/970)—did not judge it useful to write down a report of his peregrinations, he did think it necessary to compose no fewer than three catalogs that offer an "inventory of his masters."[14]

lusies en *Tārīj* de Ibn al-Faradī," in *Estudios Onomastico-Biograficos de al-Andalus*, 7 vols. (Madrid: Consejo Superior de Investigaciones Cientificas, 1988), 1:595–610.

13. Abū'l-Qāsim Tabarānī, *Al-Muʿjam al-Saghīr*, preceded by *Juzʾ fihi Dhikr Abā al-Qāsim . . . al-Tabarānī*, by Ibn Manda, ed. Kamāl Yūsūf Hūt (Beirut: Muassasat al-Rayyan, 2001), 11.

14. In his lesser *Muʿjam*, Tabarānī states: "This is the first book in which I have collected the most profitable things about the masters under whose authority I studied in various lands": ibid., 41.

In fact, Islamic men of letters preferred to confide their travel experience to an inventory rather than a travel narrative. As a genre, the inventory—which is sometimes called a "dictionary," but also a "mastery" or a "program"—is specific to Islamic scholarly culture. It arose in the ninth century thanks to the traditionists. Halfway between the biographical dictionary and the travel narrative, it was structured around the goal of meeting and studying under the largest possible number of masters, preferably those in possession of a prestigious intellectual genealogy. A determined search for a master made the genre a symbol of the consecration of the great man of letters and traveler. In his inventory Tabarānī cites almost a thousand men from whom he gathered traditions. It is understandable that, in discussing his catalog with one of his colleagues, he should confide to him that "it is the book of my life," one for which he "worked very hard."[15]

Most of these inventories are arranged in alphabetical order.[16] In spite of this structure, they managed to include a large amount of biographical information. In one such work,[17] the author tells how he persuaded his parents to let him go off on a voyage when he was still an adolescent.[18] At the age of seventeen, he had decided to leave his native Jurjān, situated in Khurasan southeast of the Caspian Sea, to study with a known master. When he arrived in Baghdad in 908, he was only nineteen, but his travels already included the fortified towns of Syria. In all, he met some 230 masters in thirty-two different cities and villages. Each time that he mentions a master, we know where and when he encountered him, and on occasion he adds the man's trade and doctrinal leanings.

In the Middle Ages, men of letters continued to compose inventories with unflagging diligence, because they served as narrative proof of their travels. That activity lasted until the day when an Andalusian jurist, Abū

15. Dhahabī, quoted in 'Abd al-Hayy Kattānī, *Al-Risāla al-Mustatrafa* (Damascus, 1964), 136.
16. Some followed the literary model of the geographical dictionary. This was the case with one of the most famous traditionists of the tenth century, Ibn Hibbān (d. 354/965), who arranged his "inventory of masters" (in no fewer than ten volumes) by city: Dhahabī, *Siyar A'lām al-Nubalā'*, ed. Shu'ayb al-Arna'ūtī et al., 25 vols. (Beirut: Mu'assasat al-Risālah, 1982–83), 16:95. Unfortunately, no inventory of this type has come down to us.
17. Abū Bakr al-Ismā'īlī, *Kitāb al-Mu'jam*, ed. Ziyād M. Mansūr, 4 vols. (Medina: Maktaba al-'Ulum wa-al-Hikam, 1990), 106. See also Heinrich Schützinger, *Das Kitāb al-Mu'gam des Abū Bakr al-Ismā'īlī* (Wiesbaden: Steiner; Mainz: Deutsche Morgenländische Ges., 1978).
18. The disciple of this doctor, Abū al-Qāsim Sahmī (d. 427/1035), returns to this narration, which he received from the mouth of his master: *Tārikh Jurjān* (Hyderabad: Matba'at Majlis Dairat, 1950), 69–70. This dictionary contains references to travel in several entries.

Bakr ibn al-'Arabī, himself the author of an inventory of masters,[19] had the idea of composing a genuine travel narrative in which he told of his travels studying in the East, and the literary genre of the *rihla* was born. Its development did not put an end to the composition of the previous fastidious lists, however. Scholars in Andalusia and the Maghreb—among other places—continued their frantic composition of inventories of their masters.

The Extraordinary in the Voyage

What are these *khabar* like? How were they put together? Because they were written in snatches, they dramatize entire segments of a voyage in a few words or a few phrases. What they note must be worth retelling. In order to satisfy that requirement, they have to communicate a strong emotional charge that will compensate for their fragmentary nature. Where to find that emotional charge? In the register of the extraordinary and the marvelous. Beginning in the ninth century, the *'Ajā'ib*—marvelous tales—made up an entire sector of knowledge and participated in both edifying literature and literature for entertainment.[20] From the moment that the voyage *khabar* arose, it tended to adopt their writing style.

More than all of the other genres with which the travel narrative had an intertextual relationship, the *'Ajā'ib* of marvels posed a problem of classification: to what genre did they belong? For us, there is no doubt that they derive from the same order of discourse as geography or history. Some have seen them as a "literary art."[21] In the late nineteenth century Carra de Vaux warned, "The word 'Marvel' does not represent something that does not exist or never has existed. Marvels are monuments, facts, and beings like those we encounter in geography and in history. It is not sure that

---

19. Ibn al-Abbār, *Al-Mu'jam fī Ashāb al-Qādī al-Imām Abī 'Alī al-Sadafī* (Cairo: Dār al-Kātib al-Arabī, 1967), 1:201.

20. On the way in which the *'Ajāib* functioned, see Mohammed Arkoun et al., eds., *L'étrange et le merveilleux dans l'Islam médiéval*, actes du colloque tenu au Collège de France (Paris: Éditions J. A., 1978).

21. See, for example, Ian Richard Netton, "Myth, Miracle and Magic in the *Rihla* of Ibn Battūta," *Journal of Semitic Studies* 29, no. 1 (1984): 131–40, esp. 131; Netton, "Rihla," in *Encyclopédie de l'Islam*, new ed. (Leiden: E. J. Brill; Paris: Maisonneuve et Larose, 1966), 8:546; and in *The Encyclopaedia of Islam*, new ed., ed. E. J. Van Donzel (Leiden: Brill, 1966), 8:528ff.; and Paule Charles-Dominique, who writes in the introduction to *Voyageurs arabes: Ibn Fadlān, Ibn Jubayr, Ibn Battūta et un auteur anonyme* (Paris: Gallimard, 1995), xix, "This literature of *mirabilia* is similar to the tale more than it belongs to the geographical genre."

they are true; it is even less sure that they are false: they are above all hard to confirm."[22] If that is the case, it would be wrong to think that studying and investigating the marvels of creation does not derive from a positive configuration of knowledge because Islam's *mirabilia* inject the extraordinary everywhere. The fact that the *'Ajā'ib*, which by nature have a great capacity for digestion, absorbed marvels very early in their career does not in any way disqualify the status of the genre as positive knowledge. As early as the mid-ninth century, Jāhiz (d. 255/868), who played a major role in the founding of the *Adab*, was saddened that the majority of men, when faced with the "strange, extraordinary phenomena, [that are] very numerous in the universe," either lacked "the passion to know them" or turned away from the *tabayyun* (clear vision of things) that permits comprehension, thus neglecting to cultivate their minds, or else they denied such phenomena as impossible. He went on to trace a entire program, reflected in part in his *Book of the Animals*.

Although those who came after Jāhiz enlarged the circle of study of the *'Ajā'ib* to include all sorts of strange things and aberrations, they were not always able to profit from the program that he had set down for the genre, even less to broaden it or move beyond it, given that most of them were jurists, fabulists, or moralists. Despite that obstacle, the genre of marvels nonetheless continued to function as a sector of medieval knowledge. That it was a form of knowledge more doxic than positive counted for little. What matters is that the *'Ajā'ib* derived from a representation of the world of porous frontiers between the visible and the invisible, nature and the supernatural, the ordinary and the extraordinary, the believable and the unbelievable, a world of permanent communication between these contrasts. Because that ambiguity never ceased to produce discourse, it continued to ensure that the intellectual activity crystallized by marvels remained a part of the *episteme* of medieval Islam.

The *'Ajā'ib* were useful when it came to trying to comprehend the elusive manifestations that lay between. In their task of meditating on the metamorphosis of beings and things, they produced a knowledge about life that captured the entire experience of the strange and foreign

22. Bernard, baron Carra de Vaux, in the introduction to the anonymous *Abrégé des merveilles*, trans. Bernard, baron Carra de Vaux (Paris: Klincksieck, 1898), xi; reprinted inthe series Islamic Geography, ed. Fuat Sezgin, vol. 196 (Frankfurt, 1994; reprint, Paris), 10. André Miquel speaks in similar terms, stating, "As aberrant as it is, the *'ajīb* is nonetheless given as true": André Miquel, *La géographie humaine du monde musulman jusqu'au milieu du 11e siècle*, 4 vols. (Paris: Mouton, 1967–), 2:484. For a description of the genre, see C. E. Dubler, "'Adjā'ib," in *Encyclopédie de l'Islam*, new ed. (1966), 1:209–10; and in *The Encyclopaedia of Islam*, new ed. (1966), 1:203–4.

through literary expression and a explicative discursive framework. This explains their configuration of discourse on the like and the unlike. As André Miquel states, "When the marvelous is decisively resistant, at least it serves to fix the limits of the human." But when he adds, "Marvels take on, marvelously, the dual function of relaxing the reader's mind and conferring the cachet of an acceptable literature on the works in which they appear,"[23] we have a right to be surprised that he should reduce the genre to amusing literary magic tricks. Not that he is not correct in pointing out the ornamental use of *'Ajā'ib* in the encyclopedias and literary anthologies, but that was not their only use. To say that the *'Ajā'ib*'s only function was pleasure is to destroy their credibility. Medieval belles lettres is full of their worn topoi, but they also entered into a number of discursive formations with other functions than that of eliciting pleasure. In geography, for example, they operated within the categories of the admirable and the believable.[24] The admirable was what is worthy of holding attention and being fixed in writing in a book that, in turn, was itself judged worthy of being read or learned by heart. The notion of the admirable derived from a way of thinking that resonated with echoes of the extraordinary—that is, of what lies beyond the reader's everyday universe and the horizon of his experience. As the *'Ajā'ib* merged with the medieval travel narrative, the categories of the admirable took on added force and authority. In the tacit pact between the "author" (if one can talk of an "author" in the Middle Ages) and the reader, it was the first who decided what the second should or should not know. The categories of the admirable were what made the "author" the only element of text that had the power to determine what was or was not worthy of interest.

It is because those categories operated to translate difference that they functioned in travel narratives as rhetorical procedures of the like and the unlike. However, as figures of the extraordinary, they did not imply leaving Islamic space in order to experience them or incorporate them into written travel accounts. Similarly, the ancient Greeks had no need to leave

23. André Miquel, preface to the anonymous *Abrégé des merveilles*, trans. Carra de Vaux (Paris: Sindbad, 1984), 14.

24. See the story of the celestial origin of the Nile that Muqaddasī offers, with a chain of authorities, in his *Ahsan al-Taqāsim fī Maʿrifat al-Aqālīm: La meilleure répartition pour la connaissance des provinces*, trans. André Miquel (Damascus: Institut Français de Damas, 1963), 58–61. Miquel observes in a note that this passage can be found almost word for word in the *Abrégé des merveilles*: ibid., 344. It had already appeared in Masʿūdī, *Murūj al-Dhahab*; Barbier de Meynard and Payet de Courteille translation, 1:268. Later, it was picked up again by Yāqūt in his *Muʿjam al-Buldān*, ed. Ferdinand Wüstenfeld, 7 vols. (Leipzig, 1855–73; reprint, 6 vols. in 11 pts., Frankfurt: Institute for the History of Arabic-Islamic Science, 1994), 4:868.

their cultural world to encounter the *thōma*. Nor did men of the medieval West need to do so in order to discover *mirabilia*. The Christian Middle Ages, heir to the ancient tradition of paradox, admittedly made marginal areas privileged places where the "topographic marvelous" proliferated, but that does not mean that they refused to let the "central territories" have their own *mirabilia*.[25] A work like the *Book of Marvels* of Gervase of Tilbury clearly attests to this.[26]

Concerning the ancient Greeks François Hartog has shown, using Herodotus as an example, the determinant use that they made of the *thōma*, the marvel or curiosity. For the Greeks, a travel narrative could not claim to be a faithful account without including material that comes under the heading of *thōma*.[27] The same might be said of Muslims of the Middle Ages, who considered that such a work had missed its target if it did not include some *'Ajā'ib*, particularly since all medieval travel narratives were programmed to end with something extraordinary. This constraint was both cultural and narrative. At times it seems the only justification for reading or listening to a travel narrative. Its role was to create an expected effect. One Eastern man of letters asked one of his Western colleagues (from Andalusia) who had "toured" a great deal (he was in fact called *"jawwāl,"* or "tourist," in the sense in which the Enlightenment used the term) to recount what he had seen in the course of his peregrinations that was the "most *'ajīb*." The man who had made a "grand tour" and who had an extraordinary tale or two in his baggage satisfied his interlocutor with one that stands out as particularly striking. The tale told changes its author as much as it strikes the person he tells it to. The voyager becomes a narrator; the listener becomes an editor. We cannot glean much from the author's biography except that he was Andalusian, had traveled widely, and in his wanderings had witnessed a scene among mystics that he thought surprising enough to be used to illustrate the singularity of his

25. Lorraine Daston and Katharine Park, *Wonders and the Order of Nature: 1150–1750* (New York: Zone, 1998), 25–26. See also Jacques Le Goff, "Le merveilleux dans l'Occident médiéval," in Arkoun et al., *L'étrange et le merveilleux dans l'Islam médiéval*, 61–79; reprinted in Le Goff, *Pour un autre Moyen Âge: Temps, travail et culture en Occident* (Paris: Gallimard, 1977, 2004), 455–76; trans. Arthur Goldhammer as *Time, Work, and Culture in the Middle Ages* (Chicago: University of Chicago Press, 1980).

26. Gervase of Tilbury, *Otio imperiale: Recreation for an Emperor*, ed. and trans. S. E. Banks and J. W. Binns (New York: Oxford University Press, 2002); trans. Annie Duchesne as *Le livre des merveilles: Divertissement pour un empereur* (Paris: Belles Lettres, 1992).

27. François Hartog, *Le miroir d'Hérodote: Essai sur la représentation de l'autre* (Paris: Gallimard, 1980), 243–48.

wide travels.[28] This proved enough to snatch him from oblivion. An Iraqi man of letters, Abū Muhammad al-Sarrāj (d. 500/1106), provides his name and his anecdote, backed up by a chain of guarantors. In this chain of transformations, we have an example of the extraordinary that, escaping oblivion, has become something remembered, which in turn has become something memorable, thanks to the magic of the written word. Everyone wins in this affair: the author of the anecdote and the listener-editors. We ourselves have a better idea of why these "tourists" had to have more than one *ʿajība* in their tour, even if they had to invent them. One anecdote, typical but forged, placed in the mouth of the celebrated jurist Shāfiʿī (d. 204/819) was published by the hagiographer Abū Nuʿaym of Isfahan (d. 430/1038):

> So-and-So told us: I have heard So-and-So say: I have head So-and-So say, according to another, according to his father, according to the latter's father:[29] I have heard Shāfiʿī say: "At the time that I was touring in search of science, I went to Yemen. There I was told of a woman who, from her feet to her pelvis, had a normal woman's body, but who, instead of having one trunk, had two separate ones, with four hands, two heads, and two faces. I learned that the two halves fought each other, struck each other, and became reconciled; they ate and drank together as well. Having left that land, I no longer heard anyone speak of them. When I went back two years later, I wanted to have news of them. Someone told me: 'May God console you for the loss of one of the two halves!' I asked for an explanation and was told: 'One of the two bodies fell ill, and when it was dead, it was solidly bound, top to bottom, with a rope and left that way until it rotted. After which, it was cut off and buried.' I was told that the body that remained alive continued to come and go in the suqs."[30]

The expression *faliʿ ahdī bi*—"I learned," or "I heard about"—seems to indicate that, in the account published by Abū Nuʿaym, Shāfiʿī did not actually see the Siamese twins, but had only heard speak of them. Yet

28. Abū Muhammad Sarrāj, *Masāriʿ al-ʿUshshāq*, 2 vols. (Beirut: Dār Bayrūt lil Tibāʿah wa-al-Nashr, 1958), 1:219.

29. The names cited here take us from Khursan, at the extreme east of the Muslim world, to Egypt, by way of Persia. This narrative appears in the *Narration of a Voyage* by Pseudo-Shāfiʿī, a tenth-century forgery.

30. Abū Nuʿaym, *Hilyat al-Awliyāʾ*, 10 vols. (Cairo: Maktabat al-Khānjī, 1932–38; new ed., 10 vols. (Beirut: Dār al-Kitāb al-Arabī, 1967–68), 9:127–28; selections trans. Muhammad Al-Akoli as *The Beauty of the Righteous and Ranks of the Elite* (Philadelphia: Pearl, 1995).

the condolences offered to him seem to attest the contrary. In the latter case, he should have said, "I saw" (*ra'aytu*), as he does in another account in which he tells of the spectacle, still in Yemen, of two blind men whom he saw in a serious dispute, being reconciled by a deaf man. He does nothing of the sort. But a later version of the same story states that Shāfi'ī saw the Siamese twins after contracting marriage with them.[31] In both instances, the narrative tells of a "marvel" (*'ajība*). There is no doubt about this: a tenth-century source tells about two male Siamese twins presented at the court of a prince of Mosul in 912.[32] The same story figures in a chapter entitled "Marvels" in a work of the late Middle Ages.[33]

There can be no doubt that the Muslim traveler going from one place to another within the "House of Islam" was moving within a familiar space in which he was everywhere as at home as he was in his paternal dwelling. It is also true, however, that the same familiarity, always and everywhere, met with unyielding obstacles. If this were not true, it would be hard to explain why or how the medieval journeyer could experience *ghurba*, an exile that took him far from his homeland, *hanīn*, which tortured the expatriate with a crushing homesickness, and *dhull*, scorn and humiliation, not a sentiment normally present in the paternal home. Moreover, the fact that it was possible to experience alterity even within Islam is attested by the use of the term *'ajīb*, which, although it expresses the concept of strangeness and extraneousness, does not always occur outside the geographical and cultural borders of Islam. Because it is ambiguous from an anthropological viewpoint, Muslim travelers could experience *'ajīb* inside or outside their own culture. Because these travelers themselves state that they have met with the extraordinary both "here" and "there," we owe it to them to take seriously the linguistic concepts within which they apprehended the world and made capital of its experience. This would make it impossible to keep repeating that "wonderment is produced only when one crosses the frontiers of the empire to venture into lands in which other cultural codes and other social burdens come into play," or that "within the borders, one encounters only particularities."[34]

---

31. Dhahabī, *Siyar*, 10:90.

32. Tanūkhī, *Nishwār al-Muḥāḍarāh*; selections trans. Youssef Seddik as *Brins de chicane: La vie quotidienne à Bagdad au Xe siècle* (Arles: Actes Sud-Sindbad, 1999), 37–39.

33. Mustawfī Qazwīnī, *The Geographical Part of the Nuzhat al-Qulūb Composed by Hamd Allāh Mustawfī of Qazwīn in 740 (1340)*, ed. Guy Le Strange, 2 vols. (Leiden: Brill, 1915–19), 284.

34. Abdelfattah Kilito, *Les séances: Récits et codes culturels chez Hamadhānī et Harīrī* (Paris: Sindbad, 1983), 21. In his *La géographie humaine*, André Miquel has shown that marvels operated both

The Travel Epistle

In the tenth century, the travel narrative had not yet found a stable and durable framework, and it took refuge in the epistle, or letter, a literary genre that it claimed as its own for nearly two hundred years.

Widespread in the mid-eighth century, the *risāla*, or letter, soon became a favorite device of the learned men of Islam.[35] Prose writers, philosophers, physicians, theologians, jurists, and traditionists used the letter to develop their various domains of knowledge. Its discourse, born of political and diplomatic needs, acquired a privileged status as a means of communication and sociability. With the coming of the 'Abbāsid empire, its spread coincided with the appearance of a new structure of literary sociability, the salon. In certain of its aspects, the letter appears as the prolongation (by means of writing) of the literary conversation, scholarly discussions, and chitchat that took places in those literary salons. Addressed to a particular individual, who is often named, the letter almost always has a real and historically identifiable addressee. Thus, as a bond of friendship and patronage it quite legitimately belongs within a sociology of social connections. Thanks to the letter, notions can be exchanged, ideas discussed, and sentiments that are judged worthy of being written down shared.

In this, the Islamic letter is hardly different from Greek, Roman, or Western models. In Islam as in the West, the voyage is linked to the letter. But whereas in Islam the travel narrative discovered the travel letter in the late ninth century, in Europe the two were fully combined only in the Renaissance. It seems, despite differences in sociohistorical context, that the joining of the two took place in the West under conditions that are structurally analogous to those in Islam.[36] If we can believe Percy G. Adams, the

------

outside Islam (2:483–514) and within its borders (4:95–124). Abū Hamīd al-Gharnātī (d. 564)/1169) says much the same thing in his *Exposé on Some Marvels of the West: Al-Mu'rib 'an Ba 'd 'Ajā'ib al-Maghrib; De Grenade à Bagdad: La relation de voyage d'Abū Hāmid al-Gharnāti* (Paris: L'Harmattan, 2006). This work lists "'*Ajā'ib* of the sea and the land" and those of Egypt.

35. On the literary genre of the letter, see J. D. Latham, "The Beginning of Arabic Prose: The Epistolary Genre," in *The Cambridge History of Arabic Literature,* ed. A. F. L. Beeston et al., 4 vols. (Cambridge: Cambridge University Press, 1983), 1:154–79. See also A. Azari and H. Ben Shammay, "Risāla," in *Encyclopédie de l'Islam,* new ed. (1966), 8:549–57; and in *The Encyclopaedia of Islam,* new ed. (1966), 8:532ff.

36. In investigating the reasons for which travel literature is cast in the epistolary narrative in Europe of the Enlightenment, Nicole Hafid-Martin offers an explanation that recalls my own, showing how, in the mid-eighth century, the invention of the literary letter coincided with the invention of the literary salon in the Muslim world. She states: "Witness to an *art de vivre,* the epistolary narrative takes on the particular character of salon conversations, from which it

letter is, with the journal and "simple narration" (transcription), "one of the three most prolific sorts of travel narration" in the West.[37] To the extent that the journal can itself function as a form of letter, we can judge the full importance of the genre for writing about travel. Jacques Chocheyras writes, "Placed under the sign of solitude—at least moral and spiritual—[the journal] was the substitute for the letter; a message to an absent person, it was a correspondence addressed to a supposedly stable double of oneself on the part of an 'I' who changed his physical place in order to give himself the illusion of changing moral space."[38] In medieval Islam as well, the travel letter joined the journal to give rise to a new form of literature of journeying.

Until the mid-nineteenth century, the West had a vast appetite for travel letters. They were not only numerous, but also for the most part available and accessible The same is unfortunately not true of the Muslim Middle Ages, for which almost all travel letters have disappeared. What remains of those that escaped obliteration is at times just an allusion, a quotation, at best a fragment, grasped from oblivion by the hazards of compilation. The letter that an eminent Andalusian writer wrote in Sicily in the late ninth or early tenth century is known to us only because it is mentioned in the biographical dictionaries of the Muslim West. All that is left of its content is the advice that the writer of the letter, who endured many hardships far from his homeland, transmits to the addressee: Never take long trips.[39] We know of another letter thanks to a twelfth-century compiler who quotes a passage from it in an entry in his geographical dictionary.[40] Composed in 1040, during the Seljuk era, by a judge from Hamadān, it describes the things that the author had seen (such as the great mosque of Damascus) and offers a portrait of the scholars whom he met. All that we have of the content of the letter is a line or two from a well-known poet whom the letter writer and traveler went to the environs of Aleppo to meet.[41] It is simply by good luck that the whole of the letter

---

cannot be dissociated; it is much less a question of confidential or private exchanges than a way to maintain a presence in a society mad for novelties": *Voyage et connaissance au tournant des Lumières (1780–1820)* (Oxford: Voltaire Foundation, 1995), 69.

37. Percy G. Adams, *Travel Literature and the Evolution of the Novel* (Lexington: University Press of Kentucky, 1983), 42. See also Michel Bideaux, "Le voyage littéraire," 187–98.

38. Jacques Chocheyras, "Lecture subversive des récits de navigateurs solitaires," in *Le désir et ses masques* (Grenoble: Université des langues et lettres de Grenoble, 1981), 146; quoted in Adrien Pasquali, *Le tour des horizons: Critique et récits de voyages* (Paris: Klincksieck, 1994), 102.

39. Ibn Sa'īd al-Andalusī, *Al-Mughrib fī Hulā al-Maghrib*, ed. Shawqī Dayf, 2 vols. (Misr: Dār al-Ma'arif, 1955–64), 1:427.

40. Yāqūt, *Mu'jam al-Buldān*, 5:48.

41. Ibn 'Asākir. *Tārīkh madinat Dimashq*, ed. 'Alī Shīrī, 40 vols. (Beirut: Dār al-Fikr, 1995–96), 2:165.

of the Christian physician Ibn Butlān (d. ca. 455/1063) about his itinerary from Baghdad to Cairo has come down to us. Two polygraphs conserved it, one in partial form in a dictionary of physicians and philosophers, the other in complete form in a geographical dictionary. Both of these compilers borrowed it from a work written in the mid-eleventh century, now lost.[42] The author of this work was aware of the letter only because it was addressed to his father, a refined man of letters and an eminent secretary of state.[43] Other, more famous letters (those of Abū Dulaf, for example) were long known only through fragments in later compilations, even though they were the work of an eminent traveler.

What were these travel letters like? To judge by what we know of them, most of them were the product of a model of appropriation of the world that we have seen at work among the tenth-century geographers. Thus, they must have told, more or less well, about the world as it entered into the travel experience of their author-narrators. Because these men strove to be scrupulous observers of the lands and regions that they visited, they did not judge it appropriate to talk about themselves as travelers in their narrations. Their mode of exposition concentrates on what they saw, which means that there is hardly any gap between seeing and telling in thir accounts. The mode that links the two is instead that of presenting what is seen and what is written as belonging to the same order of things. As a consequence, *autopsia* plays an essential (if not exclusive) role in the procedures of speaking truly. The letter of the Andalusian Abū al-Salt Umayya (d. 520?/1126?) is representative of this "realism."[44]

A humanist avant la lettre, Abū al-Salt, who was a writer, a physician, an astrologer, a mathematician, an engineer, and a musicologist, wrote a travel letter dominated by observation during a sojourn in Egypt. He tells his reader in the introduction: "I shall content myself with describing those things of which I have been a direct witness in the land of Egypt, and I shall limit myself to what I have seen, leaving aside what I might have heard, so true is it that one who says, 'I have known this or that by way of

42. This book was conceived as a supplement to Tanūkhī, *Nishwār al-Muhādarāh*. Ishān 'Abbās compiled and published the existing fragments in *Shadharāt min Kutub Mafqūda* (Beirut: Dār al-Gharb al-Islāmī, 1988).

43. Qiftī, *Ibn al-Qiftī's Tārīkh al-hukamā*, ed. Julius Lippert (Leipzig: Dieterisch'sche Verlagsbuchhandlung, 1903), 295–313.

44. Abū al-Salt Umayya's letter circulated widely among medieval historians and writers. It is published as *Al Risāla al-Misriyya*, ed. 'Abd al-Azīz Hārūn, vol. 1 of *Nawādir al-Makhtūtāt*, by 'Abd al-Salām Muhammad Hārūn, 2 vols. (Cairo: Mustafā al-Bābī al-Halabī, 1973–75), 2:11–56.

apprenticeship and audition' is not worth as much as he who says, 'I have verified it by the direct testimony [*mushāhada*] and the knowledge that one has oneself of the facts [*ittilāʿ*].'" Although it is not, strictly speaking, a travel letter, the *Book of Instruction and Teachings about Things Seen and Facts Observed in the Land of Egypt* by the philosopher ʿAbd al-Latīf of Baghdad (d. 629/1231) is composed according to the same canons.[45] To speak only of what the eye can see is the principle of these travel letters.

When, in the modern age, Europe took off to discover the world, voyage accounts asserted the weight of the gaze with equal force and energy. *Autopsia* was well at work in medieval narratives such as Marco Polo's (one of the titles of which is *Book of Marvels*),[46] but it did not operate with the same sovereignty as in the narrations of great travelers of the Renaissance such as Léry or Lescarbot. Léry writes, "If anyone finds it bad that I will speak of the ways of the savages (as if I wanted to make myself look good), I use so often that way of speaking: I saw, I found myself, that happened to me, and such things, I respond that not only . . . are these matters of my subject, but also, as is said, that is the habit of speech of science, that is, of sight and experience."[47] When Lescarbot speaks of the reasons for his voyage to Canada, he explains that he took it on uniquely because he was "desirous not so much to travel as to reconnoiter the land ocularly."[48]

---

45. ʿAbd al-Latīf al-Baghdādī, a great traveler, visited Asia Minor and Syria in the 1190s. In 1200–2001 he was in Egypt, where he observed the Nile in flood and the famine and pestilence that struck the land. His Egyptian experience was the basis for his *Kitāb al-Ifāda* (*Book of Instruction and Admonition on the Things Seen and Events Recorded in the Land of Egypt*). The two key terms of *autopsia* in Islam in this title—"direct witness" (*mushāhada*) and "visual ascertainment" (*muʿāyana*)—echo one another so strongly that the reader soon discovers the author's chosen epistemological posture. When, in fact, ʿAbd al-Latīf declares, "I thought that I could extract (from my *Relation on Egypt*) the contemporary events of which I was a direct witness and the vestiges of the past that I have personally seen," he puts truth under the control of his own observation and the thing observed under that of the categories of the admirable. Why speak only of things seen? Because, he explains, "the information concerning them is the truest." And what should one see? Monumental admirable things, which means that the most massive and imposing buildings are significative of the "most marvelous traces of the past." The "rest"—that is, what escapes the dictatorship of *autopsia*—is thrust to one side. Why speak of it, given that "it exists, in part or in whole, regrouped or dispersed, in the books of the predecessors"?: ʿAbd al-Latīf al-Baghdādī, *Kitāb al-Ifāda*, 12; trans. Kamal Hafuth Zand, John A. Videan, and Ivy E. Videan as *The Eastern Key* (London: Allen & Unwin, 1965), 13. My translation does not follow the English translation or the French translation by S. de Sacy as *Relation de l'Égypte par Abdallatif* (Paris, 1810).

46. Marco Polo, *Travels*; ed. and trans. Arthur Christopher Moule et al. as *Le devisement du monde: Le livre des merveilles*, 3 vols. (Paris: Maspero, 1980).

47. Jean de Léry, *Histoire d'un voyage fait en la terre du Brésil*; quoted in Hartog, *Le miroir d'Hérodote*, 274.

48. Marc Lescarbot, *L'histoire de la Nouvelle France* (1609); quoted in Geoffroy Atkinson, *Les nouveaux horizons de la Renaissance française* (Paris: Droz, 1935), 15.

Why should Renaissance travel narratives have emphasized *autopsia*? Because, Alphonse Dupront explains, they were under the spell of "curiosity," a curiosity that had gone beyond its medieval sense to become the "power of open eyes and submission to the diversity of the world."[49] The discovery of the strange and different, under such conditions, took on an aspect of a "peaceful inventory." The European discoverers of the New World, instead of noting things because they themselves were wonder struck, like the wide-eyed Christian (and Muslim) voyagers of the Middle Ages,[50] were not astonished; "they simply noted."[51] This means that, although both groups of travelers used vision as a major means of persuasion, and although, throughout their written appropriation of the world, they both adopted the posture of observer rather than that of the traveler, their gaze was not the same.

Not all travel letters in medieval Islam adhered to this ideology of the gaze, however. When he stayed in Rayy with the prose writer Ibn ʻAbbād (d. 385/995), who later became vizier, Abū Dulaf (a major representative of the school of the gaze in the travel letter genre) recognized his host as one of the inventors of the personalized travel narrative. Before he rose to high political office, Ibn ʻAbbād had been a great writer. Around 958 he traveled to Iraq, where he met some of the most striking figures in the belles lettres of his age. From Iraq, the young scholar sent a letter to one of his friends (who also later became a vizier) in which he reported on his stay in Baghdad. Curiously, although the letter was written in Arabic, it bears the Persian title of *Rūznāmja*, or *Journal*.[52]

Unfortunately, that "journal" has come down to us only in fragmentary form. But because it enjoyed a fairly wide audience, a certain number of fragments have been conserved, through which we learn of the worldly life that the author led in Baghdad, the atmosphere of the salons in which he shone, the ambience of the study circles that he frequented, and something about the masters to whom he listened. The fragments all reflect the determination of a young scholar curious about men and their society,

49. On the way that curiosity functioned in the premodern age, see Maria Tasinato, *Sulla curiosità: Apuleio e Agostino* (Parma: Pratiche, 1994); trans. Jean-Paul Manganaro as *La curiosité: Apulée et Augustin* (Lagrasse: Verdier, 1999).

50. In his preface to Gervase of Tilbury, *Livre des merveilles*, 10, Jacques Le Goff speaks of the "eyes (of medieval listeners and readers) that opened wide at the recital of *mirabilia*."

51. Alphonse Dupront, "Espace et humanisme," *Bibliothèque d'humanisme et Renaissance* 8 (1946): 7–104, esp. 26–27.

52. C. Cahen and C. Pellat, "Ibn ʻAbbād," in *Encyclopédie de l'Islam*, new ed. (1966), 3:692–94; and in *The Encyclopaedia of Islam*, new ed. (1966), 3:670ff., somewhat curiously describe this journal as "a collection of literary anecdotes" (694).

to the point of defying conventions and breaking social barriers. When
the whim strikes him to mingle with "beggars," he descends to the lowest
level of the social scale. This was a voyage that medieval men of letters
willingly took.[53] Ibn 'Abbād did not forget that he had come to Baghdad
in search of language and poetry, however. When he frequented beggars,
it was not so as to live like them but as a way to learn about their poetry
and their argot. In fact, after hearing a "beggar's ballad" from one of the
great vagabond poets, Banū Sāsān, he jotted it down in his travel account.
He had his eyes open for all sorts of literary curiosities (*nawādir*) and linguistic rarities (*gharā'ib*). At court a talented prose writer fascinated him
because of the "abundance of his transmissions," his "extraordinary tales"
(*'ajib*), and his "strange stories" (*gharīb*). In the mosques he was attracted
by the grammarians' study circles, among them, that of the judge Abū
Sa'īd of Sīrāf (d. 368/978). Nothing escaped his thirst for intellectual acqui-
sitions, to the point of attending sermons preaching contrition, where one
preacher (who died in 997) told a motley crowd: "Glory to God who has
given speech to flesh, sight to fat, and hearing to bones!" and of frequenting the bohemian fringe.[54] Much imitated, Ibn 'Abbād's "journal" served as
a model for an entire progeny of travel letters composed in Arabic but under the same Persian title by men of letters whose native language was Persian. Most of these "journals" have disappeared, but some have left a trace
in later compilations, as is the case of the *Rūznāmja* composed and sent
to his son in 1036 by a scribe born in Azerbaijan who also later became a
vizier.[55]

Ibn 'Abbād (and those who adopted his style of travel writing) ends the
epoch in which men of letters, once they returned home, wrote the narrative of their travels as inventories of masters. Although he does name
the masters whom he encountered, he is far from simply following the

---

53. The geographer Muqaddasī, a contemporary of Ibn 'Abbād, boasts: "I have been in the
service of judges and persons of distinction, have conversed with rulers and ministers. I have kept
company on the road with the licentious, and sold goods in the marketplaces": *Aḥsan al Taqāsīm*;
Miquel translation, III; quoted from Muqaddasī, *Aḥsan al-Taqāsīm fī Ma'rifat al-Aqālīm*, trans.
Basil Anthony Collins, reviewed by Muhammad Hamid al-Tai, as *The Best Divisions for Knowledge
of the Regions* (Reading, UK: Garnet, 1994), 46.

54. Ṣāḥib ibn 'Abbād, *al-Rūznāmajah*, ed. Muhammad Hasan Al-Yasīn (Baghdad: Dār al-Ma-
'ārif, 1958).

55. Fragments of this letter are quoted, in the mid-thirteenth century, by the Syrian historian
Ibn al-'Adīm in his biography of his famous compatriot the poet and prose writer Abū al-'Alā'
al-Ma'arrī (d. 423/1032): Ibn al-'Adīm, *Al-Inṣāf wa'l-Taḥarrī fī daf' al-Dhulm wa'l-Tajarrī 'an Abī'l-
'Alā' al Ma'arrī*, in *Ta'rīf al-Qudāmā' bi-Abī'l-'Alā*, ed. Ṭāhā Ḥusayn (Cairo: Dār al-Qawmīyah, 1965;
photo reproduction of 1944), 483–578, esp. 575.

rules of the genre of the inventory, since he places all of his encounters within a narrative situation. He also refuses to write in the style of the geographers. This means that, as the narrator, when he says "I," it is not so much to attest to the truth of what he says as it is to speak in the first person. Saying "I" appears in his "journal" as a means for "motivating" the narrative act. It refers what he is writing about to a personalized instance, expressed in his name both to identify him and offer a guarantee of what he is saying, on the one hand, and to give voice (through narration) to his subjectivity, on the other.[56] This represents a great step forward in bringing the *rihla*-voyage closer to the *rihla*–travel narration. But in order for the two to combine, narrating a voyage had to break out of the framework of the letter. Here there lies a striking difference between the West and Islam. Whereas in the West the voyage used the letter as a borrowed but nonetheless durable discursive framework, Islam found the voyage to be an obstacle to the literary development of the letter. It was precisely to liberate itself from the framework of the letter that the *rihla* emerged as an autonomous literary genre in the early twelfth century.

An Art of Travel

Pursuing what we know about the travel narrative, we need to raise other questions about its written forms. One of these, normative writing, has not been widely studied, but it seems to me essential. Studies have shown the importance normative writing took in modern Europe. According to Norman Doiron, it was part of a entire "art of travel"; hence, it should be studied as a literary genre connected with the travel narration.[57] Adrien Pasquali rose up against this argument, in defense of the notion that

---

56. René Démoris thinks that the travel account, thus conceived, participated in the constitution, after 1660, of the romanesque first-person narration: *Le roman à la première personne: Du classicisme aux Lumières* (Paris: Colin, 1975). The idea is reflected in Jean-Michel Racault, "Les jeux de la vérité et du mensonge dans les préfaces des récits de voyages imaginaires à la fin de l'Age classique (1676–1726)," in *Métamorphoses du récit de voyage*, actes du colloque de la Sorbonne et du Sénat du 2 mars 1985, ed. François Moureau (Paris: Champion; Geneva: Slatkine, 1986), 82–109, esp. 90.

57. In the early seventeenth century, "the travel account prompted the emergence of a literary genre connected with the art of the voyage, which in turn determined, in depth, the evolution of the narrative structures of the narration. This was a form of rhetorical treatise regarding the way in which one must travel, using a didactic style to exhibit the rules to be followed in order to travel usefully": Norman Doiron, *L'art de voyager: Le déplacement à l'époque classique* (Sainte-Foy, Quebec: Presses de l'Université de Laval, 1995), 85.

the difference between the narration of a voyage and the "art of travel" is purely rhetorical. According to Pasquali, there is no basic difference between the two genres, to the extent that the modalities for writing both combine "mimetic-poetic" and "argumentative" aspects of persuasive and prescriptive elements.[58]

In Islam, the normative discourse on the voyage found expression in books by the late eighth century. But we have to wait until the tenth century before the literature of the "right way to travel" becomes a genuine literary genre. Not to mention that literature would be to do violence to an entire segment of travel writing. I will not go so far as to state that an "art of travel" and the travel narrative spring from the same order of things. Where Islam is concerned, although we do indeed see the first realized within the framework of the second, we do not see them dissolve into one another. How could they do so, given that the principal rhetorical resources of the "art of travel" are the normative and the exemplary? It is hard to imagine a travel narrative that would unfold relying almost exclusively on the literary resources of the rule, the formula, and the exemplum. As we shall see, the "art of travel" could not do this without working against its own operative principles.

Sijistānī (d. 382/992), a writer, polygraph, and great traveler, wrote a book on "the good ways to travel."[59] This work is now lost, but we know that it belonged within the type of normative literature intended to inculcate in the reader the rules for the art of conduct in society. Presented as "the art and the manner of," this genre allows itself the liberty of embracing all sorts of acts, private and public (how to dress, eat, and copulate, including rules for travel and making friends), and to establish an ethical and normative code for them. Although one work can cover several topics, each subject matter can, in principle, provide matter for a separate monograph. While Sijistānī writes only of ways to travel, in Tabarsī (d. 548?/1153?) travel makes one chapter among others.[60]

The manuscript collection of the Princeton University Library includes a manuscript that, in its form and its contents, corresponds to Sijistānī's lost work. It is entitled "Light and Unveiling about What the Voyager Needs," and it is divided into three chapters, entitled "On the Significance

---

58. Pasquali, *Le tour des horizons*, 98–99.

59. Abū 'Amrū al-Sijistānī, *Kitāb Adāb al-Musāfirīn*, quoted in Yāqūt, *Irshād al-Arīb ilā Maʿrifat al-Adīb (Muʿjam al-Udabā)*, ed. David Samuel Margoliouth (1913–29); ed. Ihsān 'Abbās, 7 vols. (Beirut: Dār al-Gharb al-Islāmī, 1993), 6:324.

60. Abū Nasr Tabarsī, *Makārim al-Akhlāq* (Beirut: Muassasat al-Aʿlamī, 1972), chap. 9, "On the Voyage and on What Pertains to It," 240–67.

of the Voyage and Its Merits," "On Preparations for a Voyage," and "On Good Manners Pertaining to the Voyage."[61]

Just as a medieval man of letters would have done regarding an important act, the author of this tract begins with a discussion of the voyage and its dogmatic implications. In comparing it with Tradition, he invokes *hadīth* favorable to travel and *hadīth* unfavorable to it. He concentrates on two traditions in particular: "Travel," the first of these recommends, "and you will gain in health and in fortune." The second one warns, "The voyage is a part of hell." In order to show that these two adages are not contradictory, the author cites an eleventh-century critique of traditions that states that "suffering is nothing but fatigue and exhaustion." This, he explains, is the price to pay to attain one's goal. It can be compared to a medicine that, although bitter, helps the patient to "recover his health." This is why it has been said of the voyage that "it is health."

To sing the "virtues" of travel, the author of this manuscript refers to the authority of the Qur'an and to Tradition. He illustrates the quest for knowledge by quoting the Qur'an and traces the story of Moses traveling over land and sea in search of "wisdom." From Tradition he takes such exempla as one that shows a Companion of the Prophet taking a trip with the sole aim of collecting one word from the mouth of his master. There follows a series of secular arguments. The author borrows from an eleventh-century anthologist the statement that "among the virtues of the voyage, there is the opportunity for the traveler to know the most marvelous lands ['*ajā'ib al-buldān*, which can also be read 'the marvels of the land'], the most exotic countries, and the most grandiose monumental constructions of the past." From another anthologist he takes the dual parallel between someone "who remains comfortably installed at home" and "water that stagnates" and "is rapidly polluted," on the one hand, and a traveler loaded with "grace and good deeds" and the cloud that announces a welcome rain, on the other. Then, addressing his reader, he recommends that he procure for himself "the joy of absence and the pleasure of the return."

Travel is not just a source of advantages, however: there are also all the "inconveniences of the voyage," which the author qualifies as "faults" or as "vices" (*'uyūb*) in the manner of the jurists. The tradition that states "The voyage is a part of suffering" alludes to these.[62] Travel implies the "hardship"

---

61. Muhammad ibn Bahādur Zarkashī (d. 794/1391), *Al-Ghurar wa-al-Safāfir 'an-mā Yaḥtāju ilayhi al-Musāfir*, MS no. 4469, Yahuda Series, Princeton University Library, fols. 67b–82a.

62. Mālik ibn Anas (d. 179/795), a jurist from Medina, is the first source of this prophetic tradition: *Muwatta'*, ed. 'Abd al-Majīd Turkī (Beirut: Dār al-Gharb al-Islami, 1994), 519; trans. Aisha

of separation, the "difficulty of abandoning what is familiar," and, even more, "fear of the unknown." It is understandable that the tradition set down by Bukhārī in the mid-ninth century should bother the audience of the mystical theologian Qushayrī (d. 465/1073):

> On his arrival in Baghdad, a session of edification was organized for him, which he inaugurated with the famous tradition according to which "the voyage is a part of suffering." Someone in the audience stood up and interrupted him, asking him, "Why does the Prophet qualify the voyage as a 'part of suffering'?" When the sheikh answered, "Because of the separation from dear ones," his response so profoundly moved the audience, composed of many foreigners, that no one was able to suppress his unhappiness. Emotion rose to such a degree that the master could not continue his session of exhortation. He then had to abandon the pulpit.[63]

Travel dissolves social solidarity just as much as it destabilizes people emotionally and psychologically.[64] When he leaves his familiar space, the traveler penetrates another space that is foreign to him. This rupture engenders a more or less durable temporal parenthesis in his existence that continually bothers him. Thus, the author tells us, he can seem to his traveling companions to be irascible and insufferable. Doesn't the proverb say that you really know a person only when you have traveled with him? Because of his psycho-affective instability, the traveler is compared to an invalid. Galen, says the author, teaches that someone who falls ill far from home recovers when his native land is again close at hand: his heart is delivered from its burdens "as the earth is relieved from drought by an abundant rain." Hippocrates, who shared this opinion, said that one cannot efficaciously care for a sick person except with plants from his own land. These maternal and protective images revive homesickness in the traveler, who is compared with an infant brutally weaned from his mother's breast. They add their burden of unhappiness to the painful experience of travel.

Abdurrahman Bewley as *Al-Muwatta of Imam Malik ibn Anas: The First Formulation of Islamic Law* (London: Kegan Paul International, 1989).

63. Qushayrī, quoted in Zarkashī, *Al-Ghurar*, fol. 71a.

64. To take an example from modern times, Bronislaw Malinowski's *Diary* created a scandal among anthropologists when it was published posthumously. They were shocked that the master should use vulgar terms in speaking of "native peoples." They rejected it. The *Diary* offers a picture of a sick man, in love, and much attached to his mother, who spent too much time wishing he were elsewhere: *Diary in the Strict Sense of the Term* (London: Routledge, 1967, 2004); trans. Tina Jolas as *Journal d'ethnographe* (Paris: Seuil, 1985).

Among the inconveniences of the voyage, the author adds, is the "abasement" and "humiliation" (*dhil, dhilla, madhalla*) that the traveler suffers. A great man of letters who was asked what *dhilla* is answered that it is a sentiment about which no one can really speak unless he has felt it himself. He immediately added that one cannot experience it unless he has traveled. The only people who can speak about it are those who have known wandering "from land to land" and who have suffered separation "from the homeland." In order to dramatize this important topos, the author defers to an eminent traveler, who tells the reader that "the expatriate has the fear of the thief and the obsequiousness of the debtor." The chapter ends with a psychological portrait of the exile in prey to humiliation and suffering.

The second chapter treats the voyage more from a legal perspective. The author dogmatically separates the topic into the two aspects of "quest" and "flight." Following the classification procedures used by the jurists, each of these aspects is subdivided into five rubrics: "obligatory," "praiseworthy," "tolerated," "disapproved," and "illicit." The "quest," for example, is obligatory when it is a question of going to participate in the holy war, making the great pilgrimage, or seeking gain, with the understanding that "the means for attaining an obligation is itself just as obligatory." It is praiseworthy when it is a question of seeking out knowledge, going on a pious or sociable visit, or going to the frontier.[65] It is forbidden when it is a question of making "a voyage of transgression" and disapproved when "one exaggerates in multiplying voyages in order to enrich oneself more and more [*sic*!]." It is tolerated when the voyage is one of pleasure, business, or commerce that goes beyond what is strictly necessary, "without, however, leading to exaggeration."

One further expression related to travel is "initiative wandering." The author discusses it in a separate section in order to dispute the opinion of the mystics, whom he clearly dislikes:

Because it is without a purpose and without a precise place, the *siyāha* is forbidden by the prophetic tradition according to which "there is no monasticism in Islam." The imam Ahmad ibn Hanbal [d. 241/855] has said, "The *siyāha* has nothing to do with Islam; neither the prophets nor the saints practiced it. The voyage, which is dispersion of the heart, is not proper for the aspirant [to holiness] unless it is a question of seeking knowledge or going in search of masters to take as an example." In the Tradition, it is also said, "The *siyāha*

65. On this medieval devotional practice, see chapter 6.

of my people is fasting, and its monasticism the jihad," as Ṭabarī [d. 310/922]
relates in his commentary on the Qur'an, or, according to the version reported
by Abū Dāwud [d. 275/888]: "The *siyāḥa* of my people is the jihad, and its monasticism assiduity in the mosques."[66]

Risking travel in far-off lands meant, in all cases, confrontations with
the unknown and being exposed to dangers. To put heaven on his side,
the author recommends that the traveler prepare himself by propitiatory
rituals and conjurations. In particular, he advises that he use *istikhāra*, a
canonical technique of divination used in the Middle Ages to consult the
heavens on all sorts of questions, receiving an answer in a dream.[67] It had
to be prepared for by ritual purification and a prayer, followed by invocations. According to Tradition, it was the Prophet (as was proper) who initiated his Companions in this procedure for divination. The author warns,
however, that its use should not stop the would-be traveler from consulting
well informed people in whom he has confidence and asking their advice.
Once someone takes the decision to travel, he must make a formal con-
fession of his faults; avoid committing unjust acts; pay off his debts; leave
a written testament, duly validated by sure witnesses; and, above all, not
forget to leave his loved ones enough money to cover their needs. There
follows a series of rules regarding things to avoid, the most important of
which, whatever the reason for the trip—pilgrimage, commerce, or a stay
at the frontier—was never to leave on a Friday between "dawn and noon."
According to Tradition, the two days that were most propitious for a departure were Thursday and Monday. Still other ritual details having to do
with preparations for the trip follow. These—and the chapter—end with
all manner of invocations to be made, beginning the moment the traveler
leaves his house. All of these prayers are supposed to revive practices that
the Prophet was thought to have inaugurated. The point is clear: to travel
in proper canonical fashion is to follow the traces of the founder of Islam,
walking behind him step by step in the great book of Tradition.

The third chapter treats rules that are, for the most part, medical.[68]
The prophylactic measures that it advises add a necessary complement to

66. Qushayrī, quoted in Zarkashī, *Al-Ghurar*, fol. 74a.

67. On the use of this technique for divination in connection with travel, see Khaṭīb al-
Baghdādī, *Al-Jāmiʿ li-Akhlāq al-Rāwī wa Adab al-Sāmiʿ*, MS no. 505, Muṣṭalaḥ al-Ḥadīth, Dār
al-Kutub, Cairo, fol. 176.

68. Beginning in the ninth century, medical science composed compendiums to help travelers
medicate themselves, if need be. The most famous of these treatises is one written in the late

the rituals of conjuration by which "the traveler buys his safety from God." In order to assure his "bodily security," the traveler must follow rules of alimentary hygiene that had been tested and found efficacious by medieval dietetics. For example, he must know what products and foods to carry with him. The treatise cites, pell-mell, kohl, teas, sugar, apricots, vinegar, onion (to be "ground up with garlic"), *kishk* (which might be either a barley infusion or a food made of wheat cooked in milk), *bazarqatūna* (meaning unknown), "little *haylaj* mixed with some *safah* [*sifh?*] and sugar," biscuits, melted butter, pure oil, salt, perfume, and dates. But "one should not in any event bring along heavy foods such as *qaddīd* [dried meat] and dense sweetmeats made with jam and butter." The treatise offers its readers culinary recipes appropriate to travel in which onions occupy a prominent place.

More than foodstuffs, it is water for the traveler's consumption that prompts warnings and practical advice. The treatise suggests that the traveler carry with him a bit of clay from his homeland to purify local water.[69] If this proved impossible, a few drops of vinegar would suffice. And because the traveler would find himself drinking several kinds of water, the treatise initiated him into the secrets of each type:

> The first is muddy water, which is purified by passing it through one filter after another until it is clear and drinkable, by putting in it some biscuits or some boiled honey that you have taken care to let cool, or else by adding crushed alum from Yemen to it. The second is salt water, which must be drunk with vinegar or after having put some *kharnūb* [?], some *habb al-ās* [?], or some medlar [pits?] in it. One can also drink it while eating quinces. The third is *murlāq* [?]] water, which must be boiled in special caldrons with pieces of wood covered with wool. After boiling, the wool is squeezed out and one can drink the water thus extracted. (81b)

---

ninth century by the Christian physician, philosopher, and translator Qustā ibn Lūqā for an 'Abbāsid sovereign, on which see Gerrit Bos, *Qustā Ibn Lūqā's Medical Regime for the Pilgrims to Mecca* (Leiden: Brill, 1992). The sources note a dozen works in the genre of "the traveler's regimen," inaugurated, according to Ibn al-Nadīm, by a translation of a work on the topic by Rufus of Ephesus: see Ibn al-Nadīm, *Fihrist*, ed. Ridā al-Māzindarānī (Beirut: Dār al-Masīrah, 1988), 350; trans. Bayard Dodge as *The Fihrist of al-Nadim: A Tenth-Century Survey of Muslim Culture*, 2 vols. (New York: Columbia University Press, 1970).

69. Rāzī, the most famous Muslim physician of the tenth century, composed an entire work about the traveler carrying with him a bit of clay from his homeland to use as a remedy: see Rāzī, *Kitāb fī anna al-Tīn al-Muntaqal bihi fihi Manāfi*; quoted in Qiftī, *Tārīkh al-hukamā*, ed. Julius Lippert (Leipzig: Dieterisch'sche Verlagsbuchhandlung, 1903), 274.

After discussing the "doctrine of thirst," the author turns to "the harm done by heat and cold." Cold is mentioned only in a short chapter in which anyone traveling in humid and snowy lands is advised to "fill up with food" and drink in "sufficient quantity."[70] Turning to travelers who have to face the rigors of desert and semidesert places, the author devotes much space to water and heat, which are the two major problems in such regions. Against the heat, he recommends good water and nourishment based on "cold foods"—that is, foods that are both thirst quenching and low in calories, such as *husrum*, a term that designates unripe, green, and acidic fruit, dates in particular, to be eaten with vinegar and oil "in very small quantities." The manual ends with this description of a diet of water and foods in hot regions. What can we conclude? Two things: First, that the voyage was a highly codified social and ritual act. Second, one does not travel following one's own inclinations, but rather as society demands. The lesson thus administered to the reader is that every travel itinerary is a journey within one's own culture. The traveler never leaves the space of that culture. He thinks he is sailing over the seas, tracking through deserts, and traversing mountains, but he is really traveling through a text—the text of his own culture, through the prism of which he observes the world and gives it body. If this is the case, how can the "art of travel" be dissociated from the other literary expressions of the voyage without amputating from it the better part of its representations?

A Return to the Travel Narrative

When, on his return from the East in the early twelfth century, Abū Bakr ibn al-'Arabī of Seville composed a *rihla*, he prompted a revolution in the writing of the voyage.[71] The *rihla*-voyage, which had arisen four centuries earlier, had since then been absorbed in the inventory of masters, the epistolary narrative, and the journal, but now it could at last abandon those forms and establish itself as a genre in its own name. Counter to all expec-

70. The eleventh-century Egyptian physician 'Alī ibn Ridwān writes, "Know that in winter the body needs very consistent and very abundant nourishment": *Kitāb Kifāyat al-Tabīb*; trans. Jacques Grand'henry as *Le livre de la méthode du médecin de 'Ali b. Ridwan (998–1067)*, 2 vols. (Louvain: Université Catholique de Louvain, Institut Orientaliste, 1979–84), 16 (Arabic), 61 (French trans.); trans. Michael W. Dols as *Medieval Islamic Medicine: Ibn Ridwan's Treatise, "On the Prevention of Bodily Ills in Egypt"* (Berkeley: University of California Press, 1984).

71. On Abū Bakr of Seville (Abū Bakr ibn al-'Arabī, d. 534/1148), see J. Robson, "Ibn al-'Arabī," in *Encyclopédie de l'Islam*, new ed. (1966), 3:729; and in *The Encyclopaedia of Islam*, new ed. (1966), 3:707.

tation, the artisan of this literary innovation was not a secular writer, but a man of the law and a theologian.

The text that has come down to us in a manuscript dated 1340 is unfortunately only the summary of a more ample work, entitled *Book of the Organization of the Voyage*.[72] In this work Abū Bakr explains how, after having been "betrayed by time," he decided to "return to the pieces saved" from his earlier narration and complete them "by memory," so as to rescue from oblivion "the trace of what happened." While he had been serving as a judge in Seville, insurgents had burned his house and his books, and the narrative in question may have been destroyed in this disaster.[73]

The stripped-down text of the abridged version of this voyage is an "inventory of masters." It is clear, however, that this skeleton had been wrapped in a rich narration. Recourse to a style of writing that is explicitly seeking effects encourages this evaluation.[74] The work adheres, in fact, to an ancient form of rhythmic prose highly reliant on assonance—the *saj'*—that the great writers of the tenth century had revised to the taste of the day. Had Abū Bakr read Hamadhānī and Harīrī, the two masters of that literary style? There is every indication that he had, for we know that Harīrī at least had been a resounding success in Andalusia, even in religiously trained intellectual milieus.[75] The connection between the *rihla*-travel narrative and the *Maqāma*-adventure tale is not inopportune. My idea is that the emergence of the *rihla* as a literary genre owed much to that connection. When, half a century later, another Andalusian, Ibn Jubayr (d. 614/1217),[76] raised the travel narrative to the level of great art, he wrote under the influence of Harīrī, and it is known that his disciple

72. This summary is available in the biographical study by Sa'īd A'rāb, *Ma'a al-Qāḍī Abū Bakr ibn al-'Arabī* (Beirut: Dār al-Gharb al-Islami, 1987), 185–226. Another version of the *Rihla* figures in another manuscript work by Abū Bakr, a 1340 copy of which exists and has also been published: see Ihsān 'Abbās, "Rihlat Ibn al-'Arabī ilā'l-Mashriq kamā Sawwarahā 'Qānūn al-Ta'wīl," *Abhāt* 21 (1968): 59–91, esp. 71–91.

73. *Buyūtāt Fās al-Kubrā*, an anonymous work cited in A'rāb, *Ma'a al-Qāḍī Abū Bakr ibn al-'Arabī*.

74. The author, a theologian by training, acquired a solid knowledge of belles lettres, which was a domain in which his father before him, a politician and accomplished man of letters, had been well versed.

75. A man of letters overheard the cadi 'Iyāḍ of Ceuta, who had been a student of Abū Bakr ibn al-'Arabī, declare, "When the *Sessions of* Harīrī arrived in our land [in the early years of the twelfth century], I did not sleep the whole night through in order to read the book and finish reading it": see the biography composed by his son, Muhammad Abū 'Abd-Allah, *Tarīf bi al-Qāḍī 'Iyāḍ* (Morocco, 1982), 109.

76. On this man of letters, see C. Pellat, "Ibn Djubayr," in *Encyclopédie de l'Islam*, new ed. (1966), 3:777–78; and in *The Encyclopaedia of Islam*, new ed. (1966), 3:755ff.

Sharīshī (d. 619/1222) was a much-appreciated commentator of Harīrī's *Maqāmāt*.[77]

On the narrative level, Abū Bakr brought to the *rihla*–travel narrative a structure and elements that, for the most part, it retained from then on. Two staple themes stand out: motivating the departure and crossing the sea. In the strategy of the narration, these occupy a key position. The first, a prelude to the text proper, was charged with setting off the action, while the second provided an obstacle that added tension to the dynamics of the narration. Far from being specific to the *Rihla*, however, these had been standard features in the poetics of the narration of a sea voyage since Homer. In the modern age, they have played an essential role in the Western art of the travel narrative.[78]

Abū Bakr invokes political reasons as the cause of his departure. In Seville, the accession to power of a new dynasty resulted in dismissals and persecutions within the elite that had served the old one. His father, a high dignitary of the fallen dynasty, was forced into exile in the East, and he decided to take his son with him. This genuine drama motivated the departure. The narrator, Abū Bakr, treats that as a secondary event, however, and it enters into the dynamic of his narration only incidentally. Political themes do not carry the narrative along. Instead, what keeps things going is another pretext, books and the quest for books, which are a major feature throughout the narrative. He speaks of them in these terms:

> One day when I was with one of my tutors, my father, who was usually totally absorbed by his many activities, had managed to get free of them and come join us so as to inform himself about my progress in studies. But hardly had he arrived when visitors began to file in. Among those who had come to pay him a visit there was a book dealer who had a bundle in his hands. When he had opened his packet to spread out the contents before my father, my gaze fell on a work by [the Ash'aarite theologian] Samānī [d. 444/1052], the master of Abū al-Walīd al-Bājī [d. 494/1100]. In the discussion that followed, I heard them say, "These are the great works that contain the precious sciences brought back from the East by Bājī," words that made me shiver to the depth of my being and set my mind on fire. In their long evocation of Bājī, they said how

77. Abū'l-'Abbās al-Sharīshī, *Sharh Maqāmāt al-Harīrī*, ed. Muhammad A. Ibrāhim (Cairo, 1969).

78. See Doiron, *L'art de voyager*.

much that man had gone beyond the scholars of our own land in knowledge and in wisdom. . . . To hear them cover him with praise, I said to myself, "The day will come when I too will be master of myself, and when I will leave my homeland in quest of the high rank that Bājī attained. . . ." When that opportunity was presented to me, I grasped it with true happiness, despite the gravity of the situation. The idea of leaving on a voyage filled me with euphoria. I was happy, when anyone else in my place would have been sad to leave the comfort in which I lived.[79]

This passage is the key that explains the doxological praise with which the text begins: "I am amazed that some people could be led to wisdom by the bridle and to science by chains, whereas others, left to themselves and free of any hindrance, give themselves over to pleasures!" This is followed by a list of the subject matters and the works that the young Abū Bakr studied before he reached the age of seventeen, when he left Andalusia in the company of his father, in 1092. The passage quoted above ends this enumeration and launches the narrative. The voyage can now begin. However, between literary clichés and encounters with the masters of the places they visited, the narrative never manages to find a rhythm. It is only with the painful episode of crossing the Mediterranean from Mahdia to Alexandria, a passage that nearly cost father and son their lives, that it takes on life. The description of this episode reaches a high point equaled only later, when he describes the indignation of the inhabitants of Baghdad at the taking of Jerusalem by the Crusaders. The sea enters into the *Rihla* with a crash: "When the hour had come to leave the port [of Mahdia], we embarked on board our ship. I had taken advantage of our time in port to deepen my knowledge and jot down explanations in the proper place in my notebooks. On the high seas, God tested us by fear and tormented us by terror, to the point that, when we finished up on a shore, we were like dead men emerging from their tomb. Exhausted, we dragged ourselves, my father and I, until we reached a settlement of the Banū Sulaym Bedouins. Unrecognizable, our clothes in rags, we looked like miserable [beggars]."[80]

After having lost everything, the narrator and his father were fortunate to obtain protection and hospitality from the lord of the tribe after this

79. Abū Bakr ibn al-'Arabī, *Tartib al-Rihla*, 192–93.

80. Ibid., 198–99. Abū Bakr returns to his "torments of the sea" in his *Ahkām al-Quran*, ed. 'Ali Muhammad al-Bagawi (Cairo: 'Īsā al-Bābī al-Halabī, 1957 [1378]), 811.

double experience of the horrors of the sea and the desert.[81] It is a well-known fact that traversing the desert is a major moment in travel narratives in medieval Islam. Its fears are often expressed as a reflection of the sea, and vise versa. The *Rihla* is no exception: its images of the sea come right from the desert.

Once the two obstacles of the sea and the desert have been triumphantly surmounted, the narrator and his father arrive safe and sound in Egypt. Unfortunately, despite the fascination that the Egyptian capital exerted over men of letters of the Muslim West, we will never know anything about the journey that took them to Cairo. Where *autopsia* is concerned, their sojourn in Egyptian territory seems a narrative failure. The reader's expectations of travel narratives are not met, and the narration turns to a flat enumeration of the "inventory of masters."

Because an entire tendency of the *Rihla* made little or no attempt to produce visual results, modern scholars have scorned it. One critic complains: "These aspirants to knowledge arrive in a city, where they see nothing but sheikh So-and-So and sheikh So-and-So and do nothing but blacken pages with what they have read in the house of one or heard in the house of another. When anyone surveys their travel accounts—the *Rihla* of Ibn Rushayd [d. 721/1321], for example—he has the impression that they are operating in the void, for they see nothing except the study circles of their masters; they are in the situation of someone who walks at night and keeps his eyes on the heavens to count the stars!"[82]

Other writers were reproached for their "blindness." One such was Khatīb al-Baghdādī (d. 463/1070) who, although he spent a large part of his life in Baghdad, never spoke of the city except by way of hearsay. André Miquel blames the "deficiency" of the traditionists on their "major and formidable incapacity."[83] Thus, medieval writers are blamed for not having kept their eyes wide open to the world. They have been reproached for using their hearing but not their eyesight, after which their supposed lacks and incapacity to be part of the world have been violently denounced. However, although those authors did not see the world, they did indeed hear it. The books that they wrote proceed from that sense perception.

81. Fearing the perils of the desert, Abū Bakr writes (after having been aided by the lord of the Banū Sulaym), "See how this world, which is close to ignorance, is literally made of abundantly flowing good manners!": ibid., 201.

82. Husayn Munis, *Tārīkh al-Jughrāfiya wa al-Jughāfiyīn fi'al-Andalus* (Cairo: Maktabat Madbuli, 1986), 451.

83. Miquel, *La géographie humaine*, 1:256.

Thus, their modus operandi was governed by an epistemological orientation that quite openly conceded to the ear a cognitive superiority over
the eye. Khatīb al-Baghdādī 's *History of Baghdad* is neither a history nor a
topography of Baghdad, but rather a biographical dictionary of traditionists compiled by a writer who adheres without reservation to the way in
which knowledge functioned among those who fill the pages of his literary
monument. Why should we ask him to fulfill the narrative contract of a
literary genre that was not his?

Like all theologians, Abū Bakr was not unaware of the principle of *autopsia*. When, in Baghdad, he first met the mystical theologian Ghazālī
(d. 505/1111), whom he knew only by reputation, that principle immediately sprang to his mind: "We realized that the rule according to which information [*khabar*] concerning the absent is superior to direct testimony
[*mushāhada*, the act of seeing with one's eyes] does not apply in general. If
that were the case, Ibn al-Rūmī [d. 283/896] would not have said, 'If you
praise a prince in his absence / rather than going on and on, hold yourself
back / If you go beyond the limits that increase suppositions about him /
You think you are magnifying him and you do nothing but lower him / in
virtue of the importance that you accord to absence over presence.'"[84]

These statements show that the narrator does not deny the *mushāhada*
its heuristic value. Still, he carries out his narration by means of what he
feels and hears more than he does by trusting what he sees. If in what he
says there is a trace of *autopsia*, it enters into the narrative only margin-
ally—that is, without ever going beyond the limits that are set for it by
the principle of hearing. Thus, we have a description of study circles or
disputations, but never of the places in which they are held; we have the
description of sanctuaries or mosques, but not of the places where they
are located. Description is not only given in parcels and fragments; it is
entirely guided by an essentialist conception of the world. The narrator
fully accepts this, writing:

> At the time when I left on [my] search in [various] lands, I was continually
> preoccupied by studies and by meeting people of reason and clairvoyance,
> and I had no other aim than that of attaining the supreme goal of all signi-
> fication: knowledge of God. For this reason, when we look at the world, we
> should not do so because it is a perfect work, or because it offers to sight what
> is admirable, and still less because it is useful or an imposing body, but rather

84. Abū Bakr ibn al-'Arabī, *Tartib al-Rihla*, 219.

because it is a means. We should in fact look at it only as the work of God. Similarly, when looking at our acts, we must not apprehend them as movements inspired by the search for the good and thrusting away evil, but rather as service to God or transgression of his decrees. In all observation, all words, all action, the goal must be All-Powerful God. As concerns myself, when the road was illuminated before me and the way of verification was opened to my spirit, I acquired the certitude that the Book of God is the only guide that leads to him; it is his proof. After which, I did not hold back on ways to reach the upper levels of knowledge. For he who does not draw from God what it just and true and does not drink from his ocean will never see his efforts rewarded. Thus have I read many books of exegesis and drunk from more than one fountain of Tradition. [A list of works studied follows.][85]

Islamic culture of the Middle Ages places books into a paradoxical situation. Although it permits them to be read with the eyes (the term *nadhara* literally means "to look at"), it validates access to their content only by means of an "audition" (*samāʿ*) — that is, through the ears. In order to tell the tale of an absence that took him thousands of miles from his home for over ten years, Abū Bakr begins and ends his narration with an authorized quest for books that, if they do not all teach knowledge of God, are nonetheless in the majority religious books. Nothing outside that objective interests him (from the viewpoint of narrative, at least). Whereas other travel accounts unfolded the world like a book in which their authors, through their amazed observations, reached a full sense of the immanence of the divine, the narrative of our Andalusian traveler is a trip in books and among the masters who hold the keys to those books. Unlike Don Quixote, who "reads the world in order to prove his books,"[86] Abū Bakr deciphers books in order to authenticate the world. This means that his concept of reality became refracted and stripped of its worldly envelope. All that is to be observed must fall within or near this framework.[87]

---

85. Ibid., 224–25.

86. Michel Foucault, *Les mots et les choses: Une archéologie des sciences humaines* (Paris: Gallimard, 1966), 83; quoted from the English translation as *The Order of Things: An Archaeology of the Human Sciences* (London: Tavistock, 1970; reprint, New York: Vintage, 1994), 47.

87. One example: the meeting between Abū Bakr and Abū Bakr of Tortosa (d. 520/1126), a prominent jurist who had lived in Jerusalem before settling in Alexandria, is placed under the sign of *autopsia*. The text states that Abū Bakr and his father "left [to go] to the house of our master, Abū Bakr, which was attached to the Mosque of the Rock in a place called Ghawī, situated between Bāb al-Asbāt, the 'Gate of the Twelve Tribes of Israel,' and Zachary's Niche. As he was not there, we left in search of him, and we found him at a place called Sakīna. There I became aware of [literally: I observed for myself] his high degree of guidance. My eyes and my ears were filled with

When the narration goes beyond that essential reality and reaches out to another reality, the latter is held to be true only because it is legally defined as such.[88] In order to portray what is true, Abū Bakr has no need to make his readers see, which explains why his travel account is more narrative than descriptive.

When Ibn Jubayr composed a *rihla*,[89] a half century later, he responded better to the expectations of the modern reader of travel accounts, in that his narration belongs more resolutely to the school of the gaze. Although he is not insensitive to the almost clinical verismo of the tenth-century geographies, he remains within the path traced by Abū Bakr ibn al-ʿArabī. Still, even while following the rule of composition that an account of a voyage should be organized in terms of narrative, spatial, temporal, and societal progression, he resolves the tension between narration and description in a more balanced way than his compatriot. The result is a new conception of the travel narrative, the main orientations of which are, on the one hand, a greater exactitude in description (or truth telling by making things visible and making them come alive), and, on the other hand, the "pleasure of the text" (a pleasure never compromised by a determination to instruct). Ibn Jubayr's account stands out in this regard, even though it is true that, in his search for a pleasing writing style, he is at least in part bested by his compatriot. Still, by refining the resources of his writing, he succeeds in giving his account a more pleasing and more agreeable cast. It was in order to satisfy a similar expectation that in 1356 the globe-trotting Ibn Battūta hired a professional writer to help him compose the narrative of his travels.[90]

---

his words. . . . At that moment, I made the decision to make Jerusalem my lair and to devote myself to studies by living retired from the world and abstaining from speaking with anyone. As a solitary I spent my days and my nights at the cupola of the Chain, from where I would see the sun rise over Tawr Mountain and set over Zachary's Niche": Abū Bakr ibn al-ʿArabī, *Tartib al-Rihla*, 205.

88. Although he operates differently, leaving a large space for *autopsia*, another Andalusian traveler, Ibn Jubayr, also apprehends the world by means of the categories of the law: "Behind the descriptive modalities adopted by Ibn Jubayr," Giovanna Calasso observes, "[there is] a classification of the measurable founded on a hierarchical thought. And behind that hierarchy, [there is] a normative model borrowed from the juridical sciences": Giovanna Calasso, "Les tâches du voyageur: Décrire, mesurer, compter, chez Ibn Jubayr, Nāser-e Khosrow et Ibn Battūta," *Rivista degli Studi Orientali* 73 (2000): 69–102.

89. For a recent French translation of Ibn Jubayr's travel narrative, see Charles-Dominique, *Voyageurs arabes*. Ian Richard Netton has devoted several studies to this work, among them "Basic Structures and Signs of Alienation in the Rihla of Ibn Jubayr," *Journal of Arabic Literature* 22, no. 1 (1991): 21–37; reprinted in *Golden Roads, Migration, Pilgrimage and Travel in Medieval and Modern Islam*, ed. Ian Richard Netton (Richmond, UK: Curzon, 1993), 57–74.

90. On the connections between these two men, see H. A. Mahdi, "A Manuscript of Ibn Battūta's *Rihla* in Paris and Ibn Juzayy," *Journal and Proceedings of the Asiatic Society of Bengal* 20

Modern scholars have not always appreciated the more pleasing kind
of *rihla*–travel narrative. The translator of Ibn Battūta has mocked the
affected style of Ibn Juzayy, the writer who collaborated with Ibn Battūta
on the latter's travel narrative. His critique soon turns from acts to supposed intentions, accusing the professional writer of having "arranged
certain passages, without the tale teller's knowledge," thus falsifying the
"simplicity [of his] discourse."[91] Bolstered by this Manichaean approach,
the translator has intervened in the text to free it from what he deems the
"weight of [its] digressions" (*sic*!). This not only does violence to the text
by attacking its integrity; it also shows that its perpetrator has mistaken
the genre of the travel narrative. He fails to see that the supposed "inopportune interventions" emerge from writing about travel. They are in fact
a part of the well-known technique of the collage.

The use that Western travel literature has made of this procedure of
literary creation is a familiar story.[92] It is for other reason that Orientalists
have taken up this type of narrative, using it as a glass through which to
view the narrative achievements of Muslim travelers. When they salute
one traveler for his "descriptive talent" and the "acuity of his gaze" or compare another traveler to a "modern reporter," their judgements are (im-
plicitly or explicitly) informed by the Western model. What characterizes
that model of the travel narrative? According to Roland Le Huenen, it is
"To see, make [the reader] see, and make [him or her] know." It seems
that the Western traveler has had, "from the beginning," the aim of de-
ciphering the world by the gaze, and that his discovery is the immediate
result of what is "perceived visually." That aim gave rise to a way of narrating the voyage directly connected with the "primacy of the visual" and the
"reach of the regard":[93] the eye looks out at the world, and that knowledge
is expressed in description.[94] This explains the narrative/descriptive am-
bivalence of this type of writing and its oscillation between "the adventure

---

(1954): 49–53; Ross E. Dunn, *The Adventures of Ibn Battūta: A Muslim Traveler of the 14th Century*
(Berkeley: University of California Press, 1986), 310–18; and the entry "Ibn Djuzayy" in *Encyclopédie de l'Islam*, new ed. (1966), 3:779; and in *The Encyclopaedia of Islam*, new ed. (1966), 3:756.

91. Ibn Battūta, *Voyages et périples choisis*, trans. Paule Charles-Dominique (Paris: Gallimard,
1992), 17.

92. On the interventions of professional writers in French travel narratives of the seventeenth
century, see Jacques Chupeau, "Les récits de voyage aux lisières du roman français du XVIIe
siècle," *Revue d'histoire littéraire de la France* 3–4 (May–August 1977): 536–53, esp. 544–45.

93. Le Huenen, "Qu'est-ce qu'un récit de voyage?" 17.

94. "Admirable and noble edifice in which modern man will enclose himself": Dupront,
"Espace et humanisme," 96.

and the inventory," "the heroizing narration" and "the affirmation of a new knowledge about the world."[95]

We have already had occasion to verify that this way of writing about the voyage was not foreign to medieval Islamic culture. But it was not the only way. Instead of having just one model of writing about the voyage, Islamic tradition in fact had two. According to whether the travelers concerned *observed* the world or *listened* to it, they returned with different narrative results. Some expected from *autopsia* what others obtained from hearing. They could not have perceived the world in the same fashion. Those who speak of these two ways of putting together a travel narrative in terms of a "gap" or "decline" of one way in relation to the other forget that both approaches are rooted in fundamentally different epistemological models. But because travelers of Islam could legitimately follow one model or the other, they could say "I go, I see, and I write," or else "I come, I listen, and I write."

95. Réal Ouellet, "Héroïsation du protagoniste et orientation descriptive dans le *Grand voyage au pays des Hurons*," in *Voyages: Récits et imaginaire*, actes de Montréal, ed. Bernard Beugnot (Paris: Papers on French Seventeenth Century Literature, 1984), 219. On this tension between description and narration, see also Le Huenen, "Qu'est-ce qu'un récit de voyage?" 19–22.

·☾ CONCLUSION ☽·

THE JOURNEY TO THE END OF THE SAME

Some believe that the world no longer exists as the *place* for the voyage. Others think that it exists, but in a considerably reduced form. If it has not disappeared, it is on its way to extinction, somewhat like threatened species. After the death of God, of man, and of history, we thus are living through the death of something else that is essential: the voyage.[1] There are no more travelers; their race has disappeared. All there is left is tourists, not in the sense that Stendhal intended in his *Memoirs of a Tourist*,[2] but in the more serial sense of the "tour operators," who never take on a destination without turning it into an industrial "formula for a sojourn."[3] Aside from this mass tourism, there still are intrepid adventurers of high levels of sporting or scientific skills who explore the final frontiers of the "elsewhere," but although our nostalgic dream of distant adventures finds fulfillment in these extra-ordinary beings, their exploits should not lead us to forget that, as the twentieth century gives way to the twenty-first, geographical voyages rarely end "elsewhere." The distant has (almost) disappeared from the face of the earth, leaving nothing but the nearby.[4]

1. Claude Lévi-Strauss bade farewell to the savage in his *Tristes tropiques* (Paris: Plon, 1955); trans. John and Doreen Weightman as *Tristes Tropiques* (New York: Atheneum, 1974).

2. On Stendhal as a "tourist," see *Le journal de voyage et Stendhal*, actes du colloque de Grenoble, ed. Victor Del Litto and Emanuele Kanceff (Geneva: Slatkine, 1986).

3. One might regret the passing of the humanist and romantic ages, credited with having done more than other ages to produce "a paradoxical possibility for man to be himself by becoming others": Jean Cassou, "Du voyage au tourisme," *Communications* 10 (1967): 25–34.

4. See Gilles Lapouge, *Besoin de mirages* (Paris: Seuil, 1999).

Similarly, there are almost no geographical itineraries that do not end up, in one way or another, defining a touristic circuit.[5]

While we wait for intergalactic voyages to be developed (and they doubtless will be the great human adventure of the twenty-first century), trips back in time have become a widespread means for learning that the I is an other. Our own times summon us more and more to that sort of invitation to the voyage. Its proliferation is the sign that an entire tradition of travel and its narration have been extinguished or are in the process of being so.[6] There is no longer any place where we can compare ourselves to others; the "same" reigns everywhere. The "identical" has spread over the planet under the alienating form of the market and the fetishism of merchandising. No traveler today can explore the *oikoumene* and return with new figures of the other, as was true when Herodotus invented the "Barbarian," Jean de Léry, the "good savage," and Gérard de Nerval, the "Oriental." Because the West westernized the earth, its geographical voyagers can no longer investigate its identity in the mirror of others and, within the gap that separates *us* from *them*, give it a meaning. Since the invention of the "World Tour" in the century of the Enlightenment, what new frontier remains uncrossed? Can a travel narrative still unfold like an appropriation of the world? There is every reason to doubt it. The West no longer has anything to translate into its culture that has not already been translated, nothing to know that it does not already know, and nothing to discover that it has not already discovered. Everywhere, people speak only the language of the West, and—just as Diderot feared, as a sarcastic reader of Bougainville—the entire world now conforms to its image. This reflects, in a different key, the dramatic and narrative structure of Pierre Clastres's account of his stay among the Guayaki, which opens with a chapter entitled "Birth" and closes, with the clang of a tombstone, with another entitled "The End."[7]

---

5. In the era of mass tourism, Marc Augé writes, parodying Mallarmé, the world is made in order to produce a video: Marc Augé, *L'impossible voyage: Le tourisme et ses images* (Paris: Payot & Rivages, 1997).

6. "Today we very nearly have to acknowledge the death of travel literature," François Moureau writes in "L'imaginaire vrai," the concluding text in *Métamorphoses du récit de voyage*, actes du colloque de la Sorbonne et du Sénat du 2 mars 1985, ed. François Moureau (Paris: Champion; Geneva: Slatkine, 1986), 165–67. It should also be stressed that, by a curious paradox, the literary quality of travel narratives has never been as high as it is in the age of the "end of the voyage."

7. Pierre Clastres, *Chronicle of the Guayaki Indians*, trans. Paul Auster (New York: Zone; Cambridge, MA: MIT Press, 1998).

To be sure, it was not my intention to invite the Western readers of this book to an appreciation of the style of travel and travel writing to which the twentieth century put an end. From the *Odyssey* to modern accounts of exploration and adventure, a particular representation of the voyage has been a part of the Western reader's experience and shaped his or her intellectual horizon. It is in fact not only in the West that the travel narrative is the privileged form of written expression relating to travel. Elsewhere, in Islam for example, the travel narrative is but one way among many to write about travel, and historically speaking, it is even the last form to be attempted.

Moreover, in the West the model for the traveler is one who crosses his own cultural frontier and goes "elsewhere" to find himself and to translate his experience of the other into the text of his own culture. In Islam, those who were considered to be great travelers (and they were called, literally, *touri*sts) never or almost never went out of the geographical space of their religious belief. Moreover, rather than making exclusive use of the narrative form, they elaborated other expressions of travel writing. Thus, we are struck by the contrast between the extraordinary richness of their experience of going from one place to another and the little urgency they display about composing a narrative to tell of that experience. What we see is travelers who did not leave home, in the Western manner, in order to explore their own identity in the mirror of the other, but rather to confront what should be and adjust themselves to it. Rather than going "elsewhere," Islamic journeyers (at any event, those whom we have met in this book) traveled in the space of the same, and their chief preoccupation was to create more of the same. Rather than psychological, aesthetic, or philosophic, their main aim was dogmatic in nature.

How did someone become a *Homo islamicus*? How could the men who embodied that typical figure speak the same language throughout the entire "dwelling of Islam" (*dār al-islām*)? How did their domestic space have to be structured to be accepted everywhere as one unified and centrifugal space? How, without losing sight of their overall unity, could certain parts of that "dwelling" be admitted by all the members of the brotherhood as Chief Places? It was questions of this sort that led Muslim men of letters to travel, and in great numbers, to work collectively on the enormous enterprise of changing their geopolitical space into a dogmatic space. Here the traditionists played a major role, as early as the ninth century, by compiling canonical editions of prophetic Tradition.

The most famous of those collections opens with a *hadīth* that is still accepted and venerated by all the world's Sunni Muslims. What it says is simple: "In truth, actions [are judged] according to intentions, and everyone is responsible for what he intends to do." Yesterday as today, this statement of the Prophet has been regarded as one of the most important principles of Islam. It is in fact considered to be one of the four fundamental doctrines on which Islam turns. Although originally it had an ethical application and measured the morality of all religious acts by the intention governing that act, theologians and jurists used it to rule on religious and juridical questions. This principle, which dominated the entire Muslim theory of law, was not known throughout Islam, or at least not in the form of a tradition. Originally it had been transmitted only to Medina, which is why we are explicitly told that at the time, "it was not known either in Iraq, or in Mecca, or in Yemen, or in Syria, or in Egypt." It was only in the late eighth century that a Basra jurist could say, "It would be desirable that we insert that maxim into every chapter of the law."[8] The tradition has since become a norm of Islamic juridical doctrine. Its "Islamization," along with that of many other norms, would not have been possible without its editors, whose numbers lent it weight. Their efforts uprooted these and other norms from their regional particularism and molded them together into collective general works governed by a clear desire for uniformity reflected in the official title of *Summa*. The founders of the *Corpus traditionum* were able to accomplish this task because they agreed to the sacrifice of costly and dangerous voyages that allowed them to traverse the territories of Islam from one end to the other. Once collected, then classified independently of the place in which they had been collected, the assembled materials could be consulted and serve as rules of conduct valid for all times and all places. Without the voyages, those local materials, which came from all of the provinces of Islam, might not have been collected and stripped of their particularism.

A project of the sort quite naturally favored certain provinces over others (the Hejaz over Iraq, for example). By that same token, thanks to the techniques of writing and taxonomy, the traditions of the privileged provinces were raised to the level of norms valid for all of Islam. That means that while the voyage brought the provinces of Islam into one unified dog-

---

8. For a discussion of this tradition, see Ignaz Goldziher, *Muhammedanische Studien*, 2 vols. (Halle: Niemeyer, 1889–90); vol. 2 trans. Léon Bercher as *Études sur la tradition islamique: Extraits du tome II des Muhammadanische Studien* (Paris: Adrien-Maisonneuve, 1952), 221–22; trans. C. R. Barber and S. M. Stern as *Muslim Studies: Muhammedanische Studien*, 2 vols. (London: George Allen & Unwin, 1967).

matic space, they consecrated—in the literal sense of the word—some of those provinces as more exemplary than others.

When, in the eighth century, philologists began to travel in the desert in search of Bedouins to inform them on the pure and inalterable language of the Arabs, they may well have founded a new secular branch of knowledge, but religious motivation remained an essential element in the definition of their linguistic choices. In deciding that the linguistic horizon of the Arabic language had to be Bedouin speech, what they had in mind was that some of those idioms were very close to the language of the Qur'an. That choice not only gave them the opportunity to forge a positive body of knowledge based on the Arab nature of the Qur'an; it also gave them a legitimate reason for promoting Arabic as the language of Islam. By multiplying dictionaries, lexicographical works, monographs on linguistics, and anthologies of poetry, the founders of the *fus'ḥā*—"pure and clear language"—movement created a standard for putting order into the materials collected among the Bedouins. The new instruments they forged served to bolster a new language with both a liturgical and a professional vocation. The two classes of learned men in Islam, the religious and the secular,[9] took on the separate tasks of developing that new language within the framework of sophisticated writing models. Here too, while the voyage permitted the Arabic language to benefit from a very high status from a dogmatic standpoint, it diminished its ethnicity. I might note that the promoters of this linguistic reform were by no means all Arabs. Persian was the mother tongue and language of communication for the most famous of them.

The empire of Islam was also the framework for the intelligibility of other branches of knowledge, such as geography. Despite its manifestly secular content, we should not lose sight of geography's religious basis and apologetic intentions: the geographer's task was to draw up a coherent picture of the empire of Islam, "and also, of course, of the Arab character," in contrast to the infidel world. André Miquel sees Muqaddasī, the most famous of the tenth-century geographers, as displaying the juxtaposition of these two themes as the essential foundation of the *mamlaka*, the

---

9. "Contrary to Egypt, Babylon, or China, in Islam there developed not one but two classes of scribes—the *fuqahā*, or specialists in canon law, and the *kuttāb*, or 'secretaries.' It was the *kātib* who turned out to be the typical representative of the refined education characteristic of the Muslim world, the *adab*": Gustave E. von Grunebaum, *Studien zum Kulturbild und Selbstetverständnis des Islam* (Zurich: Artemis, 1969); trans. Roger Stuvéras as *L'identité culturelle de l'Islam* (Paris: Gallimard, 1973), 37.

domain of Islam.[10] As that geographer, who was also a great traveler, moved through the politico-religious space of Islam, he experienced it as a unified space that owed its unity, first and foremost, to being a space of belief. Thus, when he defines the eastern frontiers of the *mamlaka*, he states that Sind and Khurasan adjoin "the lands of Impiety," about which one is not expected to know anything. What interests the geographer is first and foremost "the domain of Islam, on which one must meditate."[11]

As a perfect space should, the *mamlaka* has a center. Not the Hejaz, as the traditionists claimed, nor the desert of the Arab Bedouins, as for the linguists. That center could not be either exclusively religious or exclusively cultural: geography, which is an administrative science, requires a political center above all. This was Baghdad, the circular city, "*omphalos* of the earth" (*surrat al-ard*).[12] From its founding, Baghdad was the symbol of 'Abbāsid power, but in the age of our geographer, it had already fallen from a past splendor that was by then disputed by the rival city of Cairo, ruled by a Shiite dynasty, the Fatimids. Muqaddasī, who was not fooled by this gap between and past and the present of the city, states that Baghdad was "in ruins and depopulated." At the same time, Cairo (that is, Fustāt) was "more magnificent" and was called the "abrogator of the City of Peace."[13] In other words, at the same time that Muqaddasī was painting a picture of an ideal political space, he was scratching that picture away by his own observations as a traveler who had noted for himself the gap between the domain of Islam as it willed itself to be and as it really was. Muqaddasī's entire inquiry bears the mark of a line of fracture that breaks the *mamlaka* (which no longer was a unified domain) and two spaces in constant tension, one of them normative, the other open to actual experience. Because he was in the same defensive posture as the *mutakallim* (apologetic theologian), however, he had to give a unified representation

10. André Miquel puts these two aspects in clear perspective in his introduction to his translation of selections of Muqaddasī's *Geography: Ahsan al-Taqāsīm, fī Ma'rifat al-Aqālīm: La meilleure répartition pour la connaissance des provinces*, trans. André Miquel (Damascus: Institut Français de Damas, 1963), xxii.

11. Ibid., Miquel translation,138; quoted from *The Best Divisions or Knowledge of the Regions*, trans. Basil Anthony Collins, reviewed by Muhammad Hamid al-Tai (Reading, UK: Garnet, 1994), 64.

12. For an analysis of the political and symbolic representations that presided over the foundation of the city of Baghdad, see Oleg Grabar, *The Formation of Islamic Art* (New Haven: Yale University Press, 1973, 1987); trans. Yves Thoraval as *La formation de l'art islamique* (Paris: Flammarion, 1987), 92–98.

13. Muqaddasī, *Ahsan al-Taqāsīm fī Ma'rifat al-Aqālīm*, ed. M. J. de Goeje (Leiden: Brill, 1906), 120, 147 (Arabic text); Collins translation, 109, 181.

of that pseudoentity that overcame the break. He did so by becoming a geometrician—that is, by describing the concrete spaces that he had traveled through or read about as mostly abstract geometric spaces. This enabled him to trace a unified figure. Muqaddasī himself, who knew very well that the geographical space of the *mamlaka* was "not uniform" but "quite irregular," discusses whether a geometrical space can be made out of an actual space. One can apprehend Islam by "the device of squaring it" or "by longitude and latitude."[14] What counted was to "give the description and representation" of a unified domain. The space of abstraction was surer. Consequently, if what is called *mamlaka* has no real existence, that simply signifies that the domain of Islam is not truly unified.

Although cartographic orientation is not absent in Muqaddasī, he does not follow his predecessors, the heirs and continuators of "scientific" geography after Ptolemy.[15] He does not limit his portrayal of spatial heterogeneity to a cartographic expression, for he uses another resource—himself as narrator—to attain his objective of unification and conformity. This way, he connects disparate spaces and gives them an illusory unity.

The geographer cannot organize his writing around a split representation of Islamic space. This was unthinkable because it went against the totalizing and englobing spirit of the *Weltanschauung* of medieval Islam. Consequently, Muslim men of letters could not acknowledge that such a cleavage had a structural function, even when they observed it empirically. One example of this is the famous *Biographical Dictionary* of Ibn Khallikān (d. 681/1282). Much like Muqaddasī in his *Geography*, Ibn Khallikān paints an ideal picture of a unified Muslim world, with its center in Baghdad, in which men of letters who travel—generally from the periphery toward the center—contribute to the creation of that fictive unity by their very journeys. He compares Fatimid Cairo, the center of a heterodox Islam that its Ayyūbid masters, under the leadership of Saladin had just destroyed, to Baghdad, the political center of Sunni Islam. The entire construction is, of course, just a game of images. Baghdad at the time was merely one provincial center among others.[16] The biographer, however, as a good Sunni man

14. Ibid., Miquel translation, 137; Collins translation, 63. The geographer knew of other representations of Islam's empire, for example, one that showed it in the form of a bird.

15. On the cartography of medieval Islam, see Konrad Miller, *Mappae Arabicae, Arabische Welt- und Länderkarten des 9.–13. Jahrhunderts*, 4 vols. (Stuttgart: 1926–30); and J. H. Kramers, "La question Balhī-Istakhrī-Ibn Hawkal et l'*Atlas de l'Islam*," *Analecta Orientalia* 10 (1932): 9–30, reprinted in the series Islamic Geography, ed. Fuat Sezgin, no. 31 (1992), 326–47.

16. Speaking of the age in which Khatīb al-Baghdādī composed his *History of Baghdad,* Claude Cahen writes: "Baghdad was no longer Baghdad; it had lost all memory of what it had been, and, before completely ceasing to be, it set down testimony for posterity." He adds that at the time,

of letters, insists on believing the fiction of a single caliphate operating in
that city. On the level of what Muqaddasī calls "representation and description," the picture he paints retains the fiction of a centrality embodied by an empty signifier called "Baghdad." When Ibn Battūta, who was to
the Muslim world of the Middle Ages what his contemporary, Marco Polo,
was to the West, described the city in the mid-fourteenth century, he projected onto it the old literary schemata of "city of paradise" and "capital
of Islam." He even went so far as to decree that it was the "residence of
the caliphs and the sojourn of scholars."[17] These clichés, which are the expression of an "image wish,"[18] tell us more about the Maghrebian voyager
than about the city itself. They show that Ibn Battūta was an active adept
of the ideology of a centralized and unified Islam of the *mamlaka* elaborated in the ninth century.[19] The rhetorical formulas that he uses show the
globe-trotter moving within a system of representations that, despite the
great age of its materials, were still endowed with a certain ideological efficacy. As we have seen, travelers liked to cover ground in texts. Not only
did Muqaddasī draw his "representation and description" from the great
semiotic text of Islam; he also made travel in the books and maps of his
predecessors one of the chief reasons for his own voyages. After him, Ibn
Battūta did much the same. In particular, he traveled in the book of Ibn
Jubayr, one of the founders of the literary genre of the voyage in Islam.
On several occasions, we see Ibn Battūta visiting places that he knew perfectly well for having frequented them for months, looking at them with
the eyes of his prestigious predecessor, then describing them in a style

---

"no one could have said that Baghdad was the capital of the mind. Beginning in the latter half of
the [eleventh] century, many men of letters and scholars succumbed to the attraction of Syria,
while waiting for a tomorrow in which [that attraction would pass to] Egypt, reconquered by
the Syrians, theoretically under obedience to the 'Abāssid caliphate": Claude Cahen, "Bagdad
au temps de ses derniers califes," in "Bagdad," special issue published on the occasion of the
1,100th anniversary of the founding of the city, *Arabica* 9 (1962): 289–302, esp. 296, 299. On
the representation of Baghdad as the "dome of Islam," see Françoise Micheau, "Les sources pour
les mégapoles orientales," in *Mégapoles méditerranéennes: Géographie urbaine retrospective*, actes du
colloque, ed. Claude Nicolet, Robert Ilert, and Charles-Louis Depaule (Rome: École Française de
Rome, 2000), 685–704.

17. Ibn Battūta, *Voyages et périples choisis*, trans. Paule Charles-Dominique (Paris: Gallimard,
1992), 107.

18. Ernst Bloch, *Das Prinzip Hoffnung*, 5 vols. (Frankfurt: Suhrkamp, 1985); in French translation as *Le principe espérance*, 3 vols. (Paris: Gallimard, 1976–91).

19. It is possible that commonplaces about Baghdad are not by Ibn Battūta but by Ibn Juzayy,
the coauthor of his travel account. That changes nothing, however. We would, to the contrary,
have one more attestation that the representation of Baghdad was drawn from medieval Islamic
knowledge. There was no need to visit the Iraqi city to adopt it as one's own.

that was already a century and a half old. Those who cry plagiarism[20] or who complain of the "solution of facility that consists in dipping into the works of his predecessors"[21] forget that the technique of the collage was an integral part of the travel narrative. Here the travel narrative in Islam is similar to that of other traditions, that of the West, for example, given that, as Maurice Barrès states, travelers of any culture eternally place their feet in the steps of their predecessors. Every time that happens, a chain of solidarity links the two.

Marco Polo and Ibn Battūta both visited China, and they both re-counted their voyages in books that they dictated. But whereas Marco Polo's *Book of Marvels* circulated widely in the late Middle Ages and at-tracted the attention of cartographers as early as the fifteenth century, the adventures of Ibn Battūta had only a modest echo. How can we explain this difference in reception? After the fourteenth century, both "curiosity" and "interest" urged Europe to focus on its prodigious voyager at a time when it was exercising its nascent vocation as an exploring and conquer-ing power in books and through maps. The world of Islam, wearied and folded back into itself, had no particular interest in reading Ibn Battūta. This explains the inverted image of the reception of the two men, where Marco Polo appears as the *first* of the great travelers of a West in expan-sion and Ibn Battūta as the *last* of the great voyagers of a Muslim world now broken into pieces and shriveled into itself. One represents prefigura-tion; the other, repetition; one inaugurated the "beginning" of the voyage; the other signals its "end."

What happened to make the adventures of Ibn Battūta mark the "end of the voyage" in Islam? What happened was that the construction of Is-lam became definitively fixed in structures and representations that it re-tained up to the period of colonial conquest. To the extent that there was nothing left to elaborate or construct, the voyage—as a literary practice—lost the efficacy with which it had been credited in the formative period, making it one of Islam's major intellectual acts. It is understandable that, under these conditions, the founders of Islamic knowledge should have traveled more than their later counterparts. Having almost nothing left to invent, the latter progressively abandoned the voyage. Hence the topic of the present book: I have attempted to understand and explicate the fact

20. Such as, for example, Ross E. Dunn, *The Adventures of Ibn Battūta, a Muslim Traveler of the 14th Century* (Berkeley: University of California Press, 1986), 313–414.

21. As, for example, Paule Charles-Dominique, in Ibn Battūta, *Voyages et périples choisis*, 10.

that in no period of their premodern history did Muslims travel as much, motivated by intellectual considerations, as between the eighth century and the twelfth century. In terms of distance covered and time spent, Ibn Battūta can only be compared with the globe-trotters of that epoch. His narrative had to wait until the mid-nineteenth century to be "discovered" and to enjoy an international readership. Translated into several of the world's major languages, in French translation it figures in the prestigious collection of La Pléiade, standing next to the great monuments of universal literature. The height of irony lies in the fact that he owes that broad audience to a geographical region not too far from his native Maghreb that, although he went all the way to China, he never dreamed of discovering: Western Europe.

CHRONOLOGICAL LIST OF
PRINCIPAL TRAVEL ACCOUNTS

Traveler	Work	Source
Mak'hūl (d. 730)	Fragments	Ibn Khuthayma (d. 857), *Kitāb al-'Ilm*, fol. 188b.
Kisā'ī (d. 799)	Fragments	Anonymous (10th century), *Kitāb al-Majālis*, fols. 98b–102a.
Ahmad ibn Hanbal (d. 855)	Fragments	Sālih ibn Ahmad ibn Hanbal (d. 878), *Sīrat al-Imām Ahmad ibn Hanbal* (Alexandria, 1981).
Abū Hātim (d. 890)	*Rihla*	Chapters published by his son Ibn Abī Hātim (d. 938): "What My Father Endured in his Voyages"; "What is Said About My Father's Voyages," *Kitāb al-Jarh*, 1:263–66.
Ibn Fadlān	*Risāla* (921–22)	Published in German, Russian, English, and French translation (by M. Canard; P. Charles-Dominique).
Ibn al-Qallās (d. 948)	Fragments	Edited by Ibn al-Faradī, *Tārīkh*, Spanish translation, Manuela Marín, 1994.
Ibn 'Abbād (d. 995)	*Rūznāmaja*	Fragments, edited by Muhammad Āl-Yasīn, Baghdad, 1958.
Abū Dulaf (d. late 10th century)	*Risāla II*	Edited by V. Minorski, Cairo, 1955; edited by P. Bulgakov and A. Khalidov, Cairo, 1970.

Traveler	Work	Source
Pseudo-Shāfiʿī (10th century)	*Kitāb al-Safar*	Manuscript copies and editions, Cairo, 1931; Damascus, 1995.
Ibn Sīnā (Avicenna) (d. 1037)	*Sīra*	Autobiography dictated to a student; published in Qiftī, *Tārīkh al-Hukamā*, 413–25; in English translation by W. E. Gohlman, 1974.
Ibn Butlān (d. 1063)	*Risāla*	Qiftī, *Tārīkh al-Hukamā*, 295–313.
Nāsir-ī Khusrū (d. 1088)	*Safar-nāma*	Edited and translated into French, Scheffer, Paris, 1881.
Abū al-Salt Umayya (d. 1126?)	*Risāla*	Edited by ʿAbd ʾl-Salām Hārūn, *Nawādir al-Makhtūtāt*, 1973, 2:12–56.
Abū Bakr ibn al-ʿArabī (d. 1148)	*Rihla*	Edited by Saʿīd Aʾrāb, *Maʿa al-Qādī Abū Bakr ibn al-ʿArabī*, Beirut, 1987, 185–226.
Ibn Jubayr (d. 1217)	*Rihla*	Published in English, Italian, and French translation.
ʿAbdarī	*Rihla* (1250)	Edited by Muhammad al-Fāsī, 1968.
Ibn Rushayd (d. 1321)	*Rihla*	Escurial, MS no. 1680, 1735, 1736, 1737, 1739; selections, vol. 2 edited by Muhammad ibn al-Khawjah, Tunis, 1982; vol. 5 Beirut 1988.
Ibn Battūta (d. 1368)	*Rihla*	Edited by C. Defrémery and B. R. Sanguinetti, 1853–58; published in French, English, German, Spanish, Italian, Russian, Hungarian, and Polish translation.

Note: This list does not include inventories of masters or geographical works.

GLOSSARY

abdāl: substitute saints; mystics
Adab: belles lettres
'ādil: honorable person, of high probity
āhād: "unilateral" (of traditions with only one chain)
'Ajā'ib: marvelous tales
'ajā'ib al-buldān: marvelous lands
'ajīb: extraordinary tales
'ajība: marvels
'amal: works of piety
as'hāb al-hadīth: tradition seekers
as'hāb al-ray': reasoners
autopsia: knowledge through sight

Bādiya: desert of the Arabs; steppes between Syria and Iraq
basīra: inner sight, penetration, perspicacity
bātin: hidden, esoteric

dānī', adnā': silly; vile
dār: house; territory
dhāhir: appearance
dhil; dhull: humiliation
dirāya: reflection ; reasoning
djebel (Jabal): mountain; deserted areas
djihād: jihad

faqīr: Sūfī mendicant
farā'id: law of succession; heirs' rights; legal obligation
farsakh: parasang (5.7 km)
fasāha: pure, correct language
fus'hā: clear, pure language

gharā'ib: rare word(s)
gharīb: hapax; expatriate; strange stories
ghāzī: combatant
ghazw, ghazwa: holy war, combat

haddatha: to transmit, report, narrate
hadīth: prophetic tradition(s); information; oral account

ijāza: certificate of transmission; licence
ijtihād al-ra'y: personal reasoning
ikhtibār: inspection
ikhtiyār: choice
'ilm: Islamic learning
i'rāb: case declension (vowel endings)
irsāl: incomplete chain of guarantors
isnād: chain of guarantors
'iyān: direct visual knowledge; observation

jāhiliyya: pre-Islamic times

khabar: piece of information; report; oral tradition

malāma: blame
malāmatiyya: movement of blame
mamlaka: empire; domain of Islam
manzil, manāzil: halt, stop, station
maqām: way station (on road)
maqāma; maqāmat: work(s) of fiction
maqāmāt: stages, degrees of mystical union
masālik: roads; itineraries; works about roads
mawqūf: interrupted chain of transmission
mirabilia: extraordinary occurrences
mi'rāj: Muhammad's Night Flight; Ascension
mu'ammir, mu'ammarūn: macrobiotic figure(s)
mudd: 2 lbs
mudtarr: distressed person

mujāhada: combat against oneself
mujāhid, mujāhidūn: combatant(s) for God
mujāwir; mujāwara: "neighbor(s) of God"
muqīm, muqīmūn: resident mystic(s)
murābata: a stay at the frontier
mursal: interrupted chain of transmission
musannaf: collections of traditions thematically divided into chapters
musannif: editor, author
mushāfaha: oral interchange, conversation
mushāhada: direct testimony, seeing with one's own eyes
Musnad: corpus of traditions attached to a Companion, hence to Muhammad
mutakalim: apologetic theologian
mutatawwi'a: volunteer combatants
muttasil: of *hadīth* in a complete chain

nawādir: literary curiosities

opsis: sign

qāsid, qāsidūn: one who goes (people who go) somewhere
qurrā': people who read/recite the Qur'an
qutb: mystical pole (head of "substitute" saints)

rahbāniyya: monasticism
rāhib al-umma: monk of Islam
rāwī: rhapsodist, transmitter
rāwiya: scholar, transmitter (of poetry)
ra'y: personal interpretation; legal opinion
ribāt: fortress
rihla: voyage; travel narrative
riwāya: oral transmission, memorization
Rūm: "Rome" (i.e., the Byzantine Empire)
Rūznāmaj: journal

sā'ih, sā'ihūn: vagabond saint(s)
sā'imūn: people who fast
samā': audition; hearing
sanad: guarantors; chain of authorities
sawma'a: hermitage
shadādat al-khutūt: written testimony
shadādat 'iyān: ocular testimony
shadādat samā': auricular testimony

shalshelet ha-qabbelah: Jewish chain of Tradition
silsila: chain of Tradition
silsilat al-dhahab: golden chain
silsilat al-sanad: chain of guarantors
siyāha: mystics' travel

tabayyun: lucidity
tābi'ūn: Successors, disciples of Companions
tarīqa: spiritual "road," method, way
tawakkul: abandonment to God
thagr, pl. *thugūr:* fortress(es), fortified town(s)
thiqa: person worthy of trust
thōma: a marvel, curiosity

'ulamā': doctors of law, ulemas
umma: community of Muslims
uns: social life

via: way, road

wijāda: access to knowledge without masters; permission to study a book without a
   guarantor

zuhd: mystical renunciation; asceticism

BIBLIOGRAPHY

Primary Sources: Manuscript

'Abd al-Ghānī ibn Sa'id. *Kitāb al-Mutawārīn*. MS no. 3807. Zāhiriyya, Damascus.

Anonymous. *Juz' fīhi Miḥnat al-Imām al-Shāfi'ī*. MS no. 3747. Zāhiriyya, Damascus.

Anonymous. *Kitāb al-Majālis al-Madhkūra li'l-Ulama bi'l-Lugha*. Microfilm no. 232. Ma'had a-Makhtūtāt al-'Arabiyya (Institut Arabe des Manuscrits), Cairo. 'Abd-Allah Hārūn, the editor of this manuscript, believes that the author of this work is the Iraqi philologist Abū'l-Qāsīm al-Zujājī (d. 340/951).

Ibn Khuthayma Zuhayr ibn Harb. *Kitāb al-'Ilm*. MS no. 3830. Zāhiriyya, Damascus.

Khatīb al-Baghdādī. *Al-Jāmi' li-Akhlāq al-Rāwī wa Adab al-Sāmi'*. MS no. 505. Mustalah al-Hadīth, Dār al-Kutub, Cairo.

———. *Risāla fī Ḥukm al-Ijāza lil-Majhūl wa'l-Ma'dūm* (Ahmad III, 23/624). Microfilm no. 269. Hadīth, Ma'had al-Makhtūtāt al-'Arabiyya (Institut Arabe des Manuscrits), Cairo.

Al-Sawwāy, Muhammad ibn Nāsir ad-Dīn. *Risālat Shann al-Ghāra fī Fadl Ziyārat al-Maghāra*. MS no. 4391. Zāhiriyya, Damascus.

Shāfi'ī. *Riḥla*. MS no. 578. Histoire-Taymūr, Dār al-Kutub, Cairo.

———. *Riḥla*. MS no. 9787 (microfilm no. 6137). Zāhiriyya, Damascus.

Zamakhsharī, Mahmūd ibn 'Umar. *Al-Muhādarāt wa-al-Muhāwarāt*. MS no. 6865. Zāhiriyya, Damascus.

Zarkashī, Muhammad ibn Bahādir. *Al-Ghurar wa-al-Safāfir 'an-mā Yahtāju ilayhi al-Musāfir*. MS no. 4469, fols. 67b–82a. Yahuda Series, Princeton University Library.

Primary Sources: Printed

'Abd Allāh ibn al-Mubārak. *Kitāb al-Jihād*. Ed. Nazīh Hammād. Cairo: Majma' al-Buhūth al-Islāmīyah, 1978.

―――. *Kitāb al-Zuhd wa-al Raqā'iq*. Ed. Habīburrahmā A'zamī. Beirut: Muhammad 'Afīf al-Zughbīi, [1971?].

'Abd al-Latīf al-Baghdādī. *Kitāb al-Ifāda*. Trans. Kamal Hafuth Zand, John A. Videan, and Ivy E. Videan as *The Eastern Key* (London: Allen & Unwin, 1965).

'Abd al-Razzāq. *al Musannāf*. Ed. Habīb al-Rahmān al-A'zamī.

Abū Bakr al-Hāzimī. *Al-i'tibār fī al-Nāsikh wa-al-Mansūkh min al-akhbār*. Ed. Muhammad 'Abd' al-'Azīz. Cairo, n.d.

Abū Bakr ibn Hijja. *Thamarāt al-Awrāq*. Ed. Muhammad Abū al-Fadl Ibrāhīm. Cairo: Maktabat al-Khanjī, 1971.

Abū Bakr al-Ismā'īlī. *Kitāb al-Mu'jam*. Ed. Ziyād M. Mansūr. 4 vols. Medina: Maktaba al-'Ulūm wa-al-Hikam, 1990. See also Heinrich Schützinger, *Das Kitāb al-Mu'gam des Abū Bakr al-Ismā'īlī* (Wiesbaden: Steiner; Mainz: Deutsche Morgenländische Ges., 1978).

Abū Dāwūd. *al-Marāsīl, ma'a al-asānīd*. Cairo, n.d.

―――. *Sunan Abī Dāwūd*. Ed. Muhammad Muhyī al Dīn 'Abd al-Hamīd. 4 vols. Beirut: Dār Ihya al-Sunnah al-Wabawiyah, 1970–79.

Abū Dulaf. *Ar-Risāla at-Thaniya*. Ed. Pavel G. Bulgakov. Cairo: 'Alam al-Kutub, 1970.

Abū Hāmid al-Gharnātī. *Al-Mu'rib 'an Ba'd 'Ayā'ib al-Maghrib*. Ed. Ingrid Bejarano. Madrid: Consejo Superior de Investigaciones Cientificas, 1991.

―――. *Tuhfat al-Albāb*. Ed. and trans. Gabriel Ferrand. *Journal Asiatique* 2 (1925): 1–148, 195–291.

Abū Hātim al-Rāzī. *Adāb al-Shāfī*. Ed. 'Abd al-Ghānī 'Abd al-Khāliq. Cairo: Maktabat Muhammad Najib Amīn all-Khānjī, 1953.

―――. *Marāsil fī' al-Hadīth*. Ed. Subhī al-Badrī al-Samarrā'ī. Baghdad: Maktabat al-Muthaan, 1967.

Abū Hiffān al-Mihzamī. *Akhbār Abī Nuwās*. Ed. 'Abd al-Sattār Ahmad Farrāj. Cairo: Dār Misr lil-Tibā'ah, [1953?].

Abū Husayn Ahmad ibn Fāris. *Al-Sāhibī fī Fiqh Lughah al-'Arab fī kalāmihā*. Beirut: Maktabat al-Ma'ārif, 1993.

Abū Nu'aym. *Akhbār Isbahān*. Ed. Sven Dederin. 2 vols. Leiden: Brill, 1931.

―――. *Hilyat al-Awliyā'*. 10 vols. Cairo: Maktabat al-Khānjī, 1932–38. New edition, 10 vols. (Beirut: Dār al-Kitāb al-Arabī, 1967–68). Selections trans. Muhammad Al-Akoli as *The Beauty of the Righteous and Ranks of the Elite* (Philadelphia: Pearl, 1995).

Abū al-Salt Umayya. *Al Risāla al-Misriyya*. Ed. 'Abd al-Azīz Hārūn. Vol. 1 of *Nawādir al-Makhtūtāt*, by 'Abd al-Salām Muhammad Hārūn, 2 vols., 1:11–56. Misr: Mustafā al-Bābī al-Halabī, 1973–75.

Abū Tālib al-Makkī. *Kitāb qūt al qulūb*. Ed. 'Abd al-Qādir Ahmad 'Atá. Misr: Maktabat al-Qāhirah, 1964.

Abū Zayd al-Ansārī. *Kitāb al-nawādir fī al-lughah*. Ed. Muhammad 'Abd al-Qadir Ahmad. Cairo: Dār al-Shuruq, 1981.

Abū Zayd al-Qayrawānī. *Al-Jāmi' fī al-Sunan*. Ed. Muh. Abū-Lajfān and 'Uthmān Battīkh. Beirut, 1985.

Ajūrī, Abū Bakr. *Kitāb al-Ghurabā'*. Ed. Ramadān Ayyūb. Damascus: Dār al-Bashair, 1992.

———. *Kitāb Fard Talab al-'Ilm*. Ed. Leonard T. Librande. *Bulletin d'études orientales* 45 (1993): 89–159.

Anbārī. *Nuzhat al-Albāb fī Tabaqāt al-Udabā'*. Ed. Muhammad Abū al-Fadil Ibrāhīm. Cairo: Dār nahdat Misr, 1967.

Anonymous. *Adab al-Mulūk*. Ed. Bernd Radtke. Beirut: Steiner, 1991.

Anonymous. *Ahbār as-Sin wa l-Hind*. Ed. and trans. Jean Sauvaget as *Relation de la Chine et de l'Inde rédigée en 851* (Paris: Belles Lettres, 1948).

Ansārī. *Manāzil al-Sālihīn* (and other mystical treatises). Trans. Serge de Beaurecueil as *Chemin de Dieu: Trois traités spirituels* (Paris: Sindbad, 1985; Paris: Actes Sud, 1997).

———. *Munājāt*. Trans. Serge de Beaurecueil as *Cris du coeur* (Paris: Sindbad, 1988). Trans. Lawrence Morris and Rustam Sarfeh as *Munajat: The Intimate Prayers of Kwājih 'Abd Allāh Ansārī* (New York: Khaneghah and Maktab of Maleknia Naseralishah, 1975).

Asad ibn Mūsā. *Kitāb az-Zuhd*. Ed. Raif Georges Khoury. New ed. Wiesbaden: Harrassowitz, 1976.

Asma'ī. *Fuhūlat al-Shu'arā*. Ed. Muhammad 'Abd al-Mun'im Khafājī and Taha Zaynī. Cairo: al-Matba'ah al-Munīriyah, 1953.

———. *Tārīkh Mulūk al-'Arab*. Ed. Muhammad Hasan Al Yasin. Baghdad, 1959.

Azharī. *Tahdhīb al-Lugha*. Ed. 'Abd'l-Salām M. Mārtīn. Cairo, 1964.

Balādhurī. *Kitāb Futūh al-Buldān*. Ed. M. J. de Goeje. Leiden, 1866.

Bayhaqī, Abū Bakr. *Dalā'il al-Nubuwah*. Ed. 'Abd al-Mutī Qal'ajī. 7 vols. Beirut: Dār al-Kutub al-'Ilmīyah, 1985.

———. *Kitāb al-Zuhd al-Kabīr*. Ed. Taqī al-Dīn al-Nadwī Mazāhīri. Kuwait: Dār al-Qalam, 1983.

———. *Manāqib al-Shāfi'ī*. Ed. Ahmad Saqr. 2 vols. Cairo: Makhabat Dār al-Turāth, 1971.

———. *al-Sunan al-Kubrā*. Ed. Muhammad 'Abd al-Qādir 'Atā. 11 vols. Beirut: Dār al-Kutub al-'Ilmiyah, 1994.

Bayhaqī, Dhāhir al-Dīn. *Tārīkh al-Hukamā'*. Ed. Muhammad K. 'Alī. Damascus, 1946.

Bazzār, Abū Bakr. *al-Musnad*. Ed. M. Zīn-Allāh. 5 vols. Beirut: Muassasat 'Ulm al-Quran, 1988.

Al-Bīrūnī. *Tahqīq mā li'l-Hind*. Ed. Edward C. Sachau. London, 1887. Trans. Vincent Monteil as *Enquête sur l'Inde*. Trans. Edward C. Sachau as *Alberuni's India: An Account of the Religion, Philosophy, Literature, Geography, Chronology, Astronomy, Customs, Laws and Astrology of India about AD 1030*, 2 vols. (London, 1888).

Buzurg ibn Shahriyār. *Kitāb 'Ajā'ib al-Hind*. Ed. and trans. L. Marcel Devic. Leiden, 1883–86. Trans. Jean Sauvaget in *Mémorial Sauvaget*, 2 vols. (Damascus: Institut Français de Damas, 1954), 1:189–309.

Dārimī. *al-Sunan*. 2 vols. Beirut: Dār Ihyā' al-Sunna al-Nabawāyah, 1975.

———. *Tārīkh Abi Zakarya Yahyā ibn Ma'in*. Ed. Ahmad Muhammad Nur Sayf. Damascus: Dār al-Mamūn lil-Turāth, 1980.

Dhahabī. *Kitāb Tadhkirat al-huffādh*. 3rd ed. 2 vols. Hyderabad: Dairatu L-Ma'arif-il-Osmana, 1955.

———. *Mizān al-i'tidāl*. Ed. 'Alī M. Al-Bajjāwī. 4 vols. Cairo, 1963–64.

———. *Siyar A'lām al-Nubalā'*. Ed. Shu'ayb al-Arna'ūtī et al. 25 vols. Beirut: Mu'assasat al-Risālah, 1982–83.

Hākim al-Nīsābūrī. *Al-Mustadrak 'alā al-Sahīhayn*. Ed. Yūsuf 'Abd al-Rahmān Mar'ashī. Beirut: Dār al-Ma'rifah, 1986.

Hakīm al-Tirmidhī. *Khatm al-Awliyā*. Ed. 'Uthman Yahyá. Beirut: al-Matbatah Kāthūlīkīya, 1965.

———. *Kitāb Manāzil al-'Ibād*. Ed. Muhammad Ibrahim Juyūshī. Cairo: Dār al-Nahdah, 1977.

———. *Manāzil al-Qāsidīn*. Ed. Ahmad 'Abd al-Rahim al-Sayih. Cairo, 1988).

———. *Tābā'i' al-Nufūs*. Ed. Ahmad 'Abd al-Rahīm Sāyih and Sayyid al-Jumaylī. Cairo: al-Maktab al-Thaqāfī, 1989. Trans. Bernd Radtke and John O'Kane in *The Concept of Sainthood in Early Islamic Mysticism: Two Works by al-Hakīm al-Tirmidhī* (Richmond, UK: Curzon, 1996).

Hallāj. *Akhbar al-Hallaj: Recueil d'oraisons et d'exhortations du martyr mystique de l'Islam Husayn ibn Mansur Hallaj*. Ed. and trans. Louis Massignon and Paul Kraus. 3rd ed. Paris: Vrin, 1975.

Hamadhānī. *Maqāmāt (séances)*. Selections in French translation by Régis Blachère and Pierre Masnou (Paris: Klincksieck, 1957).

Hamadhānī, Badī' al-Zamān. *al-Rasā'il*. Constantinople, 1298 AH.

Harawī al-Mawsilī. *Kitāb al-Ishrārat ilā Ma'rifat al-Ziyārāt*. Trans. Janine Sourdel-Thomine in *Guide des lieux de pèlerinage* (Damascus: Institut Français de Damas, 1952, 1957).

Harīrī. *Kitāb al-Maqāmāt*. Trans. René R. Khawam as *Le livre des malins: Séances d'un vagabond de génie* (Paris: Phébus, 1992).

Hārūn, 'Abd'l Salām, Muhammad. *Nawādir al-Makhtūtāt*. 2 vols. Misr: Mustafā al-Bābī al-Halabī, 1973–75.

Haythamī. *Majma' al-Zawā'id*. Beirut: Dār al-Kitāb, 1967.

Hujwīrī. *Somme spirituelle: Kashf al-Mahjūb*. Trans. Djamshid Mortazavi. Paris: Sindbad, 1988. Trans. Reynold A. Nicholson as *The Kashf al-Mahjub: The Oldest Persian Treatise on Sufism* (Leiden: Brill; London: Luzac, 1911; Lahore: Islamic Book Foundation, 1976).

Humaydī, Abū Bakr. *al-Musnad*. Ed. Habiburrahman A'zamī. 2 vols. Beirut: 'Alam al-Kutub; Cairo: Maktabat al-Mutanabbī, 1970–.

Ibn al-Abbār. *al-Mu'jam fī Ashāb al-Qādī al-Imām Abī 'Alī al-Sadafī*. Cairo: Dār al-Kātib al-Arabī, 1967.

Ibn 'Abd al-Barr. *Jāmi' Bayān al-'Ilm wa-fadlih*. Ed.'Abd al-Rahmān Muhammad 'Uthmān. 2 vols. Medina: al-Maktabah al-Sulfiyah, 1968.

———. *Al-Tamhīd li-mā fī al-Muwatta' min al-Ma'ānī wa'l-Asānid*. Ed. Mustafā ibn Ahmad 'Alawī and Muhammad Abdal-Kabīr Bakrī. 17 vols. Rabat, 1967.

Ibn 'Abd-Rabbihi. *Kitāb al-'Iqd al-Farīd*. Ed. Ahmad Amīn and Ahmad Zayn. 7 vols. Cairo, 1948. Trans. Arthur Wormhoudt as *Selections from al-Iqd al farid of Abu 'Umar ibn 'Abd Rabbihi*, 3 vols. (Oskaloosa, IA: William Penn College, 1985–86).

Ibn Abī al-Dunyā. *Rasā'il*. Beirut, 1986.

Ibn Abī Hātim. *Kitāb al-Jarh wa al-ta 'dīl*. 9 vols. Beirut: Dār al-Kitub al-'Ilmiyah, 1952.

———. *Al-Marāsil fī al-Hadīth*. Ed. Subhī al-Samarrā'ī. Baghdad: Maktabat al-Muthaan, 1967.

Ibn Abī Shaybah. *al-Musannaf*. Ed. 'Abd'l-Khāliq al-Afghānī. 5 vols. Hyderabad, 1967. Ed. Kamāl Y. Al-Hūt, 7 vols. (Beirut: Dār all-Tāj,1989).

Ibn Abī Usaybi'a. *'Uyūn al'Anbā' fī Tabaqāt al-Atibbā'*. Cairo, 1886. Reprint, Beirut, 1965.

Ibn Abī Ya'la. *Tabaqāt al-Hanābila*. 2 vols. Beirut: Dār al-Kutub al-'Ilmīyah, 1997.

Ibn al-'Adīm. *Al-Insāf wa'l-Taharrī fī daf' al-Dhulm wa'l-Tajarrī 'an Abī'l-'Alā' al Ma'arrī*. In *Ta'rīf al-Qudāmā' bi-Abī'l-'Alā*, ed. Tāhā Husayn, 483–578. Cairo: Dār al-Qawmīyah, 1965; photo reproduction of 1944.

Ibn al-'Arabī. *Kitāb al-Isfār 'an Natā'ij al-Asfār*. Ed. and trans. Denis Gril as *Le dévoilement des effets du voyage* (Paris: Éditions de l'Éclat, 1994).

———. *Manāqib Dhū al-Nūn al-Misrī*. Trans. Roger Deladrière as *La vie merveilleuse de Dhū' l-Nūn l'Égyptien* (Paris: Sindbad, 1988).

Ibn 'Arab-Shāh. *'Ajā'ib*. Trans. Bernard, baron Carra de Vaux, in *Abrégé des merveilles* (Paris: Klincksieck, 1898). Reprinted in the series Islamic Geography, ed. Fuat Sezgin (1994). Ed. André Miquel (Paris: Sindbad, 1984).

Ibn 'Asākir. *Tārīkh madinat Dimashq*. Ed. 'Alī Shīrī. 40 vols. Beirut: Dār al-Fikr, 1995–96.

Ibn Bashkuwāl. *Kitāb al-Sila*. 2 vols. Cairo: Dār al-Misrīyah, 1966.

Ibn Battūta. *Tuhfat al-Nudh'dhār fī Ghārā'ib al-Amsār wa 'Ajā'ib al-Asfār*. Trans. C. Defrémery and B. R. Sanguinetti as *Voyages d'Ibn Battoutah*, 4 vols. (Paris, 1853–58). Trans. H. A. R. Gibb as *Travels in Asia and Africa, 1325–1354* (London: Routledge Curzon, 2005). See also *Voyageurs arabes: Ibn Fadlān, Ibn Jubayr, Ibn Battūta et un auteur anonyme*, trans. Paule Charles-Dominique (Paris: Gallimard, 1995).

Ibn al-Faqīh al-Hamadhānī. *Baghdād Madīnat al-Salām*. Ed. Sālih Ahmad 'Alī. Baghdad: al-Jumhuriyah al-'Iraqiyah, 1977.

———. *Kitāb al-Buldān: Al-Hamadhānī's Geographie der arabischen Halbinsel*. Ed. D. H. Müller. Leiden, 1891. Trans. Henri Massé as *Abrégé du Livre des pays* (Damascus: Institut Français de Damas, 1973).

Ibn al-Faradī. *Tārīkh 'Ulamā' al-Andalus*. Ed. Ibrāhīm Ibyārī. 2 vols. Cairo: Dār al-
Kutub al-Islāmīyah, 1983.

Ibn Hajar al-'Asqalānī. *Lisān al-Mizān*. Beirut: Dār all-Fikr, 1986.

———. *Al-Rahma al-Ghaythīya fī Manāqib al-Imām al-Layth b. Sa'd*. Cairo, 1301 AH.

Ibn Hanbal. *Kitāb al-Zuhd*. Ed. Muhammad Jalāl Sharaf. 2 vols. Iskandarīyah: Dār
al-Fik al-Jāmī, 1980–84; Beirut: Dār al-Nahda al-'Arabīya, 1981.

———. *al-Musnad*. Ed. Ahmad Muhammad Shākir. 15 vols. Cairo: Dār al-Ma'ārif,
1946–56.

Ibn Hawqal. *Kitāb Sūrat al-Ard*. Ed. Johannes Hendrik Kramers. Leiden, 1939.
Trans. Johannes Hendrik Kramers and Gaston Wiet as *Configuration de la terre*,
2 vols. (Paris: Maisonneuve et Larose, 1964).

Ibn Hibbān. *Kitāb al-Thiqāt*. Ed. 'Abd'l-Mu'īn Khān. 9 vols. Hyderabad: Dār al-
Fikr, 1973–83.

———. *Mashāhīr 'Ulamā' al-Amsār*. Ed. Marzūq 'Alī Ibrāhīm. Beirut: Mu'assasat
al-Kutub al-Thaqāfiyah, 1987.

———. *al-Sahīh*. Ed. Kamāl Y. Jawf. Beirut, 1987.

Ibn al-Jawzī. *Kitāb Sifat al-Safwah*. 4 vols. Hyderabad: Matba'at Dā'irat al-Ma'ārif
al-'Uthmānīyah, 1936–37.

———. *al-Muntadham fī Tārīkh al-mulūk wa-al-umam*. Ed. Muhammad 'Abd
al-Qādir 'Atā and Mustafā 'Abd al-Qādir 'Atā. 19 vols. Beirut: Dār al-Kutub al-
'Ilmīyah, 1992.

Ibn Jubayr. *Rihla*. Ed. M. J. de Goeje. Leiden, 1907. Trans. Maurice Gaudefroy-
Demombynes as *Voyages d'Ibn Jubayr*, 4 vols. (Paris: Geuthner, 1949–56).

Ibn Jumāy' al-Saydāwī. *Mu'jam al-Shuyūkh*. Ed. 'Umar Tadmurī. Tripoli: Dār al-
Imān, 1985.

Ibn Kathīr. *Al-Bidāya wa'l-Nihāya*. 14 vols. Cairo: Matba'āt al-Sa'ādah, 1932–39.

Ibn Khaldūn. *Muqaddima*. Trans. Vincent Monteil as *Discours sur l'histoire univer-
selle*, 3 vols. (Beirut, 1967–68); 2nd ed., 3 vols. (Paris: Sindbad, 1978). Trans. Franz
Rosenthal as *The Muqaddimah: An Introduction to History*, 3 vols. (New York:
Pantheon, 1958).

Ibn Khallikān. *Wafayāt al-A'yān*. 8 vols. Cairo, 1948. Ed. Insān 'Abbās, 8 vols.
(Beirut: Dār Thāqāfa, 1968–72). Trans. William MacGuckin, baron Slane, as *Ibn
Khallikān's Biographical Dictionary*, 4 vols. (Paris, 1842–71).

Ibn Khurdādhbeh. *Kitāb al-Masālik wa'l-Mamālik*. Ed. M. J. de Goeje. Leiden, 1889.

Ibn Māja. *al-Sunan*. Ed. Muhammad Fu'ād 'Abd al-Bāqī. 2 vols. Cairo: 'Isā al-Bābī
al-Halabī, 1972.

Ibn Manda. *Musnad Ibrāhīm ibn Ad'ham*. Ed. Majdī al-Sayyid Ibrāhīm. Cairo: Maktabat al-Qur'ān, 1988.

Ibn Mansūr. *al-Sunan*. Ed. Sa'īd ibn 'Abd Allah ibn Abd al-'Azīz Āl Humayd. 5 vols.
Riyadh: Dār al-Sunay'ī, 1993.

Ibn al-Nadīm. *al-Fihrist*. Ed. Ridā al-Māzindarānī. Beirut: Dār al-Masīrah, 1988. Trans.

Bayard Dodge as *The Fihrist of al-Nadim: A Tenth-Century Survey of Muslim Culture*, 2 vols. (New York: Columbia University Press, 1970).

Ibn al-Qādi Shuhba. *Tabaqāt al-Shāfiʿīyā*. Ed. ʿAbdʾl-Halīm Khān. 4 vols. Beirut, 1987.

Ibn Qutayba. *Mukhtalaf al-Hadīth*. Cairo: Maktabat al-Kullīyāt al-Azharīyah, 1966. Trans. Gérard Lecomte as *Le traité de divergence du Hadīth dʾIbn Kutayba (m. 276/889)* (Damascus: Institut Français, 1962).

Ibn Rajab. *Kitab al-Dhaylʿalā Tabaqāt al-Hanābilah*. Ed. Muhammad Hamīd Fiqqī. 2 vols. Cairo, 1932–53.

Ibn Rashīq. *Al-ʿUmda fī Mahāsin al-Shiʿr wa-adabihi wa-Naqdihi*. Ed. Muhammad Muhyī al-Dīn ʿAbd al-Hamīd. 2 vols. Cairo: al-Maktabah al-Tijārīyah al-Kubrā, 1963–64.

Ibn Ridwān ʿAlī. *Kitāb Kifāyat al-Tabīb*. Trans. Jacques Grandʾhenry as *Le livre de la méthode du médecin de ʿAli b. Ridwan (998–1067)*, 2 vols. (Louvain: Université Catholique de Louvain, Institut Orientaliste, 1979–84).

Ibn Rusteh. *al-Aʿlāq al-Nafīsah*. Trans. Gaston Wiet as *Les atours précieux* (Cairo: Société de Géographie dʾÉgypte, 1955).

Ibn Saʿid al-Andalusī. *Tabaqāt umam*. Ed. Karl Vilhelm Zetterstéen. Leiden, 1909. 8 vols., Beirut: Dār Sādir, n.d. Trans. Régis Blachère as *Kitā tabakāt al-uman (Livre des catégories des nations)* (Paris: Larose, 1935).

———. *Al-Mughrib fī Hulā al-Maghrib*. Ed. Shawqī Dayf. 2 vols. Misr: Dār al-Maʿarif, 1955–64.

Ibn Salāh. *Muqaddima*. Ed. ʿĀʾisha ʿAbd al-Rahmān. Cairo: Wizārat al-Thaqāfah, 1974.

Ibn Sallām. *Al-Gharīb al-Musannaf*. Ed. Muhammad al-Mukht ār al-ʿAbīdī. Carthage: al-Muʾassasah al-Watanīyah, 1989–.

———. *Kitāb al-Amwāl*. Ed. Muhammad Khalīl Harrās. Beirut: Dār al-Kutub al-ʿIlmīyah, 1986. In English translation as *The Book of Revenue: Kitab al-amwal* (Reading, UK: Garnet, 2005).

Ibn Sīnā. *Sīra*. In *Tārīkh al-Hukamāʾ*, by Qiftī. Ed. Julius Lippert as *Ibn al-Qiftīʾs Tarīh al-hukamā* (Leipzig: Dietenchʾsche Verlagsbuchhandlung, 1903), 413–25. Trans. William E. Gohlman as *The Life of Ibn Sīna* (Albany: State University of New York Press, 1974).

Ikhwān al-Safāʾ. *Rasāʾil Ikhwān al-Safā wa-khullān al-wafā*. 4 vols. Beirut: Dār al-Bayrut, 1983.

Istakhrī. *Kitāb al-Masālik waʾl-mamālik (Liber viarum et regnorum)*. Ed. M. J. de Goeje. Leiden, 1870.

ʿIyād, al-Qādī. *Al-Ilmāʾ ilā Maʿrifat Usūl ar-riwāya*. Ed. Sayyid Ahmad Saqr. Cairo, 1970.

———. *Tartīb al-Madārik*. Ed. Ahmad B. Mahmūd. 5 vols. Beirut: Maktabat al-Hayāh, 1967–68.

Ja'far al-Sādiq. *Misbāh al-Sharī'ah*. Beirut: Muassasat al-A'lamī lil-Matbū'āt, 1980.

──────. *Tafsīr*. Ed. Paul Nwyia as "Le *Tafsīr* mystique attribué à Ga'far Sādiq," *Mélanges de l'Université Saint-Joseph* (Beirut) 43, fasc. 4 (1968): 179–230.

Jāhiz. *Al-Bayān wa'l-Tabyīn*. Ed. 'Abd al-Salām Muhammad Hārūn. 4 vols. Cairo: Maktabat al-Khānjī, 1968.

──────. *Kitāb al-Amsār wa 'Ajā'ib al-Buldān*. Ed. Charles Pellat. *Al-Mashriq* 60, no. 2 (March–April 1966): 169–205.

──────. *Kitāb al-Tarbī' wa-al-Tadwīr*. Ed. Charles Pellat. Damascus: Institut Français de Damas, 1955. Trans. Maurice Adad as *Le livre du carré et du rond, Arabica* 13, no. 3 (1966): 268–94.

──────. *Rasā'il al-Jahiz*. Ed. 'Abd al-Salām Muhammad Hārūn. 4 vols. Cairo: Maktabat al-Khānjī, 1964. Selections trans. Charles Vial as *Al-Gāhiz: Quatre essais*, 2 vols. (Cairo: Institut Français d'Archéologie Orientale du Caire, 1976–).

──────. *Tahdhīb Kitāb al-Hayawān*. Ed. 'Abd al-Salām Muhammad Hārūn. 7 vols. Cairo: Maktabat al-Khanjī, 1938–45). Selections trans. Lakhdar Souami as *Le Cadi et la mouche: Anthologie du Livre des animaux* (Paris: Sindbad, 1988).

Jandī, Bahā' al-Dīn. *Al-Sulūk fī Tabaqāt 'Ulamā' al-Yaman*. Ed. Muhammad ibn 'Alī ibn al-Husayn al-Akwa' al-Hiwalī. San'a: Maktabat al-Irshād, 1993, 1995.

Jawharī. *al-Sihāh*. Ed. Ahmad 'Abd al-Ghafūr 'Attār. Cairo: Dār al-Kitāb al-'Arabī, 1956.

Jazarī, Shams al-Dīn. *Ghāyat al-Nihāya fī Tabaqāt al-Qurrā'*. Ed. Gotthelf Bergstrasser. 2 vols. Cairo: Maktabat al-Khānjī, 1932–35.

Junayd. *Rasā'il*. Trans. Roger Deladrière as *Enseignement spirituel* (Paris: Sindbad, 1983).

Jūzjanī, Ibrahīm ibn Yaqūb. *Ahwāl al-Rijāl*. Ed. Subhī al-Badrī Samarrā'ī. Beirut: Muassasat al-Risālah, 1985.

Kalābādhī. *Kitāb al-Ta'arruf li-Madhhab ahl al-Tasawwuf*. Ed. A. J. Arberry. Cairo: Maktabat al-Khānjī, 1933.

Kattānī, 'Abd al-Hayy. *al-Risāla al-Mustatrafa*. Damascus, 1964.

Kharrāz, Abū Sa'īd. *Kitāb al-Sidq*. Ed. and trans. A. J. Arberry as *The Book of Truthfulness (Kitab al-sidq)* (London: Oxford University Press, 1937).

Khatīb al-Baghdādī. *al-Kifāya fī 'ilm al-Riwāya*. Beirut: Dār al-Kitāb al-'Arabī, 1985.

──────. *al-Rihlah fī Talab al-Hadīth*. Ed. Nūr al-Dīn 'Itr. Beirut: Dār al-Kutub al-Ilmīyah, 1975.

──────. *Sharaf Ashāb al-Hadīth*. Ed. Muhammad Sa'īd Khātib Ogiu. Ankara: Dār ihyā al-Sunnah all-abawīyah, 1972.

──────. *Tārīkh Baghdād*. 14 vols. Cairo, 1931.

Khushānī. *Akhbār al-Fuqahā'*. Ed. Maria Luisa Avila and Luis Molinas. Madrid: al-Majhlis al-A'lā lil-Abhāth al-'Ilmīyah, 1992. In Spanish translation as *Ajbar al-fuqaha wa-al-muhadditin: Historia de los alfaquies y tradicionistas de Al-Andalus*, ed. Maria Luisa Avila and Luis Molinas (Madrid: Consejo Superior de Investigaciones Cientificas, 1992).

Khwārizmī, Abū Bakr. *Rasā'il*. Cairo, 1279 AH/1883.

Kinānī, 'Abd al-'Aziz ibn Yahya. *Kitāb al-Haydah*. Ed. Jamil Saliba. Damascus, 1964.

Ma'arrī. *Rasā'il*. Ed. and trans. David S. Margoliouth as *Rasā'il Abī al-Alā al-Ma'arrī: The Letters of Abū'l-Alā' of Ma'arrat al-Nu'mān* (Oxford, 1898).

Mālik ibn Anas. *al-Muwatta'*. Ed. 'Abd al-Majīd Turkī. Beirut: Dār al-Gharb al-Is-lami, 1994. Trans. Aisha Abdurrahman Bewley as *Al-Muwatta of Imam Malik ibn Anas: The First Formulation of Islamic Law* (London: Kegan Paul, 1989).

Marwazī, Sharaf al-Zamān. *Abwāb fī al-Sīn . . .* Trans. Vladimir Minorski as *Sharaf al-Zamān Tāhir Marvazī on China, the Turks and India* (London: Royal Asiatic Society, 1942).

Mas'ūdī. *Kitāb al-Inbāh wa'l-Ishrāf*. Trans. Bernard, baron Carra de Vaux, as *Le livre de l'avertissement* (Paris, 1896).

——. *Murūj al-Dhahab*. Trans. Charles Barbier de Meynard and Abel Payet de Courteille as *Les prairies d'or*, 9 vols. (Paris: Imprimerie Impériale, 1861–1917). That translation reviewed and corrected by Charles Pellat, 5 vols. (Paris: Société Asiatique, 1962, 1989, 1997).

Mubash'shar ibn Fātik. *Al-Hikam wa Mahāsin al-Kalām*. Ed. 'Abd al-Rahman Badawi as *Los bocados de oro (Mujtār al hikam)* (Madrid: Instituto Egipcio de Estu-dios Islámicos, 1958).

Muhāsibī. *Al-Qasd wa-al-Rujū' ilā Allāh*. Ed. 'Abd al-Qādir Ahmad 'Atā. Cairo: Dār al-Turāth al-'Arabī, 1980.

Muqaddasī. *Ahsan al-Taqāsīm fī Ma'rifat al-Aqālīm*. Ed. M. J. de Goeje. Leiden: Brill, 1906. Selections trans. André Miquel as *Ahsan al-Taqāsīm fī Ma'rifat al-Aqālīm: La meilleure répartition pour la connaissance des provinces* (Damascus: Institut Fran-çais de Damas, 1963). Trans. Basil Anthony Collins, reviewed by Muhammad Hamid al-Tai, as *The Best Divisions for Knowledge of the Regions* (Reading, UK: Garnet, 1994).

Muslim. *Al-Jāmi' al-Sahīh*. Ed. Fu'ād 'Abd al-Bāqī. 4 vols. Beirut, 1985. In English translation as *Sahih Muslim: Being Traditions of the Sayings and Doings of the Prophet Muhammad as Narrated by His Companions and Compiled under the Title al-Jami'-us-sahir*, 4 vols. (Beirut: Dār al Arabia, 1990–).

——. *al-Tabaqāt*. Ed. Abū 'Ubayda Mashūr ibn-Hasan Āl-Salmān. 2 vols. Riyadh: Dār al-Higra, 1991.

Nāsā'ī. *al-Sunan*. Ed. 'Abd'l-Fattāh Abū Ghadda. Beirut, 1986.

Nāsir-ī Khusrū. *Safar Nāmèh: Relation du voyage de Nassiri Khosrau en Syrie, en Palestine, en Egypte, en Arabie et en Perse pendant les années de l'Hégire 437–444 (1035–1042)*. Ed. and trans. Charles Henri August Schefer. Paris, 1881. Reprint, Frankfurt am Main: Institute for the History of Arab-Islamic Science, 1994. Ed. and trans. Wheeler M. Thackston as *Nasir-i Khusrav's Book of Travels* (Costa Mesa, CA: Mazda, 2001).

Nawawī. *Le Taqrīb de en-Nawawi*. Trans. William Marçais. Paris: Imprimerie Na-tionale, 1902.

Nuʿaym ibn Hammād. *Kitāb al-Fitan*. Ed. Suhayl Zakkār. Mecca: al-Maktabah al-Tijārīyah, 1991.

Qādirī, Ibrāhīm Hilmī. *Takdhīb al-Muddaʿī bi-Sihhat Rihlat al-Imām al-Shāfiʿī*. Alexandria, 1965.

Qālī, Abū ʿAlī. *Amālī*. 3 vols. Cairo: Dār al-Kutub al-Misrīyah, 1324 AH/1926. Reprint, Beirut: Dār al-Āfāq, 1980.

Qiftī. *Ibn al-Qiftī's Tārīkh al-hukamā*. Ed. Julius Lippert. Leipzig: Dieterisch'sche Verlagsbuchhandlung, 1903.

———. *Inbāh al-Ruwwāt*. Ed. Muhammad Abū al-Fadī Ibrāhīm. 3 vols. Cairo: al-Hayah al-Misrīya al-ʿĀmmah lil- Kutub, 1981.

Qushayrī. *Latāʾif al-Ishārāt*. Ed. Ibrāhīm al-Basyūnī. 2 vols. Cairo: Dār al-Kātib al-ʿArabī, 1981.

———. *al-Risālah*. Ed. Maʿrūf Zurayq and ʿAlī ʿAbd al-Hamīd Baltah'jī. Beirut: Dār al-Jīl, 1990. In English translation as *Al-Qushayri's Epistle on Sufism: Al risala al-qushayriyya fī ʿilm al-tasawwuf* (Reading, UK: Garnet, 2007).

Rabaʿī AbūʾlʿAlāʾ. *Kitāb al-Fusūs*. Ed. ʿAbdʾ al-Wahhāb al-Tāzī Suʿūd. 3 vols. Mouhammadia, Morocco, 1993.

Rabaʿī Abūʾl-Hasan. *Al-Muntaqā min Akhbār al-Asmaʿī*. Ed. Izzeddine al-Tanoukhi. Damascus: Ibn Zeydoun, 1936.

Rāzī, Fakhr al-Dīn. *Manāqib al-Imām al-Shāfʿī*. Ed. Ahmad Hijazī Ahmad Saqqa. Cairo: Maktabat al-Kulliyat al-Azharīyah, 1986.

Ruzbehān Baqlī. *Kashf al-Asrār*. Trans. Paul Ballanfat as *Le dévoilement des secrets et les apparitions des lumières* (Paris: Seuil, 1996).

Sāhib ibn ʿAbbād. *al-Rūznāmajah*. Ed. Muhammad Hasan Al-Yasīn. Baghdad: Dār al-Maʿārif, 1958.

Sahmī, Abū al-Qāsim. *Tārikh Jurjān*. Hyderabad: Matbaʿat Majlis Dairat, 1950.

Salafī, Abū Tāhir. *Al-Wajīz fī Dhikr al-Mujāz*. Ed. Muhammad Khayr al-Biqāʿī. Beirut: Dār al-Gharb al-Islāmī, 1991.

Sālih ibn Ahmad ibn Hanbal. *Sīrat al-Imām Ahmad ibn Hanbal*. 2 vols. Alexandria: Muʾassasat Shabāb al-Jāmiʿah, 1981.

Samʿānī. *Kitāb al-Ansāb*. Ed. ʿAbd al-Rahmān ibn Yahyā Muʿallimī. Hyderabad: Matbaʿat Majlis Dairat, 1962–.

Sarrāj, Abū Muhammad. *Masāriʿ al-ʿUshshāq*. 2 vols. Beirut: Dār Bayrūt lil Tibāʿah wa-al-Nashr, 1958.

Sarrāj, Abū Nasr. *The Kitāb al-Lumaʿ*. Ed. Reynold Alleyne Nicholson. 2 vols. Leiden: Brill; London: Luzac, 1914.

Sayrafī. *Akhbār al-Nahwīyīn al-Basriyīn*. Ed. Muhammad Ibrahim Bannā. Cairo: Dār al-iʿtisām, 1985.

Shadharāt min Kutub Mafqūdah. Ed. Ihsān ʿAbbās. Beirut: Dār al-Gharb al-Islāmī, 1988.

Shāfiʿī. *al-Dīwān*. Ed. Muhammad ʿAbd al-Munim Khafajī. Cairo: Maktabat al-Kulliyat al-Azharīyah, 1980.

————. *al-Musnad*. Cairo, 1888.

————. *al-Rihla*. Ed. Muhibb al-Dīn Khatīb. Cairo, 1250 AH. Republished as *Kitāb al-Safar* (Damascus, 1995).

————. *al-Risāla*. Trans. Lakhdar Souami as *La Risāla: Les fondements du droit musulman* (Paris: Actes Sud, 1997).

Shāsī, Abū Sa'īd. *al-Musnad*. Ed. Mahfūdh 'A. Zin-Allah. 3 vols. Medina, 1993.

Shaybānī. *Kitāb al-Siyar al-Kabīr*. Ed. Salāh al-Dīn al-Munajjid, with commentary by Muhammad ibn Ahmad al-Sarakhsī. 3 vols. Cairo: Ma'had al-Makhtūtāt bi-Jāmi'at al-Duwal al-Arabīyah, 1957–60.

Sijistānī, Abū Sulaymān. *Siwān al-Hikmah*. Ed. 'Abd al-Rahman Badawi. Teheran: Bunyad'i Farhang'i Iran, 1974.

Subkī. *Tabaqāt al-Shāfi'iyyah*. Ed. Mahmūd Muhammad al-Tanāhī Al-Tānjī and Abd al-Fattāh Muhammad Al-Hilw. 4 vols. Cairo: 'Isā al-Bābī al-Halabī, 1964.

Suhrāb. *Kitāb 'Ajā'ib al-Aqālīm*. Ed. Hans von Mzik. Leipzig, 1876; reprint, Leipzig: Harrassowitz, 1930.

Sulami. *Risālat al-Malāmatiyya*. Trans. Roger Deladrière as *La lucidité implacable: Épître des hommes du blâme* (Paris: Actes Sud, 1991).

————. *Tabaqāt al-Sūfiyah*. Ed. Nūr al-Dīn Shuraybah. Cairo: Dār al-Kitāb al-'Arabī, 1953.

Suyūtī. *Bughyat al-Wu'āt fī Tabaqāt al-Lughawīyīn*. Ed. Muhammad Abū Ibrāhīm. 2 vols. Cairo: Matba'at 'Isā al-Bābī al-Halabī, 1964–65.

————. *Al-Itqān fī 'Ulūm al-Qur'ān*. 2 vols. Cairo: Matba'at al-Ma'ahid, 1935.

————. *Tadrīb al-rāwī*. 2 vols. Cairo: al Matba'ah al-Khayryah, 1307 AH/1889.

————. *Al-Muzhir fī 'Ulūm al-lugha*. 2 vols. Cairo, 1325 AH.

Tabarānī, Abū'l-Qāsim. *Al-Mu'jam al-Saghīr*. Preceded by *Juz' fihi Dhikr Abā al-Qāsim . . . al-Tabarānī*, by Ibn Manda. Ed. Kamāl Yūsuf Hūt. Beirut: Muassasat al-Rayyan, 1986, 2001.

Tabarsī, Abū Nasr. *Makārim al-Akhlāq*. Beirut: Muassasat al-A'lamī, 1972.

Tanūkhī. *Nishwār al-Muhādarāh*. Selections trans. Youssef Seddik as *Brins de chicane: La vie quotidienne à Bagdad au Xe siècle* (Arles: Actes Sud-Sindbad, 1999).

Tarsūsī 'Uthmān ibn 'Abd 'Allah. *Kitāb Siyar al-Thughūr*. Ed. Ihsān 'Abbās. In *Shadharāt min Kutub Mafqūdah*. Beirut: Dār al-Gharb al-Islāmī, 1988.

Tawhīdī. *Kitāb al-Imtā' wa-al-Mu'ānasa*. Ed. Ahmad Amīn and Ahmad Zayn. 2 vols. Cairo: Matba'at Lajnat al-ta'līf, 1958.

Tha'ālibī. *Al-Tamthīl wa al-Muhādarah*. Ed. 'Abd al-Fattāh Muhammad Hulw. Tunis: al-Dār al-'Arabīyah lil-Kitāb, 1983.

————. *Thimār al-Qulūb*. Ed. Muhammad Abū al-Fadī Ibrāhīm. Cairo: Dār Nahdat Misr Lil-tab' wa al-Nashr, 1965.

Tirmidhī. *al-Jāmi' al-Sahīh*. Ed. Muhammad ibn 'Abd Allāh ibn al-'Arabī. 13 vols. in 5 pts. Al-Azhar: al-Matba'ah al-Misrīyah, 1931–34.

Tustarī. *Tafsīr al-Qur'ān al-'adhīm*. Misr: Matba'at al-Sa'ādah, 1329 AH/1908.

'Ubayd-Allāh al-Bakrī. *Kitāb al-Mughrib fī Dhikr Bilāb Ifrīqiya wa'l-Maghrib*. Ed. and trans. William MacGuckin, baron de Slane, as *Description de l'Afrique septentrio-nale* (1859; 2nd ed., Alger, 1911, 1913).

'Uqaylī, Abū Jaʿfar. *Kitāb al-Duʿafā al-kabīr*. Ed. ʿAbd al-Muʿtī Amin Qalʿajī. 4 vols. Beirut: Dār al-Kutub al-Ilmīyah, 1984.

Wakīʿ ibn al-Jarrāh. *Kitāb al-Zuhd*. Ed. ʿAbd al-Rahmān ʿAbd al-Jabbār al-Faryawāʾī. Medina: Maktabat al-Dār, 1984.

Wasīf Shāh. *Mukhtasar ʿAjāʾib al-dunyā*. Trans. Bernard, baron Carra de Vaux, in *Abrégé des merveilles* (Paris: Klincksieck, 1898).

Yaʿqūbī. *Kitāb al-Buldān*. Trans. Gaston Wiet as *Les pays* (Cairo, 1937).

Yāqūt. *Irshād al-Arīb ilā Maʿrifat al-Adīb (Muʿjam al-Udabā)*. Ed. David Samuel Margoliouth. 1913–29. Ed. Ihsān ʿAbbās, 7 vols. (Beirut: Dār al-Gharb al-Islāmī, 1993). In English translation as *The Irshad al-arib ilá maʿrifat al-adib; or, Dictionary of Learned Men of Yáqút*, 2nd ed., ed. D. S. Margoliouth, 5 vols. London: Luzac, 1923–31.

———. *Muʿjam al-Buldān*. Ed. Ferdinand Wüstenfeld. 7 vols. Leipzig, 1855–73. Reprint, 6 vols. in 11 pts., Frankfurt: Institute for the History of Arabic-Islamic Science, 1994.

Zubaydī. *Tabaqāt al-Nahwiyyīn*. Ed. Muhammad Abū al-Fadī Ibrāhīm. Cairo: Muhammad Samī Amīn al-Khanjī al-Kutubī, 1954.

Published Works

ʿAbbās, Ihsān. "Rihlat Ibn al-ʿArabī ilāʾl-Mashriq kamā Sawwarahā ʿQānūn al-Taʾwīl." *Abhāt* 21 (1968): 59–91.

Abbott, Nabia. *Language and Literature*. Vol. 3 of *Studies in Arabic Literary Papyri*. Chicago: University of Chicago Press, 1957–72.

———. *Qurʾanic Commentary and Tradition*. Vol. 2 of *Studies in Arabic Literary Papyri*. Chicago: University of Chicago Press, 1957–72.

Adams, Percy G. *Travel Literature and the Evolution of the Novel*. Lexington: University Press of Kentucky, 1983.

Addas, Claude. *Ibn ʿArabī, ou, La quête du soufre rouge*. Paris: Gallimard, 1989. Trans. Peter Kingsley as *Quest for the Red Sulphur: The Life of Ibn ʿArabī* (Cambridge: Islamic Texts Society, 1993).

Aigle, Denise. *Saints orientaux*. Paris: Boccard, 1995.

Amir-Moezzi, Mohammad Alī. "Remarques sur les critères de l'authenticité du *hadīth* et l'autorité du juriste dans le chiʾisme imamite." *Studia Islamica* 85 (1997): 5–40.

———, ed. *Le voyage initiatique en terre d'Islam*. Louvain: Peeters, 1996.

Anastase, Père. "Un document islamique sur le monachisme au IXe siècle." *Mashriq* 12 (1908): 883–92.

Aʿrāb, Saʿīd. *Maʿa al-Qādī Abī Bakr ibn al-ʿArabī*. Beirut: Dār al-Gharb al-Islami, 1987.

Aristotle. *De generatione et corruptione*. Trans. Charles Mugler as *De la génération et de la corruption* (Paris: Belles Lettres, 1961). Trans. C. J. F. Williams as *Aristotle's De generatione et corruptione* (Oxford: Clarendon Press; New York: Oxford University Press, 1982).

———. *On the Generation of Animals*. Trans. A. L. Peck. Loeb Classical Library. London: William Heinemann; Cambridge, MA: Harvard University Press, 1943. Trans. Pierre Louis as *De la génération des animaux* (Paris: Belles Lettres, 1966).

Arkoun, Mohammed. *La pensée arabe*. Paris: Presses Universitaires de France, 1975.

Arkoun, Mohammed, et al., eds. *L'étrange et le merveilleux dans l'Islam médiéval*. Actes du colloque tenu au Collège de France. Paris: Éditions J. A., 1978.

Asín Palacios, Miguel. *Logia et agrapha Domini Jesu apud moslamicos scriptores asceticos praesertim usitata*. 2 vols. Paris: Firmin Didot, 1916–29.

Athanasius of Alexandria. *The Life of Antony*. Trans. Tim Vivian and Apostolos N. Athanassakis with Rowan A. Greer. Kalamazoo: Cistercian Publications, 2003. Trans. Benoît Lavaud as *Vie et conduite de notre père Saint Antoine* (Bégrolles en Mauges: Abbaye de Bellefontaine, 1979).

Atkinson, Geoffrey. *Les nouveaux horizons de la Renaissance française*. Paris: Droz, 1935. Reprint, Geneva: Slatkine, 1969.

Augé, Marc. *L'impossible voyage: Le tourisme et ses images*. Paris: Payot & Rivages, 1997.

———. "Voyage et ethnobiographie: La vie comme récit. *L'homme* 151 (1999): 11–19.

Aujac, Germaine. *Claude Ptolémée, astronome, astrologue, géographe: Connaissance et représentation du monde habité*. Paris: CTHS, 1993, 1997.

———. *Strabon et la science de son temps*. Paris: Belles Lettres, 1966.

A'zamī, Muhammad Mustafá. *Studies in Early Hadīth Literature* [in Arabic]. Beirut, 1968.

Azari, A., and H. Ben Shammay. "Risāla." In *Encyclopédie de l'Islam*, new ed., 8:549–57. Leiden: E. J. Brill; Paris: Maisonneuve et Larose, 1966. In English translation in *The Encyclopaedia of Islam*, new ed., ed. E. J. Van Donzel (Leiden: Brill, 1966), 8:532ff.

Bacon, Francis. *The Essayes; or, Counsels, Civill and Morall*. 1625. Trans. Antoine de La Salle as *Essais de morale et de politique* (1836; Paris: L'Arche, 1999).

Badawī, 'Abd al-Rahmān. *Shatahāt al-Sūfiyya*. Vol. 1, *Abū Yazīd Bistamī*. Trans. Abdelwahab Meddeb as *Les dits de Bistamī* (Paris: Fayard, 1989).

Baldick, Julian. "The Legend of Rābi'a of Basra: Christian Antecedents, Muslim Counterparts." *Religion* 20 (1990): 233–47.

Beaumont, M. D. "Hard-Boiled: Narrative Discourse in Early Muslim Traditions." *Studia Islamica* 83 (1996): 5–32.

Bencheikh, Jamel-Eddine. *Poétique arabe: Essai sur les voies d'une création*. Paris: Anthropos, 1975.

Benveniste, Émile. *Le vocabulaire des institutions indo-européennes*. 2 vols. Paris: Minuit, 1969. Trans. Elizabeth Palmer as *Indo-European Language and Society* (London: Faber, 1973).

Berkey, Jonathan. *The Transmission of Knowledge in Medieval Cairo: A Social History of Islamic Education*. Princeton: Princeton University Press, 1992.

Bertaud, E. "Guides sprirituels." In *Dictionnaire de spiritualité*, 6:1154–70. Paris: Beauchesne, 1932, 1960.

Bertaud, E., and A. Rayez. "Échelle spirituelle." In *Dictionnaire de spiritualité*, 17 vols., 4:62–86. Paris: Beauchesne, 1932, 1960.

Bickerman, E. "La chaîne de la tradition pharisienne." *Revue biblique* 59 (1952): 44–54.

Blachère, Régis. *Analecta*. Damascus: Institut Français de Damas, 1975.

———. *Extraits des principaux géographes arabes au Moyen Âge*. Paris: Geuthner, 1932; 2nd ed., Paris: Klinckseick, 1957.

———. *Histoire de la littérature arabe des origines à la fin du XVe siècle*. 3 vols. Paris: Maisonneuve, 1964, 1966, 1984.

———. *Introduction au Coran*. 1947. Paris: Maisonneuve et Larose, 1977, 2002.

———. "Les savants irakiens et leurs informateurs bédouins aux IIIe–IVe siècles de l'Hégire." In *Mélanges offerts à William Marçais*, 37–53 Paris: Maisonneuve, 1950.

Bonner, Michael David. *Aristocratic Violence and Holy War: Studies in the Jihad and the Arab-Byzantine Frontier*. New Haven: American Oriental Society, 1996.

———. "The Naming of the Frontier: 'Awāsim, Thughūr, and the Arab Geographers." *Bulletin of the School of Oriental and African Studies* 57, no. 1 (1994): 17–24.

———. "Some Observations Concerning the Early Development of Jihad on the Arab-Byzantine Frontier." *Studia Islamica* 75 (1992): 5–31.

Bosworth, C. E. "Karrāmiyya." In *Encyclopédie de l'Islam*, new ed., 4:694a. Leiden: E. J. Brill; Paris: Maisonneuve et Larose, 1966.

Bourgey, Louis. *Observation et expérience chez Aristote*. Paris: Vrin, 1955.

Brown, Peter. *The Body and Society: Man, Woman, and Sexual Renunciation in Early Christianity*. New York: Columbia University Press, 1988. In French translation as *Le renoncement à la chair: Virginité, célibat et continence dans le christianisme primitif* (Paris: Gallimard, 1995).

Cahen, C., and C. Pellat. "Ibn Abbād." In *Encyclopédie de l'Islam*, new ed., 3:692–94. Leiden: E. J. Brill; Paris: Maisonneuve et Larose, 1966. In English translation in *The Encyclopaedia of Islam*, new ed., ed. E. J. Van Donzel (Leiden: Brill, 1966), 3:708ff.

Carruthers, Mary J. *The Book of Memory: A Study of Memory in Medieval Culture*. Cambridge: Cambridge University Press, 1990.

Caspart, R. "Rābi'a et le pur amour." *IBLA*, 1968,71–95.

Cassou, Jean. "Du voyage au tourisme." *Communications* 10 (1967): 25–34.

Céard, Jean, and Jean-Claude Margolin, eds. *Voyager à la Renaissance*. Actes du colloque de Tours, 1983. Paris: Maisonneuve et Larose, 1987.

Certeau, Michel de. *L'écriture de l'histoire*. Paris: Gallimard, 1975. Trans. Tom Conley as *The Writing of History* (New York: Columbia University Press, 1988).

Chabbi, Jacqueline. "Remarques sur le développement historique des mouvements ascétiques et mystiques au Khurāsān." *Studia Islamica* 46 (1977): 5–72.

———. "Ribāt." In *Encyclopédie de l'Islam*, new ed., 8:510–15. Leiden: E. J. Brill; Paris: Maisonneuve et Larose, 1966. In English translation in *The Encyclopaedia of Islam*, new ed., ed. E. J. Van Donzel (Leiden: Brill, 1966), 8:493–506.

Chamberlain, Michael. *Knowledge and Social Practice in Medieval Damascus (1190–1350)*. Cambridge: Cambridge University Press, 1994.

Charles-Dominique, Paule. *Voyageurs arabes: Ibn Fadlān, Ibn Jubayr, Ibn Battūta et un auteur anonyme*. Paris: Gallimard, 1995.

Chavannes, Edouard, ed. *Les voyageurs chinois*. Paris: Comité de l'Asie Française, 1904.

Chesneau, Jean. *L'art du voyage: Un regard (plutôt . . .) politique sur l'autre et l'ailleurs*. Paris: Bayard, 1999.

Chodkiewicz, Michel. *Le sceau des saints: Prophétie et sainteté dans la doctrine d'Ibn 'Arabī*. Paris: Gallimard, 1986.

Chupeau, Jacques. "Les récits de voyage aux lisières du roman français du XVIIe siècle." *Revue d'histoire littéraire de France* 3–4 (May–August 1977): 536–53.

Clifford, James. *Routes: Travel and Translation in the Late Twentieth Century*. Cambridge, MA: Harvard University Press, 1997.

Cook, Michael. *Early Muslim Dogma: A Source-Critical Study*. Cambridge: Cambridge University Press, 1981.

Crone, Patricia. *Slaves on Horses: The Evolution of the Islamic Polity*. Cambridge: Cambridge University Press, 1980.

Daqr, 'Abd al-Ghani. *Al-Imām al-Shāfi'ī*. Damascus: Dār al-Qalam, 1972, 1987.

De Jong, Frederick, and Colin H. Imber. "Malāmatiyya." In *Encyclopédie de l'Islam*, new ed., 4:217–22. Leiden: E. J. Brill; Paris: Maisonneuve et Larose, 1966. In English translation in *The Encyclopaedia of Islam*, new ed., ed. E. J. Van Donzel (Leiden: Brill, 1966), 6:223ff.

De la Puente, Carlos. "Vivre et mourir pour Dieu: Oeuvre et héritage d'Abū 'Alī al-Sadafī (m. 514/1120)." *Studia Islamica* 88 (1998): 77–102.

Déroche, François. "À propos du manuscrit 'Arabe 6726 BN, Paris (Al-Asma'ī, *Tārīkh Mulūk al-'Arab al-Awwalīn*).'" *Revue d'études islamiques* 58 (1990): 209–12.

Detienne, Marcel. *L'invention de la mythologie*. Paris: Gallimard, 1981, 1992. Trans. Margaret Cook as *The Creation of Mythology* (Chicago: University of Chicago Press, 1986).

———. "La leçon d'histoire." In his *Dionysos mis à mort*, 51–65. Paris: Gallimard, 1977. Trans. Mireille Muellner and Leonard Muellner as *Dionysos Slain* (Baltimore: Johns Hopkins University Press, 1979).

Djaït, Hichem. *La grande discorde: Religion et politique dans l'Islam des origines*. Paris: Gallimard, 1989.

———. *Al-Kūfa: Naissance de la ville islamique*. Paris: Maisonneuve et Larose, 1986.

Doiron, Norman. *L'art de voyager: Le déplacement à l'époque classique*. Sainte-Foy, Quebec: Presses de l'Université de Laval, 1995.

Douglas, Mary. *Purity and Danger: An Analysis of Concepts of Pollution and Taboo*. New York: Praeger, 1966. New York: Routledge, 2005. Trans. Anne Guérin as *De la souillure: Essais sur les notions de pollution et de tabou* (Paris: Maspero, 1971).

Dubler, C. E. "Adjā'ib." In *Encyclopédie de l'Islam*, new ed., 1:209–10. Leiden: E. J. Brill; Paris: Maisonneuve et Larose, 1966. In English translation in *The Encyclopaedia of Islam*, new ed., ed. E. J. Van Donzel (Leiden: Brill, 1966), 1:203–4.

Dunn, Ross E. *The Adventures of Ibn Battūta, a Muslim Traveler of the 14th Century*. Berkeley: University of California Press, 1986.

Dupront, Alphonse. "Espace et humanisme." *Bibliothèque d'humanisme et Renaissance* 8 (1946): 7–104.

Eche, Youssef. *Les bibliothèques arabes publiques et semi-publiques en Mésopotamie, en Syrie et en Égypte au Moyen Âge*. Damascus: Institut Français de Damas, 1967.

Eickelman, Dale F. "The Art of Memory: Islamic Education and Its Social Reproduction." *Comparative Studies in Society and History* 20 (1978): 485–516.

Eickelman, Dale F., and James Piscatori, eds. *Muslim Travellers: Pilgrims, Migration, and the Religious Imagination*. Berkeley: University of California Press, 1990.

Encyclopédie de l'Islam. New ed. Leiden: E. J. Brill; Paris: Maisonneuve et Larose, 1966. In English translation as *The Encyclopaedia of Islam*, new ed., ed. E. J. Van Donzel (Leiden: Brill, 1966).

Enderwitz, Susanne. "Du *Fatā* au *Zarīf*, ou comment on se distingue?" *Arabica* 36, no. 2 (1989): 125–42.

Fakhrī, M. "Al-Kindī wa Suqrāt." *Al-Abhāth: The Quarterly Journal of the American University of Beirut*, 1963: 23–34.

Fayyād, 'Abd Allāh. *Al-Ijāzat al-'Ilmīyah 'inda al-Muslimīn*. Baghdad: Matba'at al-Irshād, 1967.

Ferrand, Gabriel, ed. and trans. *Relations de voyages et textes géographiques arabes, persans et turks relatifs à l'Extrême-Orient, du VIIIe au XVIIIe siècles*. 2 vols. Paris: Leroux, 1913–14. Reprint, Frankfurt: Sezgin, 1996.

Foucault, Michel. *Les mots et les choses: Une archéologie des sciences humaines*. Paris: Gallimard, 1966. In English translation as *The Order of Things: An Archaeology of the Human Sciences*. London: Tavistock, 1970. Reprint, New York: Vintage, 1994.

Fück, Johann. *Arabiya: Untersuchungen zur arabischen Sprach- und Stilgeschichte*. Berlin: Akademie-Verlag, 1950. Trans. Claude Denizeau as *'Arabīya: Recherches sur l'histoire de la langue et du style arabe* (Paris: Didier, 1955).

Geertz, Clifford, Hildred Geertz, and Lawrence Rosen. *Meaning and Order in Moroccan Society: Three Essays in Cultural Analysis*. Cambridge: Cambridge University Press, 1979.

Gentili, Bruno, and Giovanni Carri. "Written and Oral Communication in Greek Historigraphical Thought." In *Communication Arts in the Ancient World*, ed. Eric A. Havelock and Jackson P. Hershbell, 137–55. New York: Hastings House, 1978.

Gervase of Tilbury. *Le livre des merveilles: Divertissement pour un empereur*. Trans. Annie Duchesne. Paris: Belles Lettres, 1992.

Gilliot, Claude. *Exégèse, langue et théologie en Islam: L'exégèse coranique de Tabarī.* Paris: Vrin, 1990.

———. "La formation intellectuelle de Tabarī." *Journal asiatique* 276, nos. 3–4 (1988): 203–44.

Goldziher, Ignaz. *Abhandlungen zur arabischen Philologie.* 2 vols. Leiden: Brill, 1899.

———. *Muhammedanische Studien.* 2 vols. Halle: Niemeyer, 1889–90. Selections from vol. 2 trans. Léon Bercher as *Études sur la tradition islamique: Extraits du tome II des Muhammadanische Studien* (Paris: Adrien-Maisonneuve, 1952). Trans. C. R. Barber and S. M. Stern as *Muslim Studies: Muhammedanische Studien*, 2 vols. (London: George Allen & Unwin, 1967).

———. *Vorlesungen über den Islam.* 1910. Trans. Félix Arin as *Le dogme et la loi de l'Islam: Histoire du développement dogmatique et juridique de la religion musulmane* (Paris: Geuthner, 1958, 1973). Trans. Andras and Ruth Hamori as *Introduction to Islamic Theology and Law* (Princeton: Princeton University Press, 1981).

Goody, Jack. *The Domestication of the Savage Mind.* Cambridge: Cambridge University Press, 1977. Trans. Jean Bazin and Alban Bensa as *La raison graphique: La domestication de la pensée sauvage* (Paris: Minuit, 1979).

———. *The Interface between the Written and the Oral.* Cambridge: Cambridge University Press, 1987. Trans. Denise Paulme as *Entre l'oralité et l'écriture* (Paris: Presses Universitaires de France, 1994).

Grabar, Oleg. *The Formation of Islamic Art.* New Haven: Yale University Press, 1973, 1987. Trans. Yves Thoraval as *La formation de l'art islamique* (Paris: Flammarion, 1987).

Graboïs, Aryeh. *Le pèlerin occidental en Terre sainte au Moyen Âge.* Brussels: De Boeck Université, 1998.

Guichard, Pierre. *Les musulmans de Valence et la Reconquête (XIe–XIIIe siècle).* 2 vols. Damascus: Institut Français de Damas, 1990.

Guillaumont, Antoine. "La conception du désert chez les moines d'Égypte." *Revue de l'histoire des religions* 188 (1975): 3–21.

Hadj-Sadok, Mahammed. "Le genre 'Riḥ'la.'" *Bulletin des études arabes* 40 (1948): 196–206.

Haffner, Auguste, and Louis Cheiko, eds. *Dix anciens traités de philologie arabe.* Beirut: Imprimerie Catholique, 1914.

Hafid-Martin, Nicole. *Voyage et connaissance au tournant des Lumières (1780–1820).* Oxford: Voltaire Foundation, 1995.

Halm, Heinz. *Reich des Mahdi.* Trans. Michael Bonner as *The Empire of the Mahdi: The Rise of the Fatimids* (New York: Brill, 1996).

Harder, Hermann. *Le président de Brosses et le voyage en Italie au dix-huitième siècle.* Geneva: Slatkine, 1981.

Hartog, François. "Histoire." In *Vocabulaire européen des philosophies: Dictionnaire des intraduisibles*, by Barbara Cassin. Paris: Le Robert, Seuil, 2004.

———. *Mémoire d'Ulysse: Récits sur la frontière en Grèce ancienne.* Paris: Gallimard, 1996.

————. *Le miroir d'Hérodote: Essai sur la représentation de l'autre*. Paris: Gallimard, 1980.

————. "Premières figures de l'historien en Grèce: Historicité et histoire." In *Figures de l'intellectuel en Grèce ancienne*, ed. Nicole Loraux and Charles Mirallès, 123–42. Paris: Balin, 1998.

Hārūn, 'Abd al-Salām Muhammad. *Nawādir al-Makhtūtāt*. 2 vols. Misr: Mustafá al-Babi al-Halabi, 1973–75.

Hāshim Jamīl 'Abd-Allah. *Fiqh al-Imām Sa'īd ibn al-Musayyab*. 4 vols. Baghdad: Jumhurīyah al-'Irāqīyah, 1974–75.

al-Hāshimī, al-Sayyid Ahmad, ed. *Jawāhir al-Adab*. 2 vols. Cairo, 1923.

Hinds, Martin. "al-Maghāzī." In *Encyclopédie de l'Islam*, new ed., 8:549–57. Leiden: E. J. Brill; Paris: Maisonneuve et Larose, 1966. In English translation in *The Encyclopaedia of Islam*, new ed., ed. E. J. Van Donzel (Leiden: Brill, 1966), 3:1161ff.

————. "'Maghāzī' and 'Sīra' in Early Islamic Scholarship. "In *La vie du prophète Mahomet*, Colloque de Strasbourg, 57–66. Paris: Presses Universitaires de France, 1983.

Hobsbawm, Eric, and Terence Ranger, eds. *The Invention of Tradition*. Cambridge: Cambridge University Press, 1983, 1992.

Hodgson, Marshall G. S. *The Venture of Islam: Conscience and History in a World Civilization*. 3 vols. Chicago: University of Chicago Press, 1974.

Homer. *The Odyssey*. Trans. Leconte de Lisle as *L'Odyssée* (Paris: Librarie des Amateurs, 1931). Trans. A. T. Murray, 2 vols., Loeb Classical Library (Cambridge).

Hurvitz, Nimrod. "Ahmad b. Hanbal and the Formation of Islamic Orthodoxy." Ph.D. dissertation, Princeton University, 1994.

————. "Biographies and Mild Asceticism." *Studia Islamica* 85 (1997): 41–66.

Ibn Daud, Abraham. *Sefer Ha-Qabbalah: The Book of Tradition*. Trans. Gerson D. Cohen. Philadelphia: Jewish Publication Society of America, 1967.

Izeddin, Mehmed, and Paul Therriat. "Un prisonnier arabe à Byzance au IXe siècle: Haroun ibn Yahiā." *Revue des études islamiques* 15 (1941–47): 41–62. Reprinted in the series Islamic Geography, ed. Fuat Sezgin, no. 166 (Frankfurt, 1994), 149–70.

Jacob, Christian. *L'empire des cartes: Approche théorique de la cartographie à travers l'histoire*. Paris: Albin Michel, 1992. Trans. Tom Conley as *The Sovereign Map: Theoretical Approaches in Cartography through History*, ed. Edward H. Dahl (Chicago: University of Chicago Press, 2006).

Juynboll, G. H. A. "The Date of Great Fitna." *Arabica* 20 (1973): 142–59.

————. *Muslim Tradition: Studies in Chronology, Provenance and Authorship of Early Hadīth*. Cambridge: Cambridge University Press, 1983.

————. "Some Notes on Islam's First *Fuqahā*, Distilled from Early *Hadīth* Literature." *Arabica* 39 (1992): 287–314.

————. *Studies on the Origins and Uses of Islamic Hadīth*. Brookfield, VT: Variorum, 1996.

————. "Sunna." In *Encyclopédie de l'Islam*, new ed., 9:897–99. Leiden: E. J. Brill;

Paris: Maisonneuve et Larose, 1966. In English translation in *The Encyclopaedia of Islam*, new ed., ed. E. J. Van Donzel (Leiden: Brill, 1966), 9:878.

Kawtharī, Muhammad Zāhid ibn al-Hasan. *Bulūgh al-Amānī fī Sīrat al-Imām . . . al-Shaybānī*. Madīnat al-Nasr: Maktabat Dār al-Hidayah, 1980–88.

Khoury, Raif Georges. *'Abd-Allāh ibn Lahī'a, 97–174/715–790: Juge et grand maître de l'école égyptienne*. Wiesbaden: Harrassowitz, 1986.

Kilito, Abdel Fattah. *Les séances: Récits et codes culturels chez Hamadhānī et Harīrī*. Paris: Sindbad, 1983.

Kister, M. J. *Society and Religion from Jāhiliyya to Islam*. Brookfield, VT: Variorum, 1990.

Krachkovski, Ignatii Iulianovich. *Arabskaïa geografitcheskaïa literatura*. Moscow, 1957. Trans. Sālih al-Dīn 'U. Hāshim as *Tārīkh al-Adab al-Jughrāfī*, 3 vols. (Beirut: Dār al-Gharb al-Lubnani, 1987).

Kramers, J. H. "La question Balhī-Istarī-Ibn Hawkal et l'*Atlas de l'Islam*." *Analecta Orientalia* 10 (1932): 9–30. Reprinted in the series Islamic Geography, ed. Fuat Sezgin, no. 31 (1992), 326–47.

Ladeuze, Paulin. *Étude sur le cénobitisme pakhomien pendant le IVe siècle et la première moitié du Ve*. Paris: Fontemoing; Louvain: Van Linthout, 1898.

Laffranque, Marie. "L'oeil et l'oreille: Polybe et les problèmes de l'information en histoire à l'époque hellénistique." *Revue philosophique* 158 (1968): 263–72.

———. "La vue et l'ouïe: Expérience, observation et utilisation des témoignages à l'époque hellénistique." *Revue philosophique* 153 (1963): 75–82.

Lagardère, Vincent. *Les Almoravides: Le Djihād andalou (1106–1143)*. Paris: L'Harmattan, 1998.

Laoust, Henri. *Les schismes dans l'Islam: Introduction à une étude de la religion musulmane*. Paris: Fayot, 1965, 1977.

Latham, J. D. "The Beginning of Arabic Prose: The Epistolary Genre." In *The Cambridge History of Arabic Literature*, ed. A. F. L. Beeston et al., 4 vols., 1:154–79. Cambridge: Cambridge University Press, 1983.

Le Goff, Jacques. *Les intellectuels au Moyen Âge*. 1955. Paris: Seuil, 1985. Trans. Teresa Lavender Fagan as *Intellectuals in the Middle Ages* (Cambridge, MA: Blackwell, 1993).

———. *Pour un autre Moyen Âge: Temps, travail et culture en Occident*. Paris: Gallimard, 1977, 2004. Trans. Arthur Goldhammer as *Time, Work and Culture in the Middle Ages* (Chicago: University of Chicago Press, 1980).

Lestringant, Frank. *L'atelier du cosmographe ou l'Image du monde à la Renaissance*. Paris: Albin Michel, 1991. Trans. David Fausett as *Mapping the Renaissance World: The Geographical Imagination in the Age of Discovery* (Berkeley: University of California Press, 1994).

———. *Le huguenot et le sauvage*. Paris: Aux Amateurs de Livres, 1990. Geneva: Droz, 2004.

Lévi-Strauss, Claude. *Tristes tropiques*. Paris: Plon, 1955. Trans. John and Doreen Weightman as *Tristes Tropiques* (New York: Atheneum, 1974).

Levtzion, Nehemia. "Ibn Hawqal, the Cheque and Awdaghost." *Journal of African History* 9 (1968): 223–33.

Libera, Alain de. *Penser au Moyen Âge*. Paris: Seuil, 1991.

Loraux, Nicole, and Carlos Mirallès, eds. *Figures de l'intellectuel en Grèce ancienne*. Paris: Belin, 1998.

Loucel, Henri, and André Miquel, eds. *Lumières arabes sur l'Occident médiéval*. Actes du colloque "Civilisations arabes et Européenne: Deux cultures complimentaires." Paris: Anthropos, 1978.

Makdisi, Georges. *The Rise of Colleges: Institutions of Learning in Islam and the West*. Edinburgh: Edinburgh University Press, 1981.

———. "*Suhba* et *riyāsa* dans l'enseignement médiéval." In *Recherches d'islamologie*, 207–22. Louvain: Peeters, 1977.

Makhzūmī, Mahdī. *Al-Khalīl Ibn Ahmad al-Farahdi: A'māluhu wa Manhajahu*. Baghdad: Wizarat al-Maʿarif, 1960.

———. *Madrasat al-Kūfa wa Manhajuhā fī Dirāsāt al-Lughah wa'l-Nahw*. Baghdad: Matbaʿat Dār al-Maʿrifah, 1374 AH/1955.

Malinowski, Bronislaw. *Diary in the Strict Sense of the Term*. London: Routledge, 1967, 2004. Trans. Tina Jolas as *Journal d'ethnographe* (Paris: Seuil, 1985).

Maraval, Pierre, ed. *Récits des premiers pèlerins chrétiens au Proche-Orient (IVe–VIIe siècle)*. Paris: Cerf, 1996.

Marçais, Georges. "Note sur les ribats en berbérie." In *Mélanges d'histoire et d'archéologie de l'Occident musulman*, 2 vols., 1:23–36. Alger: Imprimerie Officiel du Gouvernement Général de l'Algérie, 1957.

Marin, Manuela. "*Rihla* e biografias de Ibn al-Qallās (m. 337/948)." In *Homenaje al Professor José Maria Forneas Besteiro*, 581–91. Granada, 1994.

Massignon, Louis. *Essai sur les origines du lexique technique de la mystique musulmane*. Paris: Geuthner, 1922. Paris: Vrin, 1968. Trans. Benjamin Clark as *Essay on the Origins of the Technical Language of Islamic Mysticism* (Notre Dame: University of Notre Dame Press, 1997).

———. *Opera minora*. Ed. Youkim Moubarac. Paris: Presses Universitaires de France, 1969.

———. *La passion de Husayn ibn Mansūr Hallāj, martyr mystique de l'Islam*. 3 vols. Paris: Gallimard, 1975. Trans Herbert Mason as *The Passion of al-Hallāj: Mystic and Martyr of Islam*, 4 vols. (Princeton: Princeton University Press, 1982).

Meinardus, Otto F. A. *Monks and Monasteries of the Egyptian Deserts*. Cairo: American University in Cairo Press, 1961, 1989.

M'Ghirbi, Salah. *Les voyageurs de l'Occident musulman du XIIe au XIVe siècles*. Tunis: Université des lettres, des arts et des sciences humaines, 1996.

Micheau, Françoise. "Les guerres arabo-byzantines vues par Yahya d'Antioche, chroniqueur arabe melkite du Ve / XIe siècle." In *Eupsychia: Mélanges offerts à*

Hélène Ahrweiler, 2 vols, Byzantina Sorbonensia, 2:541–55. Paris: Publications de la Sorbonne, 1998.

———. "Les sources pour les mégapoles orientales." In *Mégapoles méditerranéennes: Géographie urbaine retrospective*, actes du colloque, ed. Claude Nicolet, Robert Ilert, and Charles-Louis Depaule, 685–704. Rome: École Française de Rome, 2000.

Miller, Konrad. *Mappae Arabicae, Arabische Welt- und Länderkarten des 9.–13. Jahrhunderts*. 4 vols. Stuttgart, 1926–30.

Miller, Susan Gilson, ed. and trans. *Disorienting Encounters: Travels of a Moroccan Scholar in France in 1845–1846: The Voyage of Muhammad as-Saffār*. Berkeley: University of California Press, 1992.

Miquel, André. "L'Europe occidentale dans la relation arabe d'Ibrāhīm b. Ya'qūb (Xe s.)." *Annales (Économie, Sociétés et Civilisation)* 5 (1966): 1048–64.

———. *La géographie humaine du monde musulman jusqu'au milieu du 11e siècle*. 4 vols. Paris: Mouton, 1967–75.

———. "Ibn Battūta." In *Encyclopédie de l'Islam*, new ed., 3:758–59. Leiden: E. J. Brill; Paris: Maisonneuve et Larose, 1966. In English translation in *The Encyclopaedia of Islam*, new ed., ed. E. J. Van Donzel (Leiden: Brill, 1966), 3:735–36.

———. "Ibn al-Djuzayy." In *Encyclopédie de l'Islam*, new ed., 3:779. Leiden: E. J. Brill; Paris: Maisonneuve et Larose, 1966. In English translation in *The Encyclopaedia of Islam*, new ed., ed. E. J. Van Donzel (Leiden: Brill, 1966), 3:756.

Molina, Luis. "Lugares de destino de los viajeros andalusies en *Tārīj* de Ibn al-Faradī." In *Estudios Onomastico-Biograficos de al-Andalus*, 7 vols., 1:595–610. Madrid: Consejo Superior de Investigaciones Cientificas, 1988.

Momigliano, Arnaldo. *Problèmes d'historiographie ancienne et moderne*. Trans. Alain Tachet et al. Paris: Gallimard, 1983.

———. *Studies in Historiography*. London: Weidenfeld & Nicolson, 1966.

Moulin, Léo. *La vie des étudiants au Moyen Âge*. Paris: Albin Michel, 1991.

Moureau, François, ed. *Métamorphoses du récit de voyage*. Actes du colloque de la Sorbonne du 2 mars 1985. Paris: Champion; Geneva: Slatkine, 1986.

———, ed. *Le second voyage, ou, Le déjà vu*. Paris: Klincksieck, 1996.

"Multiple Jérusalem: Jérusalem terrestre, Jérusalem céleste." Special issue, *Dédale*, 1996, nos. 3–4.

Les mystiques du désert dans l'Islam, le judaïsme et le christianisme. Gordes, Abbaye de Sénanque: Association des amis de Sénanque, 1974.

Netton, Ian Richard. "Rihla." In *Encyclopédie de l'Islam*, new ed., 8:545–46. Leiden: E. J. Brill; Paris: Maisonneuve et Larose, 1966. In English translation in *The Encyclopaedia of Islam*, new ed., ed. E. J. Van Donzel (Leiden: Brill, 1966), 8:528ff.

———. *Seek Knowledge: Thought and Travel in the House of Islam*. Richmond, UK: Curzon, 1996.

Nicolet, Claude. *L'inventaire du monde: Géographie et politique aux origines de l'Empire romain*. Paris: Fayard, 1988.

Noth, Albrecht. *Heiliger Kreig und heiliger Kampf in Islam und Christentum*. Bonn: Röhrscheid, 1966.

———. "Les 'ulamā' en qualité de guerriers." In *Saber religioso y poder politico en el Islam*, actas del simposio internacional, 175–95. Madrid: Agencia Española de Cooperación Internacional, 1994.

Pasquali, Adrien. *Le tour des horizons: Critique et récits de voyages*. Paris: Klincksieck, 1994.

Pellat, Charles. *Études sur l'histoire socio-culturelle de l'Islam (VIIe–XVe s.)*. London: Variorum, 1976.

———. *Le milieu basrien et la formation de Gāhiz*. Paris: Maisonneuve, 1953.

Plutarch. "On Listening to Lectures." In *Moralia*, trans. Frank Cole Babbitt, Loeb Classical Library, 1:201–62. Cambridge, MA: Harvard University Press; London: William Heinemann, 1960. Trans. Pierre Maréchaux as *Comment écouter* (Paris: Payot & Rivages, 1995).

Poliakov, Léon, ed. *Hommes et bêtes: Entretiens sur le racisme*. Actes du colloque. Paris: Mouton, 1975.

Polo, Marco. *Travels*. Ed. and trans. Arthur Christopher Moule et al. as *Le devise-ment du monde: Le livre des merveilles*, 3 vols. (Paris: Maspero, 1980).

Polybius. *The Histories*. Trans. W. R. Paton. 6 vols. Loeb Classical Library. Cambridge, MA: Harvard University Press; London: William Heinemann, 1960. Trans. Denis Roussel as *Histoire* (Paris: Gallimard, 1970).

Popovic, Alexandre, and Gilles Veinstein. *Les voies d'Allah: Les ordres mystiques dans l'Islam des origines à aujourd'hui*. Paris: Fayard, 1996.

Prévost, André. "L'expression en grec ancien de la notion 'entendre.'" *Revue des études grecques* 48 (1935): 70–78.

Radtke, Bernd. *Drei Schriften des Theosophen von Tirmidh*. Beirut: Steiner, 1992.

Resch, Peter A. *La doctrine ascétique des premiers maîtres égyptiens du quatrième siècle*. Paris: Beauchesne, 1931.

Robson, J. "Hadīth." In *Encyclopédie de l'Islam*, new ed., 3:24–30. Leiden: E. J. Brill; Paris: Maisonneuve et Larose, 1966. In English translation in *The Encyclopaedia of Islam*, new ed., ed. E. J. Van Donzel (Leiden: Brill, 1966), 3:23ff.

———. "Ibn al-'Arabī." In *Encyclopédie de l'Islam*, new ed., 3:729. Leiden: E. J. Brill; Paris: Maisonneuve et Larose, 1966. In English translation in *The Encyclopaedia of Islam*, new ed., ed. E. J. Van Donzel (Leiden: Brill, 1966), 3:707.

Rohr-Sauer, Alfred von. *Des Abū Dulaf Bericht über seine Reise nach Turkestan, China und Indien*. Bonn, 1939.

Rosenthal, Franz. "From Arabic Books and Manuscripts," Pt. 1, "Pseudo-Asma'ī on the Islamic Arab Kings." *Journal of Asian and Oriental Studies* 69 (1949): 90–91.

———. *A History of Muslim Historiography*. Leiden: Brill, 1952. 2nd ed. rev., 1968.

———. "The Stranger in Medieval Islam." *Arabica* 44 (1997): 35–75.

Samarrā'ī, Fādil Sālih. *Al-Dirāsāt al-Nahwiyya wa'l-Lughawiyya 'inda al-Zamakhsharī*. Baghdad: Dār al-Nadhir, 1970.

Sanders, Paula. "Claiming the Past: Ghadīr Khumm and the Rise of Hāfizī Histori-ography in Late Fātimid Egypt." *Studia Islamica* 75 (1992): 81–104.

Sauneron, Serge. "Le temple d'Akhmim décrit par Ibn Jobair." *Bulletin de l'Institut Français d'Archéologie Orientale* 51 (1952): 123–35.

Schacht, Joseph. *The Origins of Muhammadan Jurisprudence*. Oxford: Clarendon Press, 1950. Trans. Paul Kempf and Abdel Magid Turki as *Introduction au droit musulman* (1983; 2nd ed., Paris: Maisonneuve et Larose, 1999).

Schepens, Guido. "Éphore sur la valeur de l'autopsie." *Ancient Society* 1 (1970): 163–82.

Schimmel, Annemarie. *The Mystical Dimensions of Islam*. Chapel Hill: University of North Carolina Press, 1975, 1990. Trans. Albert Van Hoa as *Le Soufisme ou les dimensions mystiques de l'Islam* (Paris: Cerf, 1977, 1996).

Seneca. *Letters to Lucilius*. Trans. Marie-Ange Jourdan-Gueyer as *Lettres à Lucilius: 1 à 29 (Livres I–III)*. Paris: Flammarion, 1992.

Smith, Margaret. *Rābiʿa the Mystic and Her Fellow-Saints in Islam*. Cambridge: Cambridge University Press, 1928.

Strabo. *Geography*. Trans. Germaine Aujac et al. as *Géographie*, 9 vols. in 10 pts. (Paris: Belles Lettres, 1966–96).

Symposium on Commemoration of the Twelfth Century of the Death of Imam Shafii. 2 vols. Kuala Lumpur, 1990.

Tamizi, Mohammad Yahya. *Sufi Movements in Eastern India*. Delhi: Idarah-i Adabiyat-i Delli, 1992.

Thucydides. *History of the Peloponnesian Wars*. Trans. Jacqueline de Romilly as *La guerre du Péloponnèse* (Paris: Presses Universitaires de France, 1965).

Todorov, Tzvetan. *Les morales de l'histoire*. Paris: Hachette, 1997. Trans. Alyson Waters as *The Morals of History* (Minneapolis: University of Minnesota Press, 1995).

Turki, ʿAbd al-Majid. *Polémiques entre Ibn Hazm et Bāqī sur les principes de la Loi musulmane: Essai sur la littérature zāhirite et la finalité mālikite*. Algiers: Études et documents, 1973.

Urvoy, Dominique. "Sur l'évolution de la notion de Gihād dans l'Espagne musulmane." *Mélanges de la Casa Velázquez* 9 (1973): 335–71.

Vajda, Georges. "Les Zindīqs en pays d'Islam au début de la période ʿabbāside." *Revista degli Studi Orientali* 17 (1937): 173–229.

Valensi, Lucette. "Anthropologie comparée des pratiques de dévotion: Le pèlerinage en Terre sainte au temps des Ottomans." In *Urbanité arabe: Hommage à Bernard Lepetit*, ed. Jocelyne Dakhlia, 33–76. Paris: Sindbad; Arles: Actes Sud, 1998.

Vasilev, Afanasii. "Hārūn ibn Yahiā and His Description of Constantinople." *Seminarium Kondakovianum* 5 (1932): 149–63. Reprinted in the series Islamic Geography, ed. Fuat Sezgin, no. 166 (Frankfurt, 1994), 117–32.

Verger, Jacques. *Les gens de savoir en Europe à la fin du Moyen Âge*. Paris: Presses Universitaires de France, 1997.

Wansbrough, John. *The Sectarian Milieu: Content and Composition of Islamic Salvation History*. Oxford: Oxford University Press, 1978.

Wilkinson, John. *Jerusalem Pilgrimage, 1099–1185*. London: Hakluyt Society, 1988.

Yahyá, 'Uthman. "Le Kitāb Khatm al-Awliyā' d'Al-Hakīm al-Tirmidhī." Dissertation for the École Pratique des Hautes Études, 1976.

Yates, Frances A. *The Art of Memory*. Chicago: University of Chicago Press, 1966. In French translation as *L'art de la mémoire* (Paris: Gallimard, 1966, 1997).

Yerushlamī, Yosef Hayim. *Zakhor: Histoire juive et mémoire juive*. Paris: La Découverte, 1984, 1991.

Zahwah, Ahmad Ibrahim. *Min Nawādir al-'Arab*. Beirut: Dār al-Nafais, 1993.

Zichy, Ernest. "Le voyage de Sallām, l'interprète, à la muraille de Gog et Magog." *Körösi Csoma Archivum*, no. 1 (1921–25): 190–204. Reprinted in the series Islamic Geography, ed. Fuat Sezgin, no. 166 (1994), 72–86.

INDEX